Managing Democratic Organizations
Volume I

Classic Research in Management
General Editor: Derek S. Pugh

Titles in the Series

Managing Democratic Organizations
Volume I

Edited by

Frank Heller

The Tavistock Institute, London

DARTMOUTH

Aldershot • Burlington USA • Singapore • Sydney

Published by
Dartmouth Publishing Company Limited
Ashgate Publishing Limited
Gower House
Croft Road
Aldershot
Hants GU11 3HR
England

Ashgate Publishing Company
131 Main Street
Burlington
Vermont 05401
USA

Ashgate website: http://www.ashgate.com

British Library Cataloguing in Publication Data
Managing democratic organizations. – (Classic research in
   Management)
   1. Management – Employee participation
   I. Heller, Frank A. (Frank Alexander), 1920–
   331'.0112

Library of Congress Cataloging-in-Publication Data
Managing democratic organizations / edited by Frank Heller.
      p.   cm. — (Classic research in management)
   A collection of 35 journal and book articles previously published
1967–1995.
   Includes bibliographical references.
   ISBN 1-84014-480-7 (hardback) (2 vol. set)
   1. Management—Employee participation.   2. Group decision making.
3. Democracy.   4. Organizational behavior.   I. Heller, Frank A.
II. Series.
HD5650 .M348   1999
658.4'038—dc21   99-41125
                                                                CIP

Printed by WBC Book Manufacturers, Bridgend

ISBN 1 84014 480 7

Contents

PART II   THE TOP MANAGEMENT DECISION MAKING PROGRAMME (TMDM)

Overview

Acknowledgements

The editor and publishers wish to thank the following for permission to use copyright material.

Academic Press Inc. for the essay: Frank A. Heller and Gary Yukl (1969), 'Participation, Managerial Decision-Making and Situational Variables', *Organizational Behavior and Human Performance*, **4**, pp. 227–41. Copyright © 1969 Academic Press, Inc.

Administrative Science Quarterly for the essay: H. Peter Dachler and Bernhard Wilpert (1978), 'Conceptual Dimensions and Boundaries of Participation in Organizations: A Critical Evaluation', *Administrative Science Quarterly*, **23**, pp. 1–39. Copyright © 1978 Cornell University.

American Psychological Association for the essay: Frank A. Heller (1969), 'Group Feedback Analysis: A Method of Field Research', *Psychological Bulletin*, **72**, pp. 108–17. Copyright © 1969 American Psychological Association. Reprinted with permission.

Blackwell Publishers Limited for the essay: Frank A. Heller (1973), 'Leadership, Decision Making, and Contingency Theory', *Industrial Relations*, **12**, pp. 183–99.

Cambridge University Press for the essays: Peter Abell (1977), 'The Many Faces of Power and Liberty: Revealed Preference, Autonomy and Teleological Explanation', *Sociology*, **11**, pp. 3–24; Frank Heller (1992), 'Decision-Making and the Utilization of Competence', in Frank Heller (ed.), *Decision-Making and Leadership*, Cambridge: Cambridge University Press, pp. 71–89.

Greenwood Publishing Group, Inc. for the essay: Bernhard Wilpert (1989), 'Participation Behavior and Personal Growth', in Edgar Krau (ed.), *Self-Realization, Success, and Adjustment*, New York: Praeger, pp. 77–90. Copyright © 1989. Reprinted by permission of Greenwood Publishing Group, Inc., Westport, CT.

Houghton Mifflin Company for the essay: Frank A. Heller (1976), 'Decision Processes: An Analysis of Power-Sharing at Senior Organizational Levels', in Robert Dubin (ed.), *Handbook of Work, Organization, and Society*, Chicago: Rand McNally, pp. 687–745.

Kent State University Press for the essays: Cornelis J. Lammers (1975), 'Self-Management and Participation: Two Concepts of Democratization in Organizations', *Organization and Administrative Science*, **5**, pp. 17–33; F.A. Heller and B. Wilpert (1979), 'Managerial Decision Making: An International Comparison', in George W. England, Anant Negandhi and Bernhard Wilpert (eds), *Organizational Functioning in a Cross-Cultural Perspective*, Kent State University Press, pp. 49–67.

Sage Publications Ltd for the essay: Frank Heller, Pieter Drenth, Paul Koopman and Veljko Rus (1988), 'Theoretical Considerations' in *Decisions in Organizations: A Three-Country Comparative Study*, London: Sage Publications, pp. 11–36. Reprinted by permission of Sage Publications Ltd.

Scandinavian University Press for the essay: William Lafferty (1975), 'Participation and Democratic Theory: Reworking the Premises for a Participatory Society', *Scandinavian Political Studies*, **10**, pp. 53–70.

The University of Chicago Press for the essay: C.J. Lammers (1967), 'Power and Participation in Decision-making in Formal Organizations', *The American Journal of Sociology*, **73**, pp. 201–16.

John Wiley & Sons Ltd for the essays Malcolm Warner (1984), 'Organizational Democracy: The History of An Idea', *International Yearbook of Organizational Democracy*, **II**, Chichester: John Wiley, pp. 5–21. Copyright © 1984 John Wiley & Sons Ltd; Frank A. Heller and Bernhard Wilpert (1977), 'Limits to Participative Leadership: Task, Structure and Skill as Contingencies – A German–British Comparison', *European Journal of Social Psychology*, **7**, pp. 61–84. Copyright © 1977 John Wiley & Sons Ltd.

Every effort has been made to trace all the copyright holders, but if any have been inadvertently overlooked the publishers will be pleased to make the necessary arrangement at the first opportunity.

Series Preface

As the history of management and management thought continues to attract greater interest among scholars, the Ashgate/Dartmouth series of collections of articles on the *History of Management Thought* has been successful in making more readily available historically important academic papers in key areas of the subject. *Classic Research in Management* complements the *History of Management Thought* by presenting the contribution of outstanding research programmes whose sustained output of work has had a defining effect on the development of the field of business and management as a discipline.

Classic Research in Management presents, for each research programme, a comprehensive set of papers which have had a major impact on subsequent research and thinking. In many cases these research reports and articles have appeared in books which are now out of print, or are in early issues of journals which are not easily available to libraries. The present series provides a new opportunity for wider access to the research. Each volume has been collected and presented by a scholar who played a leading part in the original research programme. Each chosen article is reproduced in full. The volumes enable a detailed analysis of the distinctive contribution of each research programme in its historical context. The series offers an important resource for use by academics and advanced students in the field of increasing their knowledge and understanding of the historical development of the management discipline.

DEREK S. PUGH
General Editor
Classic Research in Management
Open University Business School, UK

Introduction

How important is managing democratic organizations today and how important will it be in the twenty-first century? The evidence is uneven. On the positive side, there are a number of eminent social scientists who believe that subjects such as participation, employee involvement, empowering, semi-autonomous work groups, teamworking, cooperative work structures, quality circles and similar practices are critical to organizational health, growth and competitiveness (see, for example, Lawler, 1986; Argyris, 1957; Qvale, 1989). Some politicians, journalists, managers and economists have come to similar conclusions – for instance, Mrs Brundtland a former prime minister of Norway and now head of the World Health Organization (Brundtland, 1989), Will Hutton (1995) economist and editor of the *Observer* newspaper, Servan Schreiber (1967), a French political journalist and Wilfred Brown (1960) manager and organizational theorist.

On the negative side, the cumulative evidence from research, including the projects described in these two volumes come to more cautious and, at times, more pessimistic conclusions. The evidence for what can be called the practical or functional utility of organizational democracy is patchy, and the intensity of application lags behind the espoused rhetoric (Heller, Pusic, Strauss, Wilpert, 1998). The absence of clear-cut research data showing a causal relationship between organizational democracy measures and economic success, need not put off the enthusiast, the idealist or even the practical manager who knows that such incontrovertible causal evidence is not available for most of the other managerial and leadership tasks he is expected to carry out. Nevertheless there are, as we shall see, substantial theoretical arguments, backed by some research evidence, which encourage optimism.

In theory, our topic is embedded in the larger issue of power and the sociopolitical exercise of democracy. In practice, the relationship between power distribution at the macro-political and the micro-organizational level is not always isomorphic. Yugoslavia was an extreme example where political autocracy spawned a very decentralized organizational self-management system.[1] At the other extreme, the United Kingdom, one of the oldest political democracies, has steadfastly opposed formal legal support for influence-sharing at the organizational level.

There is a clear connection between the work described in these two volumes and the extensive literature on sociotechnology. Eijnatten (1993), under the title 'The paradigm that changed the work-place', describes a burgeoning literature of over 3500 items on this subject and divides the field into a number of tracks covering the period from 1950 to 1990. Although the sociotechnical model started from the discovery of the joint optimization principle in British coalmines in the 1950s,[2] much of the emphasis in later writing was placed on semi-autonomous group-based organization because it was this design which yielded significantly superior results compared with mines organized along Tayloristic–mechanistic designs (Trist *et al.*, 1963). From sociotechnical findings in British coalmines evolved an enormous range of experimentation with group decision-making processes described under a variety of names including: self-management, organizational democracy, participation, employee involvement, semi-autonomy, participative job design, teamworking and, more recently, empowerment. What Eijnatten calls the Participative Design and the Scandinavian Democratic Dialogue, represents this tradition particularly powerfully (see Chapter 36).

The relation of sociotechnology to our range of projects also emerges from Volume II of the Tavistock Anthology, *The Social Engagement of Social Science*, with the subtitle 'The Socio-technical Perspective' (Trist and Murray, 1993). Eric Trist's Introduction to the volume anticipates the thrust of many of the chapters presented here when he describes the findings of the important Haighmoor mine study which demonstrated the economic and social effectiveness of participative design:

> Now they had found a way, at a higher level of mechanization, of recovering the group cohesion and self-regulation they had lost and of advancing their power to *participate in the decisions concerning their work arrangements*. (Trist and Murray, 1993: 37, emphasis added)

Because the subject of democratic organization is still wide open for interpretation and discussion, it is important that scholars, consultants and other practitioners in the fields of general management, human resource management and industrial relations are aware of available evidence. The three major research programmes described in these two volumes present theory and empirical evidence relevant to any fair assessment of the current and future potential of this area of organizational studies. Unlike hardware, such as typewriters or computers, or software languages, the accumulation of experience and valid research data remains relevant even in the face of new evidence based on new contingencies. The field is not going to stand still, but there are some baseline organizational and human conditions that will change slowly or not at all. Chapter 38 by Velijko Rus in Part V attempts to anticipate events.

The three research programmes involved the collaboration of 27 research centres and approximately 37 social scientists,[3] and several of the key members of the international teams took part in more than one project. Since all three programmes involved several countries – 16 altogether – this allows comparisons to be made, although the evidence shows that the most important conclusions are not country-specific. The enquiries are based on interviews and research data from 11 600 employees, including managers, covering all organizational levels. The programmes took place over a period of 25 years and some publications based at least partly on this work have appeared up to 2000.

There were at least two circumstances which provided the impetus for these programmes. One was the extensive post-Second World War debate about the relative inefficiency of European industry compared with that of the United States. The British government, for instance, was sufficiently concerned about this problem to send a number of productivity teams across the Atlantic to discover why certain industries were not competitive with the United States. A French political journalist, Servan Schreiber, had given extensive attention to this subject and accumulated some research data. His book, *The American Challenge* (1967), was widely discussed at the time and refuted the then current belief that the difference in efficiency was based on the United States' superior financial resources. He found that the major part of the capital for US business expansion came from Europe! His explanation for US superiority was that their managers used better leadership, more democratic methods and better organizational planning; they delegated more responsibility creating positive motivation, staff flexibility and liberated initiatives. Servan Schreiber talked of the creative power of teamwork and pointed out that, because Europe lacked social integration across social classes compared with Japan and the United States, it consequently failed to establish a common set of values (Servan Schreiber, 1967). It is interesting to note that several aspects of Servan Schreiber's diagnosis have reverberated over three decades. At the time, the 'Atlantic Gap' arguments were supported by a larger number of other studies (for instance, Diebolt, 1968; Allison, 1969; Starbuck, 1971; Jamieson, 1980) and, cumulatively, these arguments persuaded a group of European scholars to launch a comparative study which is described in Part II of this book.

The second stimulus for the investigations reported here came from the work of the Commission of the European Community designed to increase employee involvement in decision making (Wilpert, 1976). The Science Centre, Berlin had become interested in an EEC suggestion to study 'the experience with different laws on industrial democracy' (IDE, 1981: 35). There were two opposing positions. One group argued that organizational behaviour cannot, or should not, be influenced by legislation; it had to develop naturally from the requirements of the situation and from the prevailing value system in each country and the culture of each enterprise. The alternative view was that organizational democracy will only rarely develop naturally and without some outside support to overcome inertia and the opposition of powerful self-serving vested interests. Even when it develops in a given enterprise, it can easily be replaced with a change of leadership unless rooted in a legal framework. It can be argued that democracy in the political system did not develop easily or 'naturally' and without a struggle. In the political system, too, it needs some legal underpinning, such as a constitution, to survive over long periods.

A group of professionals from a variety of social disciplines came together in 1972 in the beautiful medieval town of Dubrovnik to talk about these issues. They decided that the existing diversity of structural, legislative and cultural arrangements in Europe would lend themselves to a field research that could make a useful policy-relevant contribution to this polarized debate. This is how the projects described in Part III came about.

The longitudinal in-depth study called 'Decisions in Organization' (DIO), which forms the subject of Part IV developed from the need to supplement and test the outcome of the large scale cross-sectional projects described in Part III.[4] The resources to carry out a four-year processual analysis of decision-making became available in three countries, and seven companies were involved in this work.

The design of these studies was related to a number of emerging issues. In some countries, notably in the United States, Britain and Italy, trade union-based collective bargaining was seen, at least by many industrial relations academics, to be an appropriate form of participation. In these countries, unions tended to oppose legally supported industrial democracy because they thought it would reduce employee loyalty to unions. The Scandinavian countries also held this view at first, but later fell in with the rest of Europe and legislated for employee participation.

In many countries all over the world, managers were expected to use informal direct employee involvement methods including information-sharing, consultation and even joint decision-making (Likert, 1967; Tannenbaum and Schmidt, 1958; Vroom and Jago, 1988). Business schools taught these methods, and an early comparative study in 16 countries found that some lip service was paid to participative styles of management everywhere, even when managers did not believe that their subordinates had any useful contribution to make (Haire *et al.*, 1966). Japan was often held up as an exemplar of democratic practices, although there was much misunderstanding as to what actually took place (Heller and Misumi, 1987). Nevertheless, interest in democratizing organizations had grown over the years, and many companies had voluntarily introduced works councils or joint consultative committees, sometimes with and sometimes without trade union involvement.

It seems that the arguments and conditions that prompted the three programmes of research have not changed very materially over the last three decades. The belief that democratic styles of decision-making are important for global competitiveness has persisted (Lawler, 1986; Qvale, 1996); it is supported by current research, by consultancy practices and management development programmes worldwide, and government policies are generally in line with this philosophy (Reich, 1985; Brundtland, 1989).[5] European Union (EU) policy has also continued to support its original 1970 position even in the face of substantial resistance from a previous British government and some employer organizations in various countries. One of the EU's arguments is based on the need for 'harmonization' – that is, the elimination of unfair competition between countries – but, beyond that, there is the discourse which supports efficiency and social justice. One of the EU's policy and research arms, the Dublin-based European Foundation for the Improvement of Living and Working Conditions, has, for many years, carried out an extensive programme of investigation on different aspects of direct and indirect participation (see, for example, Fröhlich *et al.*, 1991; Gill *et al.*, 1993: Vols. 1 and 2; Geary and Sisson, 1994; Regalia, 1996). In September 1997 the European Union implemented part of its policy in this field by means of a Directive which requires all companies with at least 1000 employees, including at least 150 in two separate member states, to set up works councils with specific rights of information-sharing and prior consultation on certain company policies.

Norway and Sweden have taken the democratizing aspect of company management seriously for decades (Thorsrud, 1984; Emery and Thorsrud, 1976). In the 1980s Norway and Sweden launched two large-scale government-supported action research programmes on sociotechnical democratization in which the need for Scandinavian competitiveness was deeply emedded. A new long-term programme in continuation of the previous work was started in 1997 and they have developed a range of new methods for inducing change (Gustavsen, 1998; Heller *et al.*, 1998).

Among managers and human resource specialists in the United States and elsewhere there is a dispute about the relative merits of the Japanese work designs including quality circles, continuous improvement, just-in-time and total quality management, compared with the Scandinavian Volvo-derived methods and the US adaptations in the Saturn and similar programmes continues (Rehder, 1994; Womack *et al.*, 1990; Berggren, 1993, Niepce and Molleman, 1998). However, from the point of view of the material presented in this book, a degree of employee involvement is associated with all these developments.

Finally, although I have always argued that political and organizational democracy have different origins and require different approaches, it is interesting that the sudden economic crises that created turmoil in the Far East in 1997–98 has led some analysts to argue that a lack of democratic institutions and control mechanisms, particularly in banks, played a major part in the disastrous decline in investors' confidence, which precipitated the flight of capital and led to a drop in the value of national currencies and stock market collapses in Far Eastern countries. Previously, the very rapid economic growth of many of these countries had led to theories that a community culture, based on a mixture of pateralism, trust and human resource utilization through participation, was a viable alternative to Western individualistic, confrontational, short-termist capitalism. More generally, it was argued that there is an Asian value system which differs from either socialism or Western capitalism – perhaps a kind of 'third way'. Has this theory collapsed?

The jury is still out on these alternative interpretations of economic progress and the role of democracy at different societal levels. It may also be possible to evolve an accommodation between these system attributes and Buzan and Segal (1997) have proposed such a fusion theory which they term the 'westernistic civilization'. In one form or another, the subject of managing democratic organizations will not disappear quickly.

On Method

The contributors to these two volumes use a fairly simple, traditional vocabulary to describe their work, but this should not be interpreted as unawareness of current discussions and controversies derived from counterpositions such as: positivism and phenomenology (including social constructionism); modernism and post-modernism; objectivity–subjectivity; and realism–antirealism. There is a long-established tendency in philosophy, as well as in the social sciences, to fertilize polar positions and pretend that total barrenness characterizes the ground between them. We do not follow these adversarial traditions.

The projects described in these two volumes and the variety of methodologies they use do not fall neatly into these abstract categorizations, although they lean nearer to one pole than another. The nominalist fallacy of believing that a phenomenon is the same as its name must be resisted.

The study of democracy in organizations through a range of different degrees of influence or power is derived from the judgements of the people who occupy a variety of organizational positions. These judgements are clearly subjective, and the meanings attributed to them derive from their accumulated experience. Indeed, where else should they come from? They are socially constructed and not absolute. Nevertheless, the subjective judgements have a significant degree of consistency and they accommodate to specific situations. We call this contingent behaviour as contrasted with universalistically determined behaviour.

Furthermore, the subjectivity of our actors' judgement is not absolute. There is an important degree of objectivity in the social phenomenon called power. Actors who exercise power in organizations can select, dismiss, reward or punish other actors. These other (subordinate) actors experience this exercise of power subjectively as pain or pleasure as well as objectively in terms of having a job or not having a job and so on. In extreme cases, not having a job may mean not having anywhere to live and literally not having anything to eat. To the actor in question, such a situation 'simulates' reality and objectivity.

The main divide in the social sciences is between methodologies. At one extreme is the position that what cannot be measured is not worth paying attention to. At the other pole is the belief that all behaviour can be adequately studied through symbols and metaphors. Social scientists who occupy these polar value positions tend to ignore or minimize the needs of the situation and the requirements of the questions asked. The investigators who designed the three projects in this publication asked questions that required comparisons between organizations and/or between countries, and this necessarily involved a substantial number of observations. The questions related to macro-, meso- and micro-levels – that is, to national laws, organizational structure and size, as well as personal judgements. Different methods were used to engage with these issues and with cross-sectional and longitudinal designs. Most, but not all, required some quantitative assessment. The TMDM project discussed in Part II worked with small groups of between three and eight senior management personnel in eight countries and used quantitative as well as ethnographic material derived from Group Feedback Analysis (see Heller's essay presented as Chapter 10). The two IDE projects in Part III used codification of national laws, company structure information and individual judgements from questionnaires administered in the presence of a researcher. In one country an additional follow-up research used a survey research organization to collect a nationally representative sample as a way of comparing findings with more hands-on enquiry (see Chapter 24 in Volume II). The longitudinal processual DIO project used a semi-case study design, based on interviews, participant observation and written company data for the assessment of tactical and strategic decisions over a four-year period.

All four projects (TMDM, IDE I, IDE II, DIO) use cross-national data and in all cases the field work was carried out by teams in each participating country; the teams also contributed to the interpretation of the data. Moreover, in three of the projects, the national teams jointly designed the research. This approach is different from most cross-national or cross-cultural research designed and interpreted by one person or group who have no direct experience of the countries involved in the study (for instance Haire *et al.*, 1966; Frohlich *et al.* 1991; Hofstede, 1991).

When the teams used questionnaires, they achieved almost 100 per cent response rates because, with one exception, the administration was person to person with the researcher administrating the instruments during field work. Very occasionally, one of the pre-designated members of a sample was unavoidably absent; even then there was often a last minute replacement. This almost perfect response rate has to be contrasted with an increasing number of studies carried out by distributed questionnaires that achieve very low response rates, for instance 17.8 per cent in one recent case (Gill and Krieger, 1999: 575).

Design of this book

This book describes three interrelated research programmes in the form of 38 essays and lists 21 authors. Two of the books which describe the work, and several essays, are not attributed to individual authors, reflecting the collective responsibility for the design and execution of the different studies. However, as is well known, academic pressures, the preference of publishers and the tradition of journal editors combine to produce a fairly standard format of authorship which is inevitably reflected in this book.

The reader should be aware that cross-national research involving a team of people who collaborate over long periods develops a dynamic of its own. This dynamic, which is rarely described in the literature, is a major factor in the successful outcome of the three programmes and we are fortunate that Bernhard Wilpert, one of the founders of the collaborative group, has offered us a glimpse of what goes on behind the surface. In Part III the first essay, 'Inside Story' (Chapter 16), gives us an unofficial account of the informal coordinator type leadership which steered the group through many difficult situations to achieve a high level of 'group maintenance'.

The selection of essays for this book was guided by the design of the Classic Research Programme series as explained by Derek Pugh in the Series Preface. I selected essays in refereed journals and International Yearbooks and chapters from books that are no longer in print. Since the entries are printed as originally published, there is inevitably some overlap for which we ask readers' indulgence. The Overview which introduces each Part will help guide people through the available choices.

The book comprises six Parts, preceded by this Introduction. Part I consists of nine essays which develop the historic and theoretical background to the literature on democratic organizations. Part II uses six essays to describe a study of the Top Management Decision Making process (TMDM) in eight countries: Britain, France, Germany, Israel, Netherlands, USA, Spain and Sweden. The 11 chapters in Part III cover two large-scale projects on Industrial Democracy in Europe (IDE) using a sample of 12 countries in the first study (Belgium, Denmark, Finland, Italy, Israel, Netherlands, Norway, Sweden, UK, West Germany and Yugoslavia) and an almost identical sample in a follow-up study carried out ten years later to see what, if any, changes had taken place. Part IV presents nine essays describing a four-year in-depth study of routine, tactical and strategic decision-making in seven organizations in three countries (Britain, the Netherlands and Yugoslavia). Finally, Part V comprises three chapters linking major historic reviews and anticipating the future. The section entitled 'What We Have Learned' at the end of Volume II selects a few practical, policy-relevant findings that emerge from the research projects.

Each Part has its own introduction. The Biographical Appendix gives some information about the authors of the two volumes.

Frank Heller

Notes

1   Not everybody would now accept this description of self-management: see, for instance, George (1993).
2   The joint optimization principle presents the alternative to the 'technological imperative' which is said to guide most of the design thinking in engineering and similar technical topics. Joint optimization demonstrates the impossibility of achieving maximum results from concentrating on technology alone in circumstances when people have to interact with the technology and, conversely, no maximum result can emerge from a people-based design where people and technology are correlated. The exact joint optimization relationship will vary from situation to situation, but usually requires a degree of semi-autonomy or participation of the work group. For details see Heller, 2000.
3   I say approximately because, in addition to the three main programmes which feature in this book, there were a number of country-specific projects with part- and full-time staff, as well as doctoral students who contributed indirectly to the three programmes. Furthermore, several members of the international team also took part, with others, in a related study called 'The Meaning of Working' (MOW, 1986).
4   Two studies on organizational democracy are described in Part III. While the methodology in each is cross sectional, the second (IDE II) was a deliberate follow up replication of IDE I after an interval of ten years. The two studies together are therefore longitudinal, but do not involve in-depth field work as in the project described in Part IV.
5   The Federal Republic of Germany launched an ambitious Humanization of Work Programme in 1974 which has continued until today despite changes in government. Although the name given to the programme has changed over the years, it has spent about DM 100 million per year on a wide variety of projects, often designed with the collaboration of unions. The basic assumption running through most of the projects is that humanistic work is efficient.

References

Allison, D. (ed.) (1969), *The R&D Game: Technical Men, Technical Managers and Research Productivity*, Cambridge, MA: The MIT Press.

Argyris, Chris (1957), *Personality and Organizations*, New York: Harper & Row.

Berggren, C. (1993), 'Lean Production – the End of History?', *Work, Employment and Society*, **7**, pp. 163–88.

Brown, Wilfred (1960), *Explorations in Management*, London: Heinemann.

Brundtland, Gro Harlem (1989), 'The Scandinavian Challenge: Strategies for Work and Learning', in Cornelis J. Lammers and György Széll (eds), *International Handbook of Participation in Organizations*, Vol. I, Oxford: Oxford University Press.

Buzan, Barry and Segal, Gerald (1997), 'Anticipating the Future', London: Simon and Schuster.

Diebolt, J. (1968), 'Is the Gap Technological?', *Foreign Affairs*, **46** (2), pp. 276–91.

Eijnatten, Frans M. van (1993), *The Paradigm that Changed the Work Place*, Stockholm: The Swedish Centre for Working Life; Assen: Van Gorum.

Emery, Fred and Thorsrud, Einar (1976), 'Democracy at Work', *A Report of the Norwegian Industrial Democracy Program*, Leiden: Martinus Nijhoff.

Fröhlich, Dieter, Gill, Colin and Krieger, Hubert (eds) (1991), *Roads to Participation in the European Community – Increasing Prospects of Employee Representatives in Technological Change*, Dublin: European Foundation for the Improvement of Living and Working Conditions.

Geary, John and Sisson, Keith (1994), *Conceptualising Direct Participation in Organisational Change – The EPOC Project*, Dublin: European Foundation for the Improvement of Living and Working Conditions.

George, Donald A.R. (1993), *Economic Democracy: The Political Economy of Self Management and Participation*, Basingstoke: Macmillan Press.

Gill, Colin and Krieger, Hubert (1999), 'Direct and Representative Participation in Europe', *The International Journal of Human Resource Management*, **10** (4), pp. 572–91.

Gill, Colin, Beaupain, Thérèse, Fröhlich, Dieter and Krieger, Hubert (eds) (1993), *Workplace Involvement in Technological Innovation in the European Community*, Vols 1 and 2, Dublin: European Foundation for the Improvement of Living and Working Conditions.

Gustavsen, Björn (1998), 'From Experiments to Network Building: Trends in the Use of Research for Reconstructing Work Life', *Human Relations*, **51** (3), pp. 431–48.

Haire, M., Ghiselli, E. and Porter, L. (1966), *Managerial Thinking*, New York: John Wiley & Sons.

Heller, Frank (2000), 'Towards a Socioecotechnology', *Journal of Engineering and Technology Management: Special Issue*, Beyond sociotechnical systems.

Heller, F. and Misumi, J. (1987), 'Decision Making', in Bernard Bass, Pieter Drenth and Peter Weissenberg (eds), *Organizational Psychology: An International Review*, Beverly Hills: Sage Publications.

Heller, Frank, Pusic, Eugen, Strauss, George and Wilpert, Bernhard (1998), *Participation in Organizations: Myth and Reality*, Oxford: Oxford University Press.

Hofstede, Geert (1991), *Culture and Organizations*, New York: McGraw Hill.

Hutton, Will (1995), *The State We're In*, London: Jonathan Cape.

IDE (1981), *Industrial Democracy in Europe*, Oxford: Oxford University Press.

Jamieson, Ian (1980), 'Capitalism and Culture: A Comparative Analysis of British and American Manufacturing Organizations', *Sociology*, **14**, pp. 271–45.

Lawler, Edward E. (1986), *High Involvement Management: Participative Strategies for Improving Organizational Performance*, San Francisco: Jossey-Bass.

Likert, Rensis (1967), *The Human Organization*, New York: McGraw-Hill.

MOW (Meaning of Working) (1986), *The Meaning of Working*, London: Academic Press.

Niepce, Willem and Molleman, Eric (1998), 'Work Design Issues in Lean Production from a Socio-technical Systems Perspective: Neo Taylorism or the Next Step in Socio-technical Design', *Human Relations*, **51** (2), pp. 259–87.

Qvale, Thoralf (1989), 'A New Milestone in the Development of Industrial Democracy in Norway', in Cornelis Lammers and György Széll (eds), *International Handbook of Participation in Organizations*, Oxford: Oxford University Press.

Qvale, Thoralf (1996), 'Local Development and Institutional Change: Experience from a "Fifth Generation" National Programme for the Democratization of Working Life', in Pieter Drenth, Paul Koopman and Bernhard Wilpert (eds), *Organizational Decision Making under Different Economic and Political Conditions*, Amsterdam: North Holland.

Regalia, Ida (1996), 'How the Social Partners View Direct Participation: A Comparative Study of 15 European Countries', *European Journal of Industrial Relations*, **2** (2), pp. 211–34.

Rehder, Robert R. (1994), 'Saturn, Uddevalla and the Japanese Lean Systems: Paradoxical Prototypes for the Twenty-first Century', *The International Journal of Human Resource Management*, **5** (1), February.

Reich, Robert E. (1985), 'The Executive's New Clothes', *New Republic*, pp. 23–8.

Servan Schreiber, J. (1967), *The American Challenge*, London: Athenaeum.

Starbuck, William (1966), 'The Efficiency of British and American Retail Employees', *Administrative Science Quarterly*, **11**, pp. 345–85.

Tannenbaum, Robert and Schmidt, Warren (1958), 'How to Choose a Leadership Pattern', *Harvard Business Review*, March–April, pp. 95–101.

Thorsrud, Einar (1984), 'The Scandinavian Model: Strategies of Organizational Democratization in Norway', in Bernard Wilpert and Arndt Sorge (eds), *International Yearbook of Organizational Democracy*, Vol. 2, Chichester: John Wiley & Sons.

Trist, E.L., Higgin, G.W., Murray, H. and Pollock, A.B. (1963), *Organizational Choice*, London: Tavistock Publications.

Trist, E. and Murray, H. (eds) (1993), *The Social Engagement of Social Science*, Vol II: 'The Socio-technical Perspective', London: Free Association Books.

Vroom, V.H. and Jago, A.G. (1988), *The New Leadership: Managing Participation in Organizations*, Englewood Cliffs, NJ: Prentice-Hall Inc.

Wilpert, Bernhard (1976), 'Die Harmonisierung nationaler Mitbestimmungsmodelle in Europa', in *Schriften des Vereins für Socialpolitik, Neueu Folge Band 88: Die Bedeutung Gesselschaftlicher Veränderungen für die Willensbildung in Unternehmen*, Berlin: Duncker und Humblot.

Womack, J., Jones, D. and Roos, D. (1990), *The Machine that Changed the World*, New York: Rawson & Associates.

Part I
Background, History and Definitions

Overview Part I

The objective of Part I is clear from its title. The following nine essays set the scene for the description of the three research programmes in the following chapters.

The opening essay by Dachler and Wilpert (Chapter 1) has become a classic. It draws attention to the diversity of approaches and lack of theoretical coherence in the existing literature which comes from many disciplines and different value positions. Making use of several disciplines, the authors provide a coherent conceptual framework from a balanced value position.

Malcolm Warner's essay (Chapter 2) gallops through over 2500 years of selected aspects of democratic history. The author shows that there is no linear evolution and probably no progress, just diversity, some successes and many failures. Can we now do better? The arguments and evidence presented in Parts II to V attempt to answer this question.

'The Many Faces of Power and Liberty' by Peter Abell (Chapter 3) treats power from a formal and theoretical perspective derived from a sociological approach to freedom and liberty. Starting with Weber's famous conceptualization and concentrating on two actors, A and B, he distinguishes, *inter alia*, between a positive and manipulative use of influence and power. Following on from this Heller *et al.*, in Chapter 4, introduce the subject of power from a variety of political, sociological and psychological perspectives. Power and influence are related to organizational decision-making processes, giving rise to the contention that this requires a space–time open system perspective. Cross-sectional studies can make a useful contribution but, in most cases, a processual–longitudinal theoretical framework yields more profound insights. These considerations are relevant for understanding the designs of the three programmes of research described in Parts II–V.

Chapters 5 and 6 by Cornelis Lammers describe theoretical models which facilitate an understanding of the complexities of power and participation in a variety of settings. Using distinctions like structural (power equalization-oriented) and functional (effectiveness-oriented) approaches, Lammers explores the role which participation can play in relation to conflict of interests as against harmony in organizations, and he interprets the evidence to suggest that, in conditions when common objectives are accepted, increased participation can be shared at all organizational levels.

In Chapter 7, Frank Heller presents the Motivated Competence Model which relates influence-sharing to experience and skill. Based on research evidence, the model suggests that authentic influence-sharing in complex modern organizations does not take place in the absence of relevant competence. Given this prerequisite, the dynamics of participation enables the available experience and skill to be utilized or at least less underutilized. This theoretical position is reinforced by evidence and arguments in later chapters, particularly 14, 15, 29, 31 and 37.

The last two essays, by Lafferty and Wilpert respectively, put forward powerful arguments and supporting evidence to regard participation as a critical requirement for personal growth, self-fulfilment, maturity and democratic development. This humanistic approach contrasts substantially from the traditional utilitarian assumptions, now dominant in the literature, which assign a functional–mechanistic role, treating participation as a productive outcome. However, it is the participation as life goal philosophy which informs much of the subsequent work presented in the three research programmes and links up well with theories and findings that associate personal growth with the development of competence.

It is interesting that the two authors finish up with almost identical conclusions although Lafferty starts from a political science perspective and Wilpert develops the subject by digging extensively into psychological evidence.

[1]

Conceptual Dimensions and Boundaries of Participation in Organizations: A Critical Evaluation

H. Peter Dachler and
Bernhard Wilpert

This paper outlines a broad conceptual framework for participation in organizations, which provides an overview of four defining dimensions of participatory social arrangements in organizations and their often complex interdependencies. The dimensions of participation discussed in this paper include the social theories underlying participatory social systems and the values and goals each of them implies for participation, the major properties of participatory systems, the outcomes of participation in organizations, and the contextual characteristics of participatory systems which limit or enhance their potential. The view of participation presented in this paper is of a multidimensional, dynamic social phenomenon, the study of which transcends questions unique to any given discipline paradigm and which requires an integration of micro and macro questions. The implications of this conceptualization for theory building, research, and methodology are briefly discussed.*

INTRODUCTION

Participation in decision making and other topic labels which appear to designate similar content areas, like industrial democracy, worker self-management, power equalization, autonomous work groups, and democratic leadership, have created a large and rapidly expanding international literature. This literature embraces both vigorous discussions on the social policy implications of participation as well as mounting social science research on the phenomenon of participation. It has become increasingly difficult, however, to disentangle the many and often contradictory issues which are discussed in this literature. No clear set of questions, let alone a set of answers, which begin to define the nature of the participation phenomenon are discernible. Participation literature includes a plethora of undefined terms and characteristically lacks explicitly stated theoretical frameworks. The pervasive value bases underlying topic labels like industrial democracy and power equalization are not usually made explicit and are therefore rarely systematically questioned. But different value systems imply different definitions of participation, so that the term participation has a variety of meanings across investigators. In addition, the questions that are asked about participation, and the answers which are sought, are shaped by various paradigms which come from the disciplines of psychology, sociology, economics, political science, and law. As a consequence one observes a proliferation of concepts and a divergence of theoretical views. Since practice, policy-oriented discussion, and the scientific investigation of participation, transcend the purview of any given social science discipline, we find that the participation literature cuts across micro and macro issues. Thus participation is concerned with topics ranging from individual motivation and ability considerations, through leadership and group dynamic issues, to organizational factors and socio-political structures and processes within and between societies. Unfortunately, there are very few indications in the participation literature that the micro and macro issues are being integrated. We obviously do not yet have the conceptual tools for developing an integrated analytical

© 1978 by Cornell University.
0001-8392/78/2301-0001$00.75

*

This is an extensively revised version of a paper presented by the authors at the International Conference on Coordination and Control of Group and Organizational Performance in Munich, Germany, 1976, and of a brief conceptual summary by Dachler (1977). The initial versions were written while the senior author was a fellow at the International Institute of Management, Science Center, Berlin and the support of the Institute is gratefully acknowledged.

Many helpful comments on earlier drafts of this paper were provided by Erik Andriessen, Karl Delhees, Roger Dunbar, Kurt Gerl, Walter Goldberg, J. Richard Hackman, Frank A. Heller, John R. Kimberly, Frank Rambaek, Ken Smith, Benjamin Schneider, Valerie Simmons, and Wolfgang Scholl. We gratefully acknowledge their suggestions, without holding them responsible for any shortcomings of this paper.

framework that would allow the investigation of participation in its broadest sense so that the paradigms of the various disciplines could be combined.

The fragmentation of participation research and practice, the divergence of theoretical views, the inherent contradictions, and the heterogeneity in approaches, purposes, and origins of questions in principle could indicate an active, healthy, and rapidly developing area of social science, provided that the literature indicated some process of convergence. It must be emphasized that divergence of theoretical points of view and basic contradictions within a field of inquiry may be a natural outgrowth of viewing a complex and multidimensional phenomenon from fundamentally different vantage points. Orthodox approaches would argue that such divergence and contradictions, if and when they are made explicit, indicate nothing more than confusion, fragmentation, error, or an absence of meaning. Within this understanding, divergence and contradictions have to be resolved or controlled. The definition of convergent validity of psychological measures (Campbell and Fiske, 1959) or earlier arguments on convergent operationalism (Garner, Hake, and Eriksen, 1956) exemplify this view. Alternatively, it is possible to think of theoretical divergence and contradictions as an integral part of social phenomena. For example, Benson (1977) argues that according to a dialectical view of organization, contradictions grow out of socially produced change which then stands in contrast to the established social order. Furthermore, since social production is only partially or not at all coordinated and takes place in different contexts, it results in multiple and often incompatible social forms. Such a view implies that if existing contradictions and apparently divergent theoretical points of view are made explicit and *can* be integrated into a conceptual framework of the phenomenon under study, a process of convergence at some higher order of abstraction may result. Convergence in this sense may allow an integrated analysis of complex and multidimensional social phenomena which recognizes the dynamic nature of organization and the multiple vantage points from which the same complex social system can be meaningfully studied. In other words, a convergent framework must be able to encompass both divergence and contradictions. This paper begins to develop such a framework.

It is important to recognize that one can, on the one hand, think of participation as a central concept of organizing. It is difficult to specify the attributes of organizations without asking who makes what kind of decisions, and what procedures are used to make them. Rational coordination of activities for the achievement of some common goal, division of labor and function, hierarchy of authority and responsibility — all major attributes of organization — imply some or all of the issues usually subsumed under the term participation. On the other hand, participation in organizations is usually thought of as an organizational treatment or intervention strategy; that is, as a social technology (Scholl, 1976). Our analysis of participation initially concentrates on the organizational treatment view of it. But the main arguments of this paper indicate that the separation of these two views

Participation in Organizations

of participation is an artificial one and is likely to continue the fragmentation which currently characterizes the participation literature.

This paper attempts to outline the major defining dimensions of participation and their interdependencies. A broad conceptual framework is presented in which it may be possible to integrate seemingly fragmented issues on participation. This framework may help in explicating and furthering our understanding of the existing contradictions in the participation literature.

Four broad dimensions of participation and their basic interrelationships are illustrated in Figure 1.

One dimension refers to the social theories underlying participation which represent the basis for the values and assumptions of the designers and implementers of participatory social arrangements in organizations as well as the goals and objectives in participation.

The second dimension involves the properties of participatory systems, i.e., the structures and processes along which different kinds of participatory schemes may vary.

The third dimension is concerned with the contextual boundaries within which participation occurs and which limit or enhance the *potential* of participatory social systems. These three defining dimensions will each be discussed in some detail.

The fourth dimension, the outcomes of participation, is considered primarily in the examination of the first three, since outcomes and what outcomes should be considered are a function of the other defining dimensions.

What a participatory arrangement means, i.e., its potential, is considered to be a function of all the dimensions listed in Figure 1 and their complex interdependence. After analyzing

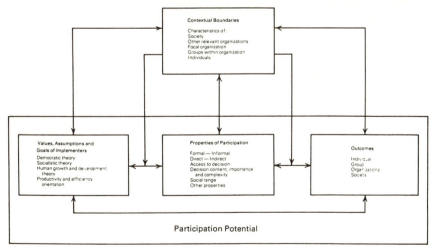

Figure 1. Overview of the defining dimensions of participation.

each of the dimensions separately and providing examples of their interrelationships, we finally discuss participation as a general dynamic system.

THEORIES AND GOALS UNDERLYING PARTICIPATION

Several authors have referred to various theories, value orientations, or ideologies as the origin for issues of participation in decision making (Pateman, 1970; Strauss and Rosenstein, 1970; Walker, 1974; Greenberg, 1975). Like Greenberg (1975), we distinguish among four major theory orientations for participation: democratic, socialist, human growth and development, and productivity or efficiency. In democratic and socialist theoretical orientations, participation is a general social phenomenon, affected by and affecting the general society, its institutions or organizations, and its individuals. Human-growth and -development and productivity and efficiency orientations focus on individual and intraorganizational issues, restricting their conception of participation to a design technique of management or to the organization meant to alleviate some dysfunctional problems within organizations.

We will only outline those major tenets of these theoretical traditions that have a direct bearing on the goals, conditions, and consequences of participation in organizational decision making. For that purpose, four search perspectives will be applied to each of the theoretical approaches:

(1) What are the basic assumptions made about human nature and social institutions that give rise to the concern with the issues of participation?

(2) What is the context in which participation will occur?

(3) What are the characteristics of participatory arrangements in organizations?

(4) What are the societal outcomes to be expected and derived from participation?

It should be noted that the discussions of these theoretical orientations are in summary form.

We have ignored the theories' points of overlap and divergence and left out many important details which are not directly, or are only tangentially, related to the issues of participation.

Democratic Theory

Historically, participatory democracy has functioned as a social value in itself. It therefore serves as an ideal model or moral standard against which social decision-making schemes can be evaluated. Self-governance as a social value, however, has traditionally been in conflict with centuries of thinking about government and social decision making in terms of various forms of autocracy and elitism. One line of democratic theory envisages a society in which members participate in every aspect of collective life. Arguments for self-determination by ordinary citizens have been based on the belief that the vast potential capacity of human beings represents a good basis for wise and effective social decision making. This potential capacity of people is seen in terms of the inherent collective wisdom and intel-

Participation in Organizations

ligence of the members of society as well as in their basic inclination to be responsible, interested in civic affairs, informed, rational, and cooperative. While it is recognized that the realization of this potential is far from perfect, traditional democratic theory argues that the democratic process not only uses the inherent capacity of participants, but also progressively develops it, giving the democratic process further impetus and direction for improving decisions. The assumption that the democratic process educates and develops implies that the process must occur and function in all social, economic, and political organizations, including the family, the school, the work place, and political institutions. Therefore participatory democracy at the political level is not sufficient for a democratic system to survive (Pateman, 1970; Thompson, 1970; Vanek, 1975).

Other analysts of participatory democracy have raised serious questions about some of the traditional assumptions underlying democratic theory (Dahl, 1956; Eckstein, 1966; Haller, 1972). With reference to recent research evidence in the social sciences, writers point out that people are frequently apathetic, unknowledgeable, irrational, easily swayed by group influences, and profoundly affected by the technology of mass communication (Bachrach, 1967; Pateman, 1970; Emery and Emery, 1976), so that the stability and effectiveness of a social system may be greatly impaired by direct and widespread participation. Furthermore, they conclude that democratic systems are greatly impaired by such contextual factors as the complexity of issues to be resolved in modern industrial nations, the power base of needed specialists, and the social dynamics of conflicting interests (Eckstein, 1966; Bachrach, 1967; Naschold, 1969; Mulder and Wilke, 1970; Scharpf, 1970).

The controversies among democratic theorists about the viability of democratic systems in the light of different assumptions about people and the context in which democratic systems do, or should exist, are also reflected in the debates about the characteristics of participatory systems. Traditional democratic theory advocates broad and direct participation of all members of a given social system. Critics of this ideal model, however, favor less intensive and more restricted participatory schemes, which characteristically include the leadership of some elite subgroup that makes social decisions under the control of some electorate. This involves establishing an institutional means to guarantee indirect, representative forms of participation controlled by periodic electoral feedback and various schemes of conflict resolution (Bachrach, 1967; Thompson, 1970).

The societal outcomes anticipated by proponents of participation within the democratic tradition are in part a function of the values emphasized. A closer approach to the value or moral standard of a free and truly democratic society is expected as a result of the educational and developmental effects of individuals participating directly in decisions in all significant institutional settings, including work organizations, where a major part of adulthood is spent, providing the opportunity to gain a growing expertise in articulating and realizing one's own interests. Other democratic theorists seek similar individual outcomes, but emphasize the stability and efficiency of social institutions as the primary expected societal outcomes of participation (Sartori, 1962).

Socialistic Theory

The extensive and heterogeneous literature on socialism also has a significant bearing on the issues of participation. Marx's concern, especially in his early writings, for a free, unalienated human existence led to theorizing on the debilitating effects of the social and economic order in the capitalistic system. Socialism gives work and the production process a central role in explaining human personality and social processes. The major arguments common to the various forms of socialism refer to the alienation of producers from themselves as a result of the dialectical relationship between capital and labor, the high degree of specialization and division of labor seen as being required by the capitalistic mode of production, and the resultant powerlessness and apathy of the producers (Kangrga, 1967). Labor in a capitalistic economy is but a commodity, and people through their labor in that economy disappropriate themselves by a process of objectification. Unable to relate to the products of their labor, workers themselves become a commodity. Therefore, the basic problem lies in the economic system of capitalism and its inherent social and production relations, which prevent the development of human potential. More recent socialist writers have extended these types of arguments also to state-monopolist, Soviet-style socialism (Vranicki, 1965).

A central assumption in the socialist literature is the potential of people to become economically liberated (Vanek, 1975) by participating actively and creatively in the production process, and ultimately controlling it. It is argued that participation accomplishes both the progressive increase in control of the production process by members of the working class, but also the education and development of workers, which is needed for workers to perform the tasks originally carried out by managers as representatives of capital (Vranicki, 1965).

Contextual variables, which affect the timing and extent of social change, are important discussion topics in the literature on socialism. Recent writers (Gramsci, 1957; Gorz, 1973), for example, have described the prevailing capitalistic conditions and value frameworks which serve as obstacles to socialist revolutionary change in Western industrialized nations. These contextual constraints, they argue, underline the necessity for developing class consciousness and confidence through worker participation in organizational decision making. These concerns are also reflected in the controversies about whether participation should be imposed on workers or granted to them, or whether participation should originate from the workers themselves as a result of political processes.

The Paris Commune of 1871 is often taken as the basic model for socialist participatory systems, the critical characteristics of which were its egalitarian values and corresponding organizational structure, its functioning simultaneously as a legislative and executive body, and its empha-

Participation in Organizations

sis on close links between its activities and the ultimate revolutionary societal goals of socialism. Therefore, self-management and self-government through workers' councils become the first step toward abolishing wage-labor relationships, in order to enable workers to control their destinies and to rearrange existing debilitating hierarchies of values (Vranicki, 1965).

The societal outcomes expected from a socialistic view of participation encompass a revolutionary change in the total societal system for the purpose of creating a proletarian culture. Such a culture is thought to be defined by cooperative, egalitarian production processes and by a social system that allows for the development of human personality and in which production represents more than merely a means for immediate survival (Vanek, 1971; Gorz, 1973). The viability and limitations of these anticipated societal outcomes, especially given party and state centralist tendencies, have repeatedly been noted (Porket, 1975).

Human Growth and Development

Several recent theories of human behavior have focused on personality growth, development of individual potential and efficiency, and mental health in the context of organizations (e.g., McGregor, 1960; Argyris, 1964; Likert, 1967). These theories have discussed participation as one among several means of overcoming debilitating effects of traditionally designed organizations on their members. These theories assume a basic hierarchy of needs which culminates in a need for self-actualizing or growth (Maslow, 1954; Alderfer, 1972). Although what is meant by self-actualization is not clear (Wahba and Bridwell, 1973), it includes people being active; independent; capable of self-control through awareness of their potential; engaged in a variety of behaviors; having long-range perspectives; and seeking equality.

Human-growth and -development theories point out that existing organizations, in search of efficiency and certainty, have usually stressed division of labor and rational coordination of activities, which imply job specialization and repetitive tasks as well as direction and control through a unified chain of command, close supervision, and a reward structure based primarily on extrinsic factors. Such an organizational context, however, is viewed as thwarting satisfaction of higher order needs, thus impeding personality development at great cost to the mental health and well-being of organization members (especially in the lower levels of organization), as well as to the economic stability and efficiency of the organization. Consequently, they argue for assigning greater importance to the intrinsic motivational properties of work itself by allowing greater employee influence, autonomy, and responsibility through such organizational redesign strategies as job enrichment, job rotation, management of objectives, employee-oriented supervision, and participation. Recent psychological research and theory have begun to broaden and specify some of the requirements for these organizational change strategies, including radically new interpersonal and organizational processes and structures (Argyris, 1969, 1975, 1976; Israel and Tajfel, 1972; Deutsch, 1973; Hackman, 1975).

It has never been clear what characteristics participatory social arrangements have (or should have) according to theories of human growth and development. Theorists of this orientation have assigned various meanings to participation and have therefore evolved or advocated various participatory structures and processes. In general, however, they have all essentially restricted participatory social systems to issues surrounding the work itself (i.e., to the actual tasks and relevant interpersonal relationships), rather than including the broad range of organizational issues in the participatory decision-making system. Furthermore, in these theories participation refers not only to decision making, but also to such processes as joint ownership of organizational change programs, and sharing of ideas, feelings, information, knowledge, and other resources.

The human-growth and -development theories do not, in principle, question the basic social, political, or economic order in a society. Their emphasis is primarily on how to arrange organizational settings in a given societal framework so as to facilitate the psychological development and growth of individuals and groups. Increases in innovative behavior and economic efficiency and productivity are seen as a correlate of individual and group development. Participation is one means, among others, to that end. Although they do not emphasize societal outcomes, the human-growth and -development theories imply that reduction of the social costs incurred by mental ill-health is an important prerequisite for the stability and efficiency of existing institutions and organizations.

Productivity and Efficiency

Contrary to the other theoretical orientations discussed so far, in which organizational productivity and efficiency are either implicit or explicit objectives among other equally important ones, productivity and efficiency are the primary or even the sole focus in this orientation. This orientation consists of isolated statements and ideas from various theoretical orientations, often oversimplifying their basic premises and implications. However, one can speak of a productivity and efficiency rationale underlying participation, in that it conforms to a paradigm which seeks an instrumental understanding of human beings and their capacities, and in which people are considered to be manipulable toward maximum output through appropriate social technologies.

Noting widespread alienation, dissatisfaction, and lack of commitment in the work force, and the resulting cost of reduced efficiency, lower quality and quantity of production, absenteeism, high turnover, and increased sabotage and labor unrest (Turner and Lawrence, 1965; Garson, 1972; U.S. Department of Health, Education and Welfare, 1973), management theorists and business leaders have looked to a variety of social science techniques — including various forms of participation — as a solution to these costs. Participation is assumed to increase general satisfaction or morale (Morse and Reimer, 1956); improve group cohesion and commitment toward issues on which people are allowed to participate (Coch and French, 1948); provide more

Participation in Organizations

accurate information about such issues (Strauss, 1963; Lowin, 1968; Lawler and Hackman, 1969); and increase productivity (Coch and French, 1948; Morse and Reimer, 1956).

Researchers have also argued that whether participation has these effects depends in part on the context. Thus, participation is expected to increase effectiveness to the extent that: (1) the issues around which participation occurs are relevant to accomplishing the task; (2) people, by participating, get more accurate information about an organizational context which in fact allows real and meaningful positive outcomes to result from effective performance; and (3) effective performance is not largely beyond the control of the worker (Katz, 1964; Lowin, 1968; Blumberg, 1969; Hackman, 1976). More generally, a great deal seems to depend upon the kinds of participatory arrangements used and how they are applied (Walker, 1974).

In view of the fragmentary treatment of participation in the productivity and efficiency orientation, it is not surprising that there are virtually no statements about the characteristics of participatory social arrangements themselves. One can observe, however, that research in the productivity and efficiency tradition limits participatory arrangements in scope and intensity, restricts them to issues surrounding task accomplishment, and characteristically leaves them under the complete control of management, so that there is no intended challenge to the basic power prerogatives of business leaders. With respect to societal outcomes, participation is seen, implicitly at least, as a relatively unimportant way to ensure the stability of the current social and economic order, to increase industrial productivity, and to avoid disruptive and costly labor unrest and sabotage.

The brief summaries of the four theoretical orientations indicate that each orientation deals with participation as a result of applying a particular value system to some real world configuration of conditions and events which are perceived as problems or emergencies. As a consequence of different roots in the historical development of social theory, each of the theoretical orientations is based on a different value system and defines different aspects of society or of organizations as problems in need of solution. These theoretical differences imply variation in the policy-oriented goals which participation is to serve. They also indicate variation in the meaning, form, and social function of participatory social arrangements. However, with respect to general characteristics of participation, the four theoretical orientations should not be considered as competing but as complementary. For example, democratic and socialist theories concentrate on societal issues, paying little attention to the organizational and group factors implied by their arguments, whereas the human-growth and -development, and the productivity and efficiency orientations emphasize organizational and group factors, with little attention to the societal implications of their arguments (Nord, 1974). But a view of participation which integrates the major questions contained in all the theoretical orientations is what is needed to provide a more complete or realistic definition of participation.

PROPERTIES OF PARTICIPATORY SOCIAL ARRANGEMENTS

Although terms like participation in decision making or power equalization are often used as if they referred to some social decision-making arrangement with known or agreed-upon properties, a bewildering variety of organizational participatory schemes is mentioned in the literature (Strauss, 1966; Walker, 1974). Furthermore, the discussions and research on participation largely fail to make explicit the connection between participatory systems with given properties and their theoretical base. Participatory schemes are often treated as if they could be identified along any one continuum, whereas the many seemingly significant and interdependent properties of participatory systems require a multidimensional analysis (Walker, 1974). We therefore discuss some of the major dimensions along which participatory systems may vary, in an attempt to develop some of the important questions these dimensions imply.

Formal-Informal Participation

Much of the research and discussion on participation implicitly considers it as an organizational treatment or intervention strategy, which in turn implies a base of legitimization or power base which some agent uses to develop and apply the treatment. The base of legitimization may vary from a formal, i.e., explicitly recorded, system of rules and agreements imposed on or granted to the organization, to an informal, i.e., nonstatutory, consensus emerging among interacting members. One can, for example, distinguish three bases of legitimization for formal participation treatments (IDE, 1976): (1) legal bases, such as clauses in a country's constitution, in national or regional laws, or in governmental executive orders; (2) contractual bases, which for most countries involve mainly collective bargaining agreements on a national, regional-sectoral, company, or shop floor level; and, (3) management policies, which are unilateral regulations about the involvement of various groups or individuals in decisions about the organization. Informal participatory schemes are based on a consensus among interacting social units or individuals and become legitimized through practice and evolving norms or customary procedures.

The degree of formality or informality of participation is closely tied to the underlying values of the designers, to the goals and objectives which participation is to serve, and to the particular organizational and societal context in which the participatory system exists. The distinction between formal and informal participation roughly coincides with the legislated, statutory tradition of industrial democracy in many continental European countries contrasted with the emerging, informally evolving participatory management and bargaining tradition in Anglo-Saxon countries. For example, there has been a greater emphasis on the development of formal participatory structures in Germany and Yugoslavia than in England and the U.S., where the greater acceptance of the human-growth or human-development orientations has been associated with fewer formal participatory structures.

Participation in Organizations

It is also appropriate here to recall that some socialist theorists have maintained that worker participation should develop from the bottom up as a result of political struggle (Gorz, 1967, 1973). The suggestion that participation should grow out of revolutionary change initiated in the lower regions of an existing social order implies that a formal participatory system may be imposed by the powerless on the holders of power. But such a process indicates nothing more than a reversal of the original social order by which the formerly powerless take on the characteristics and acquire the base of legitimization of the former holders of power. In any case, one can expect that participation imposed or granted through formal rules is likely to be different from a participatory system that emerges informally among interacting members and that is legitimized by the developmental process.

The formal-informal dimension of participation remains an issue of importance in current discussions, which are particularly heated in the European countries. For example, Sorge (1976), on the basis of a comparative historical analysis of European countries, argues that the delay in introducing institutional, statutory frameworks for participation in some countries, corresponds to particularly high levels of social and industrial unrest in those countries today. Although Scandinavian countries and Great Britain have traditionally emphasized less formal and more "grass-roots" approaches to participation (Thorsrud, Sorensen, and Gustavsen, 1976) there have been recent legislative actions and greater public pressure to introduce more formal forms of participation through national laws. On the other hand, in Germany and the Netherlands, for example, with their tradition of legislated participation, there appears a growing interest in less formal, on-the-job bargaining approaches to participation (Andriessen, 1976; Dülfer *et al.,* 1976). However, what is important is not whether formal or informal participation systems are better, according to some effectiveness criteria, but that formal and informal participatory systems differ in the questions they are meant to address, in their origin, in their developmental process, and, therefore, in their meaning and consequences. But one has to recognize that a formal participatory system is likely to develop some informal participatory social arrangements, and that a formal system may be imposed on an informal, already existing participatory system. Therefore, the search for "either-or" solutions may obscure some of the fundamental properties of participatory social systems in general.

The conceptual issues implied by the formal-informal characteristic of participation revolve around two major problems which have received very little attention. The degree of formality of a participatory social arrangement has to be considered in terms of the underlying values and basic assumptions, and the goals that participation is to serve. Equally important is the fact that whether a participatory system is formal, informal, or has characteristics of both depends on its particular setting. The preponderance of formal participatory systems in some European countries and informal participatory schemes in Anglo-Saxon countries has to be in part a function of the particular societal characteristics, the legal and political structures, and the industrial relations system. Furthermore, the mix of formal and informal participatory schemes within an organization is also likely to be a function of the particular characteristics of that organization, including its groups and its individual members.

Direct-Indirect Participation

The immediate, personal involvement of organization members in decision making is ultimately the ideal form of participation in all theoretical frameworks. The four theoretical orientations differ both in the meaning they attach to direct participation and in the extent to which they question the viability of systems of direct participation, in the light of factors believed to constrain them (Lammers, 1967). Even the arguments in democratic theory for indirect participation, i.e., mediated involvement of organization members in decision making through some form of representation, may really be thought of as an expression of compromise between pure democracy (direct participation) and autocratic social arrangements.

While direct participation may serve as a basic standard or ideal in each of the theoretical orientations, such social arrangements would still be likely to differ on other characteristics. They could vary on such characteristics as the degree to which participants have access to the decision-making process; the range and importance of issues, and the kind of decision rules to be included in the participatory decision-making process, the range of people or organizational units to be included in direct-participation systems, and the base of legitimacy on which the direct-participation system is developed. Variation on these characteristics would depend upon the theoretical orientation, on the basis of which the direct-participation system was designed and on the societal, organizational, group, and individual context of the direct-participation system.

Thus, rather than simply observing the effects of some unspecified direct-participation system, as is commonly done in American research, or continuing to enumerate all the possible constraints of direct-participation systems in today's complex and highly interdependent organizations, as European writers like to do, one might develop a more useful strategy. One might begin by specifying the characteristics of direct-participation systems in the different theoretical orientations and by systematically asking how the various contextual configurations in which such systems exist affect them. This strategy should begin to provide the kind of information necessary to understand under what circumstances direct-participation systems are viable or need to be supplemented or even completely replaced by indirect-participation systems.

Indirect or representative participation thus derives its meaning primarily with respect to direct-participation systems, which in turn are juxtaposed with autocratic social systems. This way of thinking about direct and indirect participation may oversimplify some of the important aspects of the historical development of existing participatory systems, for example, the historical bases for the existing in-

Participation in Organizations

dustrial democracy legislation in Germany and Sweden
(Pothoff, Blume, and Duvernell, 1962; Huntford, 1971).
Nevertheless, such a view seems consistent with many of
the discussions on the characteristics of participatory systems. A good example is provided by the traditional arguments about the nature of political democracy, which in
large part seem to revolve around the distinction between
direct and indirect forms of participation in the governance
of a nation and the conditions and assumptions that seem
to require one or the other form of participation (Haller,
1972). The implications of these issues at the societal and
institutional level have recently been extended to the organizational decision-making level (Naschold, 1969; Pateman, 1970; Scharpf, 1970), where indirect participation in
organizations also seems to be frequently advocated as a
result of questioning the assumptions underlying direct
participation.

Such assumptions have been criticized at every level of
analysis. Individual ability and personality factors (Strauss,
1963; Lowin, 1968), group dynamics processes (Janis,
1972), and many organizational complexities that interfere
with the effectiveness of direct participation (Lowin, 1968;
Naschold, 1969; Mulder and Wilke, 1970) have been shown
to constrain the potential of direct-participation systems.
Convincing arguments have also been presented about how
the complexities of today's interdependent, highly
technological, and rapidly changing societies, may impede
the extent to which organizations can effectively institute
systems of direct participation (Scharpf, 1970; Tannenbaum
et al., 1974). Unfortunately, there is little systematic knowledge about direct-participation systems in organizations or
about the contextual requirements for their effectiveness
and survival. Not surprisingly, this is also true for indirect-
participation systems. For example, indirect-participation systems that require the creation of new organizational roles to
represent the interests of an electorate introduce their own
complexities, often resulting in unintended consequences.
It has been found (Furstenberg, 1958; Wilpert, 1975), for
example, that the mediating role of work councils in Germany between employees, management, and unions is
likely to lead to professionalization of such roles, creating
vested interests for the mediators to keep their functions,
and often leading to estrangement and conflict between
representatives and their constituencies.

In general, it is the principle of elitism that often seems to
be at the center of the debates on the advantages or
liabilities of indirect-participation systems in organizations.
And it is not well understood what elitism means for indi-
rect- or direct-participation systems. But in light of the
interdependence of direct or indirect participation, it seems
futile to reduce the debates about these two forms of participation to the question of whether to opt for one or the
other. In practice, direct or indirect participation is usually
mixed in varying and often complex combinations, in which
the two serve different purposes and result from different
contextual requirements. For example, within the German
participatory system, the function of the works assembly,
which involves quarterly meetings of all employees, is only

as an exchange of information and consultation, whereas representatives to the work council and supervisory board have some authority to make decisions. The Yugoslav workers collective, on the other hand, together with the workers' referendum, has the right to make decisions far beyond mere exchange of information (Roggemann, 1970). Thus, the German and Yugoslav forms of participation not only differ in the mix of direct and indirect participation; they also differ in the configuration of many other characteristics. Therefore, our understanding of such differences is not well served by limiting our questions to whether one system is more effective than the other, according to criteria whose relevance is not known. As Figure 1 tries to illustrate, a conceptualization of participation — in which different properties of participation become meaningful — makes it necessary to research the developmental history of different participatory systems to make explicit the basic purposes and values which each was designed to serve, and to investigate how their properties reflect societal, organizational, group, and individual constraints or facilitators.

Access to Participation in Decisions

Although participation in decision making is often thought of as a dichotomy between involvement or noninvolvement of people in making decisions that affect them, one can, in fact, think of participation as a continuum reflecting the different access that organization members have to the actual making of a decision, or the amount of influence they can exert toward a given decision outcome. Some authors have tried to define this characteristic of participatory systems by identifying discrete behavior modes along a hypothetical "influence-power-sharing" continuum (Tannenbaum and Schmidt, 1958; Belasco and Alutto, 1969; Heller, 1971; Vroom and Yetton, 1973).

For example, one could conceive of the following behaviors along such a continuum (adapted from IDE, 1976).
(1) No (advance) information is given to employees about a decision to be taken.
(2) Employees are informed in advance of the decision to be made.
(3) Employees can give their opinion about the decision to be made.
(4) Employees' opinions are taken into account in the decision process.
(5) Employees have a veto, either negatively by blocking a decision that has been made, or positively by having to concur in advance.
(6) The decision is completely in the hands of organization members, with no distinction between managers and subordinates.

One could imagine a final reference point on this continuum which defines the situation in which decisions are exclusively in the hands of employees, with management having no access to those decisions. However, with respect to the property of participation discussed in this section, such a situation is merely the reverse of the situation indicated by behavior 1 on our influence-power-sharing continuum.

Participation in Organizations

Behavior 1 represents no formal access to the decision-making process and relatively little or no influence on the decision outcome. Critical to the analysis of participatory systems is the point at which organization members gain access to the flow of information relevant to a particular decision. In behaviors 2 through 4, all information handling remains with management and the function of participating organization members is to receive and provide information. However, the psychological meaning of behaviors 2 through 4 is likely to differ, as are the required organizational structures and processes because of differences in the degree to which employees take part in the actual decision (Lammers, 1967).

In behavior 5, organization members can manipulate information and so begin to enforce some or all of their preferences. Thus, the capacity of employees to veto a decision implies a decision-making arrangement in which participation, exclusive to superiors, ends, and a new organizational influence and power system emerges involving processes like collective and individual bargaining and negotiation.

Behavior 6 represents complete power equalization in that all members of an organization have equal access to the making of a decision and thus have an equal potential to influence the decision. Vanek (1970, 1971, 1975) has developed a general economic theory of the labor-managed firm in a labor-managed market economy, in which the distinction between managers and subordinates is no longer necessary. Also, research such as the studies by Blake and Mouton (1961) on power, ranging from complete leader control to complete delegation of control to subordinates, has provided some information about behavior 6. Of course, even in a participatory system in which all organization members have equal access and equal potential to influence a decision, one can imagine different decision rules (majority vote, consensus procedure, etc.) or certain power-based distributions among the participants (Mulder and Wilke, 1970), which would create a discrepancy between the potential access or influence of all organization members and the actual access to or influence on a decision.

Nearly all of the research on group decision making in organizations as a means of power sharing and on participatory leadership (Likert, 1967; Lowin, 1968; Vroom, 1970, 1976) is essentially restricted to behaviors 1 through 4. This focus probably emerges from the human-growth and -development, and the efficiency and productivity rationales for participation. These rationales recognize a participatory leadership style primarily in terms of its directing or manipulative characteristics, and seek to increase involvement of subordinates, but only with respect to what the leader thinks appropriate (Heller, 1971). Unfortunately, little attention has been paid to the underlying values of this research and the important paradigmatic effects on what questions are being asked.

Since the meaning of participation is confined by the set of questions asked about it, we are not likely to begin understanding what participation would mean, for example, if it originated at the bottom rather than being delegated or granted from above; if it explicitly embodied the developmental and educative functions of democratic and socialist theories; if it existed in a social system with different legal and social norms determining and regulating power and the bases from which power and authority are derived; or if it were part of what Argyris (1975) called "Model 2," a theory which calls for interpersonal relations based on cooperation, mutual trust, and shared feelings.

In the absence of participation research based on different paradigms, it is difficult to understand whether the kinds of criticisms writers, like Gilman (1962), Strauss (1963), and Leavitt (1965), have raised represent some absolute constraints for participation, or whether with a different set of assumptions and values these constraints would either vanish or become irrelevant. Such a change in the basic framework of underlying values and assumptions would also make it useful to reconsider and study Vroom and Yetton's (1973) normative model of participatory leadership in the context of a participatory system characterized by behavior 6, in which leadership remains an important issue despite the equal access of all members to decision making. But the assumptions underlying Vroom and Yetton's (1973) leadership model would need to be drastically changed, with potentially crucial insights into the psychology of leadership. Research on the drastic revisions of the influence structure in Yugoslav organizations (Obradovic, 1970; Rus, 1970) and Argyris' (1976) arguments about the deleterious effects on leadership effectiveness of inconsistencies between the action theories that researchers espouse and the theories that they actually use, illustrate the great potential of different paradigms for new insights.

In general, beginning with the point on the access continuum at which formally disenfranchized organization members can manipulate information — behavior 5 — important new and traditionally ignored questions about participation in organizations emerge. It is at this point that participation becomes a truly social phenomenon for which the traditionally used, individual-oriented paradigm no longer provides appropriate answers (Moscovici, 1972). Participatory systems which are characterized by behaviors 5 and 6 involve various decision-making and group-dynamic processes (Janis, 1972). These processes include compromise settlements among conflicting power and interest bases (Flanders, 1968) and various cooperative, antagonistic, or disjunctive decision-making strategies (Walker, 1974). However, the literature on participation in decision making does not systematically deal with these issues, apart from a few notable exceptions, like Heller (1971), Wood (1973), and Abell (1975). Instead, one most likely finds some isolated and often vague hypotheses and some empirical research results that seem pertinent but are difficult to integrate into any existing theoretical framework.

Content, Importance, and Complexity of Decisions

Research and public discussion on participation have too often ignored the attributes of the decisions in which people participate. Although the four theoretical orientations

Participation in Organizations

underlying participation are not very specific about these decision attributes, they clearly differ in the implied range of decisions and on the corresponding importance of the decision to the participants. The democratic and socialist theories imply participation in the total range of decisions that affect the participants, whereas the human-growth and -development and the efficiency and productivity orientations limit decisions to the immediate organizational roles of participants. But in each theoretical orientation some arguments have been raised in favor of restricting decisions to be in line with the current abilities, needs, or expectations of the participants (McGregor, 1960; Bachrach, 1967; Adizes, 1971; Alutto and Belasco, 1972; Vroom and Yetton, 1973; Heller and Wilpert, 1977).

In studying participatory decisions, one would have to start analyzing them into their different components which, at the very least, include the range in content and number of decisions that fall within the participatory decision-making arrangement, as well as the complexity and importance to the participants of the decisions in which they participate. Furthermore, in such an analysis, one would have to recognize that decision problems are a sequence of choices (March and Simon, 1958), which requires specification of where participation is to begin.

Equally important are questions about the determinants and consequences of different decision attributes. Although these kinds of questions are perhaps among the most central in trying to define participation, they have been completely ignored or simply skirted in research and in public discussions. For example, reference is often made to the importance of decisions by talking about employee participation in decisions which affect the employees or which are important to them (McGregor, 1960; Hackman, 1976; Strauss, 1977). However, the theories underlying participation lead to different conclusions about which organizational decisions might directly affect participants and what decisions are more or less important to participants. Thus, in America, for example, decision issues like investments, development and marketing of products, and appointments of chief executive officers have traditionally been thought to affect primarily the owners, investors, and functional specialists in the organization, rather than the main body of organization members. Interestingly, recent arguments about quality of work life, "consumerism," and the environmental impact of organizations have suggested that many of these decision issues have a much more direct effect on organization members and on people outside the organization than was previously recognized. In any case, most decisions of this kind do not ordinarily become part of the range of decisions included in participatory systems. These have characteristically included decisions about employee compensation and benefits, production methods, working time arrangements, and various hygienic factors ranging from coffee breaks to furnishing and decorating the work environment.

Apart from a few interesting but largely isolated hypotheses (Strauss, 1963; Heller, 1971; Alutto and Belasco, 1972; Vroom and Yetton, 1973), the participation literature does not provide a framework to explain this range of decisions and the importance attached to them by participants. But the development of such a framework may be helped by the lines of questions suggested in Figure 1. A comparison of decisions which are typically a part of American participatory schemes with decisions typically included in socialistic participatory systems (Roggemann, 1970; Vanek, 1971, 1975), is likely to lead to the conclusion that the values and goals which participation is to serve and the basic assumptions different theories make about people and social institutions have an important bearing on what decisions may fall into the realm of a participatory system and what decisions are explicitly excluded from it.

Equally important to the understanding of such a comparison is the context in which American and socialistic participatory systems function. The historical development of a society and its present characteristics are not only related to the prevalent values and goals which participation is to serve in that society, but also to set boundaries for the range of decisions that can be included effectively in participatory systems. Similarly, the interorganizational processes and the particular characteristics of organizations, their groups, and their individual members play a role in determining the range, complexity, and importance of decisions that are part of the participatory social arrangement.

Social Range of Participation

This refers to questions about the range of people involved in a participatory system (i.e., selected persons, certain groups or divisions, total organizational membership, affected outsiders) and the extent of their social involvement in the decision process. The definition of this participation characteristic needs to be distinguished from indirect participation, where a small set of representatives actually partakes in a decision, but they do so in the interests of their constituencies. In referring to a limited social range, for example, one implies that a particular participatory system takes into account, directly or indirectly, the interests of only some subsection of the organization. In any case, a participatory social system that includes all members in an organization is likely to involve different psychological processes and result in different individual and organizational outcomes than participatory systems confined to department heads, union members, "those immediately affected," or some other subgroup defined according to some explicit or implicit criteria. In addition to questions of where the boundaries for participants are drawn and what the determinants and consequences of those social boundaries are, the social range of participation also includes questions about the kind and intensity of social interaction processes in the participatory system. Strauss (1963), for example, made a distinction between individual participation, which emphasizes autonomy and achievement, and group participation. Group participation can involve group pressures to conform and group dynamics like "groupthink" (Janis, 1972), changes in the degree of risk taking (Davis, 1969), as well as other processes (Wood, 1973). Although a given category of participants may have equal access to the decision-making process, the psychological meaning of par-

Participation in Organizations

ticipation may change significantly because of the kind and intensity of social interaction in the process (Wood, 1970, 1973; Heller, 1971; Janis, 1972).

The literature on participation contains very little systematic research on the social range of participation. The small-group research in the social-psychology literature provides some, albeit fragmentary, information on the consequences of various group-dynamic processes (McGrath and Altman, 1966) as well as on the consequences of individual as compared to group problem solving (Davis, 1969). Walker (1974) discussed to some extent who in an organization is to participate in decision making, and Edelstein (1972) raised some of the issues that need to be addressed if interested groups outside the organization, such as consumers or trade unions, were represented in organizational participatory systems. However, there is essentially no research on what determines different social ranges in participatory systems and the consequences of participatory systems that differ in social range.

As with the previously discussed characteristics of participation, the social range of a participatory social system must in part be understood within the framework of the underlying social-theoretical orientation and the values and goals it implied, as well as with respect to the origin and developmental history of the system. Moreover, as Figure 1 illustrates, the particular social range of a participatory social system is likely to be constrained by the characteristics of the society in which an organization exists, by the relevant existing institutional and interorganizational conditions, and by the characteristics of the organization itself, its groups, and its individual members.

Some of the questions implied by the social-range characteristic of participation are also related to the questions underlying various management policies on personnel recruitment, selection, evaluation, training, and promotion, and other policies dealing with the rise of employees to upper managerial positions. While there are fairly explicit assumptions and considerable research underlying these personnel policies (Goldstein, 1974; Schneider, 1976), all bearing on the social range of participatory systems, they have never been systematically integrated with the conceptions of and research on participation.

Other Properties of Participation

We have so far discussed the major characteristics along which participatory systems may vary. There are other dimensions which a complete taxonomy of participation properties would have to include. In addition, there are other ways in which the obviously interrelated participation characteristics could be categorized. However, the principal questions that were raised remain relevant.

Scholl (1976) provides an interesting example of categorizing participatory systems according to what kind of participation process is emphasized. He argues that participation refers to the process of exchanging information, where information exists in various combinations of facts and value premises. Values are evaluated against facts of reality and against other value standards, and facts are interpreted according to held values. Therefore, one can classify participatory social arrangements into a twofold matrix, with one dimension indicating whether or not special consideration is given to the value orientation of participants, and the second dimension reflecting whether or not the factual knowledge of participants becomes an integral part of the participation process. Scholl (1976) discusses the resulting four participatory social arrangements and their differences in properties and outcomes.

Within the framework, illustrated in Figure 1, however, we would argue that each of these four participatory systems is likely to reflect a set of social-theoretical values, assumptions about people and social institutions, and goals which participation is to serve. Moreover, contextual variables are likely to be directly related to what specific properties each of the four participatory systems has, and may facilitate or constrain the degree to which each participatory system can serve the intended values and goals. For example, a participatory system which considers the values of participants but deemphasizes their factual knowledge is illustrated by employee representation in organizational decision making through an official of a national union (Scholl, 1976). In such a case, the union representative may be faced with experienced managers who are highly knowledgeable about intraorganizational matters and who, on the basis of this uneven distribution of expert power, gain greater relative influence in the decision process (Mulder and Wilke, 1970). Such a group dynamic process may not only limit the intended outcomes, it may also eventually require a change in the structural and procedural properties of the participatory system.

POTENTIAL OF PARTICIPATION

Participation as a social system is a complex and dynamic product of human action. Regardless of whether it is intentionally and rationally created or whether it emerges as a consequence of many and sometimes fortuitous factors, participation serves a variety of values and goals and takes on different structural and operational properties in various configurations, resulting in a variety of outcomes. Thus, the potential of a participatory social system, i.e., what it is capable of being and what it can ideally achieve, is defined by the sequence and interrelationships of three dimensions depicted in Figure 1: from the values, assumptions, and goals of implementers; through the properties of participatory arrangements; and to outcomes. The potential of a participatory social arrangement is a concept which takes on different meanings depending on which of the three dimensions one looks at and which factors in a given dimension one emphasizes. However, the multidimensional definition of potential stresses the importance of asking questions about what a participatory social arrangement can ideally be and what it can in consequence achieve. The total potential of a participatory system cannot be known if it is viewed from only one perspective.

This problem is illustrated by the classic participation experiment that was designed to overcome employees' resist-

Participation in Organizations

ance to periodically required changes in production tasks
(Coch and French, 1948). The potential of participation was
circumscribed by designating the main objectives for participation as "overcoming resistance to change" and eliminat-
ing all the undesirable consequences of employee resistance. Furthermore, the potential of that participatory arrangement was delineated by its particular properties (e.g.,
limited access to decisions, restricted decision content,
formally imposed participatory system, limited social range)
which were in line both with the underlying values and
goals (e.g., increase employee productivity and attraction to
the job, increase the stability of the organization as it is
currently conceived) and with the existing context (e.g., resistance to change viewed primarily as an employee problem, available labor force, competitive pressures). However,
one could argue, as Moscovici (1972) did, that resistance to
change is a consequence of the total social situation in
which the resisting group finds itself, a social context which
includes both the initiators of change as well as those who
have to carry it out, so that both groups are part of the
process of change and affected by resistance to it. Even
with the same basic goal of trying to deal with resistance to
change and its consequences, a participatory system with
very different properties and different outcomes, and therefore with a different potential, could be imagined, if one
approached the analysis of resistance from a total social-
system point of view, rather than uncritically accepting a
perspective that, on the surface, seems to fit reality as defined by some members (in this case, managers) of the
existing system.

These arguments highlight another important aspect of participation potential. The traditional scientific view which
maintains that value judgements and scientific inquiry are
basically incompatible, makes it difficult, if not impossible, to
adequately research the potential of participatory systems
(cf., Myrdal, 1969; Cattell, 1972; Bahm, 1974; Sperry, 1977).

Churchman (1968), in discussing evaluation research on social intervention programs and the study of issues arising
out of the day-to-day affairs of people or social institutions,
talks about the "pure applied" and the "heroic applied" scientist. In participation research, the pure-applied scientist
would objectively describe the attributes of a participatory
system, their determinants and consequences, and the
conditions under which these events were observed. The
heroic-applied scientist would pursue the relevance of participation for improving social systems, which requires him
to take on the moral burden of deciding what he means by
improvement. Whereas those in the current research tradition tend to conduct their discussions on participation
within either of Churchman's two roles in the social sciences, the concept of participation potential, as we have
defined it, requires an integration of both roles. In general,
the concept of participation potential, although still relatively
new and undeveloped in the participation literature (Rambaek, 1977; Seashore, 1977), seems to provide a useful
conceptual tool for better understanding the relationship between participatory systems and their environmental context.

CONTEXTUAL BOUNDARIES FOR PARTICIPATION

This defining dimension of participation refers to a broad array of both micro and macro level factors which form the context for participatory systems.

The contextual factors listed in Figure 1 can be viewed as setting boundaries for the potential of participatory systems. They do this in two ways.

First, there is a direct interdependence between the contextual factors and each of the dimensions that define the potential of participatory systems. For instance, societal characteristics form the context out of which the values and goals for participation emerge (Tannenbaum *et al.,* 1974); technological characteristics of organizations are likely to determine in part some of the properties of participatory systems (Trist and Bamforth, 1951); and group characteristics may produce some of the participation outcomes (Janis, 1972).

Secondly, the contextual factors set limits to the potential of participation by moderating the degree to which the values, assumptions, and goals of implementers are reflected in various configurations of participation properties and the degree to which the characteristics of participatory systems result in certain outcomes. For example, the amount of personality growth envisioned by human-development theorists as a result of participation is likely to be limited in part by the frame of reference of participants (Hulin and Blood, 1968) and by a variety of organizational and societal characteristics (Argyris, 1969; Nord, 1974).

Our arguments on the boundary-setting function of contextual factors seem to fit the contingency view of participation recently proposed by a number of authors (Vroom and Yetton, 1973; Heller, 1976; Heller and Wilpert, 1977). However, traditional contingency models assume an existing set of relatively static parameters which affect structures and processes of social systems in certain ways, depending on what values parameters or contingencies have. Tosi and Hamner (1974: 1), for example, say that "a 'contingency' approach . . . [assumes that] the behavior of one subunit is dependent on its environmental relationship to other units or subunits that have some control over the consequences . . . desired by that subunit." Thus a contingency is viewed as part of an existing environment, as an independent or moderating variable which affects or "controls" the behavior of the subunit in question. Such a view, however, emphasizes only simple one-way effects of the environment on the structures and processes of social systems. It ignores the fact that the very social units which are affected by environmental contingencies also actively create and change those contingencies. Theorists, both democratic (Pateman, 1970) and socialist (Gramsci, 1957; Gorz, 1973) for example, have provided convincing arguments for the importance of considering the *reciprocal* relationships between participatory social systems and their environmental context. Hence, the contextual boundaries of participation potential cannot be sufficiently understood in terms of the traditional assumptions underlying contingency conceptions of organizational phenomena.

Participation in Organizations

We started our discussion of participation by viewing it as an organizational treatment or intervention strategy, since such a view best conforms to the origin of participation as a topic for research in the real world (in contrast to its originating in a particular discipline paradigm). However, in considering the way in which contextual factors limit or enhance the potential of participatory systems, participation becomes a central concept of organizing. To ask about the boundaries of participation potential is to investigate the organizational system as it exists in and interacts with its environment. In Figure 1 contextual boundaries are represented by five general interconnected factors, from the most micro level of individual characteristics, through group and organizational characteristics, to the most macro level of interorganizational and societal attributes. Although a systematic review of all the factors implied by the context of participation is needed, for the purposes of this paper we must confine ourselves to briefly outlining examples of major issues implied by each of the five contextual factors.

Societal Characteristics

Whereas the pervasive influence of a society on its social institutions and on the social processes that govern them has received a lot of attention in the social sciences in general, participation research has only very recently begun to seriously deal with these issues. The great variety of participatory systems in different countries emphasizes the importance of societal characteristics in understanding the design and outcomes of participatory social arrangements.

One can hardly consider as a historical accident the fact that existing participatory systems in the United States, for example, characteristically limit the access of participants to the decision-making process, restrict the range and importance of decisions to be included in the participatory system, tend to be direct and informal, and usually involve a limited social range.

Similarly, the range of properties among European participatory systems must be in part a reflection of different societal characteristics in those countries. However, as is frequently the case in cross-cultural research on organizations in general (Roberts, 1970), there is little knowledge available about which of the many possible societal factors are relevant for understanding participatory social systems, at which level of abstraction these factors are best conceptualized, and how they can be operationalized. Typically, societal factors are investigated by assessing some attributes of participatory systems in different countries, including aspects of the immediate environmental context such as the technology of the organization, and noting the differences across countries. But so far these differences have not significantly contributed to any systematic framework within which the relationship between societal characteristics and participation potential can be made explicit.

A few recent cross-cultural research studies (Heller, 1971; Tannenbaum *et al.*, 1974; IDE, 1976; Heller and Wilpert, 1977; Wilpert, 1977) have begun to more systematically conceptualize and research the relationships of societal characteristics to designs and outcomes of participatory systems. Most of these studies have grown out of socio-technical systems theory (Trist and Bamforth, 1951; Emery and Trist, 1960) and have extended it by assessing societal characteristics such as turbulence of the environment and characteristics of the industrial relations system. These measures of societal characteristics of different countries were supplemented by measures of other more micro-level variables — size and technology of organizations, size of organizational departments, span of control, individual expertise — in order to investigate the effects of interacting contextual variables at different levels of abstraction on the properties and outcomes of participatory systems in different countries (Heller, 1976; IDE, 1976; Heller and Wilpert, 1977).

The boundary-setting functions of societal characteristics are becoming evident also through the analysis of the different configurations of participation properties and outcomes within a given society. For example, decisions infringing on traditional property rights would probably not be open to significant employee participation in a society based on the principles of private ownership and free-market competition. However, even in the United States, where participation has traditionally been limited, there have been a few direct-participation systems which have allowed employees not only to decide what kind of pay system was to be used in their organization, but how much they ought to be paid and what increment each employee should get.

As both Lawler (1977) and Strauss (1977) pointed out, certain factors may interact to provide the kind of immediate context that is related to whether decisions that traditionally have been the prerogatives of owners become part of a participatory system, the kinds of outcomes the system has and the structures and processes that characterize it, and the organizational system in general. Such a context may include factors like relatively small organizational size, relatively simple technologies, and a climate of trust and cooperation, as well as group processes and individual characteristics (Lawler, 1977; Strauss, 1977). Thus, although societal characteristics seem to have a strong influence on the participation potential, certain conditions and events representing other contextual factors may change the process by which society influences participatory systems and the strength of that influence.

This line of reasoning is also related to theoretical arguments about the way in which characteristics of a society set limits to participation potential as defined by the value frameworks of different social-theoretical orientations. Gramsci (1957) and Gorz (1973) clearly recognized the limiting effects of the prevailing capitalistic value frameworks and societal conditions in Western, industrialized nations for achieving the participation potential envisioned by socialist ideology.

Nord (1974), on the basis of insights gained from Marxist theory, argued that a very likely reason for the yet limited success of the human-growth and -development theories of organization was their neglect of socio-economic vari-

Participation in Organizations

ables as they affect behavior and, more importantly, as they interact with the values and goals underlying those organization theories. The basic competitiveness of interorganizational relationships in capitalistic societies and the resultant withholding of information, the distrust and development of stereotypic views of other relevant organizations, and so forth, limit the processes, climates, and structures that human-growth and -development theorists try to establish in organizations. Nord (1974) recognized that a more specific analysis of the societal characteristics, especially socioeconomic variables, would prove useful in answering whether alternative macro structures would be more supportive of the goals pursued by such organization theorists, and whether there were alternative power bases for change oriented to human growth, such as the development of proactive labor unions which could develop workers' capabilities to participate effectively in organizational decision making.

A recent article by Benson (1977) maintains that organizational and societal characteristics represent a constructed social world that needs to be understood in terms of the historical roots and the existing conflicts and contradictions among the societal characteristics. Such an analysis seems to define a crucial but mostly neglected force for change, which may provide an important source for understanding the development of participatory systems. It would indeed by difficult to understand the different potentials of participatory social arrangements in the United States, Germany, France, the Scandinavian countries, and Yugoslavia, for example, without reference to the existing societal dynamics and their historical roots.

Characteristics of Other Relevant Organizations

Both democratic and socialist arguments point to the need to relate a participatory system in an organization to the properties of other relevant organizations and to the processes by which they interact.

First, since participation in decision making may require a number of unique response and interaction capabilities, certain personality attributes, and possession of various resources, and since people tend to hold membership in various organizations, the degree to which organizations differentially develop and support the required human capabilities for participation may severely limit the potential of participatory arrangements in any given organization (Eckstein, 1966). An organization wanting to develop a participatory system in a society in which most other institutions and organizations, like family, schools, church, and government, are based on autocratic principles of interaction, might find that its members do not have the necessary capabilities. Such an organization might realize that, because of the contradictory requirements of its own participatory system to the requirements of the other relevant organizations, the potential of its participatory system is severely limited, and may not even be viable (Pateman, 1970).

Second, the way in which an organization interacts with relevant organizations in its environment and the constraints they impose on it are likely to have a bearing on the

Managing Democratic Organizations I

participation potential in that organization. The complexity of decisions resulting from dealing with many other organizations is likely to severely constrain the properties and outcomes of a given participatory system (Naschold, 1969). Such dealings may involve conflicting interests among organizations, various political and power processes between organizations, and information withholding and distortion by other organizations.

Finally there is the problem of the frequently functional equivalence of worker participation and collective bargaining (Strauss and Rosenstein, 1970). Especially in Europe, participation may refer not just to inclusion of the employees of an organization in the decisions of that organization; it may also refer to representation in organizational decision making of outside interest groups, such as labor unions or the community (Edelstein, 1972). For example, union traditions in Great Britain tend to emphasize a collective bargaining mode of furthering workers' interests even on a plant level, whereas German unions favor collective bargaining on a sectoral level, leaving intraplant bargaining to statutory work councils and their participative machinery. Such different structural conditions and strategic orientations as well as the resulting differences in interorganizational interactions are likely to set boundaries for participative processes in organizations.

Organizational Characteristics

Although this is probably the most commonly studied aspect of participation in organizations, our knowledge about the effects of organizational characteristics on the limits of participation potential is fragmentary, partly because of the often too narrow conception of participatory social arrangements in organizations. Participatory systems are often designed for one unit of an organization, with research focusing on the attitudinal, emotional, and production behavior consequences of such social arrangements (Coch and French, 1948; Morse and Reimer, 1956; Marrow, 1975). More recently some researchers (Clegg, 1960; Brown and Jaques, 1965; Likert, 1967; Naschold, 1969; Cherns, 1973; Wood, 1973; Tannenbaum *et al.,* 1974; IDE, 1976) have analyzed participation in organizations as a phenomenon that is a part of the organization as a total system. This kind of approach, still beginning and in need of elaboration, is crucial to the conceptualization of participation outlined in this paper. At present, however, it would be difficult, from the available research results, to construct interrelated hypotheses which would specify the organizational characteristics under which certain participation potentials could be achieved and maintained. We have already noted organizational boundary conditions, such as organizational size and the special demands on the organizational communication system to provide the necessary information to participants, in the value structures and goals of the human-growth and -development and of the productivity or efficiency orientations. But within the value structures of democratic and socialist orientations, our knowledge about organizational boundary conditions is almost lacking. We need much more specific information about such factors as the implications of participatory social arrangements for general manage-

Participation in Organizations

ment (Strauss, 1977), the effects and constraints of the technology used in an organization (Herbst, 1976; Thorsrud, Sorensen, and Gustavsen, 1976), and the many organizational support and maintenance mechanisms required by participatory social arrangements that arise out of different ideologies (Gyllenhammar, 1977).

Hackman (1975) warned about the probable decline of job-enrichment strategies without a much more specific and systematic analysis of the systemic organizational characteristics they imply. His arguments are also relevant to what research is required for understanding the organizational constraints for participation potential.

Furthermore, as indicated by Argyris' (1969, 1975, 1976) and Benson's (1977:1) concerns that research on organizational phenomena is based on "uncritical acceptance of the conceptions of organizational structure shared by participants," we cannot develop a full understanding of participation without starting to do comparative research on the properties of organizations that optimize the potential of participatory systems. In other words, the inevitable incompatibility, among some subsystems in an organization, requires research on how participatory systems incorporate these contradictions and change as a result of them. By ignoring these contradictions and by analyzing participatory systems only as a means of protecting the status quo, we cannot know the total potential of participatory systems in organizations.

Group Characteristics

The considerable research on intergroup and intragroup processes in decision making has a direct bearing on participatory social arrangements in organizations. Unfortunately, much of it derives from different theoretical traditions and from various, usually rather narrowly defined paradigms in social psychology, making an integration for the better understanding of organizational participatory systems a formidable task. Wood (1973) made an excellent attempt at reviewing this research for power distribution in organizations, but some examples may help illustrate the boundary conditions of group characteristics on participation potentials.

The research and conceptual work of a number of people (Deutsch, 1949; Lowin, 1968; Heller, 1971; Veen, 1972; Wood, 1972; Vroom and Yetton, 1973) have produced information that begins the integration of decision-task characteristics, individual attributes, and group processes as they affect the properties and outcomes of participatory systems. Although much of this research was carried out in the laboratory, it provides an excellent illustration of the kinds of questions that need to be asked of organizational participatory systems. The particular decision task, in interaction with the characteristics of individuals, and the resultant group processes (Hackman, 1976) set limits to the values and goals that a participatory social arrangement can serve and the kind of properties and outcomes it can have.

Janis' (1972) hypotheses about "groupthink" phenomena, and the way in which he generated these yet tentative definitions of groupthink and member-member and leader-member dynamics, as well as decision-task characteristics which may produce groupthink processes, provide another excellent example of the research questions required to start specifying the intergroup and intragroup process boundaries for participation. The reviews of Sturmthal (1964) and Peterson (1968) provide numerous research questions from the European participation context about how group dynamics may set boundaries for participation potential.

Underlying all of these questions that need research are two crucial and still very ill-defined concepts: the issue of power and influence (Abell, 1975; Scholl, 1976), and the issue of leadership (Janis, 1972; Vroom and Yetton, 1973; Heller and Wilpert, 1977; Strauss, 1977; Wilpert, 1977). Although there are some very useful conceptual bases for understanding these issues in participatory social arrangements, one of the main factors contributing to the lack of clarity about these two important concepts for participation is the neglect of differences in participation potentials and their implications for power and leadership. Thus Vroom and Yetton's (1973) integrative framework for analyzing participative leadership, for example, was confined primarily to the values and goals underlying the productivity and efficiency orientation and, to some extent, that of human growth and development. But this framework does not provide much information about how power and leadership processes set boundaries for participation potentials originating in democratic or in socialist ideologies, or in the value and goal frameworks of mixtures of the four theoretical orientations discussed in this paper.

Individual Characteristics

This set of boundary conditions for participation potential is probably among the most important and most controversial, since all the theoretical orientations underlying participation emphasize individual characteristics and make crucial and often contradictory assumptions about participation with respect to individual attributes and their interaction with various properties of participation. Equally important in all theoretical views of participation is the argument that the often-discussed education and development outcome of participation for individuals is related to the characteristics of individuals in interaction with all the other contextual boundary factors listed in Figure 1. Although current research and conceptualizing is most likely to focus on individual characteristics as preconditions or consequences of participation, there is as yet no systematic research that directly tests the various assumptions about individual characteristics in the different theoretical points of view underlying participation (Greenberg, 1975). Empirical studies and theoretical discussions on a large range of individual variables in participatory systems have provided considerable information about the boundary-setting role of individual characteristics for participation potential. Questions have been asked about individual abilities, attitudes, and values as preconditions and consequences of participation (Blumberg, 1969). Argyris (1976) discussed the learning processes that may be necessary for effective participatory

Participation in Organizations

leadership to occur. Many authors have analyzed the
decision-making process and integration of information required of individuals in participatory systems with different
properties and in different group, organizational, or societal
contexts (Scharpf, 1970; Tabb and Goldfarb, 1970; Adizes,
1971; Heller, 1976), and several studies investigated the
distribution of information and other relevant resources
among participants (Mulder and Wilke, 1970; Heller, 1971;
Wilpert, 1977). Finally, the motivational, emotional, and perceptual processes of participants as both boundaries for participation potential and outcomes of participation have received some attention (Vroom, 1960; Blake and Mouton,
1964; Meyer, Kay, and French, 1965; Hulin and Blood,
1968; Lowin, 1968; Scheflen, Lawler, and Hackman, 1971;
Argyis, 1976). Unfortunately, although the available information on individual characteristics suggests many interesting
hypotheses about participatory systems, current research on
this topic is fragmentary because it is often based on isolated hypotheses and comes out of many, often incompatible, discipline-specific paradigms.

IMPLICATIONS AND CONCLUSIONS

The view of participation in organizations developed in this
paper has some important theoretical and methodological
implications. It might be useful to summarize and integrate
these implications in order to make more explicit the underlying assumptions of this paper and their possible meanings
for research on social phenomena in organizations in general and participation in decision making in particular.

Our main intention in this paper is to provide an overview
of participation as multidimensional and dynamic which can
serve as a basis for a more systematic conceptualization of
this social phenomenon than is presently available in the
literature. The main impetus for this analysis came from the
realization that, at present, we have very few guidelines to
analyze and study participation beyond the relatively narrow
focus provided by each of the various, relevant discipline
paradigms and beyond the scope of any one theoretical or
philosophical orientation underlying participation, and there
is, therefore, a disturbing fragmentation in the conceptualization of participation and the research on it.

Although research on participation has accumulated a considerable collection of empirical data and some theoretical
insights derived from those data, one observes neither a
systematic, incremental development in the understanding
of participation as a social phenomenon, nor revolutionary
changes and fundamental shifts in the conceptualization of
participation in the way that Kuhn (1970), for example, described scientific development in the natural sciences. Instead, our analyses have repeatedly shown knowledge
about participation to be fragmentary, contradictory, and limited to a relatively few psychological and sociological preconditions and consequences of participation, such as satisfaction, commitment to decision outcomes, information
available to participants, and conflicting-interest structures.
This knowledge hardly begins to reflect the complex questions that participatory social systems pose in their real-
world setting.

Conservative Research

This paper reflects a number of problems we believe exist in how research in social science in general and research in participation in particular is often carried out. Some of these problems have been described and analyzed by a number of recent authors (Argyris, 1969, 1975; Myrdal, 1969; Weick, 1969; Israel and Tajfel, 1972; Campbell, 1974; Benson, 1977). We would like to briefly summarize what we consider to be the major problems and illustrate how the conceptualization of participation developed in this paper might help in dealing with these often interrelated issues.

Some recent papers, although containing often quite different assumptions and basic arguments, have pointed out that much of the social-organizational research, particularly in America, is politically conservative. Israel (1972: 158) argued, "The empiricist doctrine . . . has been developed in intimate contact with natural science . . . . Therefore the problem of a 'world order' has not acquired any special prominence . . . . [Empiricism] acquires a value-bias when it is applied to the social sciences . . . [in that] it accepts the 'world order' *as given,* and therefore has direct social and political implications."

Moscovici (1972) similarly pointed out that social-psychological research, in the positivistic tradition of objectively observing existing social conditions, tends to concentrate on what preserves the existing social state of affairs at the expense of questioning how the social environment is actively produced and changed by social units that are part of it. These observations certainly also apply to the study of organizational structures and processes (Benson, 1977), including participation.

Argyris' (1969, 1975) critiques of social psychology, although not based on the dialectical perspectives used by Israel (1972) and Moscovici (1972), arrived at a similar conclusion, that is, that current research in social psychology "unintentionally" preserves the status quo; consequently there is little knowledge available about how social realities change and what the changes might be. In line with these arguments is Weick's (1969: 34, 22) complaint that "a large number of organization theories could legitimately be re-labelled 'theories of crisis,' " and that "organization theory has often been stifled because it has worked on problems that managers thought were problems and has studied them using managerial concepts rather than psychological or sociological ones." Managers, as captains of organizations, represent the established order, and the tendency of the social sciences to conceptualize organizational phenomena using managerial terms and concepts only underlines the political character of social science research. Furthermore, crises indicate a threat to the status quo; so it is not surprising that current organization theory continues to think of organizational phenomena nearly exclusively in terms of forces that threaten existing organizational systems. Weick (1969: 35) was concerned that the focus on pathology implied that there were no problems with routine ongoing organizational activity, when "the statement that organizations are ongoing, an apparently innocuous assertion, in fact

Participation in Organizations

contains some of the most fascinating [and least studied] problems in organization theory." Weick (1969) cited Campbell's (1965) arguments about the importance of ecological pressures in sustaining evolved complex structures and our still hazy understanding of these pressures. But as long as our questions concentrate primarily on an established and static environmental reality, without turning our attention also to the fact that collective individuals or social units actively produce and change and must adjust to their environment, our understanding of what sustains and destroys social structures and processes will certainly remain limited.

What one might learn from these writings, which questioned the output of social-organizational research from very different points of view, is that the overriding concern with the status quo represents a strong constraint on the kind of questions social science is asking about organizational phenomena, that such an emphasis prevents us from recognizing, and therefore explicitly integrating into our conceptions, the many existing contradictions. This conservative approach stifles a critical analysis of what social science is and what its aims are. We continue to ignore the great potential for new understanding offered by the arguments that social-organizational questions derive their meaning from issues in society and that, as Moscovici (1972: 22) puts it, "the positivistic dream of a science without metaphysics — which today is often translated into a demand for science without ideology — is not likely to become a reality."

These arguments are reflected in our conceptualization of participation and in the implication this conceptualization has for research on participation. The fragmentary and difficult-to-integrate research results available on participatory social systems are a result of the different ideological frameworks in which questions about participatory social arrangements have been asked. We have argued that, since the different ideologies or social theories, and the different value and goal frameworks they imply essentially define participation differently, it may not be useful to think of participation as one homogeneous and easily delimited phenomenon. On the other hand, if one accepts the notion that different participation potentials are embedded in the total social fabric of which participatory social arrangements are a part, it becomes possible to think of participation within one conceptual framework. Therefore, as long as we make explicit the value and goal framework out of which particular questions about participation emerged, and as long as we formally integrate these ideological positions, and the stipulations (Israel, 1972) and contradictions they imply, into the overall conception of participation as a social process, then a set of general principles, as suggested by Figure 1 for example, may make possible the study of participation as a general phenomenon.

Such an approach may help in understanding that the typically restricted research questions about participation in America, for example, reflect only a part of the real-world character of participation. As we pointed out earlier, the classic study on participation by Coch and French (1948) not only reflects the positivistic tradition of social science research, it also shows that by neglecting to think of resistance to change as a social process that involves both employees and managers, a whole set of crucial questions were never asked. Our understanding then, of what resistance and change as social processes mean, was that much the poorer. Furthermore, participation viewed as an intergroup process, instead of as the intragroup process used by Coch and French (Moscovici, 1972), would certainly have allowed the researchers to understand better the wider potential of that participatory system in terms of the reciprocal power relationships between management and employees and their implications for the properties and outcomes of that participatory system.

Individual Versus Social Emphasis

The example discussed above illustrates a further crucial issue. Participation research, although obviously dealing with a social phenomenon, has primarily emphasized individual or psychological questions. Pugh (1966), Weick (1969), and others have repeatedly complained that we do not have the conceptual tools (not to mention the methodological tools) to study the social, as distinct from the individual, aspects of organizations. The social world is typically seen as an extension of the psychological world, which denies the possibility that certain social phenomena need to be explained by separate principles, which are not easily reduced to psychological laws and the physiological or physical laws which are hypothesized to underly them. Without going into the details of this long-standing problem (Simmel, 1950; Nagel, 1968; Weick, 1969; Israel and Tajfel, 1972), we may need to point out some of the implications of our conceptualizations for dealing with this problem.

Systems Concept of Participation

When we note that Figure 1 illustrates a systems conception of participation, we are not necessarily referring to all of the formal theoretical properties of organizations that the concept of system has explicitly or implicitly indicated in the literature (Katz and Kahn, 1966; Thompson, 1967; Pondy, 1976). We use the term "system," to emphasize the following basic theoretical properties and assumptions.

Participation viewed as a dynamic system above all implies complex interdependence among the various parts. Of primary importance is the identification of the different kinds of interrelationships among the defining dimensions of participation. The examples provided throughout the paper and the relationships shown in Figure 1 point to two kinds of crucial interrelationships. One is the notion of reciprocal relationships, or what Weick, following Barker and Wright (1955), referred to as "double interact," by which is meant that a variable needs to be thought of simultaneously as both a cause and an effect, so that it is not a simple matter to classify systems variables as independent or dependent variables. Rather than formulating the relationship between independent and dependent variables in terms of one-sided causal relations, the intent is on understanding the process governing interacting components. Thus, in attempting to define participation potential, for example, by seeking to es-

Participation in Organizations

tablish what social values and goals cause what kinds of participation properties and result in what kinds of outcomes, we are likely to overlook the process by which values and goals emerge out of the total social fabric and its history, and at the same time change that social fabric.

A second and closely related aspect of interdependence relates to moderated relationships among systems variables. Our discussion of the contextual boundary conditions for participation potential illustrates the need to consider other kinds of relationships in addition to direct linear effects — a necessity often ignored in current participation research.

Another important aspect in clarifying what we mean by a systems view of participation is related to one of Katz and Kahn's (1966) major reasons for advocating a systems view of organizations, namely, that the concept of a system helps in developing a set of ideas and corresponding terms designed to integrate macro and micro questions about organizations. Thinking about participation as a system also seems to be useful in dealing with such an integration of macro and micro questions.

Although both democratic and socialist theorists try to understand participation in organizations as part of a more general societal phenomenon from which it cannot be separated, they largely neglect to question systematically under what organizational, group, and individual conditions participation can in fact achieve the desired values and outcomes. On the other hand, human-growth and -development theories, as well as the productivity and efficiency orientation, focus on intraorganizational factors, without systematically questioning what individual, group, and organizational characteristics, together with a congruent set of participation properties, can achieve the values and goals inherent in their orientations. Moreover, research on participation in these two theoretical orientations has completely neglected to question whether the individual, group, and organizational conditions that might be necessary for participation to achieve the intended values and goals, require corresponding changes in the interorganizational and societal characteristics, or whether the intended values and goals are viable within the existing societal conditions. Thus a systems conception of participation may help in recognizing the interrelated levels of analyses, in which issues relevant at one level of analysis are reflected in or are directly related to variables at other levels of analyses.

However, a re-analysis is required of what conceptualizations are needed to satisfy demands for integrating micro and macro questions and studying organizations at different levels of analysis. We have to seek changes in the currently used epistemological models that define the relationship between the knowing subject and the object of his or her knowledge (Israel, 1972). And we will need a redefinition of what is currently meant by the concept of environment (Thompson, 1967; Weick, 1969; Israel and Tajfel, 1972; Nord, 1974; Pondy, 1976). These changes are required because one of the main obstacles to the understanding of social systems is the predominance of thinking about individuals primarily as biological creatures, ''as the passive party to a relationship that reaches its maturity in conforming to an immutable and pre-established model" (Moscovici, 1972: 59). We need conceptual models in which individuals are viewed as social products defined by relationships with others and whose environment is thought of "as the humanized background to the relationships in which men engage and a tool for these relationships" (Moscovici, 1972: 60).

Implications for Methodology

This brings us to some final comments about the methodological implications of the arguments presented in this paper. One can make a distinction between analytic and holistic research, and although there have been repeated arguments for either one or the other research approach, we believe that for participation research, a new look at the interdependence of these two research approaches is required. Argyris (1968) some time ago observed that our rigorous analytic research methods are based upon and perpetuate theories-in-use, which often function as self-fulfilling prophecies by creating conditions and outcomes in accordance with what is assumed. Campbell (1974: 2) reminded us of the presumptive nature of scientific knowledge, pointing out that "in any setting in which we seem to gain new knowledge, we do so at the expense of many presumptions, untestable — to say nothing of unconfirmable — in that situation. While the appropriateness of some presumptions can be probed singly or in small sets, this can only be done by assuming the correctness of the great bulk of other presumptions." Thus, scientific knowledge depends on what Campbell (1974) called the "doubt-trust ratio," which indicates the small amount that is doubted in comparison to all the knowledge we trust. But what is trusted is in fact a set of theoretical statements derived from common-sense knowing. Although Campbell (1974: 3) talks about "an evolutionary epistemology [which] may help because it portrays commonsense knowing as based upon presumptions built into the sensory/nervous system and into ordinary language, presumptions which have been well-winnowed, highly edited, and thus indirectly confirmed through the natural selection of biological and social evolution," it is important to recognize the political aspects of our theories-in-use and the ways in which social science takes its themes of research and the contents for its theories from basic issues in society (Israel, 1972). But rather than just operationalizing with all our methodological sophistication questions and answers that originate outside of scientific activities, which is basically the function of engineers, it is encumbent on science to rephrase these questions and make them more precise.

Therefore, since organizational research, in general, and participation research, in particular, have emphasized analytic research approaches in the positivistic tradition for many obvious, methodological reasons, it becomes necessary to question the process by which science decides on how to break down for analytic study a given phenomenon into its component parts and why certain components are chosen for analytic research rather than others. We submit that preoccupation with methodological requirements for

Participation in Organizations

abstraction and the resultant emphasis on analytic research may focus research questions too early on certain components of a given phenomenon, so that other components which do not emerge within the original framework for questions and which may be of far greater significance, do not enter the process of inquiry, or enter only with great difficulty.

In researching complex social phenomena, like participation, it is often difficult, within a particular discipline paradigm, to discover and abstract the crucial components because they frequently transcend any given set of discipline questions. Therefore a greater emphasis on holistic research approaches may help generate research questions more appropriate to the dynamic systems character of these phenomena. Although holistic research approaches and their techniques are by no means clear, there have recently been several promising suggestions about what such research might look like and how holistic research output may profitably interact with the more traditional analytic approaches.

Campbell's (1974: 16) "grudging consideration of qualitative program evaluation [even] in the absence of quantitative measures" and his outlines for rapprochement between qualitative and quantitative knowing is an outstanding example. The research approaches that have been used to study participation in Norway (Thorsrud, Sorensen, and Gustavsen, 1976) and the longitudinal or comparative participation research that has attempted to use group feedback analysis (Heller, 1969) as a means of integrating analytic with holistic research methods (Heller, 1976; Heller *et al.,* 1977; Wilpert, 1977) serve as additional examples of methodologies that seem to fit the view of participation outlined in this paper.

REFERENCES

Abell, Peter (ed.)
1975 Organizations as Bargaining and Influence Systems. London: Heinemann.

Adizes, Ichak
1971 Industrial Democracy: Yugoslav Style. New York: Free Press.

Alderfer, Clayton P.
1972 Existence, Relatedness, and Growth: Human Needs in Organizational Settings. New York: Free Press.

Alutto, Joseph A., and James A. Belasco
1972 "A typology for participation in organizational decision-making." Administrative Science Quarterly, 17: 117–125.

Andriessen, Jochem H. T.
1976 "Developments in the Dutch industrial relations system." Industrial Relations, 7: 49–59.

Argyris, Chris
1964 Integrating the Individual and the Organization. New York: Wiley.
1968 "Some unintended consequences of rigorous research." Psychological Bulletin, 70: 185–197.
1969 "The incompleteness of social psychological theory." American Psychologist, 24: 893–908.
1975 "Dangers in applying results from experimental social psychology." American Psychologist, 30: 469–485.
1976 "Theories of action that inhibit individual learning." American Psychologist, 31: 638–654.

Bachrach, Peter
1967 The Theory of Democratic Elitism. Boston: Little, Brown.

Bahm, A. J.
1974 Ethics as a Behavioral Science. Springfield, IL: Charles C. Thomas.

Barker, R. G., and H. F. Wright
1955 Midwest and its Children. Evanston, IL: Row-Peterson.

Belasco, James A., and Joseph A. Alutto
1969 "Organizational impacts of teacher negotiations." Industrial Relations, 9: 67–79.

Benson, J. Kenneth
1977 "Organizations: a dialectical view." Administrative Science Quarterly, 22: 1–21.

Blake, Robert, and Jane Mouton
1961 Group Dynamics: Key to Decision-Making. Houston: Gulf.
1964 The Managerial Grid: Key Orientation for Achieving Production through People. Houston: Gulf.

Blumberg, Paul
1969 Industrial Democracy: The Sociology of Participation. New York: Schocken Books.

Brown, W., and E. Jaques
1965 Clacier Project Papers. London: Heinemann.

Campbell, Donald T.
1965 "Variation and selective retention in socio-cultural evolution." In H. R. Barringer, G. I. Blanksten, and R. Mack (eds.), Social Change in Developing Areas: 19–49. Cambridge, MA: Schenkman.
1974 Qualitative knowing in action research. Kurt Lewin Award Address to the Society for the Psychological Study of Social Issues, American Psychological Association convention, New Orleans.

Campbell, Donald T., and Donald W. Fiske
1959 "Convergent and discriminant validation by the multitrait-multi-method matrix." Psychological Bulletin, 56: 81–105.

Cattell, Raymond B.
1972 A New Morality from Science: Beyondism. New York: Pergamon.

Cherns, A. B.
1973 "Conditions for an effective management philosophy of participation." In C. P. Thakur and K. C. Sethi (eds.), Industrial Democracy: Some Issues and Experiences: 93–99 New Delhi: Shri Ram Centre for Industrial Relations and Human Resources.

Churchman, C. W.
1968 Challenge to Reason. New York: McGraw-Hill.

Clegg, H.
1960 A New Approach to Industrial Democracy. London: Blackwell.

Coch, Lester, and John R. P. French, Jr.
1948 "Overcoming resistance to change." Human Relations, 1: 512–533.

Dachler, H. Peter
1977 "The problem nature of participation in organizations: a conceptual evaluation." In Bert T. King, Siegfried S. Streufert, and Fred E. Fiedler (eds.), Managerial Control and Organizational Democracy. Washington, DC: V. H. Winston & Sons (forthcoming).

Dahl, Robert A.
1956 Preface to Democratic Theory. Chicago: University of Chicago Press.

Davis, James H.
1969 Group Performance. Reading, MA: Addison-Wesley.

Deutsch, Morton
1949 "A theory of cooperation and competition." Human Relations, 2: 129–152.
1973 The Resolution of Conflict: Constructive and Destructive Processes. New Haven: Yale University Press.

Dülfer, Eberhard, Hans Peter Euler, Günter Endruweit, Hans W. Hetzler, Wolfgang H. Staehle, and Bernhard Wilpert
1976 New patterns of work organization, trends and concepts in the Federal Republic of Germany. Paper delivered at the World Congress of the International Industrial Relations Association, Geneva.

Eckstein, Harry
1966 A Theory of Stable Democracy. Princeton: Princeton University Press.

Edelstein, J. David
1972 " 'Consumer' representation on corporate boards: the structure of representation." In Participation and Self-Management, First International Sociological Conference on Participation and Self-Management, Vol. 2: 73–81. Zagreb: University of Zagreb, The Institute for Social Research.

Emery, Fred, and Eric L. Trist
1960 "Socio-technical systems." In C. W. Churchman and M. Verhulst (eds.), Management Science, Models and Techniques, Vol. 2: 83–97. New York: Pergamon.

Emery, Fred, and Merrelyn Emery
1976 A Choice of Futures, To Enlighten or Inform. Hague: Nijhoff.

Flanders, Allan
1968 "Bargaining theory: the classical model reconsidered." In B. C. Roberts (ed.), Industrial Relations: Contemporary Issues: 3–33. London: McMillan.

Fürstenberg, Friedrich
1958 "Der betriebsrat: strukturanalyse einer grenzsituation." Köllner Zeitschrift für Soziologie und Sozial Psychologie, 14: 418–429.

Garner, W. R., Harold W. Hake, and Charles W. Eriksen
1956 "Operationism and the concept of perception." Psychological Review, 63: 149–159.

Garson, D.
1972 "Luddities in Lordstown." Harpers, 244: 68–73.

Gilman, G.
1962 "An inquiry into the nature and use of authority." In Mason Haire (ed.), Organization Theory in Industrial Practice: 105–142. New York: Wiley.

Goldstein, Irwin L.
1974 Training: Program Development and Evaluation. Monterey, CA: Brooks/Cole.

Gorz, Andre
1967 A Strategy for Labor. Boston: Beacon Press.
1973 Socialism and Revolution. Garden City: Anchor.

Gramsci, Antonio
1957 The Modern Prince. London: Lawrence and Wishart.

Greenberg, Edward S.
1975 "The consequences of worker participation: a clarification of the theoretical literature." Social Science Quarterly, 56: 191–209.

Gyllenhammar, Pehr G.
1977 People at Work. Reading, MA: Addison-Wesley.

Hackman, J. Richard
1975 "On the coming demise of job enrichment." In Eugene L. Cass and Frederick G. Zimmer (eds.), Man and Work in Society: 97–115. New York: Van Nostrand.
1976 "Group influences and individuals." In Marvin D. Dunnette (ed.), Handbook of Industrial and Organizational Psychology: 1455–1525. Chicago: Rand McNally.

Haller, Walter
1972 "Grenzen der direkten demokratie." Schweizerische JuristenZeitung, 68: 265–274.

Heller, Frank A.
1969 "Group feed-back analysis: a method of field research." Psychological Bulletin, 72: 108–117.
1971 Managerial Decision Making. London: Tavistock.
1976 "Decision processes: an analysis of power sharing at senior organizational levels." In Robert Dubin (ed.), Handbook of Work, Work Organization, and Society: 687–745. Chicago: Rand McNally.

Participation in Organizations

Heller, Frank A., Pieter J. D. Drenth, Paul Koopman, and Veljko Rus
1977 "A longitudinal study in participative decision making." Human Relations, 30: 567–587.

Heller, Frank A., and Bernhard Wilpert
1977 "Limits to participative leadership: task, structure, and skill as contingencies — a German-British comparison." European Journal of Social Psychology, 7: 61–84.

Herbst, Philip
1976 Alternatives to Hierarchies. Hague: Nijhoff.

Hulin, Charles L., and Milton R. Blood
1968 "Job enlargement, individual differences, and worker responses." Psychological Bulletin, 69: 41–55.

Huntford, Roland
1971 The New Totalitarians. New York: Stein & Day.

IDE — International research group
1976 "Industrial democracy in Europe (IDE): an international comparative study." Social Science Information, 15: 177–203.

Israel, Joachim
1972 "Stipulations and construction in the social sciences." In Joachim Israel and Henry Tajfel (eds.), The Context of Social Psychology: A Critical Assessment: 123–211. London: Academic Press.

Janis, Irvin L.
1972 Victims of Groupthink: A Psychological Study of Foreign Policy Decisions and Fiascos. Boston: Houghton Mifflin.

Kangrga, Milan
1967 "Das problem der entfremdung in Marx' werk." Praxis, 3: 13–30.

Katz, Daniel
1964 "The motivational basis of organizational behavior." Behavioral Science, 9: 131–146.

Katz, Daniel, and Robert L. Kahn
1966 The Social Psychology of Organizations. New York: Wiley.

Kuhn, Thomas S.
1970 The Structure of Scientific Revolutions (2nd ed.). Chicago: University of Chicago Press.

Lammers, C. J.
1967 "Power and participation in decision-making in formal organizations." American Journal of Sociology, 2: 201–217.

Lawler, Edward E., III
1977 "Reward systems." In J. Richard Hackman and J. Lloyd Suttle (eds.), Improving Life at Work: 163–226. Santa Monica, CA: Goodyear.

Lawler, Edward E., III, and J. Richard Hackman
1969 "Impact of employee participation in the development of pay incentive plans: A field experiment." Journal of Applied Psychology, 53: 467–471.

Leavitt, Harold J.
1965 "Applied organizational change in industry: structural, technological, and humanistic approaches." In James G. March (ed.), Handbook of Organizations: 1144–1170. Chicago: Rand McNally.

Likert, Rensis
1967 The Human Organization: Its Management and Value. New York: McGraw-Hill.

Lowin, Aaron
1968 "Participative decision making: a model, literature critique, and prescriptions for research." Organizational Behavior and Human Performance, 3: 68–106.

March, James G., and Herbert A. Simon
1958 Organizations. New York: Wiley.

Marrow, Alfred J.
1975 "Management by participation." In Eugene Louis Cass and Frederick G. Zimmer (eds.), Man and Work in Society: 33–48. New York: Van Nostrand.

Maslow, Abraham
1954 Motivation and Personality. New York: Harper.

McGrath, Joseph E., and Irwin E. Altman
1966 Small Group Research. New York: Holt, Rinehart & Winston.

McGregor, Douglas M.
1960 The Human Side of Enterprise. New York: McGraw-Hill.

Meyer, Herbert H., E. Kay, and John R. P. French, Jr.
1965 "Split roles in performance appraisal." Harvard Business Review, 43: 123–129.

Morse, Nancy C., and E. Reimer
1956 "The experimental change of a major organizational variable." Journal of Abnormal and Social Psychology, 52: 120–129.

Moscovici, Serge
1972 "Society and theory in social psychology." In Joachim Israel and Henry Tajfel (eds.), The Context of Social Psychology: A Critical Assessment: 17–68. London: Academic Press.

Mulder, Mauk, and Henk Wilke
1970 "Participation and power equalization." Organizational Behavior and Human Performance, 5: 430–448.

Myrdal, Gunnar
1969 Objectivity in Social Research. New York: Pantheon Books.

Nagel, Ernest
1968 The Structure of Science (2nd impression). London: Routledge and Kegan Paul.

Naschold, Frieder
1969 Organisation und Demokratie. Stuttgart: Kohlhammer.

Nord, Walter R.
1974 "The failure of current applied behavioral science: a Marxian perspective." The Journal of Applied Behavioral Science, 10: 557–578.

Obradovic, Josip
1970 "Participation and work attitudes in Yugoslavia." Industrial Relations, 9: 161–169.

Pateman, Carole
1970 Participation and Democratic Theory. London: Cambridge University Press.

Peterson, R. B.
1968 "The Swedish experience with industrial democracy." The British Journal of Industrial Relations, 6: 193–210.

Pondy, Louis R.
1976 Beyond open systems models of organizations. Paper presented at the Annual Meeting of the Academy of Management, Kansas City.

Porket, J. L.
1975 "Participation in management in communist systems in the 1970s." British Journal of Industrial Relations, 13: 371–387.

Pothoff, Erich, Otto Blume, and Helmut Duvernell
1962 Zwischenbilanz der Mitbestimmung. Tübingen: J. C. B. Mohr (Paul Siebeck).

Pugh, Derek S.
1966 "Modern organization theory." Psychological Bulletin, 66: 235–251.

Rambaek, Frank
1977 The participative potential — a concept worth knowing for the democratization of enter-

prise? Paper presented at the Second International Conference on Participation, Workers' Control and Self-management, Paris.

Roberts, Karlene H.
1970 "On looking at an elephant: an evaluation of cross-cultural research related to organizations." Psychological Bulletin, 74: 327–350.

Roggemann, Hans
1970 Das Modell der Arbeiterselbstverwaltung in Jugoslavien. Frankfurt: Europäische Verlagsanstalt.

Rus, Veljko
1970 "Influence structure in Yugoslav enterprise." Industrial Relations, 9: 148–160.

Sartori, Giovanni
1962 Democratic Theory. Detroit: Wayne State University Press.

Scharpf, Fritz
1970 Demokratie Theorie zwischen Utopie und Anpassung. Constance: Universitäts Verlag.

Scheflen, K. C., Edward E. Lawler, III, and J. Richard Hackman
1971 "Long-term impact of employee participation in the development of pay incentive plans: a field experiment revisited." Journal of Applied Psychology. 55: 182–186.

Schneider, Benjamin
1976 Staffing Organizations. Pacific Palisades, CA: Goodyear.

Scholl, Wolfgang
1976 Theoretical reflections on influence, power and its alienating effects, and participation. Paper presented at the EGOS Symposium on Power, University of Bradford, Great Britain.

Seashore, Stanley E.
1977 Participation in decision making: some issues of conception, measurement and interaction. Paper presented at the Annual Meeting of the Academy of Management, Orlando, Florida.

Simmel, Georg
1950 The Sociology of Georg Simmel (K. H. Wolff, translator). New York: Free Press.

Sorge, A.
1976 "The evolution of industrial democracy in the countries of the European community." British Journal of Industrial Relations, 14: 274–294.

Sperry, R. W.
1977 "Bridging science and values: a unifying view of mind and brain." American Psychologist, 32: 237–245.

Strauss, George
1963 "Some notes on power-equalization." In Harold J. Leavitt (ed.), The Social Science of Organizations: 39–84. Englewood Cliffs, NJ: Prentice-Hall.

1977 "Managerial practices." In J. Richard Hackman and J. Lloyd Suttle (eds.), Improving Life at Work: 297–363. Santa Monica, CA: Goodyear.

Strauss, George, and E. Rosenstein
1970 "Workers' participation: a critical point of view." Industrial Relations, 9: 197–214.

Sturmthal, Adolf
1964 Workers Councils: A Study of Workplace Organization both Sides of the Iron Curtain. Cambridge, MA: Harvard University Press.

Tabb, J. Y., and A. Goldfarb
1970 Workers' Participation in Management. London: Pergamon.

Tannenbaum, Arnold S., B. Kavcic, M. Rosner, M. Vianello, and G. Wieser
1974 Hierarchy in Organizations. San Francisco: Jossey-Bass.

Tannenbaum, R., and W. H. Schmidt
1958 "How to choose a leadership pattern." Harvard Business Review, 36: 95–101.

Thompson, Dennis
1970 The Democratic Citizen. London: Cambridge University Press.

Thompson, James D.
1967 Organizations in Action. New York: McGraw-Hill.

Thorsrud, E., B. A. Sorensen, and B. Gustavsen
1976 "Sociotechnical approach to industrial democracy in Norway." In Robert Dubin (ed.), Handbook of Work Organization and Society: 421–464. Chicago: Rand McNally.

Tosi, Henry L., and W. Clay Hamner
1974 Organizational Behavior and Management: A Contingency Approach. Chicago: St. Clair Press.

Trist, Eric L., and K. W. Bamforth
1951 "Some social and psychological consequences of the Long-Wall method of coal-

getting." Human Relations, 4: 3–38.

Turner, A. N., and P. R. Lawrence
1965 Industrial Jobs and the Worker. Boston: Harvard Graduate School of Business Administration.

U.S. Department of Health, Education and Welfare
1973 Work in America. Cambridge, MA: MIT Press.

Vanek, Jaroslav
1970 The General Theory of Labor Managed Market Economies. Ithaca, NY: Cornell University Press.

1971 The Participatory Economy: An Evolutionary Hypothesis and a Strategy for Development. Ithaca, NY: Cornell University Press.

1975 Self-Management: Economic Liberation of Man. Harmondsworth: Penguin.

Veen, P.
1972 "Effects of participative decision making in field hockey training: a field experiment." Organizational Behavior and Human Performance, 7: 288–307.

Vranicki, Predrag
1965 "Socialism and the problem of alienation." Praxis, 1: 307–317.

Vroom, Victor H.
1960 Some Personality Determinants of the Effects of Participation. Englewood Cliffs, NJ: Prentice-Hall.

1970 "Industrial social psychology." In Gardner Lindzey and Eliot Aronson (eds.), The Handbook of Social Psychology, Vol. 5 (2nd ed.): 196–268. Reading, MA: Addison-Wesley.

1976 "Leadership." In Marvin D. Dunnette (ed.), Handbook of Industrial and Organizational Psychology: 1527–1551. Chicago: Rand McNally.

Vroom, Victor H., and Phillip W. Yetton
1973 Leadership and Decision-Making. Pittsburgh: University of Pittsburgh Press.

Wahba, Mahmond A., and Lawrence G. Bridwell
1973 "Maslow reconsidered: a review of research on the need hierarchy theory." In Thad B. Green and Dennis F. Ray (eds.), Academy of Management Proceedings: 514–520.

Participation in Organizations

Walker, Kenneth F.
1974 "Workers' participation in management: problems, practice and prospect." International Institute for Labor Studies (IILS) Bulletin, 12: 3–35.

Weick, Karl E.
1969 The Social Psychology of Organizing. Reading, MA: Addison-Wesley.

Wilpert, Bernhard
1975 "Research on industrial democracy: the German case." Industrial Relations Journal, 6: 53–64.
1977 Führung in Deutschen Unternehmen. Berlin: W. de Gruyter.

Wood, Michael T.
1970 Some determinants and consequences of power distribution in decision-making groups. Doctoral dissertation, University of Illinois.
1972 "Effects of decision processes and task situations on influence perceptions." Organizational Behavior and Human Performance, 7: 417–427.
1973 "Power relationships and group decision making in organizations." Psychological Bulletin, 79: 280–293.

[2]

International Perspectives on Organizational Democracy
Edited by B. Wilpert and A. Sorge
© 1984, John Wiley & Sons Ltd.

Organizational democracy: the history of an idea

Malcolm Warner

The origins of an idea, such as organizational democracy, are both complex and demanding. No two writers would agree on a common view. Nonetheless, an attempt to discuss the problem must not only cover possible areas of consensus but also present a subjective vision.

We cannot assume, in trying to look for the origin of contemporary notions, that there is a simple set of doctrines to be explored. The literature abounds with overlapping labels and categories. 'Organizational democracy' is a catch-all term, often divided into industrial democracy, worker participation, self-management and so on, perhaps encompassing voluntary associations and governmental forms (Crouch and Heller, 1983).

Is the history of organizational democracy a seamless web? A historian of the international labour movement such as Kendall (1975, pp. 1–23) describes the progressive implementation of its ideas. It depends on our standpoint, however, whether we accept this type of approach as a definitive account of the unfolding of organizational democracy over time. A writer interested in the evolution of economic self-management such as Vanek (1975, pp. 16–21) might present a somewhat more specialized case, than, say, a student of political theory in the age of organizations, such as Wolin (1961, pp. 352–434).

One of the problems in disentangling the disciplinary influences nourishing the idea of organizational democracy relates to the fact that the professionalization of knowledge is relatively recent. Hence the writers on this notion did not see themselves as, say, primarily economists or political scientists. This happened more recently, mostly in the present century. Many were 'men of action' rather than academics. If they were 'men of ideas', they were unlikely to be tenured scholars!

Whether the evolution of ideas via sub-sets of 'competing research programmes' (Lakatos, 1970) makes sense in this context is a moot point, but the

5

competition of notions from different disciplines has had its effect, as have events in society. Indeed, 'changes in the doctrines which practising economists regard as orthodox are more often the result of an autonomous change in the problem-situation ...' (Deane, 1978, p. xiii).

The impetus for writing this contribution to the debate on the origins of organizational democracy stems from an initial reaction to a conceptual schema drawn up elsewhere by colleagues (Dachler and Wilpert, 1978). Their paper, subsequently much cited, provides a very bold and systematic conceptual framework for looking at organizational participation. They discuss 'the social theories underlying participatory social systems and the values of goals, each of them implies for participation' (1978, p. 1), but concentrate mostly on the properties of participative social arrangements.

The theories they briefly cover include 'Democratic' ideas (1978, p. 4); 'Socialistic theory' (1978, pp. 6–7); 'Human growth and development' concepts (1978, pp. 7–8); and 'Productivity and Efficiency' notions (1978, pp. 8–10). The problem is that the historical account is highly compressed, so that it leaves out a good deal which the present writer believes to be important. We must also take issue with the 'search-perspectives' (1978, p. 4) adopted to seek out the theories and goals underlying participation, although the disagreement is one of emphasis rather than substance.

In their discussion, Dachler and Wilpert (1978, pp. 4–6) mostly confine discussion of democratic theories to recent political and social science criticisms, and set socialist theories probably unintentionally in an almost exclusively Marxist setting. Can we, in fact, 'ignore the theories' points of overlap and divergence' and leave out 'important details which are not directly, or are only tangentially, related to the issues of participation' (1978, p. 47)? While possibly appropriate for such a conceptual schema, the approach needs complementing *vis-à-vis* a fuller account of the origins of organizational democracy as an idea, or set of ideas.

We now hope to pose the following questions under a number of main headings:

(1) *Classical-versus-modern concepts*: do contemporary notions of democracy, whether in organizations or not, have only tenuous, or at best indirect, links with past ones?
(2) *Socialist theory:* do current notions of organizational democracy spring from a wide range of influences, of which any given ideological stream is only one among several, and how do we distinguish between them?
(3) *'Elite-versus-mass' notions*: do theories of elites-versus-mass membership now constitute the predominant problem to be faced in understanding organizational democracy experiments?
(4) *Theories-versus-experiments*: do theories, whether or not in any of the above categories, directly effect organizationally democratic experiments, or do ideas affect such experiments significantly at all?

Organizational Democracy: The History of an Idea   7

CLASSICAL VERSUS MODERN CONCEPTS

It is clearly difficult to pinpoint the roots of organizational democracy in antiquity, although there are 'family resemblances' between nascent notions of democracy and contemporary notions of the organizational/industrial variety.

The main difference is in the nature and scale of organizations. Greek city-states were small entities; even Renaissance cities had mostly under 50,000 inhabitants. Economic units, whether in agriculture or crafts, were also on a limited scale, *vis-à-vis* modern times. While the Athenian ideal is characterized as based on direct democracy, it was far from such a 'pure' form, according to one view. It seems:

in principle, direct and not representative, each male citizen having one vote in the Assembly which meets at stated intervals and which, in time, comes to have the final decision on all important matters. Only a fraction of the citizenry, however, usually attends meetings of the Assembly. Since rural citizens are loath to leave their farms and since many are often at war, it is rare that more than two thousand to three thousand Athenians—most of them townsmen—sit in the Assembly. Athenian democracy, however, is not as direct as some friendly stereotypes suggest, and in part for that reason is not as irresponsible and capricious as some hostile stereotypes maintain. (Gouldner, 1965, p. 135)

To draw parallels between earlier forms of participation and modern organizational involvement may be misleading. First, democracy was only confined to the *demos* in ancient Greece; thus a 'middle-class' excluding menials and slaves. Furthermore, the *polis* was in no way a 'State', a term unknown to the Greeks. Second, medieval craft guilds were dominated by the big masters and were essentially unlike trade unions. Third, if there is causality, it is in the reverse direction as we often re-invent the past to legitimize an existing phenomenon, or to seek to set up a new one.

As Sartori (1965, p. 250) points out:

The term democracy was coined almost twenty-five hundred years ago. It first appeared in Herodotus' *History* in connection with the notion of *isonomia*, equality before the law. From then on, even though it was eclipsed for a very long interval, it has remained part of the political vocabulary. But in so long a lifetime it has naturally acquired diverse meanings, referring, as it has, to very different historical situations as well as to very different ideals. So with the passing of time both its denotative and connotative uses have changed. It would be strange if this were not so; and it is therefore surprising to observe how little attention is paid to the fact that today's concept of democracy has only a very slight resemblance, if any, to the concept that was revered in the fifth century B.C. When we use the same word we instinctively tend to believe that we are referring to the same thing. However, if this ingenuousness is excusable when we are dealing with contemporary events, it is not when it makes us pass over more than two thousand years of historical achievements, as is the case with Rousseau and with Marx's and Lenin's democratic primitivism.

Thus, modern political and organizational democracy pays lip-service to its past, but discerning the intellectual and/or ideological roots of present practices and aspirations is another matter. To see current developments as *linearly* linked to past ideas and experiences, may not be as useful as distinguishing the explicit influences on recent and contemporary history.

In fact, the word 'democracy' only came into the English language in the sixteenth century as a result of Renaissance interest in Greek classics (Field, 1965, p. 275), and had little relevance at the time, except for a few Swiss cantons. It sprang up again in the seventeenth century in the guise of 'church democracy' and 'state democracy', as called for by speakers in the Puritan army. Thus:

Modern men want another democracy, in the sense that their ideal of democracy is not at all the same as that of the Greeks. And it would be strange, indeed, if this were not so. In more than two thousand intervening years Western civilization has enriched, modified and articulated its value goals. It has experienced Christianity, humanism, the Reformation, the modern conceptions of natural law, and liberalism. How can we possibly think that when we advocate democracy today we are pursuing the same aims and ideals as the Greeks? (Sartori, 1965, p. 251)

Referring to older models of self-government is also misleading. Traditionally, they involved peer groups of priests, professionals and educators. They often involved dominant or elite organizations which exercised power over their subordinates or employees, who were not really members of that body, as in the case of monasteries, and later Oxbridge colleges of dons *vis-à-vis* undergraduates and such 'lesser breeds'.

In studying the nature of both classical and modern oligarchy (see Edelstein and Warner, 1979, pp. 28 ff.), a number of models may be cited. *Within* many of these, self-government may be found, at least for the oligarchs, and particularly where it is a governing oligarchy holding power via formal office (Edelstein and Warner, 1979, p. 38).

Such cases are interesting only because their contemporary counterparts offer a model for self-government to those outside the privileged institution in question; or the organization may become extended to take in lower participants and include them in the charmed circle, or at least its procedures. Indeed, new mass organizations may develop copying the norms and rules of the restricted bodies. Even when craft unions developed they were 'exclusive', but later widened their membership; or new unions were set up to cover the unskilled.

WORK, DEMOCRACY AND SOCIALIST THEORIES: THE PAST AND RECENT PAST

The term 'organizational democracy' will be taken as relating to those democratic notions primarily relating to work organizations, although not exclusively. It goes beyond industrial bodies, to those in the agricultural and

Organizational Democracy: The History of an Idea   9

service sectors, and crosses the private/public ownership divide, covering educational, religious, and even political organizations.

Given that this is a bird's-eye view, it is necessary to stress possible *communalities* in examining the antecedents of organizational democracy; and it is inevitable that the Anglo-Saxon (or at least European) bias of the present writer will reveal itself. The reasons for this are two-fold; first, reasons of formative background and education; and second, 'facts' of general history, namely that industrialization and the ideological responses to it began in Britain, and only later spread to continental Europe and North America to a greater or lesser degree.

Before the momentous year of 1789 'the notion of popular sovereignty had been advocated by individual writers such as Winstanley and Rousseau but it had not found expression in a mass movement at a national level', according to one writer (Caute, 1966, p. 30). With initially the Girondin Revolution, then the Jacobin (as with the much later Bolshevik dictatorship), the exercise of popular will was more nominal than actual. The economic experiments, too, were peripheral, and short-lived. If there were ideas of industrial democracy afoot, they were hardly discernible at that time. Babeuf, an early communist, believed in centrally planned economy, for example. While the eighteenth century produced the 'Enlightenment', it may be argued that today's politics have been more influenced by the 'Romantic Movement' in human thought, whether 'positively or negatively' (Russell, 1961, p. 651).

The 'Romantic Movement' is characterized, as a whole, by the substitution of aesthetic for utilitarian standards (Russell, 1961, p. 653). It inspired what was to become the Left, as well as the Right, by its reaction against the emergent capitalist values. Hence it could nurture counter-tendencies to the authority of the factory owner, and often the hope of 'liberation'.

To start first with Rousseau: 'spoken of as the father of democracy, and also the father of totalitarianism, as the champion of liberty and the apologist for dictatorship' (Field, 1965, p. 39). Rousseau's notion of the Social Contract, and the emphasis on direct democracy, was set in a community rather than an organizational context; but it opened up a Pandora's Box. Transferred to the work community the General Will leads ultimately to the General Assembly as the ultimate source of legitimacy and authority of, say, the Israeli kibbutz or Yugoslav self-managed firm. Jeffersonian ideas in the emerging United States also assumed citizen involvement in decision-making. Both Rousseau and Jefferson, however, stressed property rights (Poole, 1982, p. 182), preferably with a broader distribution of such.

According to Vanek, the new machine-age was the trigger:

The modern idea of workers' participation or self-management emerged in the critical reaction to the industrial revolution which began in the eighteenth century. In England and continental Europe by the mid-nineteenth century, the intellectual reaction to industrialism had assumed a whole spectrum of different forms.

The most important figures among those whom we think of as the Utopian socialists were Saint-Simon and Charles Fourier in France, and Robert Owen in England. Saint-Simon advocated the redirecting of the industrial age under greater expertise, while Fourier and Owen placed their hopes in autonomous communities organized for the good of all who worked in them. In the Utopian communities, the producers were subordinate to the general management of the community. Although they were concerned with the organization of industry, and of agriculture, none of these men had a clear vision of workers' self-management, but each led a movement and had a school of followers, out of which sprang other movements aiming more directly at economic democracy. (Vanek, 1975, pp. 16–17)

Socialism launched its attack on two fronts, both against the specific evils of capitalist industrialism; and with an ideological onslaught on its roots in liberalism (Roll, 1938, pp. 232–3). Utopian Socialism may have had a greater impact on organizational democracy than later developments, such as the 'scientific' variety. Marx, it should be noted, 'described as utopian any form of socialist thought but his own, which he called "scientific"' (Schumpeter, 1961, p. 455, n. 8). Early socialism was associationist, and here Robert Owen and Charles Fourier were the prime candidates, with Louis Blanc and Philippe-Joseph-Baptiste Buchez in second place.

Owen, who was born in 1771, taught himself to become manager at twenty (Pollard, 1965, p. 149). He was a progressive capitalist who anticipated 'human-relations' management in the workplace. He thought that good conditions, both on and off the job, created sound workmen. He aimed to provide decent conditions of work, wages and education for the workers in his employment at the New Lanark factory in Scotland. He described it rather immodestly as 'the most important experiment for the happiness of the human race that had yet been instituted at any time in any part of the world' (see Gatrell, 1970, p. 40).

Owen wrote that:

If, then, due care as to the state of your inanimate machines can produce ... beneficial results, what may not be expected if you devote equal attention to your vital machines, which are far more wonderfully constructed? ... From experience which cannot deceive me, I venture to assure you, that your time and money so applied, if directed by a true knowledge of the subject, would return you not five, ten, or fifteen per cent for your capital so expended, but often fifty and in many cases a hundred per cent. (Gatrell, 1970, pp. 94, 95–6).

He also promoted 'the first really successful alternative to capitalist industrialism', namely the Pioneers of Rochdale in 1844, laying down the foundations for 'the first lasting cooperative of consumers' (Vanek, 1975, p. 17). Owen also influenced the setting up of experimental collective settlements in the New World, principally 'New Harmony' in 1824: but it only lasted 2 years. Charles Fourier also inspired the setting up of 'Brook Farm', Massachusetts, in 1841. It too was based on shared tasks, equality, and the simple life. It lasted just over 5 years, and collapsed soon after a major fire.

Organizational Democracy: The History of an Idea   11

Many experiments such as this ultimately failed. They were too small and too poorly run. They also went too far beyond the boundary of the system they rejected. Being utopian, they led transitory existences (Palisi, 1970), and this prevented them from influencing the mainstream of their society.

Blanc believed in workshops being set up for unemployed artisans but under state supervision; Buchez is held to have advocated, stemming from Christian egalitarianism, self-managing workmen's associations organizing production: 'The republic in the workshop' (cited in Vanek, 1975, p. 17).

Associationism of this early kind was not, however, necessarily 'extremist', nor was it a narrow, exclusive ideology. For example, this form of socialism 'was not nonsense to the Benthamite mind ... and this accounts for the cautious associationism of J. S. Mill' (Schumpeter, 1961, p. 457). Chartism, in the same epoch, must not be directly classified with the precursory notions of self-management, for it was closer to Utilitarianism as it demanded *political* reforms in the shape of the extension of the franchise. When it failed its steam was channelled into the New Model trade unions, for the most part coexisting with individual capitalist ownership. But Chartists like O'Brien, Harney and Jones were influenced by Owen, and even notions of class struggle (Thornley, 1981, p. 18).

The first modern national trade union was the Amalgamated Society of Engineers, in Britain, in 1852, largely the achievement of William Allan and William Newton, who in their own way were pioneers of organizational democracy. It was their successful advocacy which resulted in the constitution of this first national experiment being adopted in whole or part by a large number of other emerging unions between 1852 and 1875. These new bodies helped diffuse the idea of workmen running their own organizations. It was, as its name suggests, something new. Sidney and Beatrice Webb (1894) noted:

It is easy to understand the great influence which, during the next twenty years, this 'New Model' exercised upon the Trade Union world .... Scarcely a trade exists which did not, between 1852 and 1875, either attempt to imitate the whole constitution of the Amalgamated Engineers, or incorporate one or other of its characteristic features. (S. and B. Webb 1894, pp. 223–4)

Schumpeter claims that Mill was an 'evolutionary socialist' (Schumpeter, 1961, p. 532), and that he anticipated the German Revisionist position set out much later by Bernstein, with his denial of the immiseration thesis. Mill was much influenced by French associationist writers, and was emotionally attracted to Socialism, sceptical however of the Utopian variety. Conversely, Mill may have influenced Lassalle (Schumpeter, 1961, p. 457, n. 14). But he did not endorse changing the ownership and direction of industry. Mill clearly *did* believe in the *historical relativity* of social institutions, but did *not* think they would change of themselves, guided by any determinist design. He saw 'democracy as a vehicle for self-development' (Poole, 1982, p. 3).

The emphasis on work as an end in itself and having redemptive possibilities was also stressed by Carlyle, Morris and Ruskin, as well as the young Marx. Mill, unlike Owen, and possibly for this reason, accepted the 'triad' of economic theory involving the three factors of production: land, labour and capital (the latter hiring 'industrious people' (Schumpeter, 1961, p. 555), believing in the 'labour theory of value'.

Christian socialism, for its part, was represented by at least two major tributaries. The first was British and Protestant. It had its impact in the 1840s and 1850s, and through it Buchez's ideas may have been diffused in Britain (Vanek, 1975, p. 18); but its influence was limited and eventually directed into lay activities such as helping to promote the co-operative movement. The second, the Roman Catholic variety, derives from the reaction to early industrial capitalism in Europe. There is a long tradition of social criticism, even nascent Catholic Socialism of whom Buchez and Le Play were examples. Later developments influenced Papal Encyclicals such as *Rerum Novarum* in 1891, and modern Catholic ideas on co-determination (see Skalicky, 1975, pp. 110 ff.).

As for Marx, 'political economy was merely one branch (if the most important) in the study of human social behaviour in the round' (Deane, 1978, p. 126). Capitalism was to be only a stage in the unfolding of human history, according to 'the laws of motion' of the economic process, he claimed to have discovered (Deane, 1978, p. 128). Marx's chief theoretical prop was also the 'labour theory of value' (Roll, 1938, pp. 260 ff.): 'its real purpose was to serve as a basis for his theory of exploitation' (Roll, 1938, p. 266), and hence how to remedy such an evil.

Hegel's influence, via Marx, was to stress 'alienation', at least in the latter's early writings, which anticipated subsequent writers who concentrated on remedying this by advocating more involvement in the affairs of the workplace (see Blumberg, 1968, for example, for a discussion of the socio-psychological literature on alienation).

The Marxist tradition, stemming from this period, has been written about so voluminously that we cannot do more than refer to it. Selucky (1975, pp. 47 ff.) believes that it was highly ambiguous, and oscillated between the *centralist* and the *participatory*. While the Paris Commune of 1871 clearly impressed Marx, it did not last more than a few weeks. True, it exemplified egalitarian values and had a 'corresponding organizational structure' (Dachler and Wilpert, 1978, p. 6), and became a basic model for self-managing systems.

The anarchist stream derives partly from Pierre Joseph Proudhon who, apart from believing property to be 'theft', also thought value 'mad', although it is doubtful if he was as anarchist as is believed; his idea of working-men's associations was closer to the self-employed artisan federation, although his ideas on 'mutual credit' were influential. Truer to such colours was Mikhail Bakunin, whom Marx detested, and who contributed much to the anti-statist flavour of nineteenth-century radical thought. Peter Kropotkin, even more

Organizational Democracy: The History of an Idea   13

so, impelled anti-elitist communitarian theory forward, somewhat later (see Burrell and Morgan, 1979, pp. 338 ff.). He has also been seen as a precursor of the ecologists. Influenced by Darwin, he saw 'mutual aid' as the main evolutionary goal of mankind.

At the turn of the century, Socialist ideas were spreading rapidly. They were not all favourable to worker participation. The Fabian Society, set up in 1884, contained two factions; one, led by Beatrice and Sidney Webb, believed in statist notions (see Warner, 1969, pp.144–53) and was critical of producers' co-operatives; the other was a later breakaway group led by G. D. H. Cole, the founder of the British Guild Socialism. The Webbs, however, in their *Industrial Democracy* (1901), still a classic, emphasized the expansion of workplace rights via trade unions as a step towards greater democratization.

The Guild Socialists

harked back to the Christian Socialists, and even farther, to the medieval craft guilds. On the other hand they intended—as more suited to modern conditions of production—a broad vertical integration which would eventually band the workers of the nation in a given trade or industry into a single guild, which would then be the controlling power in that industry. By this method they sought to introduce what was variously called economic democracy, self-government in industry or sometimes workers' control. It was indeed an advocacy of workers' participation. (Vanek, 1975, p. 20)

Another, but more radical, movement of the period was Revolutionary Syndicalism, which was then very strong in France and neighbouring countries:

What the syndicalists meant by workers' control was markedly different, for they wanted the labour union movements to expand their power so that the syndicates would finally not only control industry but also do away with the power of the capitalist state. As part of their way to power, the syndicalists believed in the efficacy of strikes and above all else the general strike. In this they were revolutionary, but in their longing to do away with the prevailing mechanisms of government they were profoundly anarchist. Even as advocates of the proletariat, the syndicalists had no deep interest in participatory self-management; their goals were primarily political. (Vanek, 1975, p. 20)

Georges Sorel argued, for the anarcho-syndicalists' as they were called, that it 'was not science that changed the world but myth' (in McInnes (1969, p. 102)), quoted from Sorel's *Reflections on Violence* (1908). He later defended the Soviet Revolution as transferring power to the workers, believing Proudhon's self-rule had triumphed rather than Marxian state authority. Violence was inevitable to achieve progress, in his view. Sorel, in this theoretical perspective, is possibly 'father' of *direct-action*; hence, of sit-ins and factory occupations.

The Yugoslavs, it is said, derive their system of self-management from several traditions, some foreign, some domestic (Blumberg, 1968, p. 193). Whether Sorel inspired them is doubtful. The influence of the Italian

Communist thinker, Antonio Gramsci, may, however, be mentioned in this context, particularly in view of the notorious but short-lived Italian factory occupations of 1920. His aim was to develop 'a net of proletarian institutions' (cited in Burrell and Morgan, 1979, p. 290), mainly factory councils, a foundation-stone of the new workers' state (Femia, 1982).

After the First World War ideas about organizational democracy spread very widely, but in different forms. In the Russian Revolution factories had been occupied by workers, but as we shall see later this very quickly led to state control. In the Weimar Republic 'works councils' were institutionalized in law, and the foundations of the later *Mitbestimmung* system were laid, anticipating the early 1950s (see Wilpert, 1975).

The roots of this may lie much further back (Sorge, 1976; Teuteberg, 1981); indeed back to the early period of industrialization in Germany. Early social theorists, such as von Baader and others, were prominent in the 1830s. Several experiments in the mid and late nineteenth century took place, partly to counter more radical schemes. In 1919 the Weimar Republic initiated a law on works councils, in the face of revolutionary alternatives and local 'soviets' (Teuteberg, 1981, pp. 27–40).

The next section deals with some of the major debates concerning organizational democracy, relating to the conflict between notions of elite and mass membership.

ELITE AND MASS NOTIONS OF ORGANIZATIONAL DEMOCRACY

The rise of the modern political party has given rise to the notion of membership sovereignty, as ongoing polemics in the British Labour Party (and now the Social Democratic Party) testify (Whiteley, 1981). Such discussions echo, and may be relevant for the study of democratic theory as were the debates in Cromwell's New Model Army in the 1640s (Walzer, 1965; Hill, 1970).

The reality, however, first described by empirical observers such as Ostrogorski (1902) and Michels (1911), is another matter. Even in very recent experience the thesis of persistent oligarchic tendencies has been seen as operative in political parties (MacKenzie, 1963). This view has not been accepted by all writers on social and political theory.

Runciman (1963, pp. 77–8), on the other hand, has argued that the safeguards against such oligarchy are two-fold. Governing elites may be replaceable by those whose interests they represent, and the elites may be adequately diffused. A highly diffused elite would be more accessible to the membership and can perhaps be held more responsible, thus making representation more direct. But such a contention must be conditional, since oligarchies may be diffuse without being any the more democratic. In addition, one can think of a diffusion of power on routine matters, but which left top decisions in the hands of senior officials.

The notion of the 'vanguard' has, however, eroded membership rights, and

Organizational Democracy: The History of an Idea   15

Lenin's model of democratic centralism (Wolin, 1961, pp. 421 ff.) has led to party elite domination, pointing up a visible chasm between those who believe in party democracy and those who do not (see the policy statement of the Italian Communist Party, *Guardian*, 8 February 1982), mirroring the position on industrial democracy. Bottomore (1964, p. 136) believes that Marx 'never for a moment' considered the possibility of a 'new ruling class' emerging in the post-capitalist phase.

If in the heat of revolutionary zeal the workers took over factories in 1917, the Bolsheviks 'were apparently turned from this path by the exigencies of war-time production' (Vanek, 1975, p. 21), and the state bodies took the operation of the enterprises over. Henceforth 'the situation has remained substantially unchanged' (Vanek, 1975, p. 21). The moves from below towards workers' self-rule stayed latent in the Soviet system, a classic case of 'goal-displacement' (cf. Burrell and Morgan, 1979, pp. 184–9). Furthermore, 'Utopian' experiments, such as workers' control, were not to prove consistent with democratic centralism; in Lenin's words, 'the proletariat needs state power, the centralized organization of force' (cited in Wolin, 1961, p. 426); indeed 'we want no more opposition' (cited in Ionescu and de Madariaga, 1968, p. 162).

Lenin had at first paid lip service to 'workers' control' (Nove, 1972, p. 41), but deplored syndicalism and an 'authentic Workers' Opposition' (Caute, 1966, p. 173). More earnestly, he thought that the existing capitalist enterprise management could be run by the workers. It could then be perfected and purified (Wolin, 1961, p. 426). But as the revolution ran its course it was clear that a management hierarchy was needed, even if with political control superimposed. 'Taylorism' was to be diffused, for as mentioned earlier Lenin believed that combined with Socialism it would lead to Communism (Littler, 1978). By the 1930s sharp differentials had been brought back under Stalin. The dearth of trained managers was extreme. 'Foreign engineers and technical workers—American, German and some English' (Dobb, 1966, p. 258) poured in. Trade unions were even used as schools of management and administration. Incentive schemes, and especially the 'Stakhanovite' methods—called by some Taylorism in Russian clothes—became *de rigueur*.

Trotsky believed in 'workers' control' in the sense of their exercising a kind of dual power, overseeing the capitalists not yet appropriated (Blumberg, 1968, pp. 192–3). This was a transitional stage before a dictatorship of the proletariat. Trotsky was opposed to such control in the long run, and even to independent trade unions. His enthusiasm for Taylorism was, according to Merkle (1980), as great as Lenin's, although reverting in exile to supporting workers' oppositionism.

The Maoist model, relating to both party and industrial settings, has been contrasted with western capitalist, on the one hand, and Leninist notions on the other, in the sense that it offers a non-hierarchical, non-elitist alternative. On the other hand Whyte (1973, p. 163) has denied that 'China has found a route to modernization without bureaucratization, or that the Maoist ideal solves the problem of how to modernize without sacrificing revolutionary social goals'. There are still marked 'similarities between Maoist and Western organizational conceptions' (Whyte, 1973, p. 158). Mao, in this view, did not dismantle large organizations, and installed participatory democracy. Chinese organizations, like others, have goals and use the division of labour (with hierarchies and specialized roles), rewards, and rules (Whyte, 1973, p. 156). Their organized life is still co-ordinated by state, administrative, army and party bureaucracy. The survival of the notion of 'ruling class', 'elite' and familiar authority structures is not surprising. As Reisman has argued: 'We cannot be satisfied with the answers given by Marx, Mosca, Michels, Pareto, Weber, Veblen or Burnham, though we can learn from all of them' (cited in Dahrendorf, 1959, p. 302). Elitism is a residue of the past; its inertia is considerable.

THEORIES-VERSUS-EXPERIMENTS

In order to better understand the origins of organizational democracy, we must make a distinction between ideas and attempts to put them into practice. The assumption thus far has been that concepts have a primary role, and that we should trace their origins to find the roots of the institutional forms in question. Is this indeed the case?

Taking the simplest possible model, we can distinguish theories on the one hand, and experiments on the other. Moreover, we can divide each case into those which were adopted and subsequently diffused, and those which were not, as a point of departure. It is clear that there are at least four possible cases:

(1) theories which were diffused,
(2) theories which were not;
(3) experiments which were diffused;
(4) experiments which were not.

While there can be different kinds of experiments (see Warner, 1981, 1983), the main distinction we are making is between theoretical models (ideas) and practical models (experiments). *Some* theories led to experiments, but not all; *some* experiments similarly gave birth to theories. The point to be emphasized is that many ideas can be traced and identified when we look at the antecedents of organizational democracy, but it is not easy to sift out the seminal ones. There were ideas which did not lead to practical experiments, or if they did were never diffused. There are also possible candidates for the *seminal idea* category, but it is possible that each tradition will construct its own genealogy.

Moreover, even if we could establish *common* lines of evolution back into the albeit recent past, crossing frontiers, there would always be both national traditions and contexts to reckon with. In examining any one country's

Organizational Democracy: The History of an Idea   17

experience there are often local ideas and/or experiments which are put forward as the favoured candidates. A student of this field frequently encounters such national scenarios, whether historical or institutional.

It is possible that a given set of experiments may be claimed by rival ideological positions, whether on the one hand *managerial*, or on the other more *radical*. The effects of the Hawthorne experiments, for example, may be seen here as a case in point (Blumberg, 1968; Parsons, 1974; Franke and Kaul, 1978).

In the case of many experiments to be later interpreted as promoting greater democracy in the workplace, the trigger may at first take place at management's initiative, as in the case of the Glacier project (Rose, 1975, p. 177), and the original 'sociotechnical' research in the British coal mines (Trist and Bamforth, 1951), and then in an Indian textile mill (Rice, 1958; Miller, 1983). The achievements of these early *sociotechnical experiments* led to the promotion of, amongst other things, notions of participative systems, autonomous work groups and job design (see Trist, 1981). Sociotechnical experiments have probably inspired several hundreds of emulations in Sweden, let alone the rest of Scandinavia.

Although there were clearly intellectual, ideological origins of the German codetermination experiments, it is clear that the institutionalized experience has influenced ideas about organizational democracy. The fact that the 'experiment' has been going on for over 30 years has generated a vast literature on the subject, and has led to its inclusion in many management textbooks.

The Yugoslav experiments in turn have had a profound influence on recent thinking about organizational democracy (Meister, 1970; Pusić, 1973; Warner, 1976; Pusić and Rus, 1981). It may have been one of the most important organizational experiments in the postwar period, in spite of criticism. It not only involved a change on a wide scale, but the results have been monitored very closely. The experiments coupled market mechanisms with decentralized socialist forms (Pusić and Rus, 1981), and a very original concept of organization called labour management emerged from these experiments. This theory hypothesizes that labour hires capital, rather than the other way around (Vanek, 1975, pp. 33–6).

The Mondragón experiment in the Basque region of Spain has also stimulated theoretical work in the area of labour management (Oakeshott, 1980; Thomas and Logan, 1982), although on a lesser scale than the Yugoslav schemes.

The impact of theory upon experiments is thus difficult to assess. Basically where socialist notions are concerned the model of ideas leading to action appears to hold, and this is the implicit assumption of most textbooks. Keynes's 'scribblers in the attic', with their sweeping impact on history, triumph in this perspective. In any event there is a two-way traffic between theories and experiments, and the effect of the former on the latter may be as great as *vice-versa*.

CONCLUSIONS

In formulating our final remarks on organizational democracy: 'we may suspect that rather than look for a concept so dilute that communists and capitalists, liberals and socialists, republicans and Maoists, can call themselves democrats, we should do better to avoid the term ...' (Lucas, 1976, p. 9). Even so, the idea still 'sways men's minds' (Lucas, 1976, p. 9) with all its imprecisions.

Organizational democracy retains a fascination for scholars. Writers have recently expounded, for example, notions of self-management (Horvat, 1972); workers' control (Coates, 1968); de-institutionalization (Illich, 1973). Participatory democracy has also been analysed in depth (Pateman, 1970); the evolution of industrial democracy has been traced (Sorge, 1976); and empirical studies operationalized (IDE Group, 1981). Do their roots truly extend to the distant past? On balance, we can conclude only partly so.

To sum up, we have argued that at best the link between 'classical' notions and 'modern' ones is a tenuous one. Some political theorists stress the legacy of the past and like T. S. Eliot argue that:

> Time present and time past
> Are both perhaps present in time future ...

No doubt, the Greeks 'invented' political philosophy (Wolin, 1967, p. 28), perhaps our first concepts of democracy, but the distance between the *agora* and the factory floor is a long one. Their notion of democracy is theoretically distinct from our own, but may still inspire us.

Industrialization eroded the older notions of comunity; against this the classical socialists' ideas were to propose new associative forms, although there was a distinction between those which stressed traditionalist themes and those who attacked them (see Nisbet, 1966, p. 70). There were also libertarian anxieties to consider, and the possibility that socialism might engender bureaucracy was a problem that gave Marx's mind 'little trouble' (Nisbet, p. 139).

Furthermore, the conflict between 'elite' and 'mass' highlights a central contradiction in the development of organizational democracy, and applies to governmental forms as well as voluntary associations; but it gave no qualms to those who saw the *logos* of history as leading to proletarian victory. Later, 'Organization was to mass in Lenin's theory what idea had been to matter in Plato's' (Wolin, 1961, p. 421). The political was said to triumph ultimately, because the elite would see where the 'real' interests of the workers lay: hence, there was no need to bother about old-fashioned forms of democracy as such. Against this, there was the view that we would need to safeguard 'the natural rights of man' in the workplace (Laski, 1967, p. 433). This view is justified because in my view democracy is 'indivisible', whether in the

Organizational Democracy: The History of an Idea   19

workplace, voluntary association or territorial unit, even if theoretical distinctions may be drawn between the various types of governance to be found, and their origins explored.

REFERENCES

Blumberg, Paul (1968) *Industrial Democracy: The Sociology of Participation* (London: Constable)

Bottomore, Thomas B. (1964) *Elites and Society* (Harmondsworth, Middx.: Penguin Books)

Burrell, Gibson and Morgan, Gareth (1979) *Sociological Paradigms and Organizational Analysis* (London: H.E.B.)

Caute, David (1966) *The Left in Europe Since 1978* (London: Weidenfeld and Nicolson)

Coates, Ken (ed.) (1968) 'Introduction' to *Can the Workers Run Industry?* (London: Sphere Books)

Crouch, Colin and Heller, Frank (eds.) (1983) *International Yearbook of Organizational Democracy* (Chichester: Wiley) Vol. I.

Dachler, H. Peter and Wilpert, Bernhard (1978) Conceptual dimensions and boundaries of participation in organizations: a critical evaluation. *Administrative Science Quarterly*, **23**, 1–40.

Dahrendorf, Ralf (1959) *Class and Class Conflict — an Industrial Society* (London: Routledge and Kegan Paul)

Deane, Phyllis (1978) *The Evolution of Economic Ideas* (Cambridge: Cambridge University Press)

Dobb, Maurice (1966) *Soviet Economic Development Since 1917* (London: Routledge and Kegan Paul)

Edelstein, J. David and Warner, Malcolm (1979) *Comparative Union Democracy: Organization and Opposition in British and American Unions* (New Brunswick, N.J.: Transaction Books, revised edition)

Femia, Joseph V. (1982) *Gramsci's Political Thought: Hegemony, Consciousness, and Revolutionary Process* (Oxford: Oxford University Press)

Field, G. C. (1965) *Political Theory* (London: Methuen)

Franke, Richard H. and Kaul, James D. (1978) The Hawthorne experiments: first statistical interpretation. *American Sociological Review*, **43**, 623–43.

Gatrell, V. A. C. (ed.) (1970) *Robert Owen: Report to the County of Lanark. A New View of Society* (Harmondsworth, Middx.: Penguin Books)

Gouldner, Alvin W. (1965) *Enter Plato* (New York: Basic Books)

Hill, Christopher (1970) *God's Englishman: Oliver Cromwell and the English Revolution* (London: Weidenfeld and Nicolson)

Horvat, Branko (1972) An institutional model of a self managed economy, in Jaroslav Vanek (ed.), *Self Management: The Economic Liberation of Man* (Harmondsworth, Middx.: Penguin Books), pp. 127–44.

IDE (International Research Group) (1981) *Industrial Democracy in Europe* (Oxford: Oxford University Press)

Illich, Ivan (1973) *Deschooling Society* (Harmondsworth, Middx.: Penguin Books)

Ionescu, Ghita and de Madariaga, Isabel (1968) *Opposition* (London: Watts)

Kendall, Walter (1975) *The Labour Movement in Europe* (London: Allen Lane/ Penguin Books)

Lakatos, Imre (1970) *The Methodology of Scientific Research Programmes* (Cambridge: Cambridge University Press)

Laski, Harold, J. (1967) *A Grammar of Politics* (London: George Allen and Unwin), 5th edition.

Littler, Craig R. (1978) Understanding Taylorism. *British Journal of Sociology*, **29**, 185–203.

McInnes, Neil (1969) Georges Sorel, in Timothy Raison (ed.), *The Founding Fathers of Social Science* (Harmondsworth, Middx.: Penguin Books), pp. 100–9.

MacKenzie, Robert (1963) *British Political Parties* (London: Heinemann)

Meister, Albert (1970) *Où va l'Autogestion Yugoslave* (Paris: Editions Anthropos)

Merkle, Judith A. (1980) *Management and Ideology: The Legacy of the International Scientific Management Movement* (Berkeley: University of California)

Michels, Robert (1911) *Political Parties*, with an introduction by S. M. Lipset. (New York: Collier Books), 1962 edition.

Miller, Eric (1983) The Ahmedabad Experiment Revisited: Work Organization in Weaving, 1953–70, in Colin Crouch and Frank Heller (eds.), *International Yearbook of Organizational Democracy* (Chichester: Wiley) vol. I, pp. 150–180.

Nisbet, Robert A. (1966) *The Sociological Tradition* (New York: Collier Books), 1962 edition.

Nisbet, Robert A. (1966) *The Sociological Tradition* (New York: Basic Books)

Nove, Alec (1972) *Economic History of the USSR* (Harmondsworth, Middx.: Penguin Books)

Oakeshott, Robert (1980) A cooperative sector in a mixed economy, in Alasdair Clayre (ed.), *The Political Economy of Cooperation and Participation: A Third Sector* (Oxford: Oxford University Press)

Ostrogorski, Michael (1902) *Democracy and the Organization of Political Parties.* (London: MacMillan), 2 vols.

Palisi, Bartolomeo J. (1970) Some suggestions about the transitory-permanence dimensions of organizations. *British Journal of Sociology*, **21**, 200–6.

Parsons, Henry M. (1974) What happened at Hawthorne? *Science*, **183**, 922–32.

Pateman, Carole (1970) *Participation and Economic Theory* (Cambridge: Cambridge University Press)

Pollard, Sidney (1965) *The Genesis of Modern Management* (Harmondsworth, Middx.: Penguin Books)

Poole, Michael J. (1982) Theories of industrial democracy: the emerging synthesis. *Sociological Review*, 30, 181–207.

Pusić, Eugen (ed.) (1973) *Proceedings of the First International Conference on Participation and Self-management*, Dubrovnik (Zagreb: Institute of Social Research).

Pusić, Vesna and Rus, Veljko (1981) The Yugoslav industrial relations system, in IDE (International Research Group), *European Industrial Relations* (Oxford: Oxford University Press), pp. 219–32.

Rice, Albert Kenneth (1958) *Productivity and Social Organization* (London: Tavistock)

Roll, Eric (1938) *A History of Economic Thought* (London: Faber and Faber)

Rose, Michael (1975) *Industrial Behaviour* (London: Allen Lane)

Runciman, W. G. (1963) *Social Science and Political Theory* (Cambridge: Cambridge University Press)

Russell, Bertrand (1961) *A History of Western Philosophy* (London: George Allen and Unwin)

Sartori, Giovanni (1965) *Democratic Theory* (New York: Praeger)

Schumpeter, Joseph A. (1961) *History of Economic Analysis* (London: George Allen and Unwin)

Selucky, R. (1975) Marxism and Self Management, in Jaroslav Vanek (1975)

Skalicky, K. (1975) The Catholic church and workers participation, in Jaroslav Vanek (1975)

Organizational Democracy: The History of an Idea   21

Sorge, Arndt (1976) The evolution of industrial democracy in the countries of the European Community. *British Journal of Industrial Relations*, **14**, 274–94.

Teuteberg, Hans-Jürgen (1981) Ursprünge und Entwicklung der Mitbestimmung in Deutschland, in Hans Pohl (ed.), *Mitbestimmung: Ursprünge und Entwicklung* (Wiesbaden: Franz Steiner Verlag)

Thomas, Henk and Logan, Chris (1982) *Mondragon: An Economic Analysis* (London: George Allen and Unwin)

Thornley, Jenny (1981) *Workers' Cooperatives: Jobs and Dreams* (London: Heinemann Educational Books)

Trist, Eric L. (1981) *The Evolution of Socio-technical Systems*. Occasional Paper No. 2, June (Ontario: Ontario QWL Centre)

Trist, Eric L. and Bamforth, Keith W. (1951) Some social and psychological consequences of the longwall method of coal-getting. *Human Relations*, **4**, 3–38.

Vanek, Jaroslav (1975) Introduction, in Jaroslav Vanek (ed.), *Self-Management*, pp. 11–38 (Harmondsworth, Middx.: Penguin Books)

Walzer, Michael (1965) *The Revolution of the Saints* (Cambridge, Mass: Harvard University Press)

Warner, Malcolm (1969) Beatrice and Sidney Webb, in Timothy Raison (ed.), *The Founding Fathers of Social Science* (Harmondsworth, Middx.: Penguin Books), pp. 144–5.

Warner, Malcolm (1976) Further thoughts on experiments in industrial democracy and self-management. *Human Relations*, **29**, 401–10.

Warner, Malcolm (1981) Organizational experiments and social innovations, in W. H. Starbuck and P. Nystrom (eds), *Handbook of Organizational Design* (Oxford: Oxford University Press), 2 vols.

Warner, Malcolm (1983) Organizations and Experiments: *Designing New Ways of Managing Work* (Chichester: Wiley)

Webb, Sidney and Beatrice (1901) *Industrial Democracy* (New York: Kelley) (reprint 1965)

Webb, Sidney and Beatrice (1894) *The History of Trade Unionism* (London: Kelley) (reprint 1965).

Whitley, Paul (1981) Who are the Labour Activists? *Political Quarterly*, **52**, 160–70.

Whyte, Martin King (1973) Bureaucracy and modernization in China: the Maoist critique. *American Sociological Review*, **38**, 149–63.

Wilpert, Bernhard (1975) Research on industrial democracy: the German case. *Industrial Relations Journal*, **6**, 53–63.

Wolin, Sheldon (1961) *Politics and Vision* (London: George Allen and Unwin)

[3]

THE MANY FACES OF POWER AND LIBERTY: REVEALED PREFERENCE, AUTONOMY, AND TELEOLOGICAL EXPLANATION*

PETER ABELL

Abstract Concepts of bargaining power, influence, and manipulation are introduced and related to three different ways of operationalization—namely from decision-making, non-decision-making, and studying information flows. The concept of autonomy is introduced and briefly studied in the context of causal and teleological accounts of 'power play'.

Introduction

In recent years, both within the framework of general sociological theory and in the more restrictive context of organization theory, we have witnessed a resurgence of interest in the concept of 'power' and its many close relatives like influence, persuasion, manipulation, inducement, and so on. This is in part, I suspect, a reaction to functionalism which, at least in the hands of its most distinguished proponent, largely relegated issues of conflict resolution—and thus at least one conception of power—to a special case of the consensus-model of social systems (Parsons, 1967; 1963*a*, *b*). Despite, however, the increased attention the concepts have attracted, many of the old conceptual hazards remain and the seemingly intractable problems of locating operational definitions which capture the concepts in anything like their full complexity, have not been solved. Furthermore, with one or two notable exceptions, most attempts, both conceptual and operational, to use the concept are afflicted with the endemic sociological disease, namely a failure to situate the concepts in models which reflect actual social process. It is relatively easy to detail fine conceptual distinctions, but unless we can project these into models of social process which generate reasonably general explanations of social phenomena they are only of marginal interest to the sociologist.

In this paper I want to consider in detail a number of particularly thorny issues which seem to me to surround the concept of power: namely, the relative role that, on the one hand, *revealed preferences* (i.e. in decision-making), and on the other, *individual autonomy* might reasonably be permitted to play in the formulation of models designed to reflect the processes in which 'power', 'influence', and 'manipulation' serve an *explanatory* purpose. My presentation derives directly from the model of *Organisations as Bargaining and Influence Systems* (Abell, 1975) though I

*Accepted: 18.5.76

4   PETER ABELL

trust what I have to say will be of wider interest than merely to students of organizational process.

The immediate stimulus for the paper, however, has been my reading of Steven Lukes' most important and stimulating book *Power: A Radical View* (Lukes, 1974) which seems to me to raise a number of issues in a most delightful and challenging way. He contrasts three viewpoints on the conceptualization and measurement of power: firstly, the decision-making approach, perhaps most closely associated with the name of Dahl (1957, 1958); secondly, an approach usually associated with Peter Bachrach and Morton S. Baratz (1962, 1963), which centres attention upon 'non-decision-making'; and, thirdly, the viewpoint, which most pleases Lukes himself, whereby the concept of latent interest is involved in the definition of power. Thus, A's power over B becomes the extent to which A can 'affect' B in a manner contrary to B's *interests.* This latter orientation has, of course, a long history and is in some way central to the Marxist 'theory' of conflict and false consciousness. Although I do not intend to give an overview of the limitations and achievements of the three viewpoints, I will in several respects contrast them in confronting my central questions, namely the role of 'revealed preferences' and 'autonomy' in the structure of explanations from power.

An additional, but subsidiary, purpose to this paper is to try to kindle an awareness of some aspects of what we might term the 'sociology of freedom or liberty'; a neglected, not to say forgotten, sociological category. This neglect is, of course, not surprising since, as usually construed, the sociological enterprise involves a search for 'patterns', 'determinants', 'causes', and so on—ideas that do not lie at all easily with the concepts of individual or group liberty. Despite centuries-old exhortations to find 'freedom in necessity' and heroic efforts (Parsons, 1937) to preserve the voluntaristic basis of social action in the thought of our founding fathers, Durkheim's conception of a social fact as 'ways of acting, thinking, and feeling external to the individual and endowed with the power of coercion by reason of which they control him' has taken its toll. And if we are to believe Peter Berger (1963) then 'freedom is not empirically available'. More precisely, 'while freedom may be experienced by us as a certainty along with other empirical certainties, it is not open to demonstration by any scientific methods'. Be this as it may, there seems to be some robust sense in the assertion that A's power over B may be equated with A's ability to reduce B's freedom or liberty. Thus, on this count, there seems to be a reciprocal relationship between power and liberty which would inevitably lead to the conclusion that, if what Berger says of freedom is correct, it must likewise be so of the concept of power. It is part of the burden of this paper to show that Berger is not in fact correct.

Preliminary definitions

I will limit my analysis to the power interactions (relationship) between two actors only—A and B. In this respect I follow many others, finding it convenient for expository purposes, though I recognize that the extension to the many actor case introduces a number of additional conceptualizations.[1]

Most authors, at least since the time of Weber, accept as a starting point (or, as some would say, as a sensitizing-definition) that: A has power over B to the extent that A's action/behaviour[2] (to include his forbearance and lack of behaviour[3]) 'affects' B's action/behaviour (again to include forbearance and lack of behaviour) in such a manner that had it not been for A's action/behaviour, B would have acted/behaved otherwise. I do not pretend this, as it stands, is at all adequate as a definition but it does catch at least one possible intuitive notion of the concept of power.

The above very simple 'definition' seems to invite evidence concerning the following:

(P1) A's action—let us say x;

(P2) B's action—let us say y;

(P3) The way B would have acted had it not been for A's action (x). Let us say ȳ.[4]

We will see how evidence is obtained on these matters, using the three different approaches to power outlined by Lukes. In so doing, however, I will draw a tripartite conceptual distinction between 'power', 'influence', and 'manipulation'.

When considering the 'power' relationship between A and B, there are two major 'problems' (i.e. 'why' questions) which arise and potentially link A to B:

 (i) why has B changed his 'state of mind'?

(ii) why has B, despite his 'opposition' to A, not changed his state of mind, but changed his action.[5]

It is clear that an answer to (ii) can be provided in terms of evidence of the sort P1, 2, and 3, but, furthermore, (i) can also be answered in an entirely parallel manner in terms of:

(P*1) A's action (e.g. communication of beliefs);

(P*2) B's 'state of mind';

(P*3) B's 'state of mind' had it not been for A's action.

Questions (i) and (ii) effectively distinguish between a pair of social processes which link A to B. Firstly, the process whereby A changes (modifies) B's mind (attitude, sentiments, knowledge, etc.) and secondly, where A modifies B's action (without changing his state of mind). This is rather loosely expressed but if one, for the moment, reads state of mind as 'convictions' then the intent of the distinction is, I think, clear.

The English language provides a plethora of words to cover the possible nuances in such processes. However, I wish to argue for a tripartite conceptual distinction which will, in my opinion, suffice to *model* these complex processes—they are:

 (i) the process of social *influence*, whereby A changes B's state of mind (and concomitant action) but in so doing increases (or maintains[6]) B's 'autonomy';

6   PETER ABELL

(ii) the process of *manipulation*, whereby A changes B's state of mind (and con-
    comitant action) but in so doing decreases B's 'autonomy';

(iii) the process of *power*, whereby A changes B's action (obtains his compliance)
     through the agency of sanctions[7] even in the face of B's opposition (i.e. an
     opposed state of mind).

Roughly speaking, by degree of autonomy I mean an actor's range of feasible
alternatives (see below). In practice, it is difficult to conceptualize and operationalize
this idea whilst avoiding circularity, but it is nevertheless essential if we are to draw
what I believe to be a vital distinction between influence and manipulation. An
alternative formulation might appear to be one whereby we speak in terms of B's
increased or decreased basis for 'rational deliberation' (in decision-making) which,
in turn, might derive from the concept of objective or latent interest as specified by
Lukes in his third dimension of power (Lukes, 1974, p. 34). Whichever formulation
we adopt however, what is clear, is that we need, in addition to P*1, 2, and 3, a
fourth criterion enabling us to draw the distinction between what I have, admittedly
rather arbitrarily, termed 'influence' and 'manipulation'. So, provisionally, we may
add alongside P*1, 2, and 3:

(P*4) an 'estimate' of whether B's change of action (concomitant upon a change
      of mind) is associated with an increase or decrease in his 'autonomy'.

It might be argued that to draw a distinction between manipulation and influence
is an unnecessary multiplication of categories. Why should we want to separate the
two, especially when they may both have the same behavioural consequences?
Clearly the issue revolves around the concept of autonomy which to the present
remains rather opaque; but who would want to deny the importance of differentiating between, on the one hand, those processes that cripple man's very existence
as a consequence of his slavish subservience to ideas that limit his perspectives and
potential development, and, on the other hand, processes that liberate him by
awakening his awareness of new possibilities and previously unrecognized hori-
zons? Much, thus hinges on the concept of autonomy—we need ways of conceptualizing and operationalizing it—but rather than considering the problems in an
entirely abstract manner, I will situate my analyses in the context of the different
approaches to the measurement of 'power'.

Before I continue the analysis, however, I should like to make a general aside
concerning the distinction between 'manipulation' and 'influence'. What I am
driving at is a way of demarcating processes of what some would term rational as
opposed to irrational persuasion. Analysis of this distinction has, in my opinion,
become a matter of extreme urgency with recent developments in political
economy. With the increasing realization, for example, that 'consumer sovereign-
ity' can no longer be accepted as an uncontroversial assumption (e.g. Galbraith,
1974) comes the necessity of analysing those processes that shape consumer preferences. Galbraith, for instance, wishes to invert the traditionally assumed consumer/

producer relationship by suggesting the monopolistic and oligopolistic producer has the 'power' to fashion preferences. If this is so, are we not entitled to ask whether the fashioning is a case of manipulation or influence in the sense in which I am using the terms. In a number of ways theory and practice require us to develop ideas about the processes which shape people's political, social, and economic preferences. Gone are the days when we can uncritically accept a set of preferences and search for the most appropriate allocation of resources to maximize their satisfaction. Is it too much to hope that, with theories (and thus with adequate conceptualization) of the generation of preferences that we might reasonably hope to see a 'rapprochement' between economic and social theory?

Power, influence, and manipulation in decision-making

Following closely behind the reputational technique,[8] the analysis of decision-making has most frequently been used to elucidate the concept of 'interpersonal power' (Dahl, 1957). The basic idea underlying the analysis is one which considers individuals with competing preferences, bargaining to a collective outcome; and the relative success of an individual in getting his preferences embodied in an outcome is supposedly indicative of his 'power'. Most investigators have, in practice, reduced the complexity of the bargaining process to a simple win-lose, zero-sum situation, but this is not in any way conceptually necessary to the model. The literature has not, however, drawn the types of distinctions I am arguing for; in particular, the preferences of the actors party to the decision-making are taken as *given* and in this respect the models reflect practice in welfare economics. If by dint of this assumption economic theory should gain the label 'bourgeois', then accordingly the conventional decision-making models of power should likewise earn the same title. However, in the presentation that follows I have attempted to remedy the situation by seeking ways of modelling the formation of preferences.

Let us assume that A and B face a set (population) of decisions which they have to 'make' or 'take'—$D = \{d_i\}i, = 1, 2 \ldots n$.[9] How could we conceptualize and measure the concepts of 'power', 'influence', and 'manipulation' from A's and B's decision-making? First, let us get an intuitive idea of the distinction between the concepts in the spirit of the 'definitions' I gave earlier. Let us assume (i) that both A and B come to the decision-making with initial preferred outcomes (IPOs) for each of the decisions,[10] (ii) that A and B make these preferred outcomes known to each other.

If the IPOs of A and B are identical over set D, then A and B are in a *consensual posture*. (We can then ask for an explanation of why this should be so—I will return to this below.) But, for the moment, let us assume that A and B have (at least over some decisions) different IPOs. Now, putting it rather informally to start with, I will say that A has *influence* over (or manipulates) B to the extent that A can change B's IPOs, and vice versa (without the application of sanctions).

Let us assume, over set D, A's IPOs are X_{Ai} and B's are X_{Bi}. Then let us allow

8   PETER ABELL

that the influence or manipulation process, as outlined above, can take place both ways, i.e. A can 'change B's mind' and vice versa. So, let A's and B's 'influenced'/ 'manipulated' MPOs (modified preferred outcomes) be given by Y_{Ai} and Y_{Bi} respectively.

Then we postulate:

$$Y_{Ai} = f(X_{Ai}, X_{Bi}, U_{Ai}) \qquad \text{(a)}$$
and
$$Y_{Bi} = f(X_{Bi}, X_{Ai}, U_{Bi}) \qquad \text{(b)} \Bigg\} \ (1)$$

$i = 1, 2 \ldots, n$. U_A and U_B have the standard interpretation representing 'other factors' impinging on A and B respectively. In the context of each functional statement in (1) we are first interested in the variation in the MPOs accountable for by the actors' own IPOs and then how much residual variation is accounted for by the other actors' IPOs. So, for (1)(a) if we postulate, for the sake of argument, a linear relationship[11] between Y_A and X_B we obtain:

$$Y_{Ai} = \propto + I_{AA} X_{Ai} + U'_{Ai} \qquad (2)$$

$i = 1, 2 \ldots, n$.
Where, I_{AA} is, if you will, the 'degree of conviction' of A. Then we postulate a linear relationship between the rsidual U'_A and X_B

$$U'_{Ai} = \propto' + I_{AB} X_{Bi} + U''_{Ai} \qquad (3)$$

$i = 1, 2 \ldots, n$.
Where, I_{AB} is B's influence/manipulation of A.

Similar reasoning gives:

$$Y_{Bi} = \propto'' + I_{BB} X_{Bi} + U'_{Bi}$$
and
$$U'_{Bi} = \propto''' + I_{BA} X_{Ai} + U''_{Bi} \Bigg\} \ (4)$$

$i = 1, 2 \ldots, n$.
Thus with sample data on A's and B's IPOs and MPOs, we can, in principle, obtain estimates of I_{AA}, I_{BB}, I_{AB}, and I_{BA}. The coefficients I_{BA} and I_{BA} do not, however, as they stand distinguish between processes of manipulation and influence— we will return to this problem below.

Let us now turn to our third concept, namely 'power', and see how it is embodied in the decision-making approach. If we assume that A and B are not consensual (as a consequence of their mutual influencing or manipulation) over the set D then they will have to bargain over the disputed decisions to a set of *collective outcomes—* O_i. Then let:

$$O_i = f(Y_{Ai}, Y_{Bi}, U_i) \qquad (5)$$

$i = 1, 2 \ldots, n$.
Once again, for the sake of expository convenience, assuming the adequacy of a linear additive specification we obtain:

$$O_i = C + \beta_{OA} Y_{Ai} + \beta_{OB} Y_{Bi} + U_i \qquad (6)$$

$i = 1, 2 \ldots, n$.
Then, estimates of β_{OA} and β_{OB}, i.e. the marginal propensities to get outcomes

in accord with one's (modified) preferred outcomes is a convenient measure of A's and B's relative *bargaining power over decision outcomes*.[12] If one then wishes to move to a measure of A's power over B (or vice versa), it is necessary to enquire into the degree to which the stream of outcomes O_i 'affect' the behaviour/action of A and B. I have explored elsewhere, via the concept of *control-loss*, situations where the outcomes do not 'affect' the behaviour of A and B, as intended (Abell, 1975) but here, for the sake of clarity, I will assume that outcomes do 'affect' behaviour as intended.

So, we might now ask how these simple models are supposed to satisfy the evidental requirements P1, 2, and 3 and P*1, 2, and 3. Consider, first of all, A's attempt to get his MPOs embodied in the outcomes O_i (reflected in (6)). This we must assume constitutes evidence for P1; B's compliance with the outcomes (assuming $Y_{Ai} \neq Y_{Bi}$[13]) is evidence for both P2 and the counterfactual P3—the evidence for this latter component of the explanation being provided indirectly by the assumption that B, because of his differing preferences, would in the absence of A's activity have behaved differently. In this context it is most easy to construe O_i as a stream of commands constraining B's (and of course possibly A's) behaviour. The decision-making approach to power is thus, based upon a series of assumptions:

  (i) that both A and B have clearly articulated preferences;
 (ii) that they are more or less successful in getting these preferences embodied in outcomes;[14]
(iii) that the outcomes constrain A's and B's subsequent behaviour.

It might quite rightly be referred to as a *kinematic* rather than a *dynamic* model since, as it stands, it does not enquire into why it should be that one party is 'willing' to comply with or 'unable' to resist the outcomes when they do not embody his preferred line of action; merely that they do. An answer to such queries is, of course, normally provided in terms of the relative distribution of sanctions (positive and negative) available to the parties—more of which later.

A similar line of reasoning to the above applies to the influence/manipulation process P*1, 2, and 3. So far, however, I have made no attempt to distinguish between influence and manipulation, since the equations (3) and (4) are, as they stand, not able to do this—they only chart changes in A's and B's preferences (changes of mind) and we need additional evidence enabling us to say whether, in changing their preferences, they are more or less autonomous, i.e. evidence for P*4. It is important, however, to recognize that the 'shifts' in preferences X to Y must be out of conviction or 'genuine', not as a consequence of imposed sanctions or threats. Influence and manipulation are, as I use them, sanction-free.

To ask whether an individual is more *autonomous* in one 'mental state' rather than another is clearly a highly complex matter, not least because one would have to understand the—as far as I am aware not understood, but no doubt highly complex —interaction between the conscious and unconscious emotional and cognitive states of the individual in question to answer the question definitively. But what we can perhaps provisionally say is that an individual is more autonomous to the degree that:

(i) he recognizes a greater[15] range of *physically* possible alternatives open to him (i.e. loosely 'ends'). These may not be socially realizable, of course, due to the power of his adversaries;

(ii) he recognizes a greater range of feasible means physically open to him which will realize one or more of his ends;

(iii) he understands (i.e. can critically evaluate) the *implications* of selecting certain ends or means.

We might wish, in a general way to refer to these conditions as indicative of greater choice[16] or even *freedom for*.[17]

Let us examine these ideas in the context of B's shift in IPO to an MPO. Clearly (i) is satisfied if we assume that *both* preferences (and their concomitant action) are now open to him. In practice, principles (ii) and (iii) may, I think, be provisionally lumped together. Although the empirical problems of guaranteeing that they are satisfied are immense and I do not pretend that I can more than touch upon them here—it seems to me that their fulfilment can, in principle, be studied in terms of the direct or indirect *information provision* by A. If we can establish that A (intentionally or otherwise) is providing information for B which (in the process of shifting his preferences) *does not decrease* any one of: B's (i) range, (ii) means, and (iii) understanding of implications, then I would wish to regard the shift as a case of influence. If, on the other hand, there is a diminution of any one of these 'freedoms' then we should regard the shift as manipulative. I would thus wish to attempt an operational definition of the principles of autonomy in terms of information provision. Although this formulation raises almost as many problems as it solves[18] it has the distinct advantage that it ties my formulation to two of the most empirically fruitful approaches to the study of 'power' which see, on the one hand, information as a *strategic resource* (Pettigrew, 1974) and, on the other, as a bounded meaning system (Pondy, 1975). It should be noted that in adopting this sort of operational formulation we are forced to accept that A might (intentionally or otherwise) be keeping 'information' to himself that would, if it were given to B, further change his preference. Thus A may be influencing B less than he might (perhaps because it is in his interests to do so). Some might be tempted to call this manipulation but on my usage it is rather a case of, shall we say, less than possible influence. B is still more autonomous in adopting Y (rather than X) but not as autonomous as he might be (vis-à-vis A). If we believe this to be the case then we must presumably ascribe to the truth of a counterfactual—'if A were to provide this further information then B would not have adopted *either* X *or* Y'. We may be able to study evidence for such a statement by comparative method (see below).

There are, finally, a number of points which need emphasising about the decision-making approach. In deriving a measure from the full set of decisions we are, as it were, *aggregating* over the entire set. A's power, for instance, is his marginal propensity to bring collective outcomes in line with his own MPOs *over set D*. Thus, the measure points to a generalized capacity of A. We could, of course, data permitting, find more particular estimates by breaking out sub-sets of set D (by decision-type, for instance). But even then there is some implied generalized capacity—albeit of a more restricted scope.[19] Colloquially, however, we are prone to use the terms 'influence' and 'power' both in a generalized and a very specific manner. In this latter respect, we say: A influenced B over one particular issue. The model I have outlined could, in principle, give a probability measure for such individual events, but one would require a suitable sample of events to establish frequency estimates of the probability numbers. I will return to these issues below, but we might observe that some have argued that the concepts of power and influence are only of any relevance in a generalized capacity (Parsons, 1963). Thus, it is argued, we would not want to employ the concepts at all, unless they explain some general pattern, for surely as sociologists it is to patterns that we look. I believe this argument to be essentially correct but I will show below that we can render the concept of influence and power issue specific (other than in a probabilistic sense), though I still believe this of little *sociological* interest.

The 'non-decision-making' approach

A number of cogent criticisms can be made against sole reliance upon decision-making as a basis for conceptualizing and measuring power. The one that has caused the greatest stir is due to Bachrach and Baratz (1962, 1970) and delights under the title of 'non-decision-making'. The burden of their extremely penetrating argument is to the effect that the decision-making approach may (will?) give biased estimates of A's and B's power. Although it is not entirely clear whether Bachrach and Baratz want to imply biases in A's and B's *absolute* or *relative* 'power' I will assume that they are concerned with possible biases in A's power relative to B and vice versa. They believe that the decision-making fails to secure information whereby:

a person or group—consciously or unconsciously—creates or reinforces barriers to the public airing of policy conflicts,

or in a more recent formulation:

Power is also (i.e. in addition to decision-making) exercised when A devotes his energies to creating or reinforcing social and political values and institutional practices that limit the scope of the political process to public consideration of only those issues which are comparatively innocuous to A.

Thus, part of A's power, for instance, is his ability to create and maintain barriers to a full consideration of *all* decisions by B. In the most extreme case he selects those decisions which B may 'consider', keeping others to himself. A failure to incorporate this sort of social process into any operational model, will, it is argued, give unrealistic results and in Lukes' terms miss an essential 'dimension of power'. Bachrach and Baratz consequently implore us to consider the set of *potential decisions* that B could in practice, be involved in, as well as those he actually is involved in. It is easy to see that a failure to do this will almost invariably overestimate B's power in relation to A.

All this seems reasonably straightforward; however, in other places Bachrach and Baratz use a rather different argument (although they appear to regard it as identical), namely that part of A's power is his ability, in one way or another to 'curtail' what another actor 'feels' he wants out of a decision (or set of decisions). That is, in the terms of our foregoing analysis, to shape an actor's preferred outcomes. This line of argument I hope I have shown, can be accommodated within the 'decision-making approach' as either manipulation or influence, and we need, therefore, give it no further attention.

Returning, therefore, to what we might term the 'potential decision-making'[20] argument, let us note first of all, that if we are sufficiently liberal in our interpretaton of P1, 2, and 3 we can interpret the situation as follows:

P1 A's action X . . . 'A keeps the decision to himself';
P2 B's action Y . . . 'B does *not* get involved in the decision';
P3 The way B would have acted had it not been for A's action . . . 'B would have got involved in the decision'.

So, at first appearances, the non-decision-making (potential decision-making) thesis has the essential ingredients of our sensitising definition. This easy translation unfortunately clouds a number of rather complex issues—in particular on how to adduce evidence for the truth of the counterfactual P3.

As before it will be convenient to limit our attention to the two actor case facing a set of *potential* decisions. We will, furthermore, assume A is B's superordinate and is able to limit B's access to decision-making. Clearly, A's and B's access to the set of decisions in question may in turn be limited by other actors and their preferences may also be influenced or manipulated by these other actors. Thus, we encounter the *nested contingency* of power systems (bargaining-zones in terms of Abell, 1975). The important point being that we are concerned here with A's power vis-à-vis B and vice versa, *within a given power-system* (bargaining-zone).

We assume that A keeps a sub-set of the potential decisions to himself and this is indicative of his non-decision-making 'power' in relation to B.[21] It is important, I think, to draw a distinction between two rather different interpretations of A's retention of decision-making 'power'. On the first interpretation A 'makes the decision himself' (i.e. they embody his IPOs—although these may, needless to say, have been manipulated or influenced). The decision—outcomes we must assume— then carry implications for B's behaviour and it is perhaps easiest to think of them as commands or rules concerned to 'affect' or guide B's behaviour. On the second interpretation—which is a rather more subtle and challenging version of the argument—it is not so much that A takes the decisions himself (i.e. by excluding B) but rather, A prevents certain potential decisions becoming 'current'. So, in one way or another, A prevents B from either participating in or even having the opportunity *to respond to any appropriate potential outcomes.*

Let us consider the first interpretation; it is clear that we are merely dealing with a centralized decision-making mechanism and conceptually nothing of a very profound nature is involved. If B agrees with the outcome (i.e. they embody what his own preferences would have been had he been involved in the decision); then according to the decision-making approach no power is involved. B could have been manipulated or influenced by A into this posture—but that is conceptually handled within the decision-making approach and likewise calls for nothing new. If B 'disagrees' with the outcomes and once again they are supposed to dictate his behaviour, then he is accordingly potentially subject to A's power. Of course he may be able to evade the intention of these outcomes, then he has 'power' also. It is possible to formalize these matters (Abell, 1975) entirely within the framework of the decision-making approach in terms of the concepts of *control-loss.*[22] But once again there are no grounds, on this count, for claiming any conceptual distinctiveness for a non-decision-making approach to the measurement of power.

Finally, it should be noted that the truth of the counterfactual is *inferred* from the fact that B's preferred outcome is different from A's so we are willing to say, had it not been for A's 'command' B would not have done what he did do.

It seems to me that the best way of conceptualizing the second above-mentioned interpretation is in terms of A's ability to effectively *reduce the range of options open to B*. We have already encountered the concept of influence whereby A brings B's preference into line with his own preferences. Here we have a situation where B cannot form preferences as the grounds for his so doing are systematically denied to him by A. It appears conceptually to make little difference whether this is because he—(i) is not given 'information' about a potential decision, or (ii) because he 'cannot' formulate certain potential preferences about decisions in which he is directly involved. *The important point about all these situations is that we have a situation where A 'affects' B's behaviour without B's overt opposition.* They seem to be adequately captured by our concept of manipulation.[23]

Power, influence, manipulation, and latent interests

The third 'dimension' of power recognized by Lukes involves the concept of interests. He says:

A exerts power over B when A affects B in a manner contrary to B's interests.

Lukes admits that 'interests' are 'irreducibly evaluative'; be this as it may, the essential difference between this third viewpoint and the previous two is the explicit introduction of B's *interests* rather than his preferences as revealed in decision *or* potential decision-making. Of course, if B's interests are fully expressed in his revealed preferences then the distinction falls away. However, if this is not the case, then the baseline with which B's actual action should be compared is not his revealed preferences but his interests. It seems most convenient to contrast this formulation with our concepts of manipulation and influence. For, presumably Lukes would want to explain an occurrence of B not acting in accord with interests in terms of A preventing B from realizing what his latent or real interests are. Thus B's action might be quite rational in his own terms but this is only because A has, in some way, denied him realization of his true interests. So, the counterfactual takes the form—if it had not been for A doing so and so, B would have acted in a manner in accord with his 'true' interests.

Clearly then Lukes is in a position close to our concepts of influence and manipulation—but how close? My preference was to adopt B's *autonomy* as the operative concept in P*4, Lukes appears to prefer interests. We can perhaps find common ground with Lukes here in the proposal that manipulation rather than influence is the significant concept. For, adapting my concept of influence slightly, one would suspect Lukes would endorse the statement whereby 'influence' is a 'mind changing' process that makes B aware (or more aware) of his interests. So I am arguing that B is manipulated to the degree that A reduces his autonomy, whereas Lukes is (implicitly) arguing that distortions of interests is the operative concept.

Is there any significance in this difference? I think there is, but in order to make clear what is involved we need to enquire a little more deeply into the explanatory role of counterfactuals.

The problem of counterfactuals and explanatory form

To summarise: we have seen that a statement concerning the power or influence of A over B or manipulation of A by B involves evidence of four types specified in P1, 2, 3, and P*1, 2, 3, and 4.

It is in the sense of (P3) that a statement about the 'power' one actor has over another entails a counterfactual. For, according to our previous deliberations a necessary (though not sufficient) condition for the truth of the statement that A exerts power over B with respect to the action instanced in (P1) and (P2), is that we must know (or infer) the *truth* of a subjective conditional—if A had not done x then B would not have done y (would have done ȳ). It is this requirement that generates much of the operational difficulty about the concept of power and its close relatives. It is helpful to note that P1, 2, and 3 also provide the elements of an *explanation* of B's behaviour corresponding to the question—'Why did (does) B do y?'. In answer we might say 'Because A did x', it being implied that 'B did y *because* A did x'. (In what follows I shall initially concentrate upon the concept of power, though much of what I say applies to the other two central concepts also. Furthermore, for convenience, I will assume 'not having done (doing) y' is equivalent to 'doing not y' which is strictly incorrect but to draw on a deeper logic of action, at this stage, would take us too far afield.)

Now such colloquial explanations blur a basic distinction: is B's behaviour to be construed as *teleologically or causally determined?*

I wish to argue that our attitude to the evidential requirements of 'explanations from power' depends very centrally upon whether we take a teleological or causal viewpoint of such explanations. Furthermore, that an adequate analysis of the concepts of manipulation, latent interest and autonomy are also dependent on this distinction.

Consider first the case where we wish to interpret the explanation of B's behaviour in causal terms. This being the case we are searching for a *causal law* connecting A's and B's behaviour. Presumably the explanation would then depend upon the hypothesized truth of a universal proposition (law) of the form:

$$(A) \ (B) \ [Ax \Leftrightarrow By]$$

(for all A and B, if and only if A does x, then B does y.)[24]

The universal proposition will, of course, be circumscribed by a set of appropriate initial conditions describing the individuals of type A and B and perhaps some common circumstances. The explanation of B's action would then be of the classical covering-law (hypothetico-deductive) variety. Putting the relationship between A and B in this way highlights its empirical requirements; in order to 'test' an explanation based upon a causal-generalization one would need observations where (*ceteris paribus*) of the four logically possible combinations we only observe situations where:

(i) A's exhibit action x and B's exhibit action y;

(ii) A's do not exhibit action x and B's do not exhibit action y.

The role of the subjunctive conditional—if A had not done x then B would not have done y—takes on the stature of a counterfactual in any causal (hypothetico-deductive) explanation. For from the 'truth' of the 'law': 'if and only if A does x then B does y' we may deduce the truth of the subjunctive conditional, if and only if A had done x then would B have done (do) y. The interesting twist with (causal) explanations from power is that the counter-factual is naturally expressed in double negative form: 'if it had *not* been for A doing x, then B would *not* have done y'. But, of course:

$$(A) \ (B) \ [Ax \Leftrightarrow By] \Rightarrow (A) \ (B) \ [A\bar{x} \Leftrightarrow B\bar{y}]$$

is a tautology and so, *if* it is deemed legitimate to construe explanations from power as causal, then the issues surrounding the use of the counterfactual are no more controversial than those associated with the logic of causal explanations in any form of enquiry.

All this might seem rather laboured, but it seems necessary in the light of the remarks common to a number of scholars, claiming that studies of power raise special methodological difficulties whilst at the same time implicitly accepting a causal account of power relationships. For example, Lukes in praising Crenson's book (1971) claims that it is 'a real theoretical advance in the empirical study of power relations' as 'it explicitly attempts to find a way to explain things that do not happen'. I believe Crenson's book does raise a number of interesting methodological issues but not quite in the sense in which Lukes wishes to claim. Crenson's concern, working in the non-decision-making framework, is to explain why the issue of air pollution is 'raised' in some North American cities and not in others. He wishes to 'explain' the *lack* of interest in some cities in terms of the 'power' of large corporations in these cities. Despite Lukes' claims, I believe Crenson's methodology is entirely traditional for, in effect, he 'explains' what 'does not happen' by the use of simple and well established comparative methods: cities (presumably as far as possible matched on all relevant criteria[25]) are compared and it is found that those which are rather tardy in adopting pollution control are, for various historical reasons, by and large dominated by specific corporations, whereas those that are not polluted are free of such corporations. Such a research strategy is entirely in accord with the spirit of the methodology of causal explanations outlined above. *Indeed such explanations account for what 'did (does not) happen' in the sense of all suitably elaborated causal explanations.* The point is that a variance is generated across cities (some do have controls, others do not) which is 'causally' accounted for. All the other examples that Lukes cites are of the same logical structure and consequently, despite his protestations, do not, as far as I can see, take us into controversial logical terrain. However, there is a situation of special interest; suppose we believe in the *'truth' of the general causal explanation but because it is universally operative across the full population (i.e. over all known actors of type B) we can find no cases of B that did not (have not done) y.* Here we have a situation where there is no variance to explain—the causally operative 'power relation' is keeping, as it were, everybody, in line. I believe it is this sort of situation which provides us with rather unique challenges and as such deserves a name, I will (following Gramsci) call it *hegemonic control*.

It seems, therefore, that with the sole but extremely important exception of those situations where there is no variance (across relevant units) and where we take a *causal* interpretation of 'power relations', explaining what does not happen is quite a routine sociological practice. There is, however, one slight complication and this concerns *overdetermined* causal systems (Abell, 1971).

If the causal law in question takes the form:

$$(A) \ (B) \ [Ax \Rightarrow By]$$

then A's action is only a sufficient (not necessary) condition for B's action. Such a law is compatible with observations of 'B doing y' but 'A not having done x'. The law guarantees the truth of the subjunctive conditional—'if A had done x then B would have done y' but not, 'if A had not done x then B would not have done y'. So in contrast to the situation where the law is in 'necessary and sufficient' form the first counterfactual does not logically imply the second one in the double negative form. That is:

$$(A) \ (B) \ [Ax \Rightarrow By] \ \Rightarrow \ (A) \ (B) \ [A\bar{x} \Rightarrow B\bar{y}]$$

is not tautologous. Overdetermination is usually handled by supposing that a set of alternatives are severally sufficient and collectively necessary and sufficient for the given event.

So,

$$(B) \ (A) \ (A') \ldots (A^N) \ [(Ax \ v \ A'x' \ldots v \ A^N x^N) \Leftrightarrow By]$$

Then we may say that if it had *not* been for A doing x, or A' doing x' ... or A^N doing x^N then B would not have done y.

The role of teleology in explanations from power

I have already remarked upon a natural tendency to interpret explanations from power in causal terms. Lukes, for instance, seems to do this—sometimes explicitly, other times implicitly—and most of the available operational models are more or less based upon a causal interpretation.[26] Since colloquially we think of 'power' as a 'force' which changes people's action, such an interpretation is perhaps quite excusable. However, I believe causal accounts as outlined in the previous section, are not always adequate.

Let us now, therefore, turn to a *teleological* interpretation of A's power over B; once more we can fruitfully consider the issues involved by thinking in terms of an explanation of B's *action*. I will assume that teleological explanations take the form such that B's action (i.e. his doing y) can be explained in terms of a *practical syllogism* (Von-Wright, 1971) as follows:

 (i) 'B intends (wants) I' (the intentional premise);
 (ii) 'B believes in a situation he perceives as S, *only* by doing y will he bring about I' (the cognitive premises),
therefore:

(iii) 'B does y'[27]

The most significant feature about this explanatory form is its independence of the hypothesized truth of any universal proposition, analogous to the causal 'law' above. The reason being that the proposition 'B does y' (i.e. B acts y) cannot be false whilst the conjoin of propositions 'B intends I' and 'B believes (in situation S) that by doing y he will bring about I' is true; for to say that B *does* y (in situation he perceives as S) implies that he intends to do y. His action, in short, is teleological, or self-directed. Thus the relationship between the premises and conclusion of the above 'explanation' is not of a causal variety.[28] The explanatory form provides a general teleological explanation of B's *action* whereas 'explanation from power' must, in addition, make provision for some specific content to the proposition 'B intends I' which relates B's action y to A's action x.[29] This can be accomplished in a variety of ways but let us, without loss of generality, concentrate upon one rather simple wording 'B intends (wants) to secure some reward which A has at his disposal'. So we now have an explanation of B's action y of the form:

(i) B intends (wants) to secure reward W from A;
(ii) B believes that (in virtue of A's action) *only* if he does y will he secure reward W.

Therefore:

(iii) B does y.[30]

   Thus, in explaining B's action in teleological terms we need evidence of:
(i)   B's intention;
(ii) his beliefs concerning A's 'possession of W';
(iii) his belief that action will secure him the reward W in situation S;
(iv) his belief that x is signal for the truth of (iii).

   These evidential requirements are entirely in line with P1, 2, and 3 except that it is now made explicit that it is B's belief—which may of course be false—that x is indicative of A's willingness to behave in a particular way. This rather crude formulation can be much refined, and provides a general framework for the analysis of the logic of social interaction. I will not, however, pursue the details any further here as they will be covered at length in Abell (forthcoming).

   The centrally important feature of teleological explanations becomes dramatically evident when we recall that to test the 'truth' of a causal explanation we need to generate a variance across a set of actors. In particular, we need to locate some actors of the appropriate type that do not 'do y'. The query we left unresolved above was, what would happen if A was 'all powerful' across all actors of type B—for then there is no way of generating variance and thus testing a causal model—a condition I described as hegemonic control. *With a teleological explanation, however, it would be sufficient to test the scope of A's power by providing valid teleological explanations of the above type for each of the subjugated individuals. Thus teleological explanations provide a methodology for the study of lack of variance.* Admittedly, there may be rather acute problems in ascertaining the 'truth' about people's intentions, beliefs, and so on, *nevertheless we do not have to resort to the comparative method.*

   It is also worth noting, in passing, that since teleological accounts do not depend upon generalizations they likewise do not, when used in the context of 'power', entail what I earlier termed a *generalized capacity* interpretation. Teleological explanations are not incompatible with a generalized capacity of A, but by their very nature they can provide an account of the 'power' in one decision or issue.

   There are a number of points I should like to emphasise about a teleological explanation of A's power over B. First, it is often natural to interpret the first premise (i.e. the intentional premise) of the explanation in terms of the sanctions that A controls (using the term in the broadest possible sense). Thus linking our analysis with another well established approach to the measurement of power.[31] Secondly, the power of A over B is clearly not to be confused with A's ability to physically force B to comply with his wishes. For the essence of B's behaviour is one of choice where he selects to receive rewards W.[32] This could, of course, include the avoidance of anticipated negative sanctions which are 'threatened' by A. Thus, on this interpretation, explanations from power are compatible with the voluntaristic bases of social action.[33] Central to this sort of teleological account of power relations is the exchange of sanctions (however tenuous these may be) and the idea that B is guiding his own action accordingly. He can, of course, be wrong about (a) A's willingness to reward/threaten him, (b) the truth of the proposition that the situations are adequately described as S and, (c) that in those situations doing y will lead to his being rewarded. Nevertheless, the explanation of his action will still be valid. (Whether or not, in the absence of the truth, of (a) we would wish to call this an 'explanation from power' is a moot point.)

The truth of the counterfactual is inferred from the fact that B *himself* gives A's possession of W etc., as the 'reason' (necessary and sufficient) for his action, thus we are accordingly entitled to assent to the truth of the proposition that 'if it had not been for A's possession of W then B would not have done y'. If we know the explanation is valid then we know the truth of the counterfactual. Furthermore, though I have chosen to analyse 'power' relationships in terms of sanctions W, it is clear that an entirely parallel argument could be produced where B's action is teleologically dependent upon some feature in his environment which is controlled by A (see note 4).

So far, the aforegoing analysis has not explicitly brought into play the distinction between power, on the one hand, and manipulation/influence on the other. Are the distinctions between causal and teleological explanation of any use here?

If A 'changes B's mind' in the spirit of P*1, 2, and 3, then we may interpret this (from a teleological point of view) in a number of ways. Firstly, A may change B's intentional premise. Secondly, he may change B's cognitive premise in one or both of two ways. Firstly, by changing his belief that his action y will secure his objectives (intentions); secondly, by changing his belief that the circumstances he is in are adequately described as S. There thus seem to be three rather distinct ways in which A can 'change B's mind'. It will not have escaped the reader's notice that, as expressed, they appear to bear a close relationship to our three principles of autonomy mentioned above. I will examine each of them in turn, and sketch how they are intrinsically intertwined in our three central concepts.[34]

We are concerned, first of all, to explain (and in explaining to categorize) B's change in preference (objective).[35] The type of explanation we give will place the change as a case of A's power, manipulation, or influence. In the teleological framework, if we seek an answer to the question, why did B change his preference, if B's answer is, as we have analysed, in terms of sanctions that A, directly or indirectly, holds (note 29), then B has chosen to trade his *real* preference for a change in the distribution of sanctions. In this case A would not be able to control B's action if he did not control the sanctions. Needless to say the sanctions may be extremely diverse in nature.[36] If B's answer to the question as to his change in preferences does *not* involve sanctions (or conditions) that A controls then the change is a case of influence or manipulation. In both cases he will adopt his preference in terms of its own merits, expressive or instrumental; in the latter case his preference should be derivable from 'deeper' intentions (objectives) and becomes a 'means'. B has still 'chosen' between alternatives and his *range* has accordingly been increased. It is, therefore, to his cognitive premise that we must look for the differentiation between manipulation and influence. If, in the process of changing B's preferences, A intentionally or otherwise controls B's access to relevant information, such that he either (a) reduces B's understanding of his situation (S) (including implications of adopting one course of action rather than another) or, (b) reduces the perception of means open to him then A is *manipulating* B. If, however, no such reductions take place, then we must call this *influence*. A similar line of reasoning would apply to the more restrictive empirical situation of hegemonic control. Here there is no shift in preferences—everybody has the same preferences. But as we have seen we can explain this lack of variance in teleological terms. In this case we would have to show that A's information control in the sense of (a) and (b) above was sufficient to induce B to adopt certain objectives. We do this *not* by specifying an alternative objective, this must be an open question that is essentially conjectural and perhaps, therefore, subject to the contemporary emphasis on action research and/or praxis. The essential point is that the content of the counterfactual is open—B would have done 'something' else.[37]

I have argued for the rather difficult concept of autonomy as a base line (P*4) in differentiating between manipulation and influence; though I am not so sanguine as to believe that I have more than scratched the surface of the problems associated with establishing a 'sociology of freedom' but it remains finally to compare my concept of 'autonomy' with the Marxian/Lukesian concept of 'interest' as a baseline in the study of 'power'.

The Marxian/Lukesian view is disarmingly straightforward; it implies that in deciding when a shift in B's preferences, induced by A, is to be regarded as a case of A's manipulation, or influence, we merely have to ask whether the shift takes B nearer or further from his latent interests. Thus, when neither of the preferences reveal B's interests per se then we have to impose some external criterion. It cannot, by definition, be available to B, for if it were, he would clearly adopt it. The possible authoritarian implications of this viewpoint are well known and the implied justifications in over-riding preferences of those suffering from 'false consciousness' have disturbed many of a liberal frame of mind.

It seems to me that in adopting the base line 'individual autonomy' one begins to overcome these difficulties for in describing B as manipulated we do not have to take recourse in an external criterion involving his *objective interests*. Is this correct —can we specify the conditions for B's autonomy independently of B's *latent*

THE MANY FACES OF POWER AND LIBERTY   21

interests? I think we can, but to make this evident would involve a much deeper analysis of autonomy than I have space for here.

Notes

1. I have begun a discussion of these problems in Abell (1975) and they are further analysed in Abell (forthcoming). Problems also arise when we wish to consider A and B as collectivities which are not entirely consensual.

2. Although the distinction between behaviour and action has played such a central role in sociological meta-theory, it has rarely been given any detailed consideration in the context of power and influence relations. Since I am concerned with 'states of mind' and therefore more often than not with 'meaningful' behaviour, I will refer to 'action' in what follows.

3. I am using the word forebearance to mean inaction.

4. It may well be, of course, that there are very many factors 'intervening' between x and y. Thus we should not construe the power relationship between A and B as exclusively tied to a face to face sort of interaction. Indeed, if we can establish 'causal' chains of the form $x \rightarrow x_1 \rightarrow x_2 \rightarrow x_3 \rightarrow y$ then it may be that B is unaware of x, but nevertheless we would still want to say A has power over B to the extent that x ultimately determines x_3.

5. I do not pretend that the phrase 'state of mind' is at all clear. I hope what is involved will be more evident later on in the paper. For the moment it may be interpreted as B's preferences or objectives. Under (ii) we are implying that B behaves in a manner contrary to his preferences. Clearly, in one sense, B 'decides' to do this (i.e. changes his mind) but the point is he does not do this out of 'conviction', but because of some sort of sanction that (he believes) A controls.

6. We allow that A influences B by maintaining B's more autonomous state of mind in the face of other 'actors' attempting to manipulate him.

7. The distinction I am drawing, then, is one between situations where 'B does y' because it is instrumental in terms of some sanction (positive or negative) and where 'B does y' because of its intrinsic merit to him. It does not, of course, take much thought to realize that the dividing line between the two is not always as clear-cut as one would like. For example, when B follows a moral or ethical injunction promulgated by A, is this to be regarded as working through B's 'conviction' that the injunction is right (a case of influence or manipulation) or in order to avoid feelings of 'guilt' (a negative sanction)? Nevertheless, however difficult the divide may be to draw, it appears we need to do so. It should also be emphasized that the sanction involved must be so from B's point of view (see below).

8. By reputational technique I mean the method of asking suitably placed respondents to estimate various power-holders' degree of power. The technique has been much criticized, but has the advantage of being easy and cheap to use and in situations where it is cross-validated with more soundly based techniques can still be very useful (see Abell, 1975). I have not included a detailed consideration of the technique in this paper as it is not conceptually based.

9. For the sake of expository convenience I will assume that the decisions are serially independent in the sense that the outcome of one does not constrain or determine the outcome of others. This is patently an oversimplification, however; the introduction of decision dependence would complicate the presentation without adding to the basic conceptual issues I wish to discuss.

10. We might ask for an explanation of the variation in these preferences this would merely take us a stage back in the analysis—in the language of Abell (1975) into a different bargaining zone.

11. The argument is in no way dependent upon such a specification.

22   PETER ABELL

12. In practice we may wish to know how β_{OA} and β_{OB} depart from unity, not zero, as a value of unity means, in effect, perfect agreement between the outcomes and preferences (assuming they are on the same scale). The models presented in Abell (1975) are rather more complex than those presented here containing measures of *subjective salience* of each actor in each term in equation (6).

13. If preferences are identical over all decisions there is no need for power in the system.

14. One side might of course not attempt this in an active way recognizing the other's power. We must assume that the preferences involved are A's and B's 'real' preferences not necessarily those explicitly stated in the bargaining process or to the investigator. This poses a series of empirical problems, but I do not want to pursue them here. Furthermore, the model only touches on the diversity of methods that the parties can use to communicate their preferences and 'get their own way'—the content of P1 may well be highly complex.

15. A might be *maintaining*, rather than increasing B's range in the face of others who are potentially manipulating him.

16. I am trying to use the word *choose* to contrast with determination.

17. The formulation seems to come close to Berlin's (1969) classic statement.

18. Much clearly revolves on the word information and even if I were able, space precludes a detailed analysis. What is clear, however, is that it is not necessarily the 'amount' of information that matters—one can clearly manipulate by swamping somebody with information.

19. See Abell (1975) and forthcoming.

20. There are rather difficult problems in deciding what a potential decision is as Bachrach and Baratz recognize.

21. We must assume that if it were the case that the 'non-decisions' were 'given' to B he would have a preference which would be contrary to A's. Thus, Bachrach and Baratz (1970, p. 44) —'A non-decision, as we define it, is a decision that results in suppression or thwarting of a latent or manifest challenge to the values or interest of the decision maker.'

22. The idea of control-loss was first introduced by Williamson (1967).

23. It should be noted that the concept of manipulation as I have used it does not necessarily imply an intention to do so on A's behalf. It might be, therefore, useful to distinguish between intentional and inadvertent manipulation.

24. I will initially centre the argument upon propositions in the necessary and sufficient form (⇔) rather than just sufficient form—thus ruling out multiple causation. It should not be assumed incidentally that the author believes that causal explanation is unproblematic in the affairs of men.

25. That is, the initial conditions in the above presentation.

26. Dahl, for instance, not surprisingly seems to operate with an implicit causality. Indeed, since most empirical studies of power relations derive from North America, the positivist concept of power is more or less explicit in them.

27. I have again ruled out overdetermination of B's behaviour by making the doing of y a necessary and sufficient condition for I. I do this merely for ease of presentation.

28. For the relationship between the premises and conclusion to be causal it is necessary that all four combinations of truth and falsity of the premises and conclusions to be *logically* possible. From our above argument this is clearly not possible.

29. We may or may not wish to construe A's action x as teleological in terms of controlling B. Also we should recall the point I made in Note (4). x may well be remote from A's immediate action and, in fact, B may not even recognize that x is controlled by A.

30. What I said in Note (29) applies here also it may be that B wants W without realizing that it is A that controls W, etc. We could thus reformulate the analysis without specific mention of B's *recognition* of A's role in the relationship.

31. The so-called control of resources approach.

32. It may of course be instrumental to a 'deeper lying' objective of B. If this is the case then one should in principle be able to give a higher order teleological explanation starting from this objective and concluding in a statement about W.

33. The dividing line between 'force' and 'power' may in practice be rather difficult to draw; there is clearly a grey area of habitually induced behaviour lying between very clear poles. I do not, however, in an exploratory paper of this sort wish to get involved in this particular debate. The question naturally arises, though, as to whether in the teleological account (explanation), 'W' can be regarded as a 'cause' of B's action. Clearly in one sense of the word 'W' determines B's action, it is also logically possible for him not to have *chosen* to 'do y' in the presence of W, and W is temporarily prior to y. The relationship, therefore, accords with some of the standard (Humean) canons of causality. However, there is no need to link W to y in terms of a universal generalization (Law) and thus, in order to establish the 'truth' of the link, to resort to comparative method. I prefer, as a consequence, to refer to W as a 'teleological patterning factor' (see Abell, forthcoming).

34. The issues deserve a lengthy consideration, but I will only pen an outline here. Clearly there are a number of ways that an individual can be manipulated because of his emotional proclivities. I will not consider these. I admit I am in fact taking an 'over-cognitive' viewpoint.

35. We will assume that B's preferences in decision-making (and for that matter, non-decision-making) derive from his objectives. This idea is central to the concept of belief/value system which centres on the idea that there is in some sense of the word an internal logic to such systems such that preferences in 'one-off' decisions can be deductively unpacked from deep-lying beliefs/values. We know this is an over-optimistic interpretation of how individuals hold beliefs (pace cognitive consistency theories), but it would take me too far afield to introduce any complications of this sort here.

36. In fact what is and what is not regarded as a *sanction* may itself be subject to 'power play'. Thus, part of A's 'power' over B may be attributable to A's ability to implant the idea that certain rewards, etc., are worthwhile in B's mind. Thus the legitimization of sanctions is an important aspect of influence or manipulation. (I will expand these issues in Abell (forthcoming)). Furthermore, it is also possible that A and B's interpretation of sanctions are different. Our analysis rests rather heavily on B's interpretation of the sanctions involved. Clearly since I have chosen to make the provision of information a characteristic of influence and manipulation processes we must not interpret sources of information as sanctions. Nor should information flow be interpreted in purely quantitative terms—A can manipulate B by outfacing him with an abundance of information.

37. The analyst may be able, because of his understanding of B, to show that A, by virtue of additional information he controls, could increase B's autonomy if he made it available to him.

References

ABELL, PETER (1971). *Model Building in Sociology*, London: Weidenfeld and Nicholson.

—— (1975). *Organisations as Bargaining and Influence Systems*, London: Heinemann.

—— (forthcoming): *Organisations as Bargaining and Influence Systems*, Vol. II, London: Heinemann.

BACHRACH, PETER, and BARATZ, MORTON S. (1962). 'The Two Faces of Power', *American Political Science Review*, **56**, pp. 947–52.

—— and —— (1970). *Power and Poverty: Theory and Practice*, New York: Oxford University Press.

BERGER, PETER (1963). *Invitation to Sociology: A Humanistic Perspective*, London: Penguin Books.

24   PETER ABELL

BERLIN, SIR ISAIAH (1969). *Four Essays on Liberty*, London: Oxford University Press.

CRENSON, MATHEW A. (1971). *The Un-Politics of Air Pollution: A Study of Non-Decision-Making in The Cities*, London: John Hopkins Press.

DAHL, ROBERT (1957). 'The Concept of Power', *Behavioural Science*, **2**, pp. 201–5.

—— (1958). 'A Critique of the Ruling Elite Model', *American Political Science Review*, **52**, pp. 463–9.

GALBRAITH, J. KENNETH (1974). *Economics and The Public Purpose*, London: Penguin Books.

HARSANYI, JOHN C. (1962). 'Measurement of Social Power, Opportunity Costs and the Theory of Two-Person Bargaining Games', *Behavioural Science*, **7**, pp. 27–52.

LUKES, STEVEN (1974). *Power: A Radical View*, London: Macmillan.

PARSONS, TALCOTT (1957). 'The Distribution of Power in American Society', *World Politics*, **10**, pp. 123–43.

—— (1963a). 'On the Concept of Influence', *Public Opinion Quarterly*, 27, pp. 37–62.

—— (1963b). 'On the Concept of Political Power', *Proceedings of the American Philosophical Society*, **107**, pp. 232–62.

—— (1937). *The Structure of Social Action*, New York: Free Press.

PETTIGREW, ANDREW (1972). *The Politics of Organisational Decision-Making*, London: Tavistock.

PONDY, LEWIS (1975). 'The Other Hand Clapping an Information-Processing Approach to Organisational Power'. Mimeo, University of Illinois.

VON WRIGHT, GEORGE H. (1971). *Explanation and Understanding*, London: Routledge and Kegan Paul.

WILLIAMSON, O. E. (1967). *The Economics of Discretionary Behaviour: Managerial Objectives in the Theory of the Firm*, Chicago: Markham.

Biographical note: PETER ABELL, B.Sc., Ph.D.; 1967–71, Lecturer, Senior Lecturer, Department of Sociology, Essex; 1971–6, Reader (Director of Research) Industrial Sociology Unit, Imperial College; 1976–, Professor of Sociology, University of Birmingham; author of books on Model-building, Inward Investment, and Organizational Theory.

Acknowledgement

I should like to thank the following friends and colleagues for their helpful comments on an earlier version of this paper: Kerry Thomas, Sandra Dawson, Robin Cohen, Peter Lassman, Ricardo Peccèi, Norman Stockman, and Ann Westenholz.

[4]

Theoretical considerations

Decision-making and the concept of power

This book is about organizational decision-making, but in the social science literature decision-making covers several quite distinct areas of analysis. In psychology the emphasis is on cognitive processes in solving problems or making judgements, and typically these phenomena are investigated under controlled laboratory-like conditions (Nisbett and Ross, 1980; Kahneman et al., 1982; Pitz and Sachs, 1984). Most of this work is done with isolated individuals in attempts to establish preferred or optimal solutions or to discover non-rational or irrational decision outcomes.

Even when group decision-making is investigated, as in the well-known work on risky shift (Wallach and Kogan, 1965; Cartwright, 1973) the artificiality of the setting enables experimenters to exclude variables which take on a dominant role in organizational settings. Power is one such variable, but until quite recently it has received surprisingly little attention even in work on organizations. Bass (1983) in a recent review of the literature devotes less than four pages out of 190 to power although many aspects of this topic appear under different names like authority, conflict, participation rate busting and others. The reluctance to use the term power is more noticeable in Psychology than in other social science disciplines where a considerable amount of attention has been devoted to it during the last 10 years (Lukes, 1986).[1]

If even today, some management development courses and the related literature avoid talking about power, it is pobably due to the negative connotations associated with the word, so that softer substitutes like involvement, participation, autonomy, influence, persuasion and communication or leadership are preferred. However, the softer terms, some of which we will also use, can lack precision if they stand by themselves without being anchored to the core phenomenon. This is not to say that power is easily defined in theoretical terms but it seems that the average person has no great difficulty with it. One recent author goes so far as to say: 'If you don't know what power is, then perhaps you should read another book' (Mintzberg, 1983: 1).

12   *Decisions in Organizations*

We will not go to this extreme, and this chapter will review some of the major schools of thought in which power plays an important part, before presenting our own approach.

Most analyses of power concentrate on individuals and the relationship between individuals — this can be called the *interaction* aspect of power or they highlight the *dependence* aspect based on social exchange theory. An extension to groups leads to *coalition* (Child, 1972) and *bargaining* theories (Bacharach and Lawler, 1980) with the emphasis still mainly on the social actors in the situation rather than on the object or task on which people are engaged.

The actor-centred approach works well with routine and essentially short-term decisions particularly at the lower levels of organizations and maybe again at the apex of the hierarchy when personal power struggles seem to be particularly fierce. The bargaining model is particularly appropriate to the analysis of decision processes between organizations or subunits (Abell, 1975) or with a limited category of decisions relating to money, wages or salaries.

For the majority of strategic and tactical long- and medium-term decisions we have preferred to move away from a concentration on the actors by focusing on the decision task itself and studying its development over time from start-up to implementation. Of course people are involved in the tactical and strategic decision process at every stage, sometimes as individuals, sometimes as occupants of specific roles like accountants or engineers and sometimes as representatives of interest groups like directors or shop stewards. However, we believe that the focus on the task as the unit of analysis for strategic and tactical decisions has advantages which will emerge as we describe some of the schools of thought in the following pages.

One can understand why scholars have shied away from a large-scale analysis or synthesis of the literature on power.[2] There are a number of important cognate subjects which merge imperceptibly with it and are themselves the focus of a large literature. There is for instance the sociological analysis of class structure in society, the economist's study of differential income distribution, the educationalist's concern with varying career opportunities due to unequal access to prestigious educational establishments, and there is the anthropologist's assessment of the influence exerted by religious movements. With the possible exception of this last subject, the other topics are all of potential interest to the student of organization. For our own quite circumscribed objective relating to the present research, it is sufficient to give a limited overview of some major approaches that have influenced us in our thinking.

There are theories based on the individual, his propensities and resources. We will call these *inner power theories*. A second group of theories concentrates on the power relations between people. This group which can be called *inter-personal theories* makes up the bulk of the literature. Finally there are some approaches which study the role of power between groups or organizations; some of these also take account of the flow of time. We will call these *time–space theories*. While this categorization draws boundaries around a variety of ways of conceptualizing power, it should not be implied that these boundaries are impermeable. The power relationships between two people, for instance, will clearly be affected by any strong individual differences in their need for power.

Inner power theories
Philosophers, historians, novelists and psychologists have often drawn our attention to individuals who seem to have a particularly highly developed need for power. Nietzche put forward the ferocious argument that the sole force at work behind all human thought and action is the will to power.

The portrait of America's industrial empire builders in the nineteenth century gives credence to such a thesis (Josephson, 1934). An analysis of power-directed personalities in charge of four major American media institutions include William Paley at the Columbia Broadcasting System, Harry Luce of Time Inc., the Chandler family who own the *Los Angeles Times* and Phil Graham's influence on the *Washington Post*. William Manchester (1968) has written a fascinating historical account of the enormous power wielded by the Krupp family in Germany between 1650 and 1968. Although Krupps were only industrialists, Manchester shows that their cannons won the Franco-Prussian war in 1870. In World War I their cannons pulverized Verdun and shelled Paris at a range of 81 miles (130 km). They helped Germany re-arm secretly and by 1929 had perfected the famous Panzers which overran France in World War II. The Krupps financed Hitler's terror election of 1933 and during the Nazi period they ran 138 privately owned concentration camps. Hitler exempted the Krupps from taxation in a way that was apparently binding on post-1945 Germany. The Krupps survived a Nuremberg conviction and became the dynamo behind Europe's Common Market in its early stages. These are examples of personal and dynastic power.

Psychologists have taken relatively little interest in power, but some psychoanalytic theories make use of power as an explanatory variable. Zaleznic (1970) argues that an open discussion and recognition of power would help to improve the quality of

14   *Decisions in Organizations*

organizational analysis. As an example he used the power struggle between Knudson and Cole of General Motors, but in spite of extensive psychoanalytic terminology, casting chief executives into father figures and suggesting that subordinates have fantasies about what they would do if they held the top position, the approach lacks conviction.

Alfred Adler, a student of Freud, who later went his own way, used power striving as a major explanatory concept. Everybody yearns after success and some have an 'insatiable lusting after the semblance of power' (Adler, 1925: 29). If ambition and striving for power are frustrated, inferiority symptoms become the expression of maladjustment. Adler's own need for power seems to have been highly developed. In the introduction to his English translation he claims that his psychology is 'a definite science' and that 'no compromise can be admitted', nor would he ever 'agree to change the fundamentals of human psychology' (Adler, 1925: v).

Although Mulder comes from a quite different tradition, namely laboratory psychology, he too sees the power drive as a basic human characteristic and, following Stack Sullivan, speaks of 'the biological striving for power' (Mulder, 1977a: 1). The more power a person has, the more he wants. A person can become addicted to power and this 'makes it comparable to the need for hard drugs' (Mulder, 1977a: 46).

The most detailed empirical approach to the measurement of the power motive stems from psychoanalytically influenced theories of David McClelland. His interest in power motivation which took nearly 25 years to mature, is based on the theories of Freud and Erikson. Like his better-known earlier work on achievement motivation (McClelland, 1961), the empirical method uses a Thematic Aperception Test approach to scoring stories. The quantitative data are interpreted to suggest that the power drive can manifest itself in four stages. The first two relate power to the 'self', the third refers to a person's impact on others and the fourth integrates the power drive to higher-order goals like 'duty'. Unlike Freudian theory, McClelland's stages are not evolutionary but operate in what may be called a contingency framework: 'situations play a large part in determining the appropriateness of various modes of expressing the power drive' and maturity 'involves the ability to use whatever mode is appropriate to the situation. Immaturity involves using perhaps only one mode in all situations . . .' (McClelland, 1975: 24). From his analysis he concludes that 'the better managers . . . are high on power motivation and low in affiliation motivation' (McClelland and Burnham, 1976: 103).

Max Weber's use of the term charisma fits into the category of inner power theories. The word derives from New Testament Greek meaning the gift of grace. Weber uses it to describe an extraordinary quality possessed by a person which gives him an unusual degree of influence. This person-oriented use of the term must be distinguished from Weber's use of charisma to describe the nature of a bureaucratic office role (Weber, 1947: 329–42).

The term authoritarian personality is often used to describe an individual's tendency to impose his will on others. Measures of authoritarianism have sometimes been used in leadership studies, but not with great success. The famous California research, leading to the publication of the *Authoritarian Personality* (Adorno et al., 1950), emphasized social discrimination and prejudice rather than power and to the extent that there is a connection between the authoritarian type and power-striving, it is as likely to be negative as positive. In popularizing the concept, however, misunderstanding has crept in. While the 'authoritarian man' is seen to be typical of 'a highly industrialized society with irrational beliefs . . . he is at the same time enlightened and superstitious . . . and inclined to submit blindly to power and authority' (Adorno et al., 1950: ix).

This brings us to the point of recognizing that inner power theories do not take us very far unless they refer to the outer world. We now turn to theories that do this more explicitly than those we have already considered.

Inter-personal theories
Most theories recognize or stress that power is a phenomenon that intervenes in the relationship between two or more people. Such an inter-personal relationship is put forward very clearly by French and Raven's (1959) well-known description of five bases of power. The simplest bases of power are reward, coercion and expertness. Power can also result from a perception of legitimacy or from a voluntary identification with the interest of another person or group. This theory does not distinguish deliberateness or intentions. A person may submit to another without the power holder being aware of it. Wrong (1979) among others prefers to define power as connection with somebody's clear intention to exercise it.

Such a clear intention is implied in Weber's theory which has been very influential. Power (*Macht*) 'is the probability that one actor within a social relationship will be in a position to carry out his own will despite resistance, regardless of the basis on which this probability rests' (Weber, 1947: 139). While many social scientists have followed this lead, notably Dahl (1957), and to some extent Dahrendorf (1959), Weber thought that the term power was too broad and vague to serve scientific utility. For most purposes he pre-

16   *Decisions in Organizations*

ferred the more focused term *Herrschaft* (control or domination) defined as the 'probability that a command with a specific content will be obeyed by a given group of persons'. This more narrow use excludes all those situations in which power comes from a mixture of interests or from several directions.

Weber's theory lends itself to a considerable number of variations. French, following Cartwright, argues that the power relationship between A and B is equal to the maximum force that A can induce on B, minus the maximum resistance force that B can mobilize in the opposite direction (French, 1956). A few theorists have stressed the importance of resistance. Etzioni has said that 'power is the ability of partial or complete predominance'. We find out that someone has power only when he overcomes the resistance of somebody else (Etzioni, 1968: 314–15). Rus, who quotes the above passage from Etzioni, wants to go further. Deriving his approach from Hegel's philosophical dialectic, he argues that power and resistance operate in a mutual and inevitable interdependence. Everything, including power, has a positive and a negative side and the phenomenon cannot be fully understood without recognizing this inherent contradiction (Rus, 1980). Failure to recognize the legitimacy of this interdependence leads some people to use techniques like participation to reduce resistance or achieve compliance. But this, according to Rus, can be an extreme example of manipulation. This is similar to the position of Pateman (1970) and Wright Mills (1970: 50).

Bertrand Russell has made a contribution to this field in a little-known book on power. He defines it 'as the production of intended effects', and argues that this gives a measurable assessment. One can say 'that A has more power than B, if A achieves many intended effects and B only a few' (Russell, 1938: 35). In a more modern guise, this approach is developed by Abell (1975) who uses a concept derived from Hoppe's (1930) levels of aspiration theory. He calls a projection of intentions or aspirations 'initial preferred outcome', and compares it with actual outcomes whenever they can be ascertained. The bigger the difference, the lower the power of the person or group.

Several authors like to make a distinction between power and influence. While power is thought to be dependent on a measure of coercion, influence is said to depend on personal abilities, charisma and the like. A more precise distinction is put forward by Abell (1975) who says that influence is 'the ability of A to modify B's preferred outcomes'. In contrast power is defined as A's 'ability to obtain his preferred outcomes in a bargaining situation' (Abell, 1975: 15–16). Heller has moved away from the Weberian model of actors in an interpersonal power relationship, and the distinction between power and influence is based on a flow process model of decision-making. In the first place neither influence nor power can be exercised unless there is access to the decision process. Having gained access, a person exerts influence when 'as a result of direct or indirect intervention his preferences are considered in the process of arriving at a decision'. Power, however, is exerted only when 'as a result of direct or indirect intervention, his preferences are incorporated in the decision process' (Heller, 1971: xxiv). This theory moves away from the notion of power as a relation between a person A and a person B; it postulates that several people can contribute influence or power to the same decision process.

Another departure from the individualist treatment of power is taken by Emerson's (1962) power dependence theory. Power is seen to be the property of social relationship and not the attribute of a person. While it is admitted that personal traits and abilities or the ownership of property could make a contribution to a power relationship, the important dimensions reside in the dependency of the non-power holder. The power of A over B is equal to B's dependence on A, for instance for some reward. But dependencies can also be conceptualized in terms of roles or units like boards of directors and technological departments who exercise power because other roles, units or departments depend on them (Perrow, 1972; Crozier and Thoenig, 1976).

Uncertainty creates dependency on those people, roles or units that can overcome problems stemming from lack of predictability. Crozier (1964) has argued that the control of uncertainty within an otherwise routinized situation confers power. Turbulence of the environment also creates some uncertainty but, up to a certain degree, it seems to be associated with a reduced power concentration or more participative decision-making (Lorsch and Morse, 1974; Rus et al., 1977; Heller and Wilpert, 1981). It seems that more research is needed to test the effect of varying degrees of uncertainty on the distribution of power in organizations. In particular, we have to distinguish the abstract notion of uncertainty from the ability to cope with it (Hickson et al., 1974).

An analysis of relationships leading to power shifts derives from the economic theory of exchange. According to Blau (1964), power is the result of unilateral exchange. For instance, if person A supplies services to B, which B cannot reciprocate (but values), then A has power over B. Trading transactions can take place between a substantial number of people or groups but power always 'arises out of unbalanced exchanges both positive and negative and out of unbalanced trading transactions and open conflict' (Whyte, 1969: 163).

18   *Decisions in Organizations*

While Weber has been the dominant influence on the literature on power, some attempts have been made to soften his definition. Tawney, the historian, talks of 'the capacity of an individual to modify the conduct of other individuals or groups, in the manner which he desires and to prevent his own conduct from being modified in the manner which he does not' (Tawney, 1952: 175). Gradually, this softer approach is beginning to filter into a few modern textbooks of organizational behaviour (Staw, 1977). However, for the most part, the literature on organizational behaviour has preferred to use even softer terms like participation.

Participation as an alternative to power

In the next four sub-sections we will briefly review those aspects of the participation literature that are relevant to our research and, in particular, to the treatment of the short-term operational decisions in Chapter IV.

Participation and satisfaction
The assumption that participative behaviour is associated with job satisfaction and that this in turn leads to higher performance has been explored for many years. Some interpretations of the Hawthorne experiment make these connections while others have denied it. The early 'Human Relations' theory has been criticized, expanded and refined by later authors (McGregor, Maslow, Likert, Argyris, Schein and Bennis among others) but even the simple connection between participation and satisfaction is not firmly established. Wall and Lischeron (1977) who made an extensive study of the literature, and Mohr (1982) who gave this subject some critical attention, have found many conceptual and methodological difficulties. Three problems require special attention.

1 The direction of the effect could also be reversed; satisfied people will be allowed more participation. Moreover, the relation between participative leadership and satisfaction can be caused by a third variable, for instance hierarchical level.
2 Participation is often only one element of scales which measure leadership. These scales also include items such as warmth, openness and trust. Greater satisfaction through more participative leadership could then have been caused by these items, regardless of the degree of participation.
3 Scales that measure leadership behaviour often include evaluative elements. For a study of the effect of participation on satisfaction (using these scales), one needs a descriptive measure for participation and an evaluative measure for satisfaction. Correlations between two

Theoretical considerations   19

evaluations of the same phenomenon are not informative. The results are tautologous (Wall and Lischeron, 1977: 20–3).

As discussed in Chapter III, we have tried in this study to remove as far as possible the problems mentioned under points 2 and 3. The operationalization of participation was by means of a description of the way in which a working unit is involved in a dozen concrete topics of decisions. Two measures of satisfaction are used: a general indication of satisfaction, for which the Taylor and Bowers list (1972: 75–7) was translated where necessary; and a measure of satisfaction with the potential for participation in the personal work situation. The abridged list used here proved to be a valid measure of satisfaction in previous research (Koopman and Werkman, 1973).

The critical problem of causality or reverse causality (point 1 above) is more easily avoided in the four-phase longitudinal research on tactical and strategic decisions where we assessed satisfaction with the process of decision-making in phase 3 (finalization) and satisfaction with the outcome at the end of phase 4 (implementation). This approach is treated in Chapter V.

A longitudinal research covering the same individuals over half a century has led Staw et al. (1986) to believe that attitudes are stable patterns which can be traced back to early adolescence and cannot be easily changed by manipulation of the work situation, like job design improvements. It would seem to follow that this stability would also prevent attitudes from being affected by changes in participative practices.

(For a more detailed analysis of the research on participation and satisfaction see Koopman and Wierdsma, 1984.)

Participation and skill utilization
Maslow's self-actualization theory of human behaviour can be extended to argue that participative behaviour favours self-actualization and this in turn allows untapped reservoirs of 'human production resources' to be used. Likert, in particular, was convinced of the value of the motivation and creative abilities of employees. He considered these typical human production resources to be of at least as much (financial) importance to the organization as the physical means of production. In reaction to existing accounting systems, which, according to him, over-emphasize the physical means of production, he designed a new accounting system: human asset accounting (Likert, 1967). Human asset accounting tries to measure the value of the human production factors (motivation, skills) and to value them in money. This

20   *Decisions in Organizations*

amount is subsequently reflected in the financial reports on the
credit side of the balance sheet (see also Hersey and Blanchard,
1977; Carrell and Kuzmits, 1982).

Heller (1971: 32) has drawn attention to two circumstances.
Firstly that most work on skills has concentrated on the identification
and development of skills, not on their utilization. Secondly,
possibly as a result of this neglect, it has proved difficult to
demonstrate the presence of non-activated skills. Later, the
evidence of considerable under-utilization of competence at very
senior organization levels was demonstrated (Heller and Wilpert,
1981) and is further extended in the present research.

Participation and effectiveness of decision-making
Human relations theory made the simple assumptions that there is a
causal chain from participation to increased satisfaction and that
this in turn leads to a greater acceptance of authority and
consequently improved effectiveness in decision-making. Miles
(1965) explains the contrast and the advantages of the Human
Resources Model which has as its primary aim the use of people's
real capacities and in this way seeks to improve the quality of work
and decision-making.

Figure II.1

Such a model creates the relationships shown in Figure II.1
(Heller 1971: 36). A positive relation between participation and
effectiveness has been found in several studies (Likert, 1967;
Tannenbaum, 1968; Kavcic et al., 1971; Argyris, 1972; Pennings,
1976; Dickson, 1981) but not in others (Filley et al., 1976; Locke
and Schweiger, 1979; Andriessen et al., 1983). Moreover, the
limitations of operationalization and correlational methods remain
formidable.

Contingency models
Most of the early theories of participation are 'universalistic', that is
they make no specific allowance for situational differences. Fiedler
(1967) was one of the first to criticize the universalistic models. He
was able to demonstrate that the relation between participation and

outcomes was dependent on a specified number of contingencies: the relation between superior and subordinate, the task structure and the formal position of authority of the superior (Fiedler and Chemers, 1974; Fiedler, 1978).

This 'contingency thinking' has created an incentive for the formulation of more elaborate contingency theories regarding the effects of participation. One well-known study is that of Vroom and Yetton (1973) in which the required quality of the decisions and the degree to which the execution of the decision is dependent on it being accepted by those directly involved are applied as central contingency variables. This seems to be a further development of a distinction made by Maier as early as 1965: decisions may be quality dominant or acceptance dominant. A flexible contingency model has been developed which saw the decision task itself as a major situational factor and the perception of competence as another (Heller and Yukl, 1969; Heller, 1971; Heller, 1973). Contingency thinking is evident even earlier in the literature on complex decision-making. In 1959, Thompson and Tuden formulated a model in which the optimal decision-making strategy was determined by two dimensions in the decision situation: the amount of agreement on the preferences about possible outcomes and, secondly, beliefs about causation. A similar model was used by Shull, Delbecq and Cummings (1970). The foundation for these developments seems already to have been laid by March and Simon (1958). A review is given in Koopman et al. (1984b).

It seems that we have already strayed, imperceptibly, from the more clear-cut interpersonal theories of power into those that make or imply the existence of organizational space and/or the dimension of time (Hickson et al., 1971). In one very important sense all previously mentioned theories recognize space as far as the distance between levels of boss–subordinate or management–worker groups are concerned. Moreover, no theory explicitly denies the existence of time; that would be absurd. It is more a question of how essential the space–time dimension is to any given theoretical approach. While we believe that the interpersonal theories make up the bulk of the organizational literature on this topic, this is largely due to the extensive use of terms like participation, leadership involvement, control, etc. rather than to the word power.

It is not without interest for our research that the word *power* has tended to be avoided in the majority of leadership and decision-making studies until recently. Crozier, who believes that power is the dynamo as well as the foundation for all organizational analysis, has often complained about this omission.

22   *Decisions in Organizations*

Beyond the inter-personal

In contrast with the reluctance of organizational psychologists and sociologists, political scientists have developed arguments in favour of a more radical analysis of power. Such analyses often embrace societal and political dimensions and this tends to include a time perspective and in some cases also an emphasis on territorial aspects of power. Two recent approaches can be distinguished. One accepts the values and structures embedded in main-line theories, but evaluates certain behaviour and procedures within a political context. Pettigrew, for instance, seeks to emphasize the essentially 'political character of organizational life' (Pettigrew, 1975: 204) and in the same tradition is the analysis of power games (Crozier and Friedberg, 1977). We have more to say about these later.

The second approach challenges existing values and structures, usually from a marxian perspective. Barbalet (1985), for instance, argues that the traditional Weberian analysis has prevented the recognition of resistance as a distinct but interdependent aspect of power relation — a position also held by Rus (1980). Benson (1977) puts forward the view that rational assumptions about people and organizations still dominate theory but that several non-rational theories are now evolving. Interestingly, sociologists and political scientists have failed to notice the extensive psychological evidence on non-rational decision-making to which we referred earlier (for instance, Kahneman et al., 1982) and which has been frequently quoted by Simon (1984: 52). One of these theories demonstrates the importance of the external economic–social environment. Another describes organizational events as games and strategies which are played out as rituals within diversified work cultures. The goal of rationality itself becomes a ritual. It is conceivable that within such a framework 'the most potent type of power is that which is rarely exercised' (Clegg and Dunkerley, 1977). Power then becomes the submerged part of the iceberg, it 'maintains its effectiveness not so much through overt action, as through its ability to appear to be the natural convention. It is only when this taken-for-grantedness fails, . . . that the overt exercise of power is necessary' (Clegg and Dunkerley, 1977: 35). The power game can also be played more deliberately as a way of stopping latent demands for change from reaching the agenda of decision-making. For instance, 'demands for change in the existing allocation of benefits and privileges . . . can be suffocated before they can even be voiced' (Bachrach and Baratz, 1970: 44). An even more submerged part of the iceberg has been analysed by Lukes (1974) who calls it the third dimension. The most insidious use of power, he believes, is 'to prevent people . . . from having grievances by shaping their perceptions, cognitions and preferences in such a way that they accept their role in the existing order of things . . .' without conflict (Lukes, 1974: 24). The position of the French philosopher Foucault has developed along similar lines. He has argued that control over people in modern times has shifted from its earlier emphasis on physical measures through organs of state like the army and police to subtler measures which embed and control social behaviour through schools, psychiatric clinics and work organizations (Foucault, 1977; Sheridan, 1980). Such theories are not easily applied to organizational analysis through empirical data. Their function at this stage is to make researchers think about wider issues (Westerguard and Resler, 1975: 144–7).

Slightly more operational is the concept of metapower. Metapower is seen as an outside force exercising control over social relationships and social structures. It is a higher order power operating outside a given sub-system, exercising relational control and thereby imposes limitations on lower order power (Baumgartner et al., 1976). There are three control aspects to be considered. Metapower controls action opportunities, differential pay-offs and ideology (Baumgartner et al., 1975). This last category links up with Lukes' third power dimension. We will see later that in the present research we attempt an operationalization of the first metapower category, namely that concerned with the relational control from outside a sub-system over action opportunities within it.

While the rituals identified by Benson and Clegg and Dunkerley are not identical with the concept of games, there is some family likeness in these concepts. People can play games and worship myths or create images and metaphors without having specified political ideologies (Morgan, 1986). One game very frequently played by power holders in organizations as a way of preventing an opponent from introducing a change unfavourable to the power holder has been called 'why don't you, yes but' (Berne, 1973). It operates in the following way: a power holder has a problem with a group of employees and consults them because a participative style of behaviour has been highly recommended. The colleagues make a number of suggestions: 'Why don't you . . .'. In each case the power holder considers the advice, apparently with some care and then answers: 'Yes, but . . .'. Most people in positions of authority have a reasonable repertoire of games and any one of them can be played for a long time without receiving unfavourable comment (Mintzberg, 1983).

Crozier has produced an analysis of decision-making behaviour which describes games of a more advanced kind and on a more abstract level. Games are instruments for organized action. They

24   *Decisions in Organizations*

are made up of semi-ritualized patterns of interaction dominated by
the need to use and control power. Power is a relationship, not an
attribute; it creates conflicts but not because the power holders have
a stake in a given resource like expertise but because the games
people play create competitive situations surrounded by uncertainties. Uncertainties have to be resolved and actors, at any given
moment of time, have different abilities for reducing uncertainty
(Crozier and Friedberg, 1977). Games can operate at different
levels and with different degrees of formality and they are governed
by rules and regulations within a formal system. The greatest power
within a system obtains from the opportunity to operate outside the
prevalent game, that is to say, to constitute an exception. This
enables some actors or groups to operate new games at a different
level. The games created by the opportunity of flight from more
routinized games themselves develop rigidity and eventually require
a new exception (Crozier and Thoenig, 1976: 566). In our research
we will show how the ritualized power game and the use of images
operates in the budget forecasting system (see Chapter VI).

Space in decision-making research
The concept of space in the analysis of organizational life has two
facets; intra-organizational space is bounded by the area of the
triangle which we normally use to symbolize a unit or company
while extra-organizational space covers the area between triangles
and this can include governments, banks and influences from the
economic-social environment.

   Galbraith's description of decision-making in large modern
corporations using complex technology requires a consideration of
intra-organizational space. He argues that embedded in the bowels
of these organizations there is a technostructure which absorbs
problems, converts them into solutions and then sends them up the
hierarchy for scrutiny, costing and seals of approval (Galbraith,
1967: 65–70). This is a fairly rational approach, but similar space
considerations apply to models that stress the haphazardness of
decision-making or the art of muddling through (Lindblom, 1959).
Here the emphasis is on tracing the tentative or disjointed steps
which move problems from one position to another, up or down
or sideways in search of some reasonably acceptable solution.
Disjointed incrementalism is characterized by a search process
with inadequately formulated values, strained cognitive abilities,
disorganized information and difficult cost analyses (Braybrooke
and Lindblom, 1963). This unflattering description of organizational meandering has attracted much attention in recent years.
Researchers have caricatured the older more static models of

rational behaviour by descriptions of cases which resemble 'organized anarchy'. Decision-makers move about like animals in a maze,
using trial and error procedures, learning through accidents,
imitation and invention resulting from crises (Cohen and March,
1974). A garbage can model has been used to describe decisions by
oversight or by running away from the problem (Cohen et al.,
1972).

Another important departure from the analysis that sees power
residing in individuals, derives from the work of Hickson and his
colleagues. They have taken organizational units and sub-units as
their focus leading to the analysis of social relationships, the impact
of uncertainty, differences between decision tasks and the role of
organizational characteristics like the degree of interconnectedness
between sub-units (Hickson et al., 1971; Hinings et al., 1974; Butler
et al., 1979).

While organizations have always existed in an external environment, theorists have made use of this aspect of organizational space
only recently (Thompson, 1967; Burns and Stalker, 1961, Emery
and Trist, 1965; Lawrence and Lorsch, 1967). As so often happens,
the pendulum has swung from having largely ignored the external
dimension, to recent attempts to give it primacy over most others
(Leavitt et al., 1974; Starbuck, 1976; Miles et al., 1974; Pfeffer and
Salancik, 1978; Aldrich, 1979). A special aspect of environmental
space is the recent recognition that strategic decision-making takes
place between as well as within organizations. Friend looking at the
local government planning process, developed a theory of strategic
choice which related different organizations to each other (Friend
and Jessop, 1969). This was later expanded into what is now a new
field of analysis called inter-organizational decision-making. The
authors argued that 'The more comprehensively . . . organizations
seek to plan, the more they find themselves dependent on the
outcomes of other agencies, both public and private' (Friend et al.,
1974: xxii). Such inter-organizational perspectives have been used
for the analysis of power and in the broader area of industrial
relations (Berry et al., 1974; Metcalf, 1976). It is an expanding field
for research which could be applied to relatively new areas of
analysis as well as to old problems (Lammers, 1980).

Time in decision-making research
Herbert Simon's reconceptualization of the economic and psychological dimension of decisions has led to empirical work which
inevitably stressed the need to consider time as an important
element in future theories. We know from work with levels of
aspirations going back to Hoppe (1930) and Lewin et al. (1944), that

26   *Decisions in Organizations*

expectation of future events vary with subjective judgements of past events as well as with the objective knowledge of the past (Heller, 1952). The interaction between forecasts, judgements and actual events is quite complex (Cyert et al., 1958; Atkinson, 1964; Starbuck, 1963) and this leads to important shifts over time. The historic tradition of time analysis has developed quite independently from classic organization theory and failed to influence it substantially. Chandler's (1962) well-known analysis of organization structure changes over substantial time spans is a good example. Stinchcombe's environmental imprinting theory is widely quoted but rarely applied to the analysis of decision-making. He argues that certain important organizational characteristics like structures, processes and norms of behaviour can be traced back to the birth of an industry or enterprise. Once imprinted, they persist for decades, even though economic and social conditions change substantially (Stinchcombe, 1965). This characteristic appears not only to affect 'first-born' firms but also those created as the industry expands; newer organizations in a given sector imitate the imprinted characteristics of their predecessors. Although Stinchcombe's theory recognizes the importance of the environment, it provides an alternative explanation to some more recent environmental theories which take a much more restricted view of history and the effect of perseverance (Aldrich, 1979: 193–6).

A marxist view of the importance of history is well represented by Ramsay's (1977) analysis of the cycles of control in participation decision-making in British industry from about 1850 to the 1970s. He produces historical sources to trace fluctuations of acceptance and rejection of participative practices as a function of economic conditions and managerial strength. Under conditions of managerial weakness and economic stringency, including periods of war, there is an upsurge of interest in these decision practices but when management feels strong and the economy expands, joint consultative type schemes quickly collapse. While the theory is applied to Britain it would be interesting to extend it to the birth of industrial democracy schemes in other countries. A tentative step in this direction is taken in the conceptual analysis of the industrial relations and power sharing practices of twelve countries (see IDE, 1981b: Introduction). One potential weakness of the theory as developed by Ramsay is its lack of separation of the two causal variables. What happens when the economy is weak but management is aggressive and strong compared with unions? This seemed to be the position in Britain as well as other countries in the period 1978–86. It would appear that under such circumstances, managerial strength outweighs economic vulnerability. Emery (1967) also believes that the ups and downs of economic cycles affect the seriousness with which employers treat employee participation and Quality of Work Life practices. These methods are used, according to Emery, when employers are trying to get out of an economic depression but are quickly abandoned during periods of growth. This is similar to Ramsay's position.

A more conventional social science approach to time is the 'before–after' measurement of variables for which change is anticipated. This type of research often assesses the effect of training programmes. One of the best known, meticulously documented but widely ignored projects was carried out by Fleishman and associates in the early 1950s with the International Harvester Company in the United States. Using well-validated questionnaire instruments to study the leadership behaviour of first-line supervisors, they assessed their attitudes before and after they had undergone a programme of human relations training designed to increase their 'considerateness' vis-a-vis subordinates (Fleischman et al., 1955). They found that, as expected, attitudes changed substantially immediately after the training compared with the previous assessment. However, the more 'considerate' attitudes did not last after the foreman returned to his previous job. After some months, the leadership climate to which the foreman returned exerted a more powerful effect than the training. The gains in 'considerateness' were lost. This example and the next suggest that time is an integral part of a wider assessment, including organizational context and external factors.

Our final example comes from an attempt to produce organizational improvements through a carefully negotiated introduction of a new managerial philosophy (Hill, 1972). The idea started in the Employee Relations Department of Shell UK in 1963 who called in a team from the Tavistock Institute. In March 1965 the proposals were put to a two-day top management conference and were accepted. Various design changes and diffusion exercises were successfully carried out on a limited scale between 1965 and 1968. However, two developments in 1967 virtually halted the new managerial philosophy and socio-technical design programme. One was a change of the Chief Executive, who had been supportive, the second was the Suez Canal closure of 1967 and the subsequent oil crisis. An assessment of the Shell programme was undertaken by a team from the University of Lancaster in 1977–8. Their findings confirm the attenuation of the changes that were so laboriously introduced 10 years earlier with the full approval of most power holders at that time (Blacker and Brown, 1980).

28 *Decisions in Organizations*

Time–space theories

Parsons is one of the few theorists who broke away from Weber's narrow person centred definition of power by putting forward a systems focus with a process orientation. This implies the possibility of a time–space dimension. Parsons (1956) stressed the capacity of a 'system unit to actualize its interests . . . and . . . exert influence on processes in the system. However, in his elaboration of this approach and in rejecting Weber's built in conflict assumptions, he went to the other extreme and built in consensus and legitimacy as the critical dimensions' (Martin, 1977: 38).

   Our division of examples into those that have emphasized space or time properties of the decision process is somewhat artificial. Many of the studies we have cited were to some extent concerned with both, but few of them dealt explicitly with both as well as with power as an individual or organizational variable.

   A good example of the interrelation among time, space and power comes from the traditional Japanese system of decision-making. *Ringi-sei* has been described as a kind of consensus system: 'Superiors do not force their ideas on juniors; instead, juniors spontaneously lay their opinions before their superiors and have them adopted' (Nakane, 1970: 65). It is not really appropriate to call it a bottom-up system (Drucker, 1971), because it is a management decision method and does not reach down to the shop floor level (Abeggelen, 1973; Yoshino, 1968). Typically it starts three or four levels down from the top executive where a manager wants to initiate some process, product or activity. He discusses the idea with an immediate superior and later with somebody on each higher level until it reaches the top. The upward process continues only if every superior approves, that is to say, puts his seal (or *hanko*) on it. If the Chief Executive also approves, the idea or document is then returned to the originator, who is charged with putting it into practice. The circle (*ringi*) has been completed. Early American observers of this system after the Second World War were critical of the *ringi seido* approach because they thought it was inefficient and slow; they would point out that it sometimes takes several months for the *ringi* to be completed. They argued that the traditional American method of executive decision-making would often take only hours or days. There was also the problem of confusing or confounding authority relations. The enormous post-war success of Japanese business in competition with the United States and Europe renders the efficiency argument untenable. Moreover, there is no evidence that authority relations are disturbed by this system (Heller and Misumi, 1987). An experienced Japanese academic explained the success of the *ringi sei* by drawing

Theoretical considerations   29

attention to the frequent problems of communication and implementation delays which occur in the Western decision process
(Ballon).[3] Under such a system, a decision might be taken in 3 days
but its acceptance and implementation could take many months.
This seems to be the experience of Mintzberg et al. (1976) and our
own findings support this evidence.

One of the early classical pieces of research into the influence–
power dimension through leadership styles, unlike most later
studies, was conceived with a conception of the importance of the
time–space dimension. Three alternative leadership methods were
acted out by adults who were in charge of youth club sessions with
10-year olds. The objective of this complex study was to ascertain
whether 'authoritarian', 'democratic' and 'laissez-faire' leadership
method led to different behaviour in the group (White and Lippitt,
1953; Lippitt and White, 1958). The experimenters took minute-by-
minute accounts of the social interactions, the group structure and
continuous stenographic records of conversation. They deliberately
introduced tests relating to time like having the leader arrive late or
suddenly calling him out of the room to observe what happens, or
sending in a stranger after the group had started to settle down to
their tasks. The results do not concern us here directly except to
point out that group behaviour under the three styles differed
substantially over time periods and particularly in relation to the
presence, absence or recent return of the formal leader. There were
also significant differences with the changeover from authoritarian
to democratic leadership.

Good case studies describing details of life and work in
organizations inevitably use the space dimension, but time is not
always a necessary basis for analysis. The classical study of power
and bureaucracy by Crozier in a clerical agency and an industrial
monopoly makes very little explicit use of time as an explanatory
factor (Crozier, 1964). Other classical studies have made extensive
use of sequential time analysis and consideration of organizational
space without introducing power as a critical factor, for instance,
the Relay Assembly Room experiment of the Western Electric
studies (Roetslisberger and Dickson, 1949: Part I; Whitehead, 1938:
Vol. 2). However, in a later development of the same research, in
the Bank Wiring Room study (Roetslisberger and Dickson, 1949:
Part IV), power was recognized as playing an important part in
understanding social relationships. The word 'power' was never
used but there were important substitutes like 'binging'. Binging
took place when one man 'walked up to another and hit him as hard
as he could on the upper arm' (Roetslisberger and Dickson, 1949:
421). Binging was a part of an elaborate game through which

30   *Decisions in Organizations*

workers in the Bank Wiring Room controlled each other. The term 'game' was used by the Western Electric researchers and bears some resemblance to the concept 'game' more recently developed to describe similar power interactions by Crozier and Thoenig (1976: 567). In the Western Electric research's Bank Wiring Room, the space dimension in terms of the geographic layout and position of workers was seen to be important; time less so.

In some studies, the longitudinal dimension becomes a major tool for understanding power and other relationships. The three-year field study of the worker director experiment in British Steel is a good case in point (Brannen et al., 1976). The gradual changes in sentiment by top management from hostility to fairly enthusiastic acceptance of the worker director idea are traced through to the structural provisions for such a scheme. The values and political philosophies of the planner are seen to play a major part in the decision to reject the main British Steel Board and Management Committees as suitable locations for power sharing (Brannen et al., 1976: 90–5). The research then follows through the evolution of the scheme, for instance by showing how the uncertain role and power attributions of worker directors led to formal job descriptions which may have helped them gradually to infiltrate a number of committees that were previously considered to be out of bounds (Brannen et al., 1976: 145–7).

A different use of the time–space–power dimensions in the analysis of industrial democracy is made through a detailed historical account of the industrial relations system in the period preceding and immediately following the British 1976 enquiry into Industrial Democracy under the chairmanship of Lord Bullock (Elliott, 1978). Elliott shows how trade union attitudes have gradually shifted towards an acceptance of such schemes from earlier positions of scepticism.

The work on decision behaviour developed by Hickson and his colleagues has already been referred to. The difference between short-term and long-term influence of variables became important in studying the speed and severity with which the workflow of sub-units affects the final output of the organization. The timing consequences of cash forecast and the variations in predicting degrees of uncertainty became clearer and, in relation to participation, four decision stages were postulated: initiation, information provision, choice, and implementation (Hinings et al., 1974). However, little use was made of the longitudinal dimension although its theoretical importance received substantial further attention (Butler et al., 1979). The final publication (Hickson et al., 1986) describes the full 10 year study of strategic decision making which is in many ways usefully complementary to our own, because they cover larger organizations, including some in public sector industry. However, in the end they regret that they did not make use of a chronological, step by step analysis of longitudinal decision sequences (Hickson et al., 1986: 259).

A much more specific use of time stages is the basis of a field study of complex decision processes undertaken in tracing 233 decisions dealing with data processing equipment (Witte, 1972). Witte uses five sequential phases: problem recognition, gathering information, development of alternatives, evaluation of alternatives, and choice. To test his sequential assumption of time phases, he divided the decision process into ten equal time intervals and then noted the level and type of activity in each of these. His findings do not support the sequential hypothesis. Communication activity reached peaks at the beginning and end of the cycle and the number of choices increased at the end of the process. His information about the cycle came from four companies selling the equipment and did not check with the purchasers; moreover the equal interval assumption is likely to have distorted the findings since subsequent research by Mintzberg and ourselves would suggest that such a division is highly unrealistic. A different phase approach was used in the study of decision-making of a Scandinavian university. Enderud (1977) based his work on the Cohen et al. (1972) garbage can model. He puts forward four phases: an initial unstructured 'bull' session; a bargaining-coalition negotiating phase; a persuasion sequence; and a final bureaucratic phase using an 'administrative man model'. Enderud concludes that although in a broad general sense, the model of an organized anarchy applies to the total process, there is a definite movement towards greater clarification and reduced ambiguity as the decision moves from phase 1 to phase 4.

The most detailed processual analysis up to now comes from a study of 25 strategic decisions assembled by fifty teams of 4–5 students taking courses for a Masters' Degree under the direction of Mintzberg and colleagues. The longitudinal dimension was now the major consideration. The decision process was defined as 'a set of actions and dynamic factors that begins with the identification of the stimulus for action and ends up with a specific commitment to action' (Mintzberg et al., 1976: 246). The authors describe three main phases of the decision cycle: (i) identification, (ii) development, and (iii) selection. In addition, Mintzberg's study draws attention to a considerable number of subdivisions and elements, most of which have a space–time implication. A category called 'decision communication', for instance, is designed to capture an active stream of communication throughout a decision process, like

32   *Decisions in Organizations*

scanning the environment for alternatives. Several categories highlight interruptions and delays of various kinds. Decision processes are thought to be circular rather than linear, requiring movements between phases and sub-divisions; this dynamic is called comprehension cycles and was discovered in each one of the 25 decision processes described in this research. One element, called 'failure re-cycles' identifies blockages due to rejections of proposals during the evaluation and choice stages. The authors conclude that although strategic decision processes are 'immensely complex and dynamic . . . yet . . . they are amenable to conceptual structuring'. At the same time they accept that the study has barely 'scratched the surface of organizational decision-making' and that the literature still lacks 'a single acceptable theory to describe how decision processes flow through organizational structures' (Mintzberg et al., 1976: 274).

Designing the longitudinal study

The preceding review of the different concepts of power, the variations in the space and time dimensions of research and the controversies about method, serves to introduce our own approach.

The present project is the result of a desire to extend the cross-sectional analysis of decision-making and participation by obtaining a greater depth of understanding of the dynamics of the process than had been possible by the previous research (IDE, 1981a, b). At the same time we wanted to keep some of the same variables like the Influence–Power Continuum (IPC) for which a lot of interesting data had already become available. The main requirement for such an extension was to engage in a longitudinal study and a minimum of 4 years was thought to be appropriate for moving from the cross-sectional study of routine operational issues to long-term decisions. There are clearly several ways of using the additional resources available in a 4-year study. Since we were working with only seven organizations, it meant that, minimally, we could get to know each of these organizations fairly well and this would be an advantage even in using questionnaires. More specifically the term longitudinal can be applied to at least three fairly distinct approaches.

The most widely used longitudinal method, the 'time-interval method', makes two or more assessments separated by interval of days, months or years. This includes measurements of a variable-like attitude to violence 'before' and 'after' showing a war film, or economic time series measurements. It also includes follow-up studies of individuals or age cohorts over their lifetime. A second quite distinct longitudinal method is continuous assessment by participant observation or other means of living with the ongoing events. We call this method 'processual'. For obvious reasons of cost and effort it is not often used.[4]

For the third variety of longitudinal method we borrow the term 'diachronic' from the French linguistic philosopher Ferdinand de Saussure (1857–1913), who used it to describe processes of change or evolution in contra-distinction from 'synchronic' which refers to the static approach to science. Diachronic analysis is less continuous than processual methods but attempts, by a variety of means to link up the intervals between assessments in order to obtain a fairly reliable picture of events or change. Some ways of achieving diachronic analysis are described in the following chapter on the empirical design of the research. The present study uses a simple time interval longitudinal method for measuring short-term operational decisions and diachronic methods for medium- and long-term issues.

Once it is accepted that most tactical and strategic decisions are not taken instantaneously, synchronic methods are likely to produce inaccurate or misleading results. This would apply also to the use of the decision tree model which assumes that at various stages of analysis, instantaneous 'yes', 'no' alternatives can be used to simulate decision-making. While this is a convenient way of programming a computer, it is not a true representation of how organizations work.

Access, influence and power

Diachronic or processual analysis is particularly important for studying participative behaviour. For this purpose it is useful to distinguish three categories: access, influence, and power. Since decision-making is a process which involves at least one person but usually several, access to that process is a necessary preliminary step. The minimum requirement for access is information. If one does not know that a decision is in the process of being made, no influence can be exerted. Sometimes access is confined to being given information. The next step is to allow people to comment on the evolving decision through the information they have. This step is sometimes called consultation and it constitutes the minimum degree of influence. If consultation results in an opportunity to contribute to the decision, even if suggestions made during consultation are not accepted, then one can talk of increasing levels of influence or participation. Higher levels of influence or participation describe situations where some of the notions emerging from the consultative process are at least occasionally incorporated in the decision. The term power would then be reserved for the event

34 Decisions in Organizations

when, as a result of an intervention by a person or group, their preference is accepted and becomes a part of the final decision.

The various alternatives from access through information via influence through consultation to the incorporation of a preference in the final decision are captured in one of our main measurements called the influence–power continuum (IPC). It has six positions (see Figure II.2). The IPC has been used in cross-sectional research (Heller, 1971; IDE, 1981a) and gives an approximation of the extent of participative behaviour in decision-making. But in its cross-sectional use it makes the important assumption that participative behaviour does not change during the process of decision-making or that, if it does change, people are able to assess any fluctuations and give an average answer.

	Information only 2		Advice is taken into consideration 4		Complete control 6
1 No or minimal information		3 Opportunity to give advice		5 Joint decision- making	

Figure II.2 *The influence–power continuum (IPC)*

Phases of decision-making

One of the main objectives of the present research design is to test the view that variables like influence, power and conflict vary in different phases of medium- and long-term decisions.

Following on from the work of Mintzberg et al. (1976) which used the three phases described earlier, we designed one part of the research around a phase model which will be described and tested in Chapter V. Here we will only indicate that the model has four phases: (i) start-up; (ii) development (which includes a search for alternatives); (iii) finalization; and (iv) implementation (for instance the time between deciding to buy a certain machine and its becoming operational). The first three phases are similar to those of Mintzberg et al. (1976) but we often found a considerable gap between finalization and the end of the implementation cycle and important events occurred during this period. This justifies the fourth phase.

The characteristics of operational, medium- and long-term decisions

Any clear-cut distinction between types of decisions will fail to be completely satisfactory. This has also emerged from the research by Hickson et al. (1986). We have already said that the longitudinal research used two different approaches. For what are called operational decisions, two administrations of questionnaires were used separated by about 18 months. The twelve operational decisions were aimed at the workshop level and the questionnaires were filled in by workers and foremen in the presence of a researcher. Two examples of operational decisions are: 'deciding on who works on which shift' and 'deciding on the layout of your workplace (position of machinery, desk and the like)'. It was not assumed that decisions at this level have no time dimension, but that the longitude of hours or maybe days is not a major factor in the process. In any case the research method required a feedback process some time after the administration of the questionnaires during which one would pick up special problems (see Chapter III).

Medium- and long-term decisions were selected on the basis that they would require a fairly lengthy process of not less than a month for the medium-term and not less than a year for the long-term issues and that middle and senior management would normally contribute to this process. Examples of medium-term issues relate to 'job grading procedures' and 'safety procedures' while examples of long-term issues are 'setting up of a new consultative procedure' and 'budget forecasting'.

In the literature, decision-making in organizations is usually stratified into three levels and each is treated differently. According to Mesarovic (1970) short-, medium- and long-term decisions do not differ only in the time dimension, but they have different functions in the system. He envisages organizational systems to have a three-level decision-making hierarchy: (i) policy-making decisions, (ii) coordinative decision-making and (iii) productive-executive decision-making. Qualitative differences have been stressed by other organizational theorists. Mulder (1971) for instance has argued that top level leadership is more oriented toward environmental issues and to the management of boundary conditions, while middle management is more concerned with internal decision problems. This distinction makes a space dimension an essential feature of decision-making analysis. Carter's work would support this. He describes long-term strategic decisions as the outcome of sequential bargaining at various levels in the organization, rather than as a result of group consensus (Carter, 1971).

For Simon (1977) the organization is like a 'three layer cake' composed of: (i) basic work processes at the bottom, (ii) programmed decision-making processes that govern their operation at the middle, and (iii) non-programmed decisions that design and monitor the entire system at the top of organizations. This distinction relates not only to function, but also to the cognitive

36   *Decisions in Organizations*

structure of decisions. Since cognitive structures are different, methods for dealing with them should take this into account. According to Simon, analytical techniques can only be used with programmed decisions which are mainly factual. More complex, strategic non-programmed decisions are no longer predominantly factual; they require value judgements, use intuition and are not based on sequential linear analytic ways of thinking. Traditional habits, standard operating procedures, modern operational research methods and linear dynamic programming are proper techniques for programmed, that is to say operational decisions. Idiosyncratic judgements or the General Problem-solving Programs are more appropriate for non-programmed strategic decisions.

Mintzberg follows along similar lines in distinguishing strategic from operational decisions. Using the term structure rather than programme he shows that strategic decisions change their form as they proceed from phase to phase. They take place in a different context and are significantly less predictable. They operate in an ambiguous environment where almost nothing is given or easily determined (Mintzberg et al., 1976: 251).

Summarizing these various distinctions, we can say that medium- and long-term decisions differ from operational decisions on three dimensions: (i) a different time concept; (ii) a different social space; and (iii) different levels of uncertainty. The operationalization of these ideas and the results are described in Chapter V.

Notes

1. The pioneering work goes back to the 1950s and 1960s (Lasswell and Kaplan, 1950; Dahl, 1957; French and Raven, 1959; Emerson, 1962; Parsons, 1963; Crozier, 1964; Kahn, 1964; March, 1966; Whyte, 1969).
2. Some useful attempts at synthesis are available. See Wrong (1979) and Martin (1977).
3. Professor Ballon, personal communication.
4. Methodological purists would also doubt that objectivity can be maintained by this method.

References

Abeggelen, J.C. (1973) *Management and Worker: The Japanese Solution*. Tokyo: Sophia University and Kodanska International.

Abell, P. (ed.) (1975) *Organizations as Bargaining and Influence Systems*. London: Heinemann.

Adler, A. (1925) *The Practice and Theory of Individual Psychology*. London: Kegan Paul. (Revised edition 1929; reprinted 1932, 1940, 1945.)

Adorno, T.W., Frenkel-Brunswik, E., Levinson, D.J. and Nevitt Sanford, R. (1950) *The Authoritarian Personality*. New York: Harper & Brothers.

Aldrich, H.E. (1979) *Organizations and Environments*. Englewood Cliffs, N.J.: Prentice-Hall.

Andriessen, J.H.T.H., Drenth, P.J.D. and Lammers, C.J. (1983) *Medezeggenschap en Invloed in Nederlandse Ondernemingen: Resultaten van een onderzoek naar participatie- en invloedsverhoudingen*. Amsterdam: North-Holland.

Argyris, C. (1972) *The Applicability of Organizational Theory*. Cambridge: Cambridge University Press.

Atkinson, J.W. (1964) *An Introduction to Motivation*. Princeton, New Jersey: Van Nostrand.

Bacharach, S.B. and Lawler, E. (1980) *Power and Politics in Organizations*. San Francisco: Jossey-Bass.

Bachrach, P. and Baratz, M.S. (1970) *Power and Poverty: Theory and Practice*. New York: Oxford University Press.

Barbalet, J.M. (1985) 'Power and resistance', *British Journal of Sociology* 26: 513–48.

Bass, B. (1983) *Organizational Decision Making*. Homewood, Illinois: Richard Irwin.

Baumgartner, T., Buckley, W. and Burns, T. (1975) 'Meta power and relational control in social life', *Social Science Information* 14: 49–78.

Benson, K. (1977) 'Organizations: a dialectical view', *Administrative Science Quarterly* 12: 1–21.

Berne, E. (1973) *Games People Play*. New York: Ballantine Books.

Berry, D.F., Metcalf, L. and McQuillan, W. (1974) 'Neddy: an organizational metamorphosis', *Journal of Management Studies* 11: 1–20.

Blacker, F.H.M. and Brown, C.A. (1980) *Whatever Happened to Shell's New Philosophy of Management?* Farnborough: Saxon House.

Blau, P.M. (1964) *Exchange and Power in Social Life*. New York: Wiley.

Brannen, P., Batstone, E., Fatchett, D. and White, P. (1976) *The Worker Directors: A Sociology of Participation*. London: Hutchinson.

Braybrooke, D. and Lindblom, C.E. (1963) *A Free Strategy of Decisions: Policy Evaluation as a Social Process*. New York: Free Press.

Burns, T. and Stalker, G.M. (1961) *The Management of Innovation*. London: Tavistock.

Butler, R.J., Astley, W.G., Hickson, D.J., Mallory, G. and Wilson, D.C. (1979) 'Strategic decision making in organizations: concepts of content and process', *International Studies of Management and Organization* 9: 5–36.

38   References

Carrell, M.R. and Kuzmits, F.E. (1982) *Personnel: Management of Human Resources*. Toronto: Merrill.

Carter, E.E. (1971) 'The behavioural theory of the firms and top-level corporate decisions', *Administrative Science Quarterly* 16: 413–28.

Cartwright, D. (1973) 'Determinants of scientific progress: the case of research on the risky shift', *American Psychologist* 28: 222–31.

Chandler, A. (1962) *Strategy and Structure: Chapters in the History of Industrial Enterprises*. Cambridge: The MIT Press.

Child, J. (1972) 'Organizational structure, environment and performance: the role of strategic choice', *Sociology* 6: 1–22.

Clegg, S. and Dunkerley, D. (1977) *Critical Issues in Organizations*. London: Routledge & Kegan Paul.

Cohen, M.D. and March, J.G. (1974) *Leadership and Ambiguity*. New York: McGraw-Hill.

Cohen, M.D., March, J.G. and Olsen, J.P. (1972) 'A garbage can model of organizational choice', *Administrative Science Quarterly* 17: 1–25.

Crozier, M. (1964) *The Bureaucratic Phenomenon*. London: Tavistock.

Crozier, M. and Friedberg, E. (1977) 'Organization as means and constraints of collective action', in M. Warren (ed.) *Organizational Choice and Constraint*. Farnborough: Saxon House.

Crozier, M. and Thoenig, J-C. (1976) 'The regulation of complex organizational systems', *Administrative Science Quarterly* 21: 547–70.

Cyert, R.M., Dill, W.R. and March, J.G. (1958) 'The role of expectation in business decision making', *Administrative Science Quarterly* 3: 307–40.

Dahl, R. (1957) 'The concept of power', *Behavioral Science* 2: 201–15.

Dahrendorf, R. (1959) *Class and Class Conflict in an Industrial Society*. London: Routledge & Kegan Paul.

Dickson, J. (1981) 'The relation of direct and indirect participation', *Industrial Relations Journal* July/August: 27–35.

Drucker, P. (1971) 'What we can learn from Japanese management', *Harvard Business Review* 49: 110–22.

Elliott, J. (1978) *Conflict and Cooperation: The Growth of Industrial Democracy*. London: Kogan Page.

Emerson, R. (1962) 'Power dependence relations', *Administrative Science Review* 27: 31–40.

Emery, F.E. and Trist, E.L. (1965) 'The causal texture of organizational environments', *Human Relations* 18: 21–31.

Enderud, H. (1977) *Two Views on Participation in Organizational Decision Making*. Institute for Organization and Industrial Sociology, Copenhagen.

Etzioni, A. (1968) *The Active Society: A Theory of Societal and Political Processes*. New York: Free Press.

Fiedler, F.E. (1967) *A Theory of Leadership Effectiveness*. New York: McGraw-Hill.

Fiedler, F.E. (1978) 'The contingency model and the dynamics of the leadership process', in L. Berkowitz (ed.) *Advances in Experimental Social Psychology (II)*. New York: Academic Press.

Fiedler, F.E. and Chemers, M.M. (1974) *Leadership and Effective Management*. Glenview, Illinois: Scott, Foresman.

Filley, A.C., House, R.J. and Kerr, S. (1976) *Managerial Process and Organizational Behavior*. Glenview, Illinois: Scott, Foresman.

Fleischman, E., Harris, E. and Burtt, H. (1955) *Leadership and Supervision in Industry*. Ohio State University Educational Research Monograph.

Foucault, M. (1977) *Discipline and Punish: The Birth of the Prison*. London: Allen Lane.

French, J.R.P. (1956) 'A formal theory of social power', *Psychological Review* 63: 181–94.

French, J.R.P. and Raven, B. (1959) 'The bases of social power', in D. Cartwright (ed.) *Studies in Social Power*. Ann Arbor, Michigan: Institute for Social Research.

Friend, J.K. and Jessop, W.N. (1969) *Local Government and Strategic Choice*. London: Tavistock.

Friend, J.K., Power, J.M. and Yewlett, C.J. (1974) *Public Planning: The Inter-Corporate Dimension*. London: Tavistock.

Galbraith, K. (1967) *The New Industrial State*. Boston: Houghton Mifflin.

Heller, F.A. (1952) 'Measuring motivation in industry', *Occupational Psychology* 26: 1–10.

Heller, F.A. (1971) *Managerial Decision Making: A Study of Leadership Styles and Power Sharing among Senior Managers*. London: Tavistock.

Heller, F.A. (1973) 'Leadership, decision-making and contingency theory', *Industrial Relations* 12: 183–99.

Heller, F.A. and Misumi, J. (1987) 'Decision making', in B. Bass, P. Drenth and P. Weissenberg (eds) *Advances in Organizational Psychology: An International Review*. Beverly Hills: Sage.

Heller, F.A. and Wilpert, B. (1981) *Competence and Power in Managerial Decision Making*. Chichester: Wiley.

Heller, F.A. and Yukl, G. (1969) 'Participation and managerial decision making as a function of situational variables', *Organizational Behavior and Human Performance* 4: 227–41. Also in E. Williams (ed.) *Participative Management: Concepts, Theory and Implementation*. Atlanta: Georgia State University.

Hersey, P. and Blanchard, K.H. (1977) *Management of Organizational Behavior: Utilising Human Resources*. Englewood Cliffs, N.J.: Prentice-Hall.

Hickson, D.J., Hinings, C.A., Schneck, R.E. and Pennings, J.M. (1971) 'A strategic contingencies theory of intraorganizational power', *Administrative Science Quarterly* 16: 216–29.

Hickson, D.J., Hinings, C.R., McMillan, C.J.M. and Schwitter, J.P. (1974) 'The culture-free context of organization structure: a tri-national comparison', *Sociology* 8: 59–80.

Hickson, D., Butler, R., Gray, D., Mallory G. and Wilson, D. (1986) *Top Decisions: Strategic Decision Making in Organizations*. Oxford: Basil Blackwell.

Hill, P. (1972) *Towards a New Philosophy of Management*. London: Gower Press.

Hinings, C.R., Hickson, D.J., Pennings, J.M. and Schneck, R.E. (1974) 'Structural conditions of intraorganizational power', *Administrative Science Quarterly* 19: 22–24.

Hoppe, F. (1930) 'Erfolg und Misserfolg: Untersuchungen zur Handels und Affektpsychologie', *Psychologische Forschung* 14: 1–62.

IDE (1981a) *European Industrial Relations*. London: Oxford University Press.

Josephson, M. (1934) *The Robber Barons: The Great American Capitalists 1861–1901*. New York: Harcourt Brace.

40 *References*

Kahneman, D., Slovic, P. and Tversky, A. (1982) *Judgment under Uncertainty Heuristics and Biases*. Cambridge: Cambridge University Press.

Kavcic, B., Rus, V. and Tannenbaum, A.S. (1971) 'Control, participation and effectiveness', *Administrative Science Quarterly* 16: 74–86.

Koopman, P.L. and Werkman, B. (1973) 'Het verhoudingsmodel bij de meting van satisfaktie', in P.J.D. Drenth, P.J. Willems, and C.J. De Wolff (eds) *Arbeids- en Organisatiepsychologie*. Deventer: Kluwer.

Koopman, P.L. and Wierdsma, A.F.M. (1984) 'Work consultation as a channel of communication and as a consultative framework', in P.J.D. Drenth, H. Thierry, P.J. Willems, and C.J. de Wolff (eds) *Handbook of Work and Organizational Psychology*. Chichester: Wiley.

Koopman, P.L., Broekhuysen, J.W. and Meijn, M.O. (1984b), 'Complex decision making at the organizational level', in P.J.D. Drenth, Hk. Thierry, P.J. Willems and C.J. de Wolff (eds) *Handbook of Work and Organizational Psychology*. Chichester: Wiley.

Lammers, C. (1980) 'Industrial relations from an interorganizational perspective', Mimeographed, Institute of Sociology, University of Leyden.

Lawrence, P.R. and Lorsch, J.W. (1967) 'Differentiation and integration in complex organizations', *Administrative Science Quarterly* 12: 1–47.

Leavitt, H., Pinfield, L. and Webb, E. (eds) (1974) *Organizations of the Future: Interactions with the External Environment*. New York: Praeger.

Lewin, K., Dembo, T., Festinger, L. and Sears, P. (1944) 'Levels of aspiration', in J. McV Hunt (ed.) *Personality and Behavior Disorders*. New York: Ronald.

Likert, R. (1967) *The Human Organization: Its Management and Value*. London: McGraw-Hill.

Lindblom, Ch. E. (1959) 'The science of "muddling through"', *Public Administration Review* 19: 79–99.

Lippitt, R. and White, R. (1958), 'An experimental study of leadership and group life', in E. Maccoby, T. Newcomb and E. Hartley (eds) *Readings in Social Psychology*, 3rd edn. New York: Henry Holt.

Locke, E.A. and Schweiger, D.M. (1979) 'Participation in decision-making: one more look', in B. Staw (ed.) *Research in Organizational Behavior*. Greenwich, Conn.: Jai Press.

Lorsch, U.W. and Morse, J.J. (1974) *Organizations and Their Members*. New York: Harper & Row.

Lukes, S. (1974) *Power: A Radical View*. London: Macmillan Press.

Lukes, S. (1986) *Power*. Oxford: Blackwell.

McClelland, D. (1961) *The Achieving Society*. New York: Van Nostrand.

McClelland, D. (1975) *Power: The Inner Experience*. New York: Irvington.

McClelland, D. and Burnham, D.H. (1976) 'Power is the great motivation', *Harvard Business Review* 54: 100–10.

Maier, N.R.F. (1965) *Psychology in Industry*. Boston: Houghton Mifflin.

Manchester, W. (1968) *The Arms of Krupp 1587–1968*. Boston: Little, Brown.

March, J.G. and Simon, H.A. (1958) *Organizations*. New York: Wiley.

Martin, R. (1977) *The Sociology of Power*. London: Routledge & Kegan Paul.

Mesarovic, M.D. (1970) *Multilevel Systems and Processes*. Ohio: System Research Centre.

Metcalf, J.L. (1976) 'Organizational strategic and interorganizational networks', *Human Relations* 29: 327–43.

Miles, R.E. (1965) 'Human relations or human resources', *Harvard Business Review* 43: 148–63.

Miles, R.E., Snow, C.C. and Pfeffer, J. (1974) 'Organization–environment concepts and issues', *Industrial Relations* 13: 244–64.

Mintzberg, H. (1983) *Power in and around Organizations*. Englewood Cliffs, N.J.: Prentice-Hall.

Mintzberg, H., Raisinghani, D. and Theoret, A. (1976) 'The structure of "unstructured" decision processes', *Administrative Science Quarterly* 21: 246–75.

Mohr, L. (1982) *Explaining Organizational Behavior: The Limits and Possibilities of Theory and Research*. San Francisco: Jossey-Bass.

Morgan, G. (1986) *Images of Organizations*. Beverly Hills: Sage.

Mulder, M. (1971) 'Power equalization through participation', *Administrative Science Quarterly* 16: 31–8.

Mulder, M. (1977a) *The Daily Power Game*. Leiden: Martinus Nijhoff.

Nakane, C. (1970) *Japanese Society*. Berkeley and Los Angeles: University of California Press.

Nisbett, R. and Ross, L. (1980) *Human Inference: Strategies and Shortcomings of Social Judgment*. Englewood Cliffs, N.J.: Prentice-Hall.

Parsons, T. (1956) 'Suggestions for a sociological approach to the theory of organization', *Administrative Science Quarterly* 1: 63–85, 225–36.

Pateman, C. (1970) *Participation and Democratic Theory*. London: Cambridge University Press.

Pennings, J.M. (1976) 'Dimensions of organizational influence and their effectiveness correlates', *Administrative Science Quarterly* 21: 688–99.

Perrow, C. (1972) *Complex Organizations: A Critical Essay*. Glenview, Illinois: Scott, Foresman.

Pettigrew, A. (1975) 'Towards political theory of organizational intervention', *Human Relations* 28: 191–208.

Pfeffer, J. and Salancik, G. (1978) *The External Control of Organizations: A Resource Dependence Perspective*. New York: Harper & Row.

Pitz, G. and Sachs, N. (1984) 'Judgment and decision: theory and application', *Annual Review of Psychology* 35: 139–63.

Ramsay, H. (1977) 'Cycles of control', *Sociology*, 2: 481–506.

Roethlisberger, F.J. and Dickson, W. (1949) *Management and the Worker: An Account of a Research Programme conducted by the Western Electric Company, Hawthorne Works, Chicago*. Cambridge, Mass.: Harvard University Press.

Rus, V. (1980) 'Positive and negative power: the dialectical thought on power', *Organization Studies* 1: 3–19.

Rus, V., Odar, M., Heller, F., Brown, A., Drenth, P.J.D., Koopman, P.L., Wierdsma, A.F.M., Bus, F.B.M. and Kruyswijk, A.J. (1977) 'Participative decision making under conditions of uncertainty', Second International Conference on participation, workers' control and self-management, Paris, September.

Russell, B. (1938) *Power: A New Social Analysis*. London: George Allen & Unwin.

Sheridan, A. (1980) *Foucault: The Will to Truth*. London: Tavistock.

Shull, F.A., Delbecq. A.L. and Cummings, L.L. (1970) *Organizational Decision Making*. New York: McGraw-Hill.

42   *References*

Simon, H.A. (1977) *The New Science of Management Decision*. Revised edn. Englewood Cliffs, N.J.: Prentice-Hall.

Simon, H. (1984) 'On the behavioral and rational foundations of economic dynamics', *Journal of Economic Behavior and Organizations* 5: 35–55.

Starbuck, W. (1963) 'Level of aspiration theory and economic behavior', *Behavioral Science* 8: 128–36.

Starbuck, W. (1976) 'Organizations and their environments', in M.D. Dunnette (ed.) *Handbook of Industrial and Organizational Psychology*, pp. 1069–123. Chicago, Illinois: Rand McNally.

Staw, B.M. (ed.) (1977) *Psychological Foundations of Organizational Behavior*. Santa Monica: Goodyear.

Staw, B., Bell, N. and Clausen, J. (1986) 'The dispositional approach to job attitudes: a lifetime longitudinal test', *Administrative Science Quarterly* 31: 56–77.

Stinchcombe, A. (1965) 'Social structure and organizations', in J. March (ed.) *Handbook of Organizations*. Chicago, Illinois: Rand McNally.

Tannenbaum, A. (1968) *Control in Organizations*. New York: McGraw-Hill.

Tawney, R.H. (1952) *Equality*, 4th edn. London: George Allen & Unwin.

Thompson, J. (1967) *Organizations in Action*. New York: McGraw-Hill.

Thompson, J.D. and Tuden, A. (1959) 'Strategies, structures, and processes of organizational decision', in J.D. Thompson, P.B. Hammond, R.W. Hawkes, B.H. Junker and A. Tuden (eds) *Comparative Studies in Administration*. Pittsburgh: Pittsburgh University Press.

Vroom, V.H. and Yetton, P. (1973) *Leadership and Decision-Making*. Pittsburgh: University of Pittsburgh Press.

Wall, T.D. and Lischeron, J.A. (1977) *Worker Participation: A Critique of the Literature and Some Fresh Evidence*. London: McGraw-Hill.

Wallach, M.A. and Kogan, M. (1965) 'The role of information, discussion and consensus in group risk taking', *Journal of Experimental Social Psychology* 1: 1–19.

Weber, M. (1947) *The Theory of Social and Economic Organization*. New York: Oxford University Press.

Westerguard, J.H. and Resler, H. (1975) *Class in a Capitalist Society*. London: Heinemann.

White, R. and Lippitt, R. (1953) 'Leader behavior and membership reaction in three "social climates"', in D. Cartwright and A. Zander (eds) *Group Dynamics: Research and Theory*. London: Tavistock.

Whitehead, N. (1938) *The Industrial Workers*, Vol. 1 and 2. London: Oxford University Press.

Whyte, W.F. (1969) *Organizational Behavior*. Homewood, Ill.: Dorsey Press.

Witte, E. (1972) 'Field research on complex decision making processes: the phase theorem', *International Studies of Management and Organization* 2: 156–82.

Wright Mills, C. (1970) *The Sociological Imagination*. Harmondsworth: Penguin.

Wrong, D. H. (1979) *Power, Its Forms, Bases and Uses*. Oxford: Basil Blackwell.

Yoshino, M.Y. (1968) *Japan's Managerial System*. Cambridge, Ma.: MIT Press.

Zaleznic, A. (1970) 'Power and politics in organizational life', *Harvard Business Review* 48: 47–60.

[5]

SELF-MANAGEMENT AND PARTICIPATION: TWO CONCEPTS OF DEMOCRATIZATION IN ORGANIZATIONS

Cornelis J. Lammers
University of Leyden
The Netherlands

The dual character of the title of this article reflects two styles of thinking about ways and means to enhance the opportunities for human beings to control the conditions under which they work, learn, live, play, and strive for ideals. The very term "participation" apparently refers to something—some activity, process, or system of decision making—in which designated participants can "take part," but which they cannot, will not, or should not "take (over) as a whole." "Self-management," to the contrary, denotes a "something" which is, can be, or ought to be wholly under the control of the participants themselves.

One naturally wonders to what extent participation and self-management can be viewed as genotypically related or as completely separate ideals, procedures, or processes. To settle this question, it will be necessary to examine more precisely the nature of the phenomena under scrutiny.

THE STRUCTURAL AND THE FUNCTIONAL VIEW OF DEMOCRATIZATION

Some years ago, a journalist in one of our Dutch dailies reported a statement by a well-known politician to the effect that "participation does not form an aim in and by itself. It is a means for an apparatus to function more adequately," and he himself commented: "Indeed: democratization . . . is a matter of efficiency, not of ideological necessity" (Heldring, 1969).

Anyone familiar with developments and issues in large-scale organizations during recent decades will recognize this view, which I shall call the "functional" concept of democratization. It is widely prevalent among those who advocate shop-floor participation by employees in industry, the introduction of patient councils in mental hospitals, encouragement of

Revised version of the paper read at the First International Sociological Conference on Self-Management and Participation, Dubrovnik, Yugoslavia, December, 1972. My sincere thanks to Peter A. Clark and Stanley E. Seashore for their helpful criticisms and suggestions on an earlier version of this paper, and to Inez Seeger for editing the manuscript. Other elaborations and applications of the ideas presented in this article can be found in Lammers, 1970a; 1970b: Ch. 6; and 1971.

It was common practice in the sixties to define one type of (functional) democratization in terms of its results and the other one (structural democratization) in terms of its objectives. This is not very logical and, therefore, later on I preferred to define both types of democratization in terms of the process itself. When less powerful members become more powerful due to a loss of power on the part of the higher echelons - in other words, in case of a zero-sum game - I call it 'structural democratization'. When, however, the power increase on the part of the lower participants is the consequence of an overall increase in the total amount of power for all concerned - that is, in case of a positive sum game - one can characterize this process as 'functional democratization'. For further details on this view, see Lammers (1992).

initiative by students, by soldiers, and by rank-and-file members in all kinds of political, religious, and cultural associations. The functional argument is in all likelihood most often used by managers and administrators or by those who aspire to be in leading positions. It relies heavily on the potential benefits to the organization from increasing the influence of lower-level members on any or all of a variety of decisions or policies.

The contrary view—which I shall label the "structural" concept of democratization—is usually cast not in terms of organizational efficiency or effectiveness, but in terms of power equalization (the reduction of systematic and enduring differences in power between various categories of members or employees in an organization) as an "ideological necessity." The most vociferous exponents of this view at present are, of course, the activist students who have insisted that government of the people, by the people, for the people, has perished from the earth—or never existed for long anywhere—and ought to be (re)instated here and now. In the most succinct form I have heard thus far, this view was expressed to me by a student who said: "My ideal is that you have as little power as I have!" For a somewhat more sophisticated wording of this concept, we can take, for example, the first three principles outlined in the manifesto of the *Enragés de Caen* (Cohn-Bendit and Cohn-Bendit, 1969:90):

—To take collective responsibility for one's own affairs, that is, self-government.

—To destroy all hierarchies which merely serve to paralyze the initiative of groups and individuals.

—To make all those in whom any authority is vested, permanently responsible to the people.

Similar ideas upholding democracy as a way of life worthwhile in itself, or as valuable to the quality of life it engenders for the individuals concerned, have long been encountered among students, intellectuals, and artists who identify with the New Left. In modern times, however, one can also observe a growing number of European trade unionists, skilled workers, technicians, teachers, social workers, etc., professing the ideal of "structural" democratization.

In spoken or written debates, most advocates of the structural orientation toward democratization will naturally not go to such lengths as the *Enragés de Caen* and demand self-government without regard to the organizational or general societal costs involved. Likewise, most champions of the functional view will not be completely oblivious to the notion of democracy as valuable in itself. Consequently, these two views of democratization can shade off into one another and also be held simultaneously as equally important considerations. Nevertheless, I want to maintain that many people definitely do give priority to either "functional" or "structural" considerations, and that it is therefore valid to differentiate analytically between these two views.

It is not only in the practice of modern Western organizations, but also in the theories of social scientists who have studied organizational

TWO CONCEPTS OF DEMOCRATIZATION   19

processes that one encounters a differentiation of meanings attached to the concept of democratization, a differentiation corresponding roughly to the distinction between the structural and the functional views. The literature of behavioral science subsumed under the headings of "human relations" and "revisionist" schools (Bennis, 1959) abounds with statements suggestive of the functional approach to democratization. For example, Slater and Bennis (1964) argue that "democracy is inevitable . . . because it is the only system which can successfully cope with the changing demands of contemporary civilization, in business as well as in government" (p. 51). They add: "We will argue that democracy has been so widely embraced, not because of some vague yearning for human rights, but because under certain conditions it is a more efficient form of social organization. (Our concept of efficiency includes the ability to survive and prosper)" (p. 51). Furthermore, they emphasize: "We are not necessarily endorsing democracy as such" (p. 52).

In this literature the term democratization is used in a rather general sense, meaning any increase in the influence of subordinate employees on their work, their working conditions, etc., and/or any increase in recognition by their superiors of the worth of their (potential) initiatives.[1] However, whether due to some vague yearning for human rights or for some other reason, certain authors use the term democracy in a more restricted sense. For instance, according to Katz and Kahn (1966:45): "The essential difference between a democratic and an authoritarian system is not whether executive officers order or consult with those below them but whether the power to legislate on policy is vested in the membership or in the top echelons." These authors specify their model of a democratic organization in terms of three criteria: (a) the separation of legislative from executive power; (b) the locus of the veto; and (c) the selection of officers in the hands of the membership. They state that these criteria "reflect the principle of government by the active and expressed consent of the governed" (p. 213).

Similarly divergent views of democracy also play a role in political science. To take one example, Pateman (1970), in her critical account of

---

[1] As Pateman (1970:71) has observed, the terms democracy and participation are often used interchangeably. In this context she refers to a definition by French, Israël and Aas (1960:3), which is often adopted in its original or in a modified form by various authors, and which says that participation refers to "a process in which two or more parties influence each other in making plans, policies or decisions." Most authors who see democratization as effective participation with potentially functional consequences for the organization (and also for the members of that organization, to the extent that they have a stake in a well-functioning organization, in the form of material and immaterial gains), refer to an influence-gain on the part of lower-level participants and *not* to a shift in the influence-*distribution* across hierarchical levels.

An exception to the rule is Strauss (1963:41), who defines power equalization as "a reduction in the power and status differential between supervisors and subordinates," and then goes on to state (p. 60) that: "participation, however defined, is well accepted as a form of power equalization." Strauss's observation is quite wrong, in my opinion, probably because he does not take into account the possibility that increased influence among subordinates can be accompanied by an increase in the influence exerted by their supervisors.

20   *Cornelis J. Lammers*

work by Berelson, Dahl, Eckstein, Sartori, and other followers of Schumpeter's views on democracy as a "method," concludes that these authors have resigned themselves to the parliamentary democratic system as it functions today, particularly in Anglo-Saxon countries. She feels they have abandoned hope of the "classical" ideal of democracy as maximum participation by all the people in decisions about their own affairs (Pateman, 1970:15–16). Again, I have the impression that Berelson and the others judge—rather positively—the practice of democracy in the West primarily in terms of its *functions* for the political system and for society at large (among other things its stability, flexibility, and potential for conflict regulation in a pluriform society). But Pateman evaluates—rather negatively—the actual structure and functioning of Western democratic institutions in light of the ideal *structure* of a truly participatory society (Pateman, 1970: especially Chs. I and 6).

To round off this section, let me briefly note that in all likelihood one can find examples of such differences in views on the value of grass-roots democracy in organizational settings, not only in the Western, but also in the Socialist world. The "structural" preference for power equalization comes to the fore in critical writings directed against social-democratic and likewise against state-socialistic conceptions (of Lenin, for example) by the so-called Left-Communists in Russia after the Revolution (Ertl, 1968:42–49; Anweiler, 1958a:Ch. 5), by the German theoreticians of the "pure" *Räte-system* (von Oertzen, 1963:Ch.4), and by the Dutch school of *Rätekommunisten* (Mandel, 1971:295–301). Anton Pannekoek, one of the most articulate exponents of this latter point of view, later delineated his vision of a "workers' democracy" in terms of a complete fusion (even at the level of shop-floor rule) between legislative and executive control in the hands of the workers concerned, and a system of representative councils with no authority or powers to enforce a policy against the wishes of their constituents (Aartsz, 1971:35–41/132–42).

Of course, a variety of anarcho-syndicalistic and communistic theories contain comparable conceptions of a society democratically structured from the base. Most noteworthy, both in this context and from the point of view of theories that are presently being tried out in practice, is undoubtedly the Yugoslav concept of self-management. It is interesting that, according to various authors (Adizes, 1971:221–23, Broekmeyer, 1969:15–23; Kavčič, Rus, and Tannenbaum, 1971:74; Meister, 1970:363–65), the Yugoslavs have founded their broad-scale thrust toward realizing self-management not only on "structural" but also on "functional" grounds.

The "functional" view favoring democratization at the grass-roots level is less prevalent in the East than in the West. It goes without saying that a negatively toned "functional" concept of democratization looms large in both the capitalist and the socialist worlds among many managers, administrators, politicians, and scientists. One seldom encounters opponents of democratization who base their arguments on their esteem for autocracy, unity of command, élite rule, and similar principles. A case against democratization is usually made by first paying lip service to democratic ideals in order to clear the way for a detailed *exposé* of all the economic, administrative, and political disadvantages of such democratic endeavors.

DEMOCRATIZATION AS AN OBJECTIVE
AND AS A RESULT

Democratization can be defined as "a process by which the originally less powerful members of a collective entity obtain more power over the management of that entity."[2] This minimum definition is, of course, quite comprehensive. It covers a mild form of "de-autocratization" (such as occurred, for instance, when the Czar granted some rather nominal powers to the *Doema*), as well as a form of "excess democratization" (such as occurs in a self-managed factory when the director loses his very last miniscule remnant of executive authority).

Those who advocate democratization for the sake of its supposed effectiveness or efficiency would probably be less hesitant to accept this definition than would proponents of a democracy founded on principles. Nevertheless, irrespective of the appropriateness of the term for such a process, few adherents to the "structural" view will deny that democratization also involves at least a rather sizeable "power-raise" for those members of the entity who at the outset could exert little or no power to modify the forms and goals of their activities. This means that whenever the process of increasing power among formerly less powerful members is operating, it will be hard to infer from the nature of the process itself whether it represents structural or functional democratization in the work group. Whether a process can be characterized, in terms of the two concepts I have outlined, as "structural" or "functional" (or as both at the same time), can only be settled by examining the *intentions* of those who propagate or initiate the process or by investigating the *consequences*.

One finds not only in practical and ideological debates about these matters but, alas, also in many scientific discussions of the subject, that both defendants and critics of various forms of democratization outdo one another (although for opposite reasons!) in blurring the distinction between objectives and results. Thus, both "human relations" authors and radical critics of shop-floor participation are equally apt to take the *intentions* of the advocates of these changes as constitutive evidence of the *effects* of more considerate forms of leadership, group consultation, and the like on productivity, morale, etc. In actual fact, of course, a program of organizational

---

[2] I prefer to use the term "power" rather than "influence" in this definition because "power" usually implies the exertion of influence by one party on one or more other parties *in accordance with the objectives of that (first) party*. Compare, for example, Weber's (1947:28) famous definition *"Macht bedeuted jede Chance, innerhalb einer sozialen Beziehung den eigenen Willen auch gegen Widerstreben durchzusetzen, gleichviel worauf diese Chance beruht."* In other words, to use the term power rather than "influence" in a definition of democratization makes the definition somewhat more precise because in this way one excludes all kinds of unwitting and unintended influence-exertions on the part of those who acquire more influence. For a similar distinction between "influence" and "power," see Heller (1971:26).

Finally, as I have argued before (Lammers, 1967:203), power in this sense is very similar to the notion of "control" as used by Tannenbaum (1968) and others.

change might have no functional significance whatsoever, while a process of increased participation could tend toward the structural effect of power equalization.

In similar fashion, efforts deliberately undertaken to further self-management in a factory might produce no structural effects but result in improvement or deterioration of workers' motivation and thereby undermine or contribute to the viability of their organization. All this amounts to the old adage that "One can do the right thing for the wrong reason and the wrong thing for the right reason." It should be added that people can also do (1) nothing, and (2) both the right *and* the wrong thing for either the right or the wrong reasons. Therefore, we should apply Merton's (1936) famous advice to look for the "unanticipated consequences of purposive social action," and for "latent" as distinct from "manifest" functions (Merton, 1957:Ch.I).

Taking for a moment the somewhat simplified view that those who set in motion a process of democratization can do so on the basis of either structural or functional considerations,[3] one can expect the results to be: (1) only structural effects; (2) only functional effects; (3) structural and functional effects; (4) no effects whatsoever. As indicated in Exhibit 1, this yields eight types of democratization.

Exhibit 1

TYPES OF DEMOCRATIZATION

Effects	*Objectives*	
	structural	functional
—only structural	a	b
—only functional	c	d
—structural and functional	e	f
—no structural and functional effects	g	h

We can now try to characterize the two concepts of democratization already outlined, clarify some of the confusion occurring in current debates about democratization issues, and analyze the relationships between various kinds of democratization.

The distinction between structural and functional views of democratization can be cast in terms of Weber's (1947:12–13) two well-known forms of rationality, *Wertrationalität* and *Zweckrationalität*. A rationality of values is typical of the "structural" view, in which democratization is seen as

---

[3] Of course, as indicated already with reference to the Yugoslav case, democratization might be undertaken with *both* structural and functional objectives in mind. One can, therefore, extend Exhibit 1 and add four more types.

TWO CONCEPTS OF DEMOCRATIZATION 23

a movement toward an ideal; a rationality of ends comes to the fore in the "functional" view, in which democratization is seen as the "technical" application of potential means toward specified ends. In other words, completely different forms of rationality and thus of reasoning and criteria are involved in these two views—such that advocates or opponents of a "structural" concept are at a loss in debating with adherents of the "functional" view, and *vice versa*. When supporters of these two concepts try to communicate, one of them might be talking about type "a" democratization (see Exhibit 1) as a point of reference, while the other might have type "d" in mind. At worst, they are not even aware that they are talking about quite different things; at best, they are aware but try in vain to convince each other that type "a" or type "d" is the "real," "authentic" type of democratization. Likewise, in discussions between someone "for" and someone "against," it happens quite often that a "structurally" oriented champion of democratization will attack a particular provision or experiment on the grounds that it does not fulfill the requirements of type "a" democratization, only to find himself in cordial (though nonsensical) agreement with a skeptic of "functional" inclinations who also denounces the same state of affairs because it does not fit type "d."

These examples indicate that a social-scientific approach helps to establish a somewhat detached frame of reference which enables one to clarify prevalent confusions in practical, ideological, and scientific debates on these issues. It might also be of some use in that it shows which kinds of processes tend to be neglected. One could hypothesize, for instance, that due to ideological preferences, types "a" and "d" receive the most attention. Types "b" and "c" might rate second in public attention. Confirmed believers in the "structural" concept probably wish to demonstrate that measures with "functional" intentions have negative structural effects, "b," while their counterparts with a "functional" viewpoint are perhaps fond of showing that structurally intended measures have "only" yielded functional fruits or have "naturally" resulted in functionally disastrous consequences, "c." Cynics of all sorts will probably see to it that types "g" and "h" are and will forever be focused upon as the most likely outcome of any efforts at democratization. The least popular might be the "mixed" types, "e" and "f," which do not furnish outspoken opponents or proponents of either concept with really good ammunition. Nevertheless, these types might very well prove to be of considerable practical as well as theoretical interest, as will be argued in due course!

Turning now to the potentialities of this conceptual scheme for social-scientific theory and research, the first question is: can one define structural and functional democratization not only as styles of thinking, but also as observable processes? It is feasible but not very advisable to characterize processes of power gains for initially rather powerless members of a social system on the basis of the objectives of the initiators involved. The problem is, naturally, that there might be quite different parties with varying objectives who take part in the design, and/or the introduction, and/or the legitimation of the introduction, and/or the maintenance of the democratization process, once it is introduced. Furthermore, there might be the habitual discrepancy between the officially professed and the actually pursued aims (Etzioni, 1964:6–7). All this implies that it might prove a rather complicated procedure to determine unequivocally the "structural" and/or "functional" character of a democratization process by following this logic. Particularly from a researcher's point of view, it could therefore be more productive to focus on the results of their collective actions rather than on the objectives of the actors involved.

Consequently, taking as a minimal core definition of democratization the one given above, structural democratization might be defined as: *democratization tending toward power equalization.* In a similar vein, functional democratization can then be defined as: *democratization contributing toward the efficiency and/or effectiveness of the entity in question.* One might call this the "objective" approach. The "subjective" approach would entail a definition of this kind: democratization is structural when the actors involved aim at power equalization, and functional when the actors involved aim at increased efficiency or effectiveness.

To conclude this section, I submit that no matter how one defines democratization, a meaningful analysis should in general take into account both the objectives and the results. Nevertheless, not only for scientific but also for practical purposes, I believe a one-sided focus on the objectives is more misleading than a one-sided focus on the results attained. One final comment as regards the categorization of results indicated in Exhibit 1. This is admittedly a rather crude way of subdividing the results of a democratization process. Usually, one will also want to look for the *direction* (positive or negative functions; reduction or increase of power differences), the *size* (of the functional or dysfunctional consequences; of the reduction or increase of power differences), and the *kind* of results (consequences for what parts or aspects of the system? power equalization in what spheres of decision making?).

RELATIONSHIPS BETWEEN STRUCTURAL AND FUNCTIONAL DEMOCRATIZATION IN ORGANIZATIONS

Since by definition democratization implies a power gain for the less powerful members of an organization, one might wonder whether functional democratization does not by definition also always include structural democratization. However, the studies of Likert, Tannenbaum, and other investigators of Michigan's Institute for Social Research indicate that an increase in power for the less powerful does not always mean a decrease in power for the more powerful (Tannenbaum, 1968). In other words, the relationship between democratization and power equalization in organizations is indeterminate. In terms of power equalization, the net effect of a "power raise" for the less powerful members of a collective entity can be positive, zero, or negative, all depending on other conditions. Therefore, it appears sensible to analyze "the" relationship between structural and functional democratization in organizations as a set of contingent relationships between democratization, its antecedent determinants, and its structural and functional consequences (see Exhibit 2).

TWO CONCEPTS OF DEMOCRATIZATION 25

In this paper no attempt will be made to present a full-fledged theory with a detailed system of propositions based on the available empirical evidence. We will, instead, examine one or two propositions about each of the five relationships mentioned in Exhibit 2.

Exhibit 2

DEMOCRATIZATION, DETERMINANTS, AND CONSEQUENCES

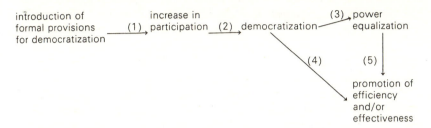

Mulder (1971) has hypothesized that under the condition of relatively large differences in expert power in a system, an increase in participation will increase the power differences between members of that system. Now, it might prove profitable to distinguish between the introduction of democratic *forms* (instituting certain organs, procedures, rules, etc.), democratization *attempts* (by means of participation or in the form of militant action on the part of less powerful members to acquire more power), and the actual process of *democratization* (in the sense of a power gain for the less powerful, as defined earlier). The instituting of formal provisions (e.g., for joint consultation in industry, for student codetermination in the universities) only provides institutional opportunities for initially less powerful members (workers, students)—which they need not use in attempts at making democracy work. Finally, when they do make such attempts, there is no guarantee that they will succeed in gaining more power.

Consequently, Mulder's hypotheses pertain to relationships (2) or (3) in Exhibit 2, and can mean

either *Under the condition of relatively large differences in expert power between members of a system, an increase in participation will usually lead not to democratization (a power increase for the less powerful), but rather to a power gain for the more powerful members of that system (2a).*

or *When relatively large differences in expert power prevail between members of a system, democratization will have a negative effect on power equalization because the power gain of the more powerful will exceed the power gain of the less powerful members of that system (3a).*

I suspect that most of the findings referred to by Mulder—deriving from both field investigations and laboratory experiments—pertains to hypothesis (2a), not to hypothesis (3a). At least his experiments, as he himself has remarked (Mulder and Wilke, 1970:444), did not allow for an increase in expert power for the powerful and thus cannot be taken as evidence in relation to hypothesis (3a). In any case, on the face of it, it does not appear very likely that this latter hypothesis is valid.

Mulder also formulates a proposition concerning relationship (1). He suggests that motivation to participate is required for increasing participation, and points to various data indicating that such motivation is often absent (Mulder, 1971:35). A similar line of reasoning is to be found in the work of other authors (Clark, 1972:32–35, for example, in his criticism of the so-called "human resource" approach). In terms of our scheme, this train of thought can be reformulated as follows: *formal provisions for democratization will lead to participation only if the less powerful members of the system in question are sufficiently motivated to participate* (1a).

However plausible this proposition may look, it has to do with a controversial issue. Pateman (1970:82), for instance, also concludes that most of the available evidence indicates that workers are not much interested in utilizing opportunities for codetermination at higher levels of decision making in industry, but suggests that this could be due to their lack of opportunities to participate in shop-floor level decision making. A similar suggestion, but formulated positively, has been made by van Beinum and de Bel (1968:14) and Emery and Thorsrud (1969:30), who see shop-floor participation as a precondition for effective participation in policy making at the plant level. On the basis of this point of view, one could propose with respect to relationship (1), as an alternative to hypothesis (1a): *formal provisions for democratization will lead to participation only if the less powerful members of the system in question participate in other settings as well* (1b).

This more general formulation leaves open the question of what kind of participative experience is likely to be most effective as training for organizational participation, and also what kind of intervening variables are involved. As regards the latter point, it is perhaps best to assume that there is no one-way causal influence on participation by motivation, but rather that participation, the acquisition of certain skills (in communication and decision making), and motivation all constitute interdependent processes.

Under what condition does democratization lead to power equalization (relationship (3) in Exhibit 2)? Since by definition democratization implies a power gain for lower-level participants, power equalization in an organization can occur only if higher-level participants are unable to expand their power at the same rate as their subordinates. In other words, democratization can lead to power equalization only when an organization's chances to expand its total amount of power are rather limited.

The total amount of power can best be represented as the "discretion" of an organization, its amount of "self-determination." This means that the better "grip" organizational decision makers have on their own system—on its resources in particular and on their environments in general—the better the chances for higher-level decision makers to experience a power gain

TWO CONCEPTS OF DEMOCRATIZATION 27

themselves (in the form of better internal and external control of their organizations) in conjunction with any power gain made by their subordinates. However, as indicated by Tannenbaum (1968) and others, there is a strong correlation between the total amount of power of an organization and its effectiveness and/or efficiency. This correlation is understandable on the basis of the foregoing reasoning, since "external grip" corresponds with effectiveness, and "internal grip" with efficiency.

This argument leads to two hypotheses that indicate a rather appalling dilemma, since

first: *Democratization can only promote power equalization when the organization does not stand much chance of improving its efficiency and/or effectiveness by improving its human organization (3b).*

second: *The less chance there is for power equalization to occur, the better chance there is for a democratization process to yield positive results for the efficiency and/or effectiveness of an organization (4a).*

So the dilemma is that we cannot have our cake and eat it too, in the sense that, at least in the short run, democratization generally cannot yield functional benefits and at the same time reduce power differences between various hierarchical echelons. This would imply that structural democratization has the best chance in a more or less stagnant organization, and that functional democratization can proceed when no simultaneous efforts at structural democratization are made (or when made, fail).

What are some of the economic, technical, and political circumstances that permit increases in external "grip," and what earmarks an organizational system that permits increases in internal "grip"? Many researchers, including Burns and Stalker (1961), Lawrence and Lorsch (1967), and Gater, *et al.* (1965), have stated that in an expanding market economy, industrial organizations have relatively favorable opportunities to grow if technological inventions occur and can be utilized at a rapid rate.

Whether or not enterprises are able to make use of such external opportunities depends on the way they are organized. Management systems that are not too bureaucratically organized and that make frequent use of "horizontal" forms of consultation and decision making, encourage initiative from below, and process facts and figures in an objective manner, are in a rather favorable position to avail themselves of such opportunities. Although not much research has been done on this point, I suspect that such open, dynamic systems of management have more potential for generating power and are therefore more prone to develop forms of functional democratization than are closed, static systems of management.

Proposition (3b) — (that power equalization can occur only under rather nonelastic conditions of the relevant environmental and organizational factors) implies that efforts at structural democratization will usually meet with such fierce opposition from both internal and external powers-that-be that, on the whole, nothing short of revolution can bring about such a change. Historical evidence supports this conclusion, for the only examples of fundamental dehierarchization of existing organizations[4] are found in times of revolution. Examples of efforts at self-government by workers in their plants—and also to some extent by soldiers and sailors in military units—occurred in Russia, Germany, Hungary, and Italy after World War I (Anweiler, 1958a; von Oertzen, 1963; Mandel, 1971:Chs. 2 and 3), in Spain during the civil war (Chomsky, 1969:62–105; Leval, 1971; Mandel, 1971:335–46; Souchy:Ch. 5), and incidentally after World War II in some Eastern European countries (Anweiler; 1958b, 1958c), and in Bolivia, Algeria, and France (Mandel, 1971:Ch. 5). Such efforts at power equalization almost always involve a seizure of power by the ruled. Then, severe struggles follow between the newly formed plant committee or workers' council on the one hand, and the indispensable technical, commercial, and managerial functionaries (for day-to-day direction of the plant) and governmental or party agencies (for control of general policy making) on the other hand. More often than not, these stories end with the final defeat of the revolution.

Yugoslavia after World War II might represent an exception to this general rule, although the available evidence does not unequivocally demonstrate that power equalization between various hierarchical levels in industrial organizations has been effected as a result of the democratization process which undoubtedly took place.[5] In other words, in terms of proposition (3b), the chances for Yugoslav industry to improve efficiency and effectiveness by improving on the human organization might have been so good that the gains in external and internal "grip" of higher-level decision makers (which includes the workers' council![6]) might to some extent have kept pace with the power gains of lower-level participants.

You may recall my earlier reference to types "e" and "f" in Exhibit 1. These represent the simultaneous occurrence of structural and functional effects of democratization processes. From all that has been said thus far, it follows that one would rather seldom find a combination of positive structural and positive functional effects due to the same democratization process in organizational contexts. In principle, however, a combination of positive structural and negative functional consequences or of positive

---

[4] Of course, organizations newly erected along democratic lines (producer cooperatives, utopian communities, etc.) do not involve dehierarchization (there being no hierarchy at the outset), and can come into being more peacefully. In that case, no pre-existing legal rules, property rights, or power and status privileges are violated. Moreover, the powers-that-be in society at large can easily defend themselves against such a threat to the social order by ignoring or ridiculing such experiments.

[5] At least in terms of the "control graph," the slope of the line of influence found in Yugoslav enterprises does not deviate too markedly from what is usually found in Western enterprises (Rus, 1970; Kavčič, Rus, and Tannenbaum, 1971). Likewise, Kamušič (1970), after his survey of the reward and authority structure of Yugoslav enterprises, concludes that "the pluralistic model of self-managed enterprises and the pluralistic system of self-managing relations generally does not differ essentially from the capitalist model of enterprises and from the modern type of mixed capitalist economic system" (p. 112).

[6] The fact that the workers' council does appear to be actually perceived as one of the most important decision-making bodies in Yugoslav enterprises is quite significant and too often overlooked. I submit that this is an indication that perhaps

TWO CONCEPTS OF DEMOCRATIZATION   29

functional and negative structural effects might very well emerge in the wake
of democratization. Such a concurrence of de-hierarchization and lowered
efficiency/effectiveness on the one hand, and hierarchization and improved
efficiency and effectiveness on the other, would mean that relationship (5) in
Exhibit 2 is negative. Are there reasons to propose such a hypothesis?

It is probable that a severe reduction of power differences does indeed,
at least at the outset, curb an organization's productivity because of the
conflicts and initial chaos ensuing from such a *coup d' organization* by
lower-level participants. But in terms of *survival*, an egalitarian organization
might well be effective in a revolutionary situation (Naschold, 1969:26–28).
Moreover, it is a moot point whether in the long run such a form of power
equalization necessarily implies definite constraints on the promotion of
efficiency and/or effectiveness. The answer hinges on the viability of a
drastically egalitarian organization. Sufficient evidence from historical
sources or current sophisticated social research is not available simply
because, as already stated, revolutionary efforts to experiment with structurally
democratized organizations are almost invariably crushed.

On theoretical grounds, Naschold (1969:26–28) has rather convincingly
defended the position that in the long run an organization making revolutionary efforts at industrial self-government does not stand much chance
of survival in modern societies. The characteristics of such a Rätesystem,
i.e., no clearcut division of labor between legislative and executive functions,
maximal participation of all workers in decision making, etc.—are, according
to Naschold, well suited to the general requirement for survival in a revolutionary situation. They are, however, completely inadequate in normal times.
This is primarily because of a general principle (Ashby's Law of Requisite
Variety) that in a highly complex, differentiated environment, a viable
organization must show a corresponding degree of differentiation and
complexity in its own structure.

Therefore, the main question becomes: is it possible to have a highly
complex, functionally specialized organization which shows a more or less
fixed pattern of power differences between the various categories of its
members? Naschold (1969:56–94) has outlined a model of intraorganizational democratization which allows for quite a bit of functional democratiza-

---

Yugoslavia has a more democratic system of (representative) government on the
macro-level of society than do many Western nations. Although *at any one point
in time* there is just as great a power difference between hierarchical levels in formal
organizations in Yugoslavia as in the West, the fact that all Yugoslavs have *access*
to such high-level power positions, and that *in the course of time* in their work and in
other organizations many lower-level participants do indeed occupy such positions,
is quite important. It could very well mean that as a *class*, Yugoslav blue and white
collar workers on the whole have more societal power than do Western workers as a
class. When most people in a society circulate frequently enough between lower
(executive) posts and higher-(legislative) level organizational positions, there is a
"classless society" in the sense that society is no longer differentiated into strata of
people who during their lifetime belong to the category of the ruled, while others
permanently occupy the position of a ruling èlite. On this notion of a "classless
society due to mobility," see Dahrendorf (1957:182) and von Oertzen (1963:331).
For some data as to the rather considerable amount of circulation in works-councils
and even in managerial positions, see Roggemann (1970:114–117).

tion, but does not eliminate structural power differences. I fear that the main obstacle to any attempt at reconciling complexity with democracy is formed by the endless variety of opportunities for differentiations of power and status that any division of labor always offers. It would not be surprising if, in the future, a model of organizational democracy were to be invented and put into action, one that finally eliminated lasting power differences between categories of personnel, but nonetheless showed sufficient differentiation to cope with a complex environment. In any case, the search for such a model should continue by all means. However, given the present state of our knowledge and the present state of our society (East and West!), we are forced to conclude that drastic efforts to achieve a simplified egalitarian organization will in all probability reduce the effectiveness and/or efficiency of the organization.

Perhaps even more problematic than the viability of egalitarian organizations is the coordination of a system of such organizations on the societal level as a whole. For example, the failure of self-government by workers' councils in Russia between 1917–1921 was probably also due to the lack of "self-coordination" by self-managing enterprises (Ertl, 1968:33–56; Anweiler, 1958a:Ch.5).

For the time being, therefore, let me formulate the following proposition with respect to relationship (5) in Exhibit 2: *power equalization tends towards simplification of structure and thus hinders organizational efficiency and/or effectiveness* (5a). It is dubious whether one can reverse this proposition. The thesis that in general the promotion of efficiency and/or effectiveness—particularly when resulting from democratization—increases organizational differentiation and fortifies power differences, is dear to the hearts of many radical critics of present-day society. In crude form this idea is often presented as a popularized version of what Marcuse called "repressive tolerance." It is couched in terms of a sinister conspiracy among managers to manipulate the workers by "human relations" tricks and other forms of mock democracy so as to enslave them more subtly but therefore more firmly to the system. In more sophisticated form, this idea has been propagated by Touraine (1969:14), who sees *participation dépendente* (herein termed democratization with functional effects only, presumably type (d) in Exhibit 1) as the most authentic and thus worst form of alienation of lower-level participants in modern organizations.

Given the correlation between total amount of power and efficiency/effectiveness measures, negative consequences of promoting efficiency/effectiveness for power equalization would imply that there is a general, negative relationship between the total amount and the distribution of control in organizations. However, there is usually *no* correlation between these two aspects of the organizational power structure (Tannenbaum, 1968:83, 159). Therefore, empirical evidence does not support the proposition that promoting efficiency and/or effectiveness would generally tighten up the hierarchical nature of organizations. This tallies with theoretical considerations. The mechanism of functional democratization consists of increased "vertical" and "horizontal" coordination of efforts directed toward joint goals and interests by both higher-level *and* lower-level participants.

Higher- and lower-level participants jointly generate more power over their organization in relation to its environment, and there is no reason why, under such circumstances, one party engaged in a joint enterprise of this kind would necessarily always gain more than the other party.

A final word of caution must be added. In the form presented here, the propositions are admittedly crude. As already Indicated, they usually pertain to the short-term effects of democratization, and they apply to organizations. This means that the long-term effects of democratization, especially when analyzed at a macro-societal level, would have to be viewed theoretically in a modified or even in a completely different conceptual framework.

DILEMMAS OF PARTICIPATION AND SELF-MANAGEMENT

The conclusion that participation and self-management cannot be maximized simultaneously, but only optimized, appears to be inescapable according to propositions (3b) and (4a). The optimal solution would appear to be an alternation of efforts at power equalization and efforts to increase functional democratization. This solution again confronts us with another dilemma, of course, because serious attempts to reduce power differences in existing organizations might reduce the level of effectiveness and/or efficiency (proposition 5a). Perhaps this is the price we must be willing to pay for experiments along the lines of structural democratization, not only because of the values involved, but also because of the dilemma of the alternative solution: forgetting about "structural" and concentrating on "functional" democratization only.

Various authors, such as Touraine (1969:8–31), have pointed to the societal impact of the growth and dominance of modern organizations. If functional democratization usually involves an increase in external power for an organization, this could mean that whatever we gain in intraorganizational power as participants, we might lose in our roles as parts of the various "publics" that become more and more powerless, and more at the mercy of flexible but uncontrollable organizations. This dangerous prospect is valid only when the "cake of power" is a fixed entity in any particular society. Whether or not the total amount of societal power can expand depends perhaps on the degree to which we can successfully achieve some sort of machinery at the level of society as a whole with respect to the macroscopic design and planning of the societal network of organizations and of their interrelations.

It goes without saying that at the moment—even in countries where such machinery exists—it is hard to visualize ways and means to plan and design our organizational infrastructure with an eye to determining the priorities of such incomparable matters as the welfare of the populace (which is also a result of large-scale organization), on the one hand, and the value of realizing what Mannheim (1940:44–49) called "the principle of fundamental democratization," on the other hand. However, since we have developed the organizational machinery required to go to the moon,

32   *Cornelis J. Lammers*

why could we not design and plan for a more democratic and at the same time relatively prosperous society?

Given the difficulties mentioned as regards the structural democratization of existing organizations, it would then be worthwhile to include "planning for freedom" (Mannheim, 1940:Part V). Perhaps techniques could be developed for the "mercy killing" of old and societally overdominant organizations and for the establishment of new, experimental organizations structured in more egalitarian forms.

REFERENCES

Aartsz, P. (Anton Pannekoek). *De Arbeidersraden*. Amsterdam: Van Gennep/De
1971   Vlam (or. ed., 1946).

Adizes, I. *Industrial Democracy: Yugoslav Style. The Effect of Decentralization on*
1971   *Organizational Behavior.* New York: Free Press.

Anweiler, Oskar. *Die Rätebewegung in Ruszland 1905–1921*. Leiden: Brill.
1958a

——————. "Die Arbeiterselbstverwaltung in Polen." *Osteuropa*, 8:224–32.
1958b

——————. "Die Räte in der Hungarischen Revolution 1956." *Osteuropa*, 8:393–400.
1958c

van Beinum, H. J. J., and P. de Bel. "Improving Attitudes to Work Especially by
1968   Participation." Paper presented at the 16th International Congress of the
          International Association of Applied Psychology. Amsterdam, August.

Bennis, W. G. "Leadership Theory and Administrative Behavior: the Problem of
1959   Authority." *Administrative Science Quarterly*, 4:259–301.

Broekmeyer, M. "De Arbeidersraden in Joegoslavië." In M. Broekmeyer and
1969   I. Cornelissen (eds.), *Arbeidersraad* of *Ondernemersstaat. Macht en
          Machtsstrijd in Nederland en in Joegoslavië*. Amsterdam: Van Gennep.

Burns, T., and G. M. Stalker. *The Management of Innovation.* London: Tavistock.
1961

Chomsky, N. *American Power and the New Mandarins*. Harmondsworth, Middlesex:
1969   Penguin Books.

Clark, P. A. *Organizational Design, Theory and Practice*. London/Assen: Tavistock/
1972   Van Gorcum.

Cohn-Bendit, G., and D. Cohn-Bendit. *Obsolete Communism, The Left Wing
1969   Alternative*. Middlesex: Penguin Books.

Dahrendorf, R. *Soziale Klassen und Klassenkonflikt in der Industriellen Gesellschaft*.
1957   Stuttgart: Ferdinand Enke.

Emery, F. E., and E. Thorsrud. *Form and Content in Industrial Democracy: Some
1969   Experiences from Norway and Other European Countries*. London/Assen:
          Tavistock/Van Gorcum.

Ertl, E. *Alle Macht den Räten?* Frankfurt am Main: Europäische Verlagsanstalt.
1968

Etzioni, A. *Modern Organizations*. Englewood Cliffs, N.J.: Prentice-Hall.
1964

French, J. R. P., J. Israël, and D. Aas. "An Experiment on Participation in a Norwegian
1960   Factory." *Human Relations*, 13:3–19.

Gater, A., et al. *Attitudes in British Management: A.P.E.P. Report.* Harmondsworth,
1965   Middlesex: Penguin Books (Pelican Book A 825).

Heldring, J. L. "Dezer Dagen." *Nieuwe Rotterdamsche Courant*, September 15.
1969

Heller, F. A. *Managerial Decision Making: A Study of Leadership Style and Power-
1971   sharing among Senior Managers*. London/Assen: Tavistock/Van Gorcum.

Kamušič, M. "Economic Efficiency and Workers' Self-Management." In
1970   M. J. Broekmeyer (ed.), *Yugoslav Workers' Self-Management*:76–116.

TWO CONCEPTS OF DEMOCRATIZATION 33

Proceedings of a Symposium held in Amsterdam January 7–9, 1970. Dordrecht, Holland: Reidel.

Kavčič, B., V. Rus, and A. S. Tannenbaum. "Control, Participation, and Effectiveness
1971 in Four Yugoslav Industrial Organizations." *Administrative Science Quarterly*, 16:74–86.

Katz, D., and R. L. Kahn. *The Social Psychology of Organizations*. New York:
1966 Wiley.

Lammers, C. J. "Power and Participation in Decision Making in Formal Organiza-
1967 tions." *American Journal of Sociology*, 73:201–17.

————. "Democratisering van Bedrijf en Universiteit." In A. van Braam (ed.),
1970a *Actuele Sociologie*. Assen: Van Gorcum.

————. *Studenten, Politiek en Universitaire Democratie*. Rotterdam: Universitaire
1970b Pers.

————. "Democratisering: Evolutie of Revolutie?" *Sociologische Gids*, 18:4–17.
1971

———— "Organizational Democracy" in György Széll (ed.) *Concise Encyclop-
1992 aedia of Participation and Co-Management*, pp.585-97, Berlin, de Gruyter.

Lawrence, Paul R., and Jay W. Lorsch. *Organization and Environment: Managing
1967 Differentiation and Integration*. Cambridge, Mass.: Division of Research, Graduate School of Business Administration, Harvard University Press.

Leval, G. *Espagne Libertaire 1936–1939: L'oeuvre Constructive de la Révolution
1971 Espagnole*. Editions du Cercle/Editions de la Tête de Feuilles.

Mannheim, K. *Man and Society in an Age of Reconstruction: Studies in Modern
1940 Social Structure*. London: Routledge and Kegan Paul.

Mandel, Ernest. *Arbeiterkontrolle, Arbeiterräte, Arbeiterselbstverwaltung*. Frankfurt
1971 am Main: Europäische Verlagsanstalt.

Meister, A. *Où Va L'Autogestion Yougoslave?* Paris: Editions Anthropos.
1970

Merton, Robert K. *Social Theory and Social Structure*. Glencoe, Ill.: Free Press.
1957

————. "The Unanticipated Consequences of Purposive Social Action."
1936 *American Sociological Review*, 1:894–904.

Mulder, Mauk. "Power Equalization Through Participation?" *Administrative Science
1971 Quarterly*, 16:31–38.

Mulder, Mauk, and H. Wilke. "Participation and Power Equalization." *Organiza-
1970 tional Behavior and Human Performance*, 5:430–48.

Naschold, Frieder. *Organisation und Demokratie: Untersuchung zum Demokratiesie-
1969 rungs Potential in Komplexen Organisationen*. Stuttgart: Kohlhammer.

von Oertzen, Peter. *Betriebsräte in der Novemberrevolution*. Düsseldorf: Droste
1963 Verlag.

Pateman, Carole. *Participation and Democratic Theory*. Cambridge: Cambridge
1970 University Press.

Roggemann, H. *Das Modell der Arbeiterselbstverwaltung in Jugoslawien*. Frankfurt
1970 am Main: Europäische Verlagsanstalt.

Rus, V. "Influence Structure in Yugoslav Enterprise." *Industrial Relations*, 9:148–60.
1970

Slater, Philip E., and Warren G. Bennis. "Democracy is Inevitable." *Harvard Business
1964 Review*, 42:51–59.

Strauss, George. "Some Notes on Power-Equalization." In Harold J. Leavitt (ed.),
1963 *The Social Science of Organizations: Four Perspectives*. Englewood Cliffs, N.J.: Prentice-Hall.

Tannenbaum, A. S. *Control in Organizations*. New York: McGraw-Hill.
1968

Touraine, A. *La Société Post-Industrielle*. Paris: Editions Denoël.
1969

Weber, Max. *Wirtschaft und Gesellschaft*. Tübingen: Mohr (or. ed., 1921).
1947

[6]

Power and Participation in Decision-making in Formal Organizations

C. J. Lammers

ABSTRACT

The notion that influence (power) is not a fixed amount at the disposal of an organization but rather a potentially expanding resource is developed in two directions. First, it is argued that "power raises" for lower-level participants and their effects on the total amount of power available to managers and managed are comparable to wage raises and their effects as described by modern economists. Second, a review of some European research, most of it relating to *indirect* participation (joint consultation), leads to the conclusion that the theorem of expanding power (and, therefore, of the relativity of the conflict of power interests) serves as an explanatory scheme for these forms of participation as well as for the forms of direct participation on which most U.S. research is focused.

The controversy in industrial sociology about the degree to which the interests of labor, management, and other (more or less) organized groups in enterprises are compatible has gradually become institutionalized. Again and again in the last twenty years the advocates of the "functionalistic" approach or the "human relations" philosophy, and usually both, have been castigated for neglecting power and income differences and conflict and competition between contending parties within industry. They are charged also as ultimately playing into the hands of the "powers that be."[1] In medical sociology the battle has started afresh in recent years, along similar lines and with the same rather disappointing results.[2] In both fields the arguments seem to lead to the conclusion that there are two irreconcilable theoretical models in terms of which organizational life can be explained.[3]

[1] E.g., R. Bendix and L. H. Fisher, "The Perspectives of Elton Mayo," *Review of Economics and Statistics,* XXXI (1949), 312–19; reprinted in A. Etzioni (ed.), *Complex Organizations, A Sociological Reader* (New York: Holt, Rinehart & Winston, 1961), pp. 113–26; R. C. Stone, "Conflicting Approaches to the Study of Worker-Manager Relations," *Social Forces,* XXXI (1952), 117–24; W. A. Koivisto, "Value, Theory, and Fact in Industrial Sociology," *American Journal of Sociology,* LVII (1953), 564–72; W. Hield, "The Study of Change in Social Sciences," *British Journal of Sociology,* V (1954), 1–11; H. L. Sheppard, "Approaches to Conflict in American Industrial Sociology," *British Journal of Sociology,* V (1954), 324–41; L. A. Coser, *The Functions of Social Conflict* (London: Routledge & Kegan Paul, 1956), esp. chap. i; L. A. Coser, "Social Conflict and the

Theory of Social Change," *British Journal of Sociology,* VIII (1957), 197–207; C. Kerr and L. H. Fisher, "Plant Sociology: The Elite and the Aborigines," in M. Komarovsky (ed.), *Common Frontiers of the Social Sciences* (Glencoe, Ill.: Free Press, 1957), pp. 281–309; R. Dahrendorf, *Gesellschaft und Freiheit. Zur soziologischen Analyse der Gegenwart* (Munich: Piper, 1961), "Die Funktionen sozialer Konflikte," pp. 112–31; L. Baritz, *The Servants of Power. A History of the Use of Social Science in American Industry* (Middletown, Conn.: Wesleyan University Press, 1960).

[2] E.g., A. Etzioni, "Interpersonal and Structural Factors in the Study of Mental Hospitals," *Psychiatry,* XXIII (1960), 13–22; A. W. Gouldner, "Anti-Minotaur: The Myth of a Value-Free Sociology," *Social Problems,* IX (1962), 199–213; A. Strauss, L. Schatzman, D. Ehrlich, R. Bucher, and M. Sabshin, "The Hospital and Its Negotiated Order," in E. Freidson (ed.), *The Hospital in Modern Society* (Glencoe, Ill.: Free Press, 1963).

[3] To be sure, some of the critics mentioned above (e.g., Stone *op. cit.*, and Coser, *The Functions of Social Conflict* and "Social Conflict and the Theory of Social Change") do point out possibilities of integrating both approaches. However, in analyses of

Particularly now that the comparative sociology of organizations is making headway as a unifying conceptual framework, it is crucial to know whether our research should be guided by one or by two sociological theories of organization.

In this paper an effort is made to point out the possibility of a theoretical integration of some basic postulates of the "functional" and "conflict of interest" approaches by taking recourse to economic theory and to notions derived from the research done on control structures by the University of Michigan's Institute of Social Research. These theoretical insights are then applied to the problems of direct and indirect participation (joint consultation) in decision-making in formal organizations.

CONFLICT OR HARMONY OF INTEREST?

We can define interests as the goals of persons, groups, or organizations to maintain or improve their chances of acquiring income, power, or prestige. The basic question then appears to be whether these goods are scarce. Taking it for granted that some inequality in this distribution is inevitable in formal organizations, one wonders whether the critics of the "functional" and/or "human relations" theories, usually following in the footsteps of Marx, rightly assume that organizational life is in this respect a *zero-sum* game. Those who earn less and those who have less status and less say in organizational policy than others will always be inclined to suffer, if not absolute, then at least relative, deprivation. Therefore—so these critics apparently argue—the limited supply of power, prestige, and income is for now and evermore a potential bone of contention.

However, when treating the problem of income distribution, modern economics no longer takes its starting point from the scarcity but from the affluence postulate,[4] at least for advanced Western economies. The income of the enterprise or industry is seen as a growing rather than as a constant quantity. In the long run, therefore, wage raises wrested from management by governments or trade unions may turn out in practice to heighten the level of income of the company or industry, to the extent that such wage raises stimulate labor productivity and/or purchasing power.

A conflict of economic interest between labor and management may be mitigated not only by the objective consequences of wage raises in the form of increased total income for all parties concerned but also by the "subjective," sociopsychological implications of a raising wage level. When workers become accustomed to regular wage raises, the relative deprivation they experience from comparing their income with that of those who are better off may be tempered somewhat by a relative elation resulting from comparing their present with their past earnings.[5]

Of course, all this by no means implies that all conflict of interests between labor and management as to the distribution of income is erased in an expanding economy. To regard the distributable income not as a fixed but as a potentially growing quantity leads only to the conclusion that under certain conditions no severe conflict of interests exists between the contending parties. Put more precisely, one should not

---

industrial or medical organizations usually either some sort of "functional" or some sort of "conflict" model is applied to the data. Examples of the latter approach: M. Dalton, *Men Who Manage. Fusions of Feeling and Theory in Administration* (New York: John Wiley & Sons, 1959); A. Strauss, L. Schatzman, D. Ehrlich, R. Bucher, and M. Sabshin, *Psychiatric Ideologies and Institutions* (Glencoe, Ill.: Free Press, 1964). Examples of the functional approach in industrial and medical sociology are so well known that no references need be given here.

[4] J. K. Galbraith, *The Affluent Society* (Harmondsworth, Middlesex: Penguin Books, 1962), esp. chap. vii; J. Pen, *Harmonie en conflict* (Amsterdam: Bezige Bij, 1962), chap. v; forthcoming English translation of this publication: J. Pen, *Harmony and Conflict in Modern Society* (New York: McGraw-Hill Book Co.).

[5] See Galbraith, *op. cit.*, pp. 79–80.

POWER AND PARTICIPATION IN DECISION-MAKING 203

presume that in organizations (and in market relations for that matter) either conflict or harmony of interests prevails. Conflict and harmony are merely the two ends of a continuum; they represent the degree to which the economic interests of various parties converge or diverge.

To turn now to the problem of *power distribution*, in sociological theory the advocates of the "conflict of interest" approach customarily have no doubt that power is a scarce commodity. In the expositions of Dahrendorf, for example, there is a fundamental dichotomy between those who wield and those who undergo power, so that in any hierarchically stratified organization a permanent tug of war between "powers that be" and "powers that would like to be" would be either manifest or present as a latent force.[6]

This conception resembles the *static* approach of the older type of economics, in which income was regarded as a constant entity. Applying a more dynamic perspective, power, too, is not necessarily a fixed quantity. Now, this is precisely what Likert, Tannenbaum, and their colleagues postulate as a likely supposition on the basis of their research concerning the influence or control structures of formal organizations.[7]

[6] R. Dahrendorf, *Soziale Klassen und Klassenkonflikt in der industriellen Gesellschaft* (Stuttgart: Ferdinand Enke, 1957), esp. chaps. iv and v. See also Dahrendorf, *Gesellschaft und Freiheit*, esp. chaps. iv, v, and ix. In the work of Dahrendorf, and also in that of his numerous predecessors who emphasized power distribution as a salient variable in social relations, the postulate of scarcity as regards the total amount of power available to an organization or to a social system in general is, on the whole, an implicit assumption. The only explicit statement on this score I have come across stems from Clark Kerr: "The power 'pie,' however, is always fixed in dimensions" ("Industrial Conflict and Its Mediation," *American Journal of Sociology*, LX [1954], 231, n. 3. This "zero sum" postulate also looms large in that branch of the theory of games which is apparently most suitable for application to the sociological study of conflict. See J. Bernard, "The Theory of Games of Strategy as Modern Sociology of Conflict," *American Journal of Sociology*, LIX (1954), 411–24, esp. 412.

The definitions given and indexes used by the Michigan researchers for "control" or "influence" justify the inference that they are dealing with the same phenomena that are labeled "power" by other social scientists.[8] Their studies show that "total amount of power" was generally a more effective predictor of organizational productivity and organizational morale than "hierarchical distribution of power." The resulting notion of expanding instead of fixed amounts of power in an organization, put forward particularly by Likert, can be conceptualized in a way similar to the notion of expanding income in economics. Granting more power to subordi-

[7] See A. S. Tannenbaum, "Control Structure and Union Functions," *American Journal of Sociology*, LXI (1956), 536–45; R. Likert, "Influence and National Sovereignty," in J. Peatman and E. Hartley (eds.), *Festschrift for Gardner Murphy* (New York: McGraw-Hill Book Co., 1960), pp. 214–27; R. Likert, *New Patterns of Management* (New York: McGraw-Hill Book Co., 1961), esp. chap. xii; A. S. Tannenbaum, "Control in Organizations: Individual Adjustment and Organizational Performance," *Administrative Science Quarterly*, VII (1962), 236–57; C. G. Smith and A. S. Tannenbaum, "Organizational Control Structure. A Comparative Analysis," *Human Relations*, XVI (1963), 299–316. The view of power as a potentially expanding property of social systems is already present in the work of Mary Parker Follett, who stated in 1925: "The division of power is not the thing to be considered, but that method of organization which will generate power"; see H. C. Metcalf and L. Urwick (eds.), *Dynamic Administration. The Collected Papers of Mary Parker Follett* (London: Pitman, 1941), p. 111. The same insight, although conceptualized in quite a different manner, may be found in T. Parsons, "On the Concept of Influence," *Public Opinion Quarterly*, XXVII (1963), 59–62.

[8] Compare, e.g., the definition of control given by Tannenbaum, "Control in Organizations," p. 239, and by Smith and Tannenbaum, *op. cit.*, p. 299—"any process in which a person (or group of persons or organization of persons) determines or intentionally affects what another person (or group or organization) will do"—with M. Weber's famous definition of power—"Macht bedeutet jede Chance, innerhalb einer sozialen Beziehung den eigenen Willen auch gegen Widerstreben durchzusetzen, gleichviel worauf diese Chance beruht" (*Wirtschaft und Gesellschaft* [3d ed.; Tübingen: Mohr, 1947], p. 28).

nates, for example, by giving them effective opportunities to participate in the preparation and/or making of significant decisions, may boost the joint power of superiors and subordinates alike, in that as a consequence of such procedures subordinates may become more willing and able to carry out decisions in the intended way. In the words of Likert, it is not only the decision but also the implementation of a decision that counts.[9] By ceding power to workers, management improves the chances that its decisions (influenced by or taken jointly with workers) will become effectuated. Therefore, the initial "loss" of power by management can eventually be transformed into a power gain in the sense of a better grip on the organizational apparatus and an increase in external power.

The "mechanism" at work here is not solely the potential motivation of increased upward influence. Giving subordinates more chances to make decisions or to participate in the decisions of higher authorities may also bear fruits because the increased amount of information made available in this fashion to higher levels may easily produce more workable decisions. At this point the analogy with processes of income redistribution no longer holds. Wage raises may increase productivity by providing incentives but not by yielding more data relevant to a decision. "Power raises," to the contrary, can have favorable productivity effects by mobilizing intellectual as well as motivational energy.

With respect to the "mechanism" of increased purchasing power as a consequence of wage raises, for obvious reasons no parallel can be found with respect to the

distribution of power. However, as to the "mechanism" of the subjective consequences of a rising wage level, an obvious analogy can be drawn. A power hierarchy is perhaps perceived as less depriving and unjust by those who experience gradual increments of power than it seems to those who cannot look back at and forward to a betterment of position in this respect.[10]

To sum up, managers and managed in organizations can at the same time come to influence each other more effectively and thereby generate joint power as the outcome of a better command by the organization over its technical, economic, and human resources in the service of certain objectives. Naturally, this happens only when the parties concerned have some goals in common. Therefore, the clash of power interests will *ceteris paribus* be more serious the less the principal parties in an organization adhere to common objectives in terms of which the organization's resources can be mobilized more effectively.[11]

The same line of argument may be valid for the prestige distribution. To the extent that the output or social climate of an organization is a source of its prestige in the community or society at large, in the long run prestige raises for the lower ranks may heighten the total amount of prestige the organization can dispose of. This in turn means a status gain of superiors as well as inferiors, so that the potential conflict of prestige interests is also to a variable extent tempered by the mutual interest the contending parties have in raising the total prestige of their organization.

Seldom do the income, the power, and the prestige of an organization depend primarily on the organization itself. Even

[9] Likert, *New Patterns of Management*, pp. 179–80. A quite similar argument to the effect that participation by subordinates not only expands the upward influence of lower echelons in organizations but also increases chances for management to participate more fully in the decision-making process (by heightening its control over the evocation of alternatives) can be found in J. G. March and H. A. Simon, *Organizations* (New York: John Wiley & Sons, 1958), p. 54.

[10] Of course, whether or not this hypothesis is valid can only be established on the basis of research.

[11] Some evidence on this point may be found in the study by C. G. Smith and O. N. Ari, "Organizational Control Structure and Member Consensus," *American Journal of Sociology*, LXIX (1964), 623–38.

POWER AND PARTICIPATION IN DECISION-MAKING   205

in the case of enterprises, external agents (governments, consumers, other enterprises, etc.) limit the degree to which the income, power and prestige available to an organization are expandable. Consequently, there is usually *some* conflict of interests between the parties contending within an organization for these at any rate *relatively* scarce goods. On the other hand, their interests usually also converge to some extent, since all organizational participants have in common an interest in jointly acquiring more income, power, or prestige. This can be achieved in two ways: The first way is by raising the level of effectiveness and/or efficiency[12] of the organization. This may bear fruits in the way of increased income, power, or prestige either automatically or because external agents become more willing to grant raises in income, power, or prestige to the organization as a whole because they are impressed by its achievements.[13] In this case there is a clear mutuality of interests. In the second way the parties concerned may try to wrest from the external agents more income, power, or prestige by putting some kind of direct pressure on them. This can be done jointly (in which case there are again common interests at stake) or separately (then, of course, there often will be a conflict of interests).

For a comparative sociology of organizations, it remains a challenging task to specify the conditions making for more or less conflict of interests within organizations. The renewed emphasis on power interests should be welcomed in this context; since power (and also prestige) issues are at stake in any formal organization, generalizations cutting across the traditional divisions into industrial, military, medical, and other organizations can be sought. In some respects the same applies to differences in income. It is true that only in industrial and commercial enterprises does income depend directly to some extent on productivity, so that only in such organizations can direct conflicts occur between the various producing parties about the distribution of the income available to the organization. However, the less free the individual enterprise becomes in disposing of its own income (increased concentration, more government regulation, etc.), the more competition for income between contending parties takes the form of a separate or joint attempt to manipulate outside agencies. This means that economic organizations become in this respect increasingly comparable to non-economic organizations, where the fight for the spoils of income has always taken place either by joint or by competing pressure(s) of the parties involved on outside decision-makers.

[12] These terms are used in this article in the same sense as Barnard applies these concepts in chap. i of his classic *The Functions of the Executive* (Cambridge, Mass.: Harvard University Press, 1938), e.g., pp. 43–45.

[13] If it is legitimate to take the percentage of the general public in the community who have heard about a certain organization as an index of its reputation, its external prestige, then research by Kahn, Tannenbaum, and Weiss on the League of Women Voters provides some evidence on this point. They found a positive correlation between the relative power of membership vs. officers in this organization, on the one hand, and the percentage of the public who had heard of the organization, on the other hand. This could mean that the external prestige and even the external power of this civic association depend to some extent on its total amount of internal power. See A. H. Barton, *Organizational Measurement and Its Bearing on the Study of College Environments* (New York: College Entrance Examination Board, 1961), p. 13.

DIRECT PARTICIPATION IN DECISION-MAKING

Participation in decision-making may be defined as the *totality of such forms of upward exertion of power by subordinates in organizations as are perceived to be legitimate by themselves and their superiors*. Participation in this sense can be of two varieties, direct (personal) or indirect (representative). The degree to which individual subordinates in organizations can and do legitimately influence in a direct way the decisions made by their supervisors or managers is obviously closely connected with the *style of leadership* prevalent in the organization in question, while the degree to which the lower ranks collectively possess legitimate means of indirectly influencing decisions taken at higher levels is an aspect of the *system of government* of the organization. The latter topic has been emphasized more often in European, the former more often in American studies. Before jumping to conclusions about "pro-managerial" and "human relations" biases, one should keep in mind that joint consultation and comparable forms of indirect participation are not (any longer) widespread in U.S. work organizations.[14] Consequently, the European sociologist has more opportunities to focus on collective participation than his American colleague. It seems rather clear, however, that to some extent the emphasis on leadership coincides with a "functional" or "human relations" approach, while the conflict-of-interest view is more often found in studies dealing with systems of government of organizations.

To what extent does the theorem of the relativity of conflicting interests in organizations, as outlined above, hold for both direct and indirect participation in decision-making?

There seems little doubt that forms of leadership that allow for *direct participation* (either by the individual alone or by the individual as a member of his colleague group in contact with his superior) often do contribute to the productivity and morale of the employees concerned.[15] Even if such "power raises" make subordinates not more satisfied but simply less dissatisfied,[16]

such leadership practices as delegation of authority, consulting one's men, or taking decisions jointly with one's subordinates have been shown to lead to more effective goal attainment in terms of the (not necessarily coinciding) objectives of both the upper and the lower ranks.

It may be mentioned here that several studies carried out in the Netherlands during recent years have yielded the same type of results as the American ones.

Philipsen reports on the results of surveys among blue- and white-collar employees of a factory and among supervisory personnel in public agencies and in hospitals.[17] Three degrees of presence of successful group meetings between superiors and subordinates are distinguished to indicate the perceived opportunities for direct participation in decision-making at higher levels: (1) meetings felt to be always or usually worthwhile, (2) absence of meetings, (3) meetings felt to be always or usually unsatisfactory.

The question used in Dutch ("Are there any meetings with your supervisors in which you can discuss freely what goes on?") was an almost literal translation of a corresponding question in the Michigan research. As in the Michigan studies, it was predicted that unsatisfactory meetings would be "worse" than an absense of such meetings. This prediction was entirely corroborated by the results.

[14] D. C. Miller and W. H. Form, *Industrial Sociology. The Sociology of Work Organizations* (2d ed.; New York: Harper & Row, 1964), p. 759, where it is mentioned that labor-management committees to speed up production flourished in the United States during World War II but have disappeared since.

[15] See, e.g., the overview of the Michigan research along these lines in Smith and Tannenbaum, *op. cit.*

[16] See F. Herzberg, B. Mausner, and B. B. Snyderman, *The Motivation To Work* (New York: John Wiley & Sons, 1959); M. M. Schwartz, E. Jenusaitis, and H. Stack, "Motivational Factors among Supervisors in the Utility Industry," *Personnel Psychology*, XVI (1963), 45–54; M. S. Myers, "Who Are Your Motivated Workers?" *Harvard Business Review*, XLII (1964), 73–88; T. M. Lodahl, "Patterns of Job Attitudes in Two Assembly Technologies," *Administrative Science Quarterly*, VIII (1964), 482–519; F. Friedlander and E. Walton, "Positive and Negative Motivations toward Work," *Administrative Science Quarterly*, IX (1964), 194–207.

[17] H. Philipsen, "Medezeggenschap in de vorm van werkoverleg," in C. J. Lammers (ed.), *Medezeggenschap en overleg in het bedrijf* (Utrecht and Antwerp: Het Spectrum, 1965), pp. 90–126.

POWER AND PARTICIPATION IN DECISION-MAKING   207

It is apparent from the data that, in the first place, the (perceived) chances for upward communication correlate with style of leadership. Socio-emotional or human-relations leadership is in all four samples significantly associated with the perceived presence of successful group meetings, and other indexes of supervisory behavior in several cases point in the same direction.

In the second place, there is evidence that satisfaction with one's management, perception of the degree of co-operation in one's department, and feeling at ease in one's work organization have something to do with opportunities for participation in the decision-making of one's higher authorities.

Furthermore, as can be seen from Table 1, similar correlations came to the fore when the department rather than the individual.was taken as unit of analysis. In the factory from which two samples of blue- and white-collar employees were drawn, again socio-emotional leadership and employee morale covary with the success of group meetings in the departments studied. What is even more important, an "objective" measure (or, rather, a measure derived from sources other than questionnaire answers given by employees) also provides evidence regarding the effects of opportunities to participate in decision-making for lower levels. Department productivity, as judged by management and as evidenced by records, seems to be associated with successful group meetings, although according to customary standards the latter correlation is not quite statistically significant.

This analysis yields some evidence, lastly, that not only style of leadership but also aspects of the formal organization determine the degree to which participation becomes institutionalized in the work situation. The higher the level of mechanization of a department, the less the department's employees report successful group meetings.

Another Dutch study, done by Teulings, is of interest because in the Royal Netherlands Blast Furnaces and Steelworks studied formal records were available concerning the presence and frequency of group meetings between supervisors and their workers.[18] Teulings divided the departments into three groups: (1) those in which the committee(s) had met five or more times during the past year, (2) those in which no such committees had ever existed, (3) those in which such committees

TABLE 1

Correlations between Successful Group Meetings (as Reported by Employees) and Morale, Leadership Practices, and Productivity in Eight Departments of a Firm

Variables	Correlations of Group Meetings with Variables[a]
Leadership practices:[b]	
Technical and administrative leadership	.19
Human-relations leadership	.81*
Morale:[c]	
Satisfaction with work and working conditions	.67*
Productivity:	
Objective data	.62
As judged by management	.66*
Characteristics of work process:	
Level of mechanization	−.86*

Source: Table adapted from Philipsen (see my n. 17).

[a] Numbers in the body of the table designate Spearman rhos. All tests are one-sided. The index of presence of successful group meetings is explained in the text.

[b] Indexes used are a combination of scores for the eight departments given by employees, by management, and by the investigator.

[c] Index consists of nineteen items.

* Significant at the 10 per cent level.

had been instituted but were later abolished or had met fewer than five times during the past year. These sixty committees in thirty-one departments of twelve factories aim at increasing productivity; they are composed of and presided over by department heads and are rewarded for workable proposals.

[18] A. W. M. Teulings, "Leiderschapsklimaat en werkoverleg," in Lammers (ed.), *op. cit.*, pp. 142–51. The frequency distribution was clearly bimodal, with three and nine times as the most common frequencies.

Several indexes of leadership practices of the executives concerned and of the quantity and quality of the productivity of their units were obtained by interviewing the factory managers. The results, given in Table 2, indicate that (according to their superiors) in departments with active productivity committees the executives show the leadership qualities that most people deem desirable more than their

of leadership and the organization of work and that the presence of such chances may contribute to the effectiveness and efficiency of the organization. By the same token there is reason to suppose that, in a European country like the Netherlands, under certain conditions (e.g., a certain amount of effective socio-emotional leadership, work processes providing the employees with some scope for initiative) the

TABLE 2

DIFFERENCES BETWEEN DEPARTMENTS WITH AND WITHOUT
ACTIVE PRODUCTIVITY COMMITTEES WITH RESPECT TO
LEADERSHIP PRACTICES AND LEVEL OF PRODUCTIVITY

	SCORES FOR DEPARTMENTS WITH:		RESULT OF STATISTICAL TESTS[a] (P)
	Active Committees (N=11)	Inactive Committees (N=9)	
Leadership practices:[b]			
Instrumental leadership..	9.0	7.8	.06
Social leadership.........	8.4	7.3	.04
Stable leadership........	9.6	7.7	.002
Dynamic leadership......	9.0	7.1	.002
Level of productivity:			
As judged by factory managers[c]..............	2.5	2.4	.10

Source: Table adapted from Teulings (see my n. 18).

[a] Willcoxon's two-sample test (one-sided).

[b] Indexes used consist of short (three-item) scales per variable and are based on answers given by factory managers concerning leadership behavior of their department heads. The scales in question were developed in research of the Netherlands Institute of Preventive Medicine, Leiden, by H. Philipsen and C. J. Lammers, and form an adaptation of Fleishman's Ohio State Leadership scales.

[c] Combined for quality and quantity of production; high score is high on productivity.

colleagues in departments with inactive committees. Factory managers also have a no-less-favorable impression of the productivity of departments in which the aforementioned committees flourish than of the output of departments in which these committees are rather passive.

We may conclude that in spite of all the supposed "cultural differences" between the United States and the Netherlands, the Dutch data corroborate the American findings that the chances for individual employees to partake in decision-making by supervisors depend on the style

granting of power to subordinates is in their interest as well as in the interest of their superiors. Although further research on this point is of course needed, serious doubt is justified regarding the postulate of an unavoidable and omnipresent cleavage of power interests between management and employees. It is more likely that in both American and European work organizations the total amount of organizational power is a potentially expanding force and that thereby the conflict of power interests between rulers and ruled can be mitigated, although not eliminated.

POWER AND PARTICIPATION IN DECISION-MAKING 209

INDIRECT PARTICIPATION IN
DECISION-MAKING

With respect to the problems of *indirect participation* by employees in managerial decision-making, it is imperative to be clear as to the differences in setup between both forms of upward influence. In Table 3 a rough comparison is made.

The setup of *indirect* participation (joint consultation) usually implies that the subordinate participants *speak for their constituents* with *top managers* about the *general policy* of the organization; *procedures are formalized* (by laws and bylaws), and *outside agencies* (government, trade unions) often *do influence* to some extent

As a result, in many cases managements (and, sometimes for quite different reasons, unions too) obstruct the legal requirements of joint consultation lest they lose their freedom of action. A great variety of such "defense tactics" is found in practices on the Continent.[19] A most simple device to prevent joint consultation from functioning as an opportunity for participation by employees in managerial decision-making is not to institute it at all or to institute it and fail to convene regularly. Using joint consultation not for upward but only for *downward* communication (such as explaining management's actions or exhorting the employees to work harder

TABLE 3

COMPARISON BETWEEN DIRECT AND INDIRECT PARTICIPATION

	Direct Participation	Indirect Participation
Subordinate party........	Employees *à titre personnel*	Representatives of groups or categories of personnel
Superordinate party......	Supervisors	Top management
Issues..................	Work or work-related matters	General policy of firm
External influences.......	Absent	Present (government; unions)
Degree of formalization...	Low	High (laws; regulations)

what goes on. *Direct* participation, on the other hand, customarily entails that the subordinate participants *speak for themselves* with *supervisors* about *work or matters related to work;* in general, aims, rules, and means are *not codified,* and *external influences* are normally absent.

Consequently, in principle there is more at stake for both management and employees in indirect than in direct participation. In joint consultation the participating parties are more powerful, the topics that can come to the fore are of greater significance, and the chance for management to operate at its own discretion (unhampered by formal requirements or by outside interferences) is not as great as in forms of personal consultation between a supervisor and his subordinates.

and better and to drop certain demands) is equally effective as a means of preventing joint consultation from growing into indirect participation.

However, many cases are also encountered in which managerial resistance has deformed indirect into *pseudo-direct* participation in one or more of the five respects

[19] The following account is based on widely scattered evidence of varying reliability (personal experiences, research reports on the work councils in the Netherlands, various sources pertaining to joint consultation in other European countries, etc.) and therefore cannot be regarded as more than the author's general impression. For a description of the systems of collective participation in Germany and France, see A. Sturmthal, *Workers Councils. A Study of Workplace Organization on Both Sides of the Iron Curtain* (Cambridge, Mass.: Harvard University Press, 1964), chaps. ii and iii. See also Miller and Form, *op. cit.*, pp. 757–64.

mentioned above (as variables differentiating between direct and indirect participation; see Table 3). For example, (1) the employer, who both in the Netherlands and in France must preside over the works council, may treat the members not as representatives but as individual employees (taking their expressed viewpoints as "just a personal opinion," trying to manipulate them by means of the positive or negative sanctions at his disposal in the manager-employee relationship, etc.). (2) The general manager may avoid attending meetings himself and send a lower authority, thus lowering the hierarchical level on which the council can exert influence. (3) He may take care that only unimportant problems are dealt with in the council's meetings. (4) He may resist outside interference, for example, by not permitting employee councilors to consult their union experts about complex problems. (5) He can finally try to keep a free hand by not co-operating in drafting the necessary by-laws or by refusing to keep official and detailed minutes of the meetings.

All such practices clearly indicate that joint consultation is often *perceived* by managers as a serious threat to the authority structure of their organizations. However, empirical evidence from Britain, Germany, and France bears out that indirect, just like direct, participation can and sometimes does in the long run benefit management by way of increased power of the organization as a whole. W. Brown, president of the Glacier-Metal Company with its elaborate machinery of a representative system, wonders why managers so greatly fear giving shareholders, boards, consumers, and representatives a say in their plans. Discussion with such interested groups, according to Brown, is indispensable for the simple reason that such groups can prevent the execution of such plans. "It is clear," states Brown, "that many managers who think they have a choice in such matters, and criticize the idea of discussing resistance to their plans with

their own people, in fact spend much time doing precisely what they so vehemently oppose. They attempt to initiate change of some sort that gives rise to great anxieties and precipitate strike action. Then they get down to the discussions which might have been so much easier to conduct if held before trouble arose."[20]

It all comes down to the fact that enabling works councils and similar bodies to participate effectively in managerial policies may turn out to be a solid investment that will pay off for management in the form of heightened chances to take adequate decisions and to see certain decisions through.

A "mechanism" similar to the one we encountered in relation to direct participation is at work here: a "power raise" for the lower ranks contributes toward employee motivation and releases relevant information for the upper managerial levels, so that not only do employees become more powerful with respect to their superiors but also managers acquire more power over their subordinates for agreed-upon ends. The increased joint power of the organization yields increased effectiveness and efficiency (see scheme below).

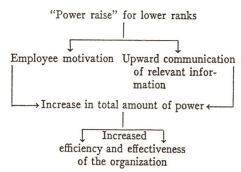

However, in spite of this similarity there is still, as was pointed out in the comparison between these two forms of upward influence (see Table 3), a basic difference between direct and indirect participation with respect to the *kind* of de-

[20] W. Brown, *Exploration in Management* (London: Heinemann, 1960), pp. 223–24.

cisions in which the lower ranks partake and in the *structure* of this process. The "power raise" in direct participation consists of more say regarding work and work-related matters, so that the employee's motivation regarding his *work* or work-related matters is furthered, while a greater amount of relevant *work* information becomes available to executives. In indirect participation, on the other hand, the "power raise" implies to a greater extent the right of groups or categories of personnel *to promote their interests and to present their views concerning general managerial policies.* Consequently, joint consultation can contribute toward employee motivation in the sense of heightened trust on the part of the employees that their interests and views are well represented at top levels. Joint consultation can release relevant information to top executives, not primarily in the form of productivity suggestions, but rather in the form of insight into possible resistance to or alternatives for the managerial actions under consideration.

Now, the main point Brown makes is that no management can avoid some sort of collective influence by its personnel on its central policies. Top executives can only choose between an officially recognized system of representative participation or an irregular, non-legitimated one. Wherever management thwarts the functioning of any kind of indirect participation, an unofficial, non-regulated indirect influence on organizational policy (in the form of work stoppages, restriction of output, high levels of turnover, absenteeism, grievances, etc.) comes to the fore. It follows that from the point of view of management a representative system has potential value primarily because it provides a less costly means to accommodate conflicting interests and viewpoints than non-institutionalized forms of influence exerted by its personnel on the formation and execution of its policy. The available empirical evidence offers some support for this inference, although no definite conclusion can be reached for

lack of adequate research seeking an answer to this question. Moreover, systems of collective participation vary greatly not only between but also within western European countries, so that any generalization made on the basis of a few studies is bound to be too sweeping.

As regards *Great Britain*, Brown is clearly convinced on the basis of his experiences with the Glacier Metal's representative system that this is for the company a more effective and for its personnel a more efficient approach to labor-management controversies than any other. Evidence pertaining to this question can also be found among the results of the survey on joint consultation in British industry, carried out between 1948 and 1950 by the (British) National Institute of Industrial Psychology. It appears that joint consultation is less successful (as determined by the investigators on the basis of an elaborate scoring procedure) when matters such as "quality of workmanship," "training," "work tempo," "methods of production," and "reduction of waste" are discussed than when labor conditions, work rules, safety and accidents, and similar topics are taken up in the representative bodies.[21] This corroborates the notion that, for both parties concerned, indirect participation is primarily useful as a way of dealing with potentially controversial subjects and matters of general company policy that are of joint interest to management and labor.

In *France*, Montuclard and his collaborators made a detailed content analysis of the minutes of meetings of the *comités d'entreprise* in eight concerns from about 1945 up to 1958. They recognize four categories of topics considered by these committees:[22] (*a*) the *committee* itself (its organization, budget, relations with the

[21] National Institute of Industrial Psychology, *Joint Consultation in British Industry* (London: 1952), pp. 182–83.

[22] M. Montuclard, *La dynamique des comités d'entreprise. Exploration sociologique de quelques effets de l'institution des comités d'entreprise sur les relations industrielles* (Paris: Centre National de la Recherche Scientifique, 1963), pp. 110–14.

personnel at the disposal of the committee, relations with the workers of the enterprise and with the unions), (*b*) *social affairs* (canteens, leisure-time activities, festivities, co-operative societies, and other social provisions for the workers' benefit; the committee has sole responsibility for the administration of such affairs), (*c*) *working conditions* (salaries, employment conditions, and security), and (*d*) *the enterprise* (technical matters regarding the organization of the production process or the equipment and matters concerning the economic and commercial policy of the enterprise).

The authors assumed that in discussions about "working conditions" *conflicting* interests between management and labor are usually involved, whereas discussions about "enterprise" indicate attempts to solve general problems of the enterprise in the light of the *joint* interests of labor and management. The data show that the more attention the committees, at various points in their history, pay to the promotion of the workers' interests ("working conditions"), the more attention they simultaneously pay to the problems of the enterprise as a whole ("enterprise").[23] The investigators had expected the contrary. Because the representatives serving on the committees are in general militant union members and because of the Marxist orientation of the French labor movement, it would have come as no surprise if in the course of their development the committees had gravitated toward either the status of an instrument in the class struggle or the status of a management-oriented body of "loyalists." However, neither proved to be the case. Even in France, joint consultation can function effectively both as a means to accommodate conflicting management-worker interests and as a means to obtain the co-operation of workers' representatives in pursuing the general welfare of the company. It is quite likely that the two tendencies reinforce one another. The more management is willing and able to have general desires and grievances

[23] *Ibid.*, chap. xvi.

dealt with in the *comité d'entreprise,* the more workers' representatives become motivated to partake in joint efforts to promote the interests of the enterprise. The more the employee representatives are willing and able to co-operate with management in the formulation and execution of its general policy, the more management may be inclined to pay serious attention to workers' interests as brought forward in the committee.

In *Germany,* indirect participation (*Mitbestimmung*) is institutionalized to a higher degree than anywhere else in western Europe. All companies with more than five hundred employees are required to have a works council (*Betriebsrat*), while one-third of the members of the Board of Supervision (*Aufsichtsrat*) must be workers' representatives. In the iron, steel, and mining industries there is parity on the board between representatives of the stockholders and of the workers.[24] Moreover, the heavy industries know the institution of the labor director (*Arbeitsdirektor*); this functionary is appointed by the board and must be reappointed every five years. Because of the composition of the supervisory board, the labor director cannot be appointed or retained against the wishes of the workers' representatives. The labor director, together with the technical and commercial directors, carries the *joint* responsibility for management of the enterprise in all respects.

Most of the research done in Germany on *Mitbestimmung* consists of surveys concerning the opinions and attitudes of workers and of their representatives. On the whole, it appears that workers are positively inclined toward *Mitbestimmung*, do not know much about it, expect mainly benefit to their own position, but are not very satisfied with the fruits of *Mitbestimmung* thus far.[25] Their representatives are usually

[24] This is true in practice, not in principle. See, e.g., Sturmthal, *op. cit.*, p. 56.

[25] R. Dahrendorf, *Das Mitbestimmungsproblem in der deutschen Sozialforschung. Eine Kritik* (Munich: Piper, 1965), pp. 31–46.

more optimistic about the effectiveness of co-determination. They feel that, on the whole, a betterment of position (wages, security of employment, etc.) has been achieved as a result of this representative system, while at the same time labor-management relations have improved. Of course, workers and their representatives are in general more satisfied with the results of *Mitbestimmung* in the heavy industries than elsewhere.[26]

Obviously, the judgment of the participants in the representative system and that of their constituents provide only tentative evidence regarding the outcome of co-determination. This gives special interest to an elaborate study done under the guidance of Voigt, because in this project not only workers and their representatives but also other informants (technical and commercial directors, board members representing stockholders' interests, trade-union and government officials) were questioned; using at the same time various kinds of documents and statistics (about strikes, wages, prices, investments), Voigt tried in the first place to gauge the *economic* effects of the *Mitbestimmungs* institutions. Although one gets the impression that no very rigorous methods of quantitative analysis were applied, this investigation still is the best available source of data concerning the consequences of the mass "power raise" the German labor movement was able to obtain after World War II through an odd constellation of circumstances.[27]

Voigt reports that in the iron, steel, and mining industries *Mitbestimmungs* institu-

tions have proved to be advantageous for the workers in terms of elevated wage levels, improved employment conditions (e.g., better protection of employee interests in hiring and firing practices) and all kinds of fringe benefits.[28] Particularly under the condition that works council, personnel director, and workers' representatives on the board co-operate closely, indirect participation is a powerful force shaping managerial policy.[29]

To what extent have the fruits of co-determination for labor jeopardized the profitability and expansibility of German industry? Voigt indicates that so far no serious malfunctioning of the German economy has resulted from this system of indirect participation. Apparently, expansion and concentration processes in German enterprises have in no way been hampered by the increased power of labor representatives.[30] Voigt is even inclined to conclude that on the whole *Mitbestimmung* has proved beneficial to German industry.[31] This judgment is based on two grounds. In the first place, the author points to the effects of wage raises on purchasing power and improvement of the quality of labor as a production factor. In the second place, Voigt feels that *Mitbestimmung* has achieved a degree of conflict regulation which ultimately has had positive effects on industrial productivity. The drastic re-

[26] Surveys among labor directors and labor representatives in works councils and Boards of Supervision, which show this result: O. Blume, "Zehn Jahre Mitbestimmung," in E. Potthoff, O. Blume, and H. Duvernell, *Zwischenbilanz der Mitbestimmung* (Tübingen: Mohr, 1962), pp. 277–79; O. Blume, *Normen und Wirklichkeit einer Betriebsverfassung* (Tübingen: Mohr, 1964), chaps. iv, v, and vi.

[27] For an excellent account of the genesis of German co-determination in the heavy industries, see E. Potthoff, "Zur Geschichte der Mitbestimmung," in Potthoff *et al., op. cit.*, pp. 1–54.

[28] F. Voigt, "Die Mitbestimmung der Arbeitnehmer in den Unternehmungen. Eine Analyse der Einwirkungen der Mitbestimmung in der Bundesrepublik Deutschland auf die Unternehmungsführung," in F. Voigt and W. Weddigen, *Zur Theorie und Praxis der Mitbestimmung* (Berlin: Duncker & Humblot, 1962), chaps. vii–xi and pp. 500–518 (Summary).

[29] *Ibid.*, e.g., pp. 225, 280–81, 294, 331–32, and 429.

[30] *Ibid.*, pp. 272–87, 373–86.

[31] This is the general theme running through Voigt's conclusions (see *ibid.*, pp. 500–518). It should be emphasized, however, that Voigt repeatedly warns that his conclusions pertain only to the present time with its favorable economic conditions. The crucial test for *Mitbestimmung*, Voigt feels, will come in times of depression.

Managing Democratic Organizations I

duction of strike activity, primarily in the iron, steel, and mining industries, constituted a direct economic gain in that large-scale interruptions of the production process and a relative loss of purchasing power (due to diminished income of the strikers) are avoided. The institutionalization of labor-management conflicts also contributes indirectly to making industry thrive. The tensions which usually precede a strike and the strained relations between management and workers which often follow its settlement probably have an equally negative impact on productivity. Once indirect participation functions as a substitute for real or threatened work stoppages in settling labor-management disputes, there is less chance that such tensions and strains in labor-management relations will affect productivity in a negative manner.

Lastly, it should be reported that Voigt, in view of his findings, repeatedly denies the applicability of a simplistic model presuming an omnipresent cleavage of interests between management and labor. He concludes, for instance, that the majority of personnel directors manage quite well to overcome the potential role conflict following from their double allegiance (to management, on the one hand, and to the workers and unions, on the other).[32] On the basis of this evidence the view of authors like Dahrendorf,[33] who claim that the *Arbeitsdirektor* is faced with an insoluble dilemma—being just another manager or being a bad manager (as a result of the hopeless task of trying simultaneously to serve workers' interests)—can be rejected. Since, at least under present conditions in Germany, the interests of managers and managed are to a large extent compatible, particularly in terms of long-range policy, the labor director can quite well "serve two masters."

Although the above conclusions refer particularly to German heavy industries,

Voigt is of the opinion that similar effects are also valid to a lesser, but by no means negligible, extent for the rest of German industry. In this connection it is worthwhile to note a finding from a survey made by Blume. German enterprises with more than one hundred employees are required to institute a so-called economic committee (*Wirtschaftsausschusz*) in addition to the *Betriebsrat*. This economic committee is a purely advisory body with equal representation of management and labor. Management can inform and consult labor representatives concerning economic and technical affairs pertaining to the enterprise. On the whole, in most enterprises this committee is not a flourishing institution.[34] Blume, however, found that in some cases meetings of the *Wirtschaftsausschusz* were the scene of serious controversies and conflicts between labor and management. Interestingly enough, it appeared that such battles in the economic committee were far more typical of enterprises in which the works' council appeared to be *active* and where on the whole quite *positive* relationships between management and labor prevailed than of enterprises in which the *Betriebsrat* was *inactive* and labor-management relations were of a *negative* nature![35]

By way of summarizing, one might say that the German experiences with institutions of *Mitbestimmung* have shown, as in the case of the French *comités d'entreprise* described by Montuclard, that under certain circumstances the goals of workers and management can both be served by indirect participation, since this institution can be used to accommodate conflicting interests and at the same time, or rather thereby, function to promote the effectiveness of the organization as a whole. It does not seem too farfetched to interpret this state of affairs in terms of the notion of expanding power dealt with at the beginning of this paper.

---

[32] *Ibid.*, pp. 215–16.

[33] Dahrendorf, *Soziale Klassen und Klassenkonflict*, p. 232.

[34] See, e.g., Voigt, *op. cit.*, chap. x.

[35] See Blume, *Normen und Wirklichkeit einer Betriebsverfassung*, pp. 176–78.

DISCUSSION

This article constitutes an attempt to elaborate in two directions the notion of expanding rather than fixed amounts of power being at the disposal of formal organizations. In the first place it was argued that this theorem of the relativity of the conflict of *power* interests bears a fairly strong resemblance to the theorem of the relativity of the conflict of *economic* interests. In the second place, the implications of this notion of expanding amounts of power as developed by Tannenbaum, Likert, *et al.* for *direct* participation were examined for *indirect* participation (joint consultation) and found, *mutatis mutandis,* to be valid in this area as well.

The primary focus of this exposition of similarities in structure and of effects of power processes in direct and indirect participation should, however, not lead to the erroneous conclusion that these two forms of participation in decision-making by lower level participants of organizations are for all practical purposes the same. As was pointed out (see Table 3), there are considerable differences between the "mechanisms" at work in direct participation and those operative in indirect participation. Moreover, detailed research may prove that specific effects of influence by subordinates on higher-level decision-making are quite variable for the participation system of both the personal and the representative variety.

Some scattered research evidence points to the likelihood that effective direct participation in industrial organization bears little or no relationship to effective forms of indirect participation.[36] Obviously, this would mean that different forces are conducive to the functioning of these two kinds of participation. Another inference from the lack of strong correlation between direct and indirect forms of participation would be that the personal, on-the-job influence of the employee and the collective influence of employees via representatives do not reinforce each other to any appreciable ex-

tent. This state of affairs implies that it is both possible and desirable to study not only the consequences of direct and indirect participation separately but also, as Patchen did,[37] the consequences of the *joint* operation of both kinds of participation.

Analysis of the *dys*functions of various forms of participation may turn out to be another line of fruitful research. As reported above, the Michigan researchers in the United States and we in the Netherlands found "mock participation" (meetings of superiors and subordinates felt to be always or usually unsatisfactory) less effective and/or efficient than the absence of participation. Interestingly enough, research by Drenth *et al.* in seventeen Dutch factories shows no relationship whatsoever between the "quality" (as judged both by

[36] In Philipsen's still unpublished study of the level of sick absenteeism and various organizational characteristics of eighty-five Dutch firms, there appeared to be a correlation of only .13 (.19 when size is controlled; significant at the 5 per cent level) between an index of indirect participation (the number of labor-management committees convening more than four times a year) and an index of direct participation (combined opinions of the head of the personnel department and of the production manager concerning the degree to which successful meetings between first-line supervisors and their subordinates, and between those first-line supervisors and their superiors, occur).

In another article, "Medezeggenschap in een tiental bedrijven" (*Sociologische Gids,* XII [1965], 269–86), a study of ten firms by A. W. M. Teulings and C. J. Lammers, what are in general not-significant correlations of comparable size were found with respect to the relationships between various indexes of direct and indirect participation.

Finally, a study by M. Patchen, "Labor-Management Consultation at TVA: Its Impact on Employees," *Administrative Science Quarterly,* X (1965), 149–74, perhaps supplies some data on this point. If one takes the "discrepancy in influence between employees and their immediate supervisor" as an index of direct participation, and "participation of work group in cooperative program" as a measure of indirect participation, it can probably be inferred from the numerals in parentheses in Patchen's Tables 3 and 4 that there is little or no correlation between these two kinds of participation.

[37] Patchen, *op. cit.,* pp. 163–65, 170–72.

management and labor representatives) of the works council and such variables as the frequency or duration of meetings of the council.[38] As in the case of direct participation, the sheer activity of a representative system may perhaps have functional as well as dysfunctional consequences for an organization and its members. In what respects precisely do such dysfunctional forms of participation differ from the functional ones? Research on this question is badly needed, since up till now we know only that people who participate in such participation systems feel more satisfied when the meetings are more successful in terms of other criteria as well—a plausible but hardly enlightening finding.

Finally, in terms of the attempted reconciliation between "functional" and "conflict of interest" theories, the question under what conditions a conflict of interests between managers and managed in formal organizations prevails is of crucial impor-

tance. As already stated, goal consensus between the major parties involved seems to be one such prerequisite for the mitigation or institutionalization of such conflicts.[39] What factors, however, are conducive to such communality in outlook between rulers and ruled?

For one thing, a rapidly expanding economy seems both in the United States and in western Europe to have been such a precondition for labor and management to discover the common interest in generating their joint power. Perhaps, in general, a high rate of social change in society at large may foster organizational parties' awareness of the fact that joint efforts may prove beneficial to all. The intriguing question then arises of to what extent more goal consensus and less conflict of interests are attained at the level of the individual organization at the price of less consensus and heightened conflict of interests at the level of interorganizational relationships.[40]

UNIVERSITY OF LEIDEN

[38] P. J. D. Drenth and J. C. W. van der Pijl, *De ondernemingsraad in Nederland* (The Hague: Commissie Opvoering Productiviteit of the Sociaal-Economische Raad, September, 1966), Part I, pp. 5 and 75–77. Some results of the study by Teulings and Lammers, *op. cit.*, also indicate that the amount of participating activity in an organization is more or less independent of the degree to which such participation is perceived as successful.

[39] See Smith and Ari, *op. cit.*, and Patchen, *op. cit.*, p. 172, where a correlation of .77 between participation in the co-operative program of TVA and feelings of common purpose with management is reported.

[40] Some remarks on this question may be found in Pen, *op. cit.*

[7]

DECISION-MAKING AND THE UTILIZATION OF COMPETENCE

FRANK HELLER

ABSTRACT

A considerable literature discusses the extent to which power and influence is shared in managerial decision-making. A critical question is whether influence and power sharing (IPS) has positive consequences for the organization. For example, are organizations which practise high levels of IPS more productive or profitable? And, if they are, why?

The thesis of this chapter is that, other things being equal, IPS does increase organizational efficiency. It achieves this result through three related processes: first it makes better use of organizational members' existing competence (experience and skill), secondly it helps develop new competence, and thirdly it liberates dormant motivation. The theoretical framework to describe these relationships is called the Motivated Competence model, which also suggests that attempts to use IPS when relevant experience and skill are absent results in inauthentic or manipulative participation.

INTRODUCTION

This chapter will analyse the role of competence as one of the conditions which operates both as a constraint and an opportunity in the process of IPS.

There is a large social science literature investigating different influence-sharing methods of decision-making (DM) or styles of leadership (for instance Allport, 1945; Stogdill and Coons, 1957; Blake and Mouton, 1964; Likert, 1967; Heller and Yukl, 1969; Vroom and Yetton, 1973; Misumi, 1985). The extensive attention given to this topic in several areas of social science, including organizational behaviour, theories of change, and leadership, is often commented on (Macy *et al.*, 1989) and has led to a proliferation of terms used to describe the influence-power-sharing (IPS) process, including: participation, initiating structure versus consideration, industrial democracy, involvement, power equalization, co-

71

determination, performance-maintenance behaviour, empowering, and decentralized leadership.

IPS covers a wider range of leadership styles than participation. It starts with access to the decision-making process through sharing information and goes beyond consultation and consensus decision-making to delegation or autonomy. Nevertheless, because the term participation is so widely used in the literature, it will also be used in this chapter.

Most researchers share the assumption that IPS has some identifiable advantage over more centralized decision methods, at least in some circumstances. The advantages of IPS are frequently based on values and ideologies (Strauss, 1963) as much as on practical considerations, like economic efficiency (Warner, 1984), and analogies are drawn between political and organizational democratic systems (Pateman, 1983) which may be inappropriate. Critical assessment of IPS can also be influenced by politically informed beliefs (Locke and Schweiger, 1979).

The emphasis on ideology has had positive and negative effects. On the positive side, it has undoubtedly led to a greater volume of research and experimentation (much of it of high quality) than would otherwise have occurred. On the negative side, apart from poorly designed investigations, there has been a tendency to assume that the appropriate antecedent and consequential conditions that most people accept as legitimate for political democracy can be translated into organizational life without much adaptation. The similarities and differences between political and organizational democracy have not received sufficient conceptual and empirical attention (Pusic, 1984), and since it is as difficult to argue against motherhood as against democracy, academics have been reluctant to probe sufficiently into the limiting and contingency factors which distinguish between feasible and non-feasible applications of IPS. These value positions are not easily substituted by more analytically based rational approaches, but it is hoped that a model of DM which pays special attention to the role of experience and skill and its relation to IPS will clarify many of the issues that at the moment rely on little more than good sense and personal values.

This chapter will analyse the role of competence as one of the conditions which operates both as a constraint and an opportunity in the process of participative decision-making.

EVIDENCE ABOUT SKILL JUDGEMENTS AND PARTICIPATION

One of the earliest pieces of evidence about the relationship between competence and participative DM comes from the fourteen country study of Haire *et al.* (1966). They found that in their sample of 3,600 managers there was a consistent tendency for managers to have little faith in the

The utilization of competence   73

competence of other managers, while at the same time they approved of participative DM. The authors were conscious that this finding drew attention to a major inconsistency in attitudes, since participation only made sense if one could assume that there was sufficient experience and skill among participating members to improve the quality of decisions.

A few years earlier, Miles (1964) had found a similar negative assessment by managers of their lower level employees: 'although managers have few doubts about their own abilities, they have serious reservations concerning the abilities of those below them' (p. 78). Nevertheless, 'the typical manager generally endorses participative policies, whether or not he has faith in the capacities of those below him' (p. 89). The managers' judgements about their subordinates' capabilities may, of course, be wrong. In our own research on senior management in eight countries, we used different instruments from Haire *et al.* (1966) and Miles (1964), but again found that, on average, senior managers thought that their immediate subordinates, who were also senior managers, had substantially lower skills and would take a very long time to reach the level of competence of the next higher level (Heller and Wilpert, 1981). However, we also had objective measures of experience and qualifications and these objective indices showed that the subordinates were, on average, equal to their superiors and in some dimensions, like formal education, scored higher. We used a method called Group Feed-back Analysis (GFA) to confront our groups of managers with their own judgements and asked them to elaborate on them. It then emerged that, on reflection, most groups felt some discomfort about their negative assessment of subordinates. Since our research involved both levels with identical questions and procedures, we felt confident that in reality, the difference in competence between the two senior levels was very small. For instance, it emerged that, in a large number of cases, the senior managers travelled extensively through the year and, during such absences, the subordinate made all relevant decisions. In each case, the decisions were accepted as satisfactory.

While judgements about competence may be quite incorrect, they are nevertheless likely to influence behaviour. In Miles' early work he found a small but statistically significant relationship 'between managers' attitudes towards participation with subordinates and attitudes towards their subordinates' abilities' (Miles, 1964, p. 88). Attitudes towards participation were more favourable as the perceived skill gap between the manager and his subordinates decreased. Since then we have evidence that this relationship is not confined to attitudes, but affects leadership behaviour, particularly in relation to the methods used for making decisions.

74   *Frank Heller*

CONTRASTING MODELS OF THINKING

A study of decision-making of 260 top managers in fifteen large American companies used a list of twelve specific tasks to describe the decision behaviour by two interlocking boss-subordinate pairs of managers (Heller, 1971). At both levels each member of the dyad was asked to give scaled judgements of the minimum skills required for their own job and separately for the job on the other level. Later, managers on both levels described how each of the twelve decisions was taken. The findings show 'that senior managers are willing to share more influence and power with subordinates whose skills they perceive to be similar to their own' (p. 107).

Ten years later, an eight country study of 1,600 senior managers in 129 large companies (Heller and Wilpert, 1981) extended the inquiry, but retained the same measurements of skill judgements and decision-making with a larger and more diverse sample. The research again came to the conclusion that judgements about competence significantly affect managerial behaviour.[1]

The early work by Miles (1964) and Haire *et al.* (1966) required a reassessment of the theoretical model used to describe the participative process. Miles came to the conclusion that the starkly inconsistent managerial attitudes reflected genuine alternative models of thinking. One model expresses a manager's judgement about himself, the other refers to lower levels of the hierarchy. The model that describes how managers conceptualize the reaction of subordinates has been called the human relations model (HREL). It is the result of a movement away from the classical theories of 'scientific management' championed by Frederick Winslow Taylor and his followers, who advocated a highly centralized autocratic style. Taylor's writings (Taylor, 1911) show that he had a very low opinion of the ordinary employee and devised a system which sought to accumulate all competence at higher levels. Managers were expected to give orders and to be obeyed without question. The human relations philosophy, influenced by the work of Elton Mayo and others (Trahair, 1984) revolted against autocracy and viewed employees in more humanistic terms. Employees should be given information about management plans and have opportunities to feel that they participate in a common endeavour. Participation is a way of softening the effect of centralized structures by building cooperative work teams that will not resist managerial initiatives. Participation, in this model, is thought to be an effective way of increasing work motivation and satisfaction. The emphasis is on oiling the wheels and getting decisions accepted, not on producing a better mechanism and improving the quality of DM.

In contrast, the human resources (HRES) model, as described by Miles

The utilization of competence   75

(1965), starts from a different set of assumptions. Employees are seen as having a substantial reservoir of untapped resources which they are eager to make available to the organization. Not being involved in the decision process is then seen as a frustration as well as a loss of potential. The untapped resources include a wide spectrum of experience and skill, including creativity and the ability to work responsibly for the good of the organization, rather than narrowly in the pursuit of self-interest. The basic value underlying this model, is that people at all levels of the hierarchy want to fulfil themselves by realizing their potential through the process of DM.

The research mentioned earlier in fifteen American companies (Heller, 1971) as well as the larger comparative research (Heller and Wilpert, 1981) found extensive evidence to support both the HRES and HREL models. Senior managers consistently judged their competence levels to be substantially higher than that of their immediate subordinates, although our evidence, and their own admission later, showed this perceptual skill gap to be unrealistic and, in practical terms, also unworkable. For instance, the senior level believed that their most experienced subordinate would need twenty-one months to acquire the minimum skills necessary for the senior position. During feed-back discussion it was widely accepted that this would, in most cases, lead to inefficiency and frequently to bankruptcy. Despite their negative judgements on subordinates, they claimed to support a philosophy of participation and in this way demonstrated their adherence to the HREL model.

However, other parts of the same study supported the HRES model. Managers at both levels were asked to rank in order of importance five reasons for using participative DM. The results are shown in table 5.1.

With very few exceptions, managers at both levels and in nearly all countries gave as the most important reason for participation, the improvement of the technical quality of the decision. The two motives attributed to the HREL philosophy: increasing satisfaction and facilitating change were given much lower priority. Increasing satisfaction came third or fourth, and facilitating change came last at both organizational levels in nearly all countries. These results support the HRES model. Further evidence to support the HRES philosophy came through their judgements on the utilization of competence. The 1,600 managers in the 1981 study were asked how much of their current job-relevant experience and skill they were unable to use in their organization. The average under-utilization of their competence was about 20 per cent at both levels (Heller and Wilpert, 1981, p. 117). This figure varied significantly in the eight industrial sectors covered by the study, reaching 27 per cent in public transport (p. 118). More importantly, high under-utilization reached 52 per cent among the most qualified senior managers and nearly 62 per cent

76 *Frank Heller*

Table 5.1. *Reasons for using participation rank orders of senior and subordinate levels in eight countries*

	Countries								
	US	GB	NL	D	F	S	IS	E	All
Level 1									
To increase satisfaction	2	3	2	3	4	3	3	3	3
To improve technical quality of decision	1	1	1	1	3	1	1	1	1
To train subordinates	4	4	5	4	2	4	4	4	4
To improve communications	3	2	3	2	1	2	2	2	2
To facilitate change	5	5	4	5	5	5	5	5	5
Level 2									
To increase satisfaction	3	3	3	3	4	3	4	3	3
To improve technical quality of decision	1	1	2	1	2	1	1	1	1
To train subordinates	4	4	4	4	3	5	3	4	4
To improve communications	2	2	1	2	1	2	2	2	2
To facilitate change	5	5	5	5	5	4	5	5	5

Notes: US = USA, GB = Britain, NL = Netherlands, D = Germany, F = France, S = Sweden, IS = Israel, E = Spain, All = average of eight countries.

among those under forty years of age (p. 121). There was clearly a very substantial loss of perceived competence in the 129 companies of our sample. Similar results come from O'Brien (1986, p. 26) who describes an extensive study of Australian employees who reported under-utilization varying from 29 per cent to 45 per cent.

Managers at both organizational levels answered some questions eliciting values and others describing specific decision behaviour. The inconsistency of their answers applied to values as well as to behaviour description. These inconsistencies could explain why participative practices are often contrived and inauthentic.

LONGITUDINAL RESEARCH

Most studies of decision-making, leadership, and participation are cross-sectional. This makes it impossible to come to any firm conclusions about cause and effect. Is skill utilization an antecedent to IPS or a consequence, or does it play a role in both directions? A four-year longitudinal research in three countries tried to address itself to this issue and concentrated on tracing the decision process over time with 217 specific tactical and strategic issues (Heller *et al.*, 1988). Some aspects of this study are described in the chapter by Drenth and Koopman.

We made the assumption that all strategic and tactical decisions can be traced through a cycle of events from start-up through development and finalization to implementation. During this progress, various people exert

The utilization of competence   77

influence as long as they have access to the DM process. What we have called IPS (influence and power sharing) can be assessed on a continuum with six positions from no or minimal information being given to potential participants, via opportunity to give advice and joint decision-making, to delegation or complete control. We assessed the antecedent conditions to the IPS process and its consequences. Skill utilization was one of five postulated consequences of the IPS–DM process. The others were satisfaction, efficiency, achievement, and duration of the cycle.[2]

The results support a model in which skill utilization is an outcome of IPS. In particular, it could be shown that the utilization of experience and skill was significantly predicted by the way influence was distributed between senior management and lower levels of the organization. When top management exercised a very high degree of influence and prevented the participation of lower levels and reduced the influence of the works council, then the existing reservoir of experience in the organization was under-utilized (see Heller *et al.*, 1988, figure VII.2, p. 220 for a summary of results). The ethnographic material based on being present during committee meetings and individual discussions with staff at all levels, supported the statistical analysis. In the twelve month cycle of budget forecasting, for instance, senior management relied extensively on quanti-fied predictions by chiefs of division, but failed to solicit inputs from lower levels that were more closely in touch with the customer. Substantial error in forecasting could be traced to this non-participative process (Heller *et al.*, 1988, pp. 165–78).

The failure to obtain lower level inputs into budget forecasts is further evidence to support the contention that the HREL philosophy is alive and well and the inconsistency in attitudes and behaviour is as noticeable today as it was four decades ago.

The HREL model lends itself to manipulation because it is content with creating a 'feeling of participation' rather than the reality. Many writers have observed this; Etzioni (1969) calls it inauthentic participation, Pateman (1970) talks of pseudo participation, which she describes as creating an impression of involvement when in reality no influence is shared. 'It is used to persuade employees to accept decisions that have already been made by management' (Pateman, 1970, p. 68). Hopwood (1976, p. 77) describes situations where managers induce a 'feeling of participation in situations which provide little freedom'; Heller (1971, pp. 97–9) came to the conclusion that 'participatory techniques were frequently used manipulatively' and in particular when managers described their behaviour as 'prior consultation', it frequently turned out that it would have been more accurate to call it 'post facto' participation.

Pseudo or manipulative participation would make no sense to people who genuinely espoused the HRES way of thinking, because involving people without using their experience and skills, would not contribute to the main objective, which is to achieve superior overall results based on the use of all available resources.

What makes people adopt two very different and inconsistent ways of thinking? Is it possible that the contrast between these models is too great, that there are other factors not accounted for and that the complexity of the situation is substantially greater than the models suggest? Is it possible that the human relations model takes too gloomy a view of human nature while the human resources model portrays an unrealistic ideal?

What follows is a tentative attempt to reassess the evidence we have reviewed and to suggest the need for amendments to the human resources model (HRES).

THE COMPETENCE MODEL

The strength of the HRES model is its stress on the under-utilization of available skills, but its weakness is in the assumption that most people have a very extensive portfolio of experiences and abilities, including creativity and an understanding of the substantial complexities of modern organizations. This idealistic assumption which underpins the HRES model is not supported by sufficient evidence. There are occasions when this competence is present, but there are at least as many when it is not. The literature on participation is replete with idealistic values showing, as Strauss noted: 'the earmarks of its academic origin' (Strauss, 1963, pp. 48–9). Mulder (1971) made a similar analysis.

Two recent examples will illustrate the need for an adaptation of the model to bring it closer to reality. They both come from Germany: one from the advanced economy of the Federal Republic in the west, and the other from the technologically less advanced German Democratic Republic, before their merger in 1990. A three-year research in the Federal Republic covered twelve companies using computer-aided production planning and control. The report describes in detail the difficulty trade unions and works' councils have in taking an active and useful part in the decision process of these organizations (Hildebrandt, 1989). Although management gave prompt and extensive information, the author concludes that, due to a lack of relevant competence, 'the works' councils have little to show for their activity, even in plants with a high degree of organization in an area where unions are strong' (p. 194). He also observed that many works' councils were not interested in taking part in technical aspects of decision-making, although they had important consequences for their members. This lack of motivation is underlined by the fact that the unions did not make use of their legal rights

The utilization of competence   79

under the Works Constitution Act, to use the advisory services of experts, even though the cost of such advice would have been borne by management.

The research in East German companies using information technology came to similar conclusions (Meier, 1989). The qualifications of their labour force are said to be high. Only 15 per cent have no formal vocational training and 20 per cent are professionals with diplomas or degrees. Nevertheless, the opportunities for effective participation did not exist. Meier concludes that 'for democratic control of new technologies, two types of knowledge are indispensable: general job competence, including the necessary level of skills, experience and education ... and specialized information on prerequisites, strategy' (p. 201). More generally, Meier claims that, 'without competence based on knowledge which can be used for specific purposes, it seems impossible to turn potential opportunities for participation into real influence' (p. 204).

It should not be thought that this problem is confined to high technology companies. It exists over a wide range of activities but has received inadequate research attention. Mulder's (1971) well-known contribution to the participation literature cites evidence, mainly from Dutch research, that works' council members were not very interested in taking an active part in decision-making unless the subject fell within their personal sphere of interest. He also cites evidence from Yugoslavia, which had the most highly structured and legally supported scheme of self-management, to show that employees without special skills make very little contribution to council discussions and, in general, motivation to contribute, even to problems of very great importance, is low. Mulder's laboratory research supports the hypothesis that, when there are large differences in expert power between people, an increase in participation will increase the difference in power rather than reduce it. Much earlier, in experiments with teachers and students, Asch (1951) had shown that participation did not improve performance when the teacher rather than the students had the required skills. Calvin *et al.* (1957) found from laboratory studies that participative decision-making was successful in increasing productivity with competent students, but unsuccessful when competence was absent.

THE DUAL ROLE OF COMPETENCE

It seems that in analysing the relationship between influence and power sharing (IPS) in the decision-making (DM) process we have to distinguish two distinct roles for competence. In the first place as an antecedent, and in the second place as an outcome (see figure 5.1). As an antecedent to the IPS–DM process, competence is a prerequisite for genuine rather than pseudo participation. Without the relevant experience and skill, people

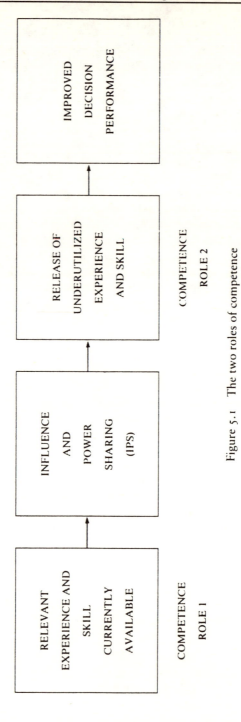

Figure 5.1   The two roles of competence

The utilization of competence   81

are neither motivated nor able to make a contribution to the DM process. However, there are circumstances when pseudo participation succeeds in giving people a feeling of being involved and this can lead to increases in satisfaction.

We do not know how long this induced satisfaction lasts, though there is some evidence that subordinates become aware of the inauthentic nature of IPS and then react against it (Heller, 1971, pp. 98–9).

There is a third position between IPS based on competence and inauthentic participation. This occurs when people take part in committees or other participative arrangements as a way of acquiring experience and skill which would subsequently allow them to switch to IPS based on competence. There is no systematic information about the use of this learning motivated form of participation, but it can play an important part in the total cycle of events (see figure 5.2). Where IPS is used as a learning experience, the subsequently acquired competence (Box 3) like the liberated competence (Box 2) would result in improved decision performance (Box 4). The competence released or created as a result of IPS then becomes the antecedents for further useful IPS. This is illustrated in the feed-back loop of figure 5.2.

We have seen that the limitation of the HRES model is due to its unrealistic assumption about people's experience and abilities. Many research projects have shown that employees are motivated to participate on subjects with which they have direct experience, but are reluctant or unwilling to take part or to assume responsibility over issues that are outside their competence (Mulder, 1971; Hespe and Wall, 1976; IDE, 1981; Drenth and Koopman, 1984). It would follow that, where people are expected or persuaded to be present in discussions on subjects outside their experience, they would take as little active part as possible (Obradovic, 1970) and would show little satisfaction. The important consequence of omitting competence as a necessary precondition for meaningful participation has been to encourage manipulative IPS and to neglect the critical role of training.

The literature on participation has paid almost no attention to the creation of experience and skill as a prerequisite to influence sharing and there are several well-documented examples where this neglect probably played a decisive role in the failure of major attempts by industry to involve inexperienced people in high-level decision-making (Brannen *et al.*, 1976; Batstone *et al.*, 1983). It seems likely that similar problems have occurred at the national level when legislation prescribed an active and important role for workers without giving them the necessary experience and training. The failure of self-management in Yugoslavia could be a consequence of this (Lydall, 1989). On the other hand, there is evidence that, where competence creation was taken seriously, influence sharing

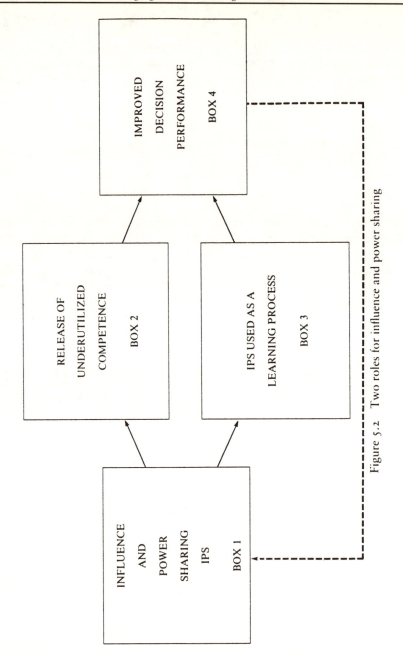

Figure 5.2   Two roles for influence and power sharing

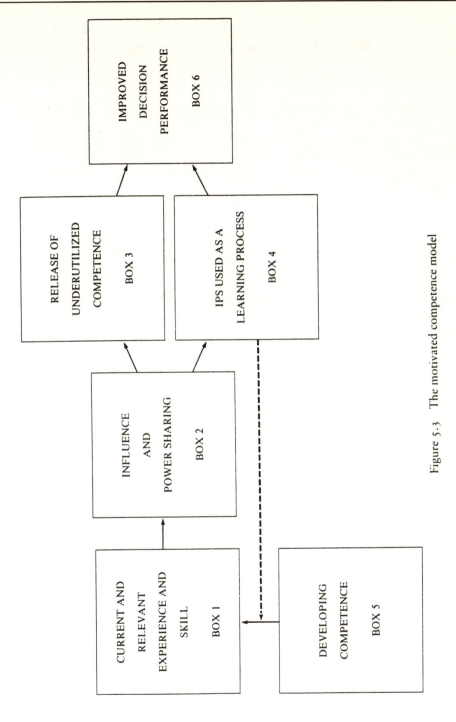

Figure 5.3   The motivated competence model

can be effective and satisfying. This is the lesson of the successful cooperative movement in the Basque country (Aurrezkia, 1986; Bradley and Gelb, 1981; Whyte *et al.*, 1983) and is probably the reason why semi-autonomous group work and its related quality circle movement in Japan has scored some successes (O'Brien, 1986, p. 277; Mohr and Mohr, 1983; Trist, 1981).

I have argued that there is a need to extend and amend the HRES model to include competence creation as well as competence utilization and to distinguish between IPS as a release of experience and skill and as a deliberate learning experience. These conditions are incorporated in the motivated competence model (MCM) (figure 5.3). The term 'motivated' is used on the assumption that merely providing opportunities for being involved in DM without relevant experience and skill is not enough. There is plenty of evidence that, as McCarthy (1989) shows, 'a major problem is that many employees when offered the responsibility of participation, choose not to become involved' (p. 115).

It is, of course, quite likely that, even if all the conditions of the MCM are met, some people will prefer to stay outside the DM process, but I believe that the number who will choose this option will be reduced.

HOW TO ASSESS OUTCOMES

Given the bewildering array of research approaches and ideologies, it is not surprising that global evaluation studies find it difficult to come to clear conclusions (Wagner and Gooding, 1987; Macy *et al.*, 1989). I want to mention three problems that explain the diversity of results. One is the choice of the outcome variable. Productivity and efficiency measures can usually be influenced by changes in a variety of circumstances apart from IPS. The output of a work unit producing soft drinks, for instance, will be decisively determined by changes in demand consequent on variations in weather rather than by participative work design. This may be an extreme case, but the principle holds. Secondly, we have seen that changes in IPS may leave employees unmotivated for a variety of reasons or may increase their job satisfaction without affecting other output measures. Thirdly, very few experiments apart from those described by O'Brien (1986) have taken account of changes in skill utilization which would explain changes in outcome according to the HRES model. Even fewer studies have taken note of the extent to which IPS is preceded by or requires skill development in its execution as demanded by the MCM.

Strauss (1982) realizes the limitations of some of the most widely used outcome measures and implicitly accepts the MCM when he argues that it is hardly surprising 'that the totally untrained workers in Peru and Algeria proved unequal to the demands of worker participation in management'

The utilization of competence   85

(p. 50). Strauss puts forward the view that IPS should be assessed by the effect it has on the wider society outside the factory gate, rather than on the narrow criterion of productivity and worker satisfaction (p. 174). For those who are content only with hard measures of success or failure, such a global approach would cause problems.

One alternative is to confine research to outcome measures that are largely or entirely controlled by IPS decision behaviour. Skill utilization would be an obvious candidate. One could put forward the view analogous with the engineer's concept of machine utilization that – other things being equal – better utilization of human competence should improve the quality of DM and ultimately the effectiveness of the operation. With this in mind, the three-country longitudinal research used two other outcome measures: efficiency (as an input/output measure of the decision process) and achievement (measuring the extent to which expected goals, objectives, and desired outcomes of the DM process were achieved). Efficiency was predicted by skill utilization and achievement by IPS variables (Heller *et al.*, 1988, pp. 149–60. See also the evidence reviewed by O'Brien, 1986, p. 65).

Although a great deal more evidence will have to accumulate, the MCM shown in figure 5.3 is a reasonable representation of the data currently available and the hypothesized relationships derived from the conceptual analysis presented in this chapter.

SUMMARY AND CONCLUSIONS

This chapter is concerned with leadership and decision-making processes and the use of influence and power. Influence and power sharing (IPS) has antecedents and consequences and I have isolated competence (experience and skill) as a major factor in the before and after events of decision-making (DM). It is, however, necessary to distinguish between situations where competence is present and where it is not.

It has been shown that, when people have the appropriate experience and skills, they are often prevented from using them. Excessively centralized, non-participative DM is largely responsible for the resulting wastage of human resources and consequent inferior decisions. This evidence supports the human resources (HRES) model. The previous human relations (HREL) model saw the main function of IPS as increasing job satisfaction and in this way, boosting organizational performance. By omitting competence, the human relations (HREL) model lends itself to manipulative behaviour. It allows, or even encourages, people to have a 'feeling' of being involved in the DM process, when in fact they have little or no influence over events.

We have seen that managerial beliefs oscillate between these two

86   *Frank Heller*

models of thinking; they apply the HRES model to themselves, because in their judgement they have the necessary competence and want to be genuinely involved in the DM process. At the same time, they prefer the ideas of the HREL model for lower levels of the organization because they have great doubts about the competence of their subordinates.

The weakness of the HRES model is that it makes unrealistic assumptions about competence and therefore neglects the need to develop further experience and skill resources. At all levels of organization there are potential or actual limits to the experience and skill currently available. While this has always been true, it has shown up more clearly in recent decades because of the enormous speed of technological change.

Influence and power sharing can be used as one method among many for creating relevant experience and skills, but the people designing and taking part in IPS with this objective have to be aware of what is happening. In many circumstances, more formal methods of training will be necessary to create the competence that would allow genuine IPS and achieve improved decision outcomes.

In this analysis, competence plays two distinct roles. One is as an antecedent to IPS behaviour. As an antecedent one has to make sure that the relevant experience and skill is currently available or is being developed through training. If the antecedent conditions are met, then IPS will draw on these resources of competence and this should enable the quality of decisions and organizational performance to improve. If the antecedent conditions are not fulfilled, IPS will fail to achieve improved performance, even if, at least for a time, job satisfaction may improve.

The dual role of competence requires an extension of the HRES model which I have called the motivated competence model (MCM) illustrated in figure 5.3 above. Some evidence in support of this model has been given, but more research is needed to test its main assumptions.

ACKNOWLEDGEMENTS

The material used in this chapter owes a great deal to the extensive financial support of the Economic and Social Research Council of Britain on two cross-national studies. In addition to the author, Professors Pieter Drenth, Paul Koopman, Veljko Rus and Bernhard Wilpett participated in some aspects of the various research studies.

I am grateful to Professors George Strauss and Raymond Miles for useful critical comments on previous drafts relating to the evidence on under-utilization of competence.

The utilization of competence　　　　　87

NOTES

1 Although the statistics used were based on concurrent correlations which do not allow one to interpret directional effects, the interpretation is based on tape recorded and content-analysed data from Group Feed-back Analysis.
2 For definition of these variables and detailed analysis and statistical results, see Heller *et al.* (1988).

REFERENCES

Allport, Gordon (1945), 'The psychology of participation', *Psychological Review*, 53, 117–32.

Asch, M. J. (1951), 'Non-directive teaching in psychology: an experimental study', *Psychological Monographs*, 65, 4.

Aurrezkia, Lan Kide (1986), *The Mondragon Experiment*, Caja Laboral Popular.

Batstone, E., Ferner, A., and Terry, M. (1983), *Unions on the Board* (Oxford: Blackwell).

Blake, R. and Mouton, J. (1964), *The Managerial Grid* (Houston, Texas: Gulf Publishing Co).

Bradley, K. and Gelb, A. (1981), 'Motivation and control in the Mondragon experiment', *British Journal of Industrial Relations*, 19, 2.

Brannen, P., Batstone, E., Fatchett, D., and White, P. (1976), *The Worker Directors: A Sociology of Participation* (London: Hutchinson).

Calvin, A. D., Hoffman, F. K., and Hardin, E. E. (1957), 'The effect of intelligence and social atmosphere on group problem solving behaviour', *Journal of Social Psychology*, 45, 61–74.

Drenth, Pieter and Koopman, Paul (1984), 'A contingency approach to participative leadership: how good?', in James Hunt, Dian-Marie Hosking, Chester Schjriesheim, and Rosemary Stewart (eds.), *Leaders and Managers: International Perspectives on Managerial Behavior and Leadership* (New York: Pergamon Press).

Etzioni, A. (1969), 'Man and society: the inauthentic condition', *Human Relations*, 22, 325–32.

Haire, M., Ghiselli, E., and Porter, L. (1966), *Managerial Thinking* (New York: Wiley).

Heller, F. A. (1971), *Managerial Decision-Making: A Study of Leadership and Power Sharing among Senior Managers*, (London: Tavistock Publications).

Heller, Frank and Wilpert, Bernhard (1981), *Competence and Power in Managerial Decision Making: A Study of Senior Levels of Organization in Eight Countries* (Chichester: Wiley).

Heller, F. A., Drenth, P., Koopman, Paul, and Rus, Veljko (1988), *Decisions in Organizations: A Longitudinal Study of Routine, Tactical and Strategic Decisions* (London and Beverly Hills: Sage).

Heller, F. A. and Yukl, G. (1969), 'Participation and managerial decision-making as a function of situational variables', *Organizational Behavior and Human Performance*, 4, 227–41. Also in Ervin Williams (ed.), *Participative Management: Concepts, Theory and Implementation* (Georgia State University, 1976).

88   *Frank Heller*

Hespe, G. and Wall, T. (1976), 'The demand for participation among employees', *Human Relations*, 29, 411–28.

Hildebrandt, Eckart (1989), 'From codetermination to comanagement: the dilemma confronting works councils in the introduction of new technologies in the machine building industry', in Cornelis Lammers and Gyorgy Szell (eds.), *International Handbook of Participation in Organizations*, vol. I (Oxford University Press).

Hopwood, Anthony (1976), *Accounting and Human Behaviour* (Englewood Cliffs, New Jersey: Prentice-Hall).

IDE (Industrial Democracy in Europe Research Group) (1981), *Industrial Democracy in Europe* (Oxford University Press).

Likert, R. (1967), *The Human Organization* (New York: McGraw-Hill).

Locke, Edwin and Schweiger, David (1979), 'Participation in decision making: one more look', in Barry Staw (ed.), *Research in Organizational Behavior* (Greenwich, Connecticut: JAI Press).

Lydall, Harold (1989), *Yugoslavia in Crisis* (Oxford: Clarendon Press).

Macy, Barry, Peterson, Mark, and Norton, Larry (1989), 'A test of participation theory in a work re-design field setting: degree of participation and comparison site contrasts', *Human Relations*, 42, 1095–165.

McCarthy, Sharon (1989), 'The dilemma of non-participation', in Cornelis Lammers and Gyorgy Szell (eds.), *International Handbook of Participation in Organizations*, vol. I (Oxford University Press).

Meier, Artur (1989), 'In search of workers' participation: implementation of new technologies in GDR firms', in Cornelis Lammers and Gyorgy Szell (eds.), *International Handbook of Participation in Organizations*, vol. I (Oxford University Press).

Miles, R. E. (1964), 'Conflicting elements in managerial ideologies', *Industrial Relations*, 4 (1), 77–91.

Miles, R. E. (1965), 'Human relations or human resources?', *Harvard Business Review*, 43, 148–63.

Misumi, Jyuji (1985), *The Behavioral Science of Leadership: An Interdisciplinary Japanese Research Program* (Ann Arbor: The University of Michigan Press).

Mohr, William and Mohr, Harriet (1983), *Quality Circles: Changing Images of People at Work* (London: Addison-Wesley).

Mulder, Mauk (1971), 'Power equalization through participation', *Administrative Science Quarterly*, 16, 31–8.

Obradovic, Josip (1970), 'Participation and work attitudes in Yugoslavia', *Industrial Relations*, 9, 161–9.

O'Brien, Gordon (1986), *Psychology of Work and Unemployment* (Chichester: Wiley).

Pateman, Carole (1970), *Participation and Democratic Theory* (Cambridge University Press).

   (1983), 'Some reflections on participation and democratic theory', in Colin Crouch and Frank Heller (eds.), *International Yearbook of Organizational Democracy*, vol. I (Chichester: Wiley).

Pusic, Eugen (1984), 'The political impact of organizational democracy', in Bernhard Wilpert and Arndt Sorge (eds.), *International Yearbook of Organizational Democracy*, vol. II (Chichester: Wiley).

The utilization of competence　　　　　89

Stogdill, R. M. and Coons, A. E. (1957), *Leadership Behavior: Its Description and Measurement* (Columbus: Ohio State University, Bureau of Business Research).

Strauss, George (1963), 'Some notes on power equalization', in H. J. Leavitt (ed.), *The Social Science of Organizations* (Englewood Cliffs, NJ: Prentice-Hall).

Strauss, George (1982), 'Worker participation in management', in *Research in Organizational Behavior*, vol. IV, (JAI Press).

Taylor, F. W. (1911), *The Principles of Scientific Management* (New York: Harper).

Trahair, R. C. S. (1984), *The Humanist Temper: The Life and Work of Elton Mayo* (New Brunswick, NJ: Transaction).

Trist, Eric (1981), 'The evolution of socio-technical systems: a conceptual framework and an action research programme', *Issues in the Quality of Work Life*, No. 2, June, Ontario Ministry of Labour.

Vroom, Victor and Yetton, Philip (1973), *Leadership and Decision-Making* (University of Pittsburgh Press).

Wagner, John A. and Gooding, Richard (1987), 'Effects of societal trends on participation research', *Administrative Science Quarterly*, 32, 241–62.

Warner, Malcolm (1984), 'Organizational democracy: the history of an idea', in Bernhard Wilpert and Arndt Sorge (eds.), *International Yearbook of Organizational Democracy*, vol. II (Chichester: Wiley).

Whyte, William Foote, Hammer, Tove Helland, Meek, Reed Nelson, and Stern, Robert N. (1983), *Worker Participation and Ownership: Cooperative Strategies for Strengthening Local Economies* (Ithaca, NY: ILR Press).

[8]

Participation and Democratic Theory: Reworking the Premises for a Participatory Society*

WILLIAM LAFFERTY
Institute for Social Research, Oslo

Every academic discipline has certain core problems which, by their very nature, seem to define and give structure to research activity. One such problem for political science is the ancient and continuing debate over the nature of democratic theory and praxis. At present, the argument is dominated by two lines of thought, which can be broadly characterized as the 'elitist' and 'participatory' theories of democracy. The major contributions to both sides of the debate are listed in Carole Pateman's recent book, *Participation and Democratic Theory*, and I will use this work as a point of departure for formulating yet another contribution to the problem.[1]

1. Elitist versus Participatory Democracy

Pateman addresses herself critically to the 'theory of democratic elitism' and offers her own recommendations for an alternative model and theory of a 'participatory society.' Her treatment of the elitist theory is based mainly on the works of Schumpeter, Berelson, Sartori, Dahl, and Eckstein. Briefly, this theory can be described as the response of liberal social scientists to two sets of circumstances which developed in the decades immediately preceding and following World War II. First, there was the spread and threat of totalitarian regimes and totalitarian ideas and, second, there was the rather shocking realization that the 'people,' when finally asked in sample surveys, gave no indication of being the type of 'common man' upon which liberal democrats had always assumed that democracy safely rested. With threat from without and disillusionment from within, the group of theorists in question set about making both theory and practice safe for democracy or, if you will, to protect democracy from the double dangers of Utopian cynicism and subversion from below.

The result was a 'realistic' rewriting of the 'classical' theory of democracy to

---

* This article is based on the work of Ernest Becker, whose death in March of 1974 represents a major loss for social science and humanism in general. This piece, and all subsequent work in his spirit, is dedicated to his memory.

comply with the liberalist standards of the cold-war era. The major planks of
this new democratic platform were as follows:

(1) The masses of democratic citizens are in fact anything but democratic,
showing instead strong latent tendencies toward authoritarianism, which occasionally break out in active support of the likes of a Hitler, a Mussolini, or a
Joe McCarthy.

(2) The spirit of democracy, and the source of the values and inspiration necessary to sustain it, do not rest, therefore, with the common man but rather with
popular elites, who, for one reason or another, have proved their ability to rule
in the name of the people.

(3) The mandate thus rendered is, and *should* be, endorsed in a mutual process
whereby elites formulate alternative courses of action for periodic approval or
disapproval by an informed electorate. Voting between a pluralism of interest
options is the citizen's major function, and the carrying out of these options in a
'responsible' manner is the elite's (representative's) major duty.

(4) Participation beyond voting is not really necessary for the average man as
long as access to elite positions is open to all, so that those who *will* get more
deeply involved in politics have the opportunity. Furthermore, most citizen interests are doubly taken care of through interest groups which manage to exert
influence on the decision-making process between public elections. This provides
the desirable situation of a maximum of interest 'output' with a minimum of
citizen 'input'.

(5) These various aspects of an updated theory of democracy serve to preserve
one of the most vital features of the democratic system, i.e., its *stability*. History
has shown – for example in Athens, the Weimar Republic, and, more recently,
on university campuses – that excessive participation is often the forerunner of
chaos. In an age of demagogues and irrational needs, a viable democracy requires as many institutional safeguards as possible.

(6) Even if one does not accept any of the above arguments, it should be clear
to all that advanced techno-industrial societies simply cannot *afford* excessive
levels of participation if they are to function with a reasonable amount of
efficiency. The sufferings inflicted upon the populace through a breakdown in
the decision-making processes of these systems would be much more severe than
any benefits gained by increased participation. Besides, there is a large body of
evidence which shows that the majority of people in industrial societies don't
like to participate anyway; that they would rather devote their time to family
and recreation. In short, images of the Greek polis and the New England town
meeting are both undesirable and unrealistic for modern industrial democracies.

These points by no means cover all of the subtleties or ramifications of the
'contemporary' theory of democracy (Pateman's term), but they serve to give
the general drift of the argument.[2] Pateman's answer to these views does not
take the form of a direct refutation, but is rather based on an attempt to formulate a stronger argument *for* a participatory society.

She starts off by showing that the so-called 'classical' theory of democracy against which the contemporary theorists rail, is, in fact, a myth. She shows first, that few of the elitist theorists actually specify to whom they are referring when they use the term 'classical' theory, and, second, that the theories they do attack are actually straw men having little to do with those theories which *might* reasonably be associated with the notion of genuine participatory democracy. Going to the classical theorists themselves, Pateman shows that, Schumpeter at any rate – and she sees him as the tone setter – has totally missed the fact that there are not one but at least *two* theories implicit in their works and, further, that Schumpeter's attack hits *neither* of them.[3]

The theories of the elder Mill, Bentham, and Locke did call for universal participation, but only as a limited 'protective function' of other, *more important,* institutional arrangements. There was nothing 'unrealistic' to attack in these ideas, since they were, after all, quite similar to the emphasis on *representative* democracy that the contemporary theorists themselves have arrived at. Other classical theorists, such as the younger Mill and Rousseau, *did* put forth notions of a truly participatory society, but these are notions that the contemporary theorists are either unaware of or systematically not interested in. It is from these theorists, along with G. D. H. Cole, that Pateman derives the key ideas for her own theory of a participatory society.

Her point of departure is Rousseau's ideal participatory system as stated in the *Social Contract.* In highly capsulized form, the internal logic of this system states that if all participate in such a manner as to impose only those conditions on each other which they would want imposed upon themselves, they will then have operationalized a 'general will' which serves both individual and group well-being. By submitting his personal interests to those of the group, and assuming that other members do likewise on an equal basis, the individual participant contributes to an increase of freedom for all, since each is then free from encroachments by the others at the same time that each member's control is increased *through* the greater efficiency of group cooperation. It is from this general argument that Pateman derives the first major proposition of her scheme, which she summarizes as the idea that there is an interrelationship between the authority structures of institutions and the psychological qualities and attitudes of individuals, and . . . 'that the major function of participation is an educative one'.[4]

The second major proposition is taken from G. D. H. Cole, who, for Pateman, is the participatory theorist most relevant for modern industrial society. Cole extends many of Rousseau's ideas to the highly differentiated labor structure resulting from industrialization, stressing the notion of a 'complex of associations held together by the wills of their members'. These associations arise in relation to the *functions* which each carries out, and it is a form of functional representation which Cole stresses as the core of democracy in the modern era. This system of functional representation implies 'the constant participation of the ordinary man in the conduct of those parts of the structure of society with which he is directly concerned, and which he has therefore the best chance of understanding'.[5]

Cole thus makes explicit an idea which was originally put forth by John Stuart Mill, i.e., that the 'democratic principle' both can and should be applied to

55

spheres of social action other than those considered strictly 'political'. It is in areas such as the industrial workplace that basic questions of superiority and sub-ordination are crucial, and they should therefore be considered as optimal settings for the educative effects of participation. Furthermore, since economic in-equality lies at the basis of political inequality, the only way to attain conditions of equal participation in the political system is by demanding equal participation in the functional-economic system.

Pateman sums up her two major propositions as follows:

> The existence of representative institutions at national level is not sufficient for democracy; for maximum participation by all the people at that level socialization, or 'social training', for democracy must take place in other spheres in order that the necessary individual attitudes and psychological qualities can be developed. This development takes place through the process of participation itself. The major function of participation in the theory of participatory democracy is therefore an educative one, educative in the very widest sense, including both the psychological aspect and the gaining of practice in democratic skills and procedures.
>
> The second aspect of the theory of participatory democracy is that spheres such as industry should be seen as political systems in their own right, offering areas of participation additional to the national level. If individuals are to exercise the maximum amount of control over their own lives and environment then authority structures in these areas must be so organized that they can participate in decision making. A further reason for the central place of industry in the theory relates to the substantive measure of economic equality required to give the individual the independ-ence and security necessary for (equal) participation; the democratizing of industrial authority structures, abolishing the permanent distinction be-tween 'manangers' and 'men' would mean a large step toward meeting this condition.[6]

These two ideas, which Pateman calls the *educative function of participation* and the *crucial role of industry,* are to be regarded as hypotheses upon which the theory of participatory democracy 'stands or falls'. The remainder of Pateman's book is devoted to secondary analyses of the literature in search of support for these two major ideas. Briefly, she finds considerable evidence for the posited relationship between increased participation and increased feelings of political efficiency and personal well-being. The idea that industrial participation *per se* is an effective means of political education is more difficult to establish, how-ever, since, as she points out, there are so few cases where full participation has been effectively implemented on both higher and lower levels of decision making. Those cases which do exist, however, such as the system of industrial democracy in Yugoslavia, seem to point in the proper direction and, in general, she feels that 'the evidence shows no obvious, serious impediments to economic efficiency that would call into question the whole idea of industrial democracy'.[7]

Pateman's plea for a participatory society is thus based on the two related ideas: (1) that participation in decision making is *per se* good and necessary for both individuals and society, and (2) that industrial participation is an especially fruitful area for educating responsible and critical citizens. In the following section, I want to look briefly at Pateman's premises for these hypotheses and then go on to the development of a complementary approach.

2. Power and Participation

The core of Pateman's argument seems to be a tautological proposition, derived from Rousseau, to the effect that a good system of participatory democracy is dependent on a certain type of participatory personality, and that this type of personality is best developed within a properly functioning participatory system. On the input side of this tautology is the premise as to *equality* in decision-making power, and on the output side is the production of more politically effective individuals who then go on to spread the demands of greater participation to other subsystems of the total system. One need not be a supporter of 'contemporary' democratic theory to see the problem inherent in this formulation. If equality in power is necessary for meaningful participation and if, further, it is obvious to all that equality of power does not exist in any of the present-day democracies, is it not also obvious that Pateman's propositions *are* hopelessly Utopian?

Well, yes and no. Yes, in that Pateman herself stresses the prescriptive nature of her ideas *in the face of* the lack of power equality; no, in that her plea for the expansion of 'the political' to cover industrial and other nonelectoral structures is meant as a definite technique for the *correction* of the unequal distribution of power. Pateman, like Bachrach, stresses the goal of a participatory society as *both* end and means.[8] Both authors refuse to allow their theorizing to be unduly affected by 'what is', because they are convinced that the more depressing aspects of current democratic practices – citizen apathy, ritualism, and political alienation – are largely a result of structures and legitimations arising from a combination of social injustice and contemporary democratic theory itself. The goal is, therefore, to attack social injustice and the unequal distribution of power *through* participation.

This perspective gives rise to its own set of problems, however. First, if the conditions of Rousseau's system are not present in contemporary democracies, how are we to argue for participation without in reality arguing for power? Why, that is, must participation *per se* take precedence over interest-group tactics? Second, if it is really the act of participation itself which is so essential, just what *are* the characteristics of this act which make participation work in the direction posited by Pateman? What is the psychological nature of the 'educative effect' and how does it actually work?

In what follows, I will try to answer both of these questions by building up an argument for participation along lines quite different from Pateman's approach.

57

Instead of relying on premises at the level of the social system – such as equality of power – I will try to build up a case based on a normative model of individual needs. It is a model which reduces the question of need to a simple requirement for organismic action and then shows how this requirement must be met by the sociocultural system if the notion of 'human' is to be maximally preserved and engendered. I believe that it is a model which not only makes certain forms of participation mandatory for personal growth, but which, through its own dynamic, also serves to bring forth to both group and individual consciousness the bases of power underlying group interaction. It is thus a model for both political participation and political consciousness, with the latter being offered here as both the major result of Pateman's educative effect and the major reason, in and of itself, for maximizing participation in democratic systems.

3. Action and Meaning

The model to be proposed is derived from Ernest Becker's 'full field theory of alienation.'[9] Becker's project has been to construct a theory of alienation and social injustice based on the idea of what it is to be human. Drawing on material from philosophy, psychology, psychiatry, sociology, anthropology, and history, he builds up an integrated and logically consistent 'theory of the nature of the social bond' which, by its scope of synthesis alone, poses a unique challenge to the current state of specialized social science. His goal is nothing less than the attempt 'to show the dependence of private troubles on social issues', and he avoids no discipline or theorist who seems to shed light on the task. The result is a perspective on the human condition which is so rich, variegated, and complex that it is impossible to apply more than certain relevant key aspects to any one problem. The following presentation is, therefore, mainly my own synthesis of Becker in relation to the problem of participation and by no means does justice to the full scope of his ideas.[10]

Organismic Action

As an initial simplification, it can be said that Becker's scheme builds upon six basic elements: *action, objects, anxiety, self-esteem, symbols, and meaning.* All organisms have *to act.* They must move forward through their environments under their own biological impetus or they are not organisms. For an organism to be hindered in its mode of action is to die, to cease being. But action alone is not enough to define life. Organisms must act within specific environments which contain the minimum of *objects* necessary for the progression of an epigenetic growth cycle. Organisms thus have specific modes of 'reactivity' which determine the range of objects with which they can successfully 'interact', and these object-action ranges make up the experiential field of the organism. Within the unlimited potential range of objects there will always exist for each organism some objects which sustain and promote growth and some which stunt and hinder growth.

Interactions with objects of the former type can be said to be accompanied by a general warm feeling of the 'rightness' of organismic development, while interactions with objects of the latter type can be said to be accompanied by feelings of danger and impending nonbeing. The organismic experience of the first feeling can be called *self-esteem,* while the experience of the second feeling can be called *anxiety.*

Everything said up to this point applies equally well to both animals and humans; everything, that is, except the application of the term *self*-esteem to the warm feeling of successful, forward-moving action. Without quibbling over semantics, it can be said that it is the existence of a *linguistic self-system* which truly differentiates man from the higher primates. Due to the combination of a prolonged state of infant dependency and the evolution of a large brain, the human infant is the only neonate which cognitively objectifies its own body *before* it knows what to do with it. For a period of several years, the human child is totally dependent on some form of 'mothering' if it is to survive. This unique situation of instinct proverty means that the human organism develops a realm of experience and a mode of object reactivity that is premised on the contingent *symbols* (including gestures) accompanying parental socialization. The requisite element of self-esteem is thus not determined solely by the organism but rather by a type of bargaining process between organism and mothering object, in which the organism gradually *learns* what reaction is necessary to maintain a warm feeling of development. It is the unique combination of objects-as-action-possibilities, symbols, and shades of anxiety vs. self-esteem which constitutes the *meaning* of the human organism's realm of experience.

Meaning is thus seen as an overarching category which describes the integration between object, symbol, action-potential, and emotion. An object has meaning for an individual when a behavioral response can be called forth which facilitates action in relation to the object. Without this behavioral response and its accompanying symbol, the organism will tend not 'to see' the object in its perceptual field, i.e., it will be a 'meaningless' object for which the organism has neither action-potential nor emotion. Symbols thus serve to differentiate the environment for the actor, calling forth some objects for attention, action, and emotion, and relegating other objects to an epistemologically neutral background.

A further function of symbols is to enable the individual to generalize single-object responses to a wider range of phenomena so that the organism can continue to move forward through the environment with a maximum amount of safety, prediction, and self-esteem. Since initial or single-object responses are always learned in a unique setting composed of object-quality, specific symbol, and emotional set (anxiety/self-esteem), each individual's world of meaning is peculiarly unique and, as we shall see, peculiarly binding. (This does not mean, of course, that classes of individuals cannot share broadly similar meaning characteristics.) The learning of meaning can be either constricting or liberating, depending on how object-responses and symbols are acquired by the organism and depending on how they are linked together in increasingly more complex structures of consciousness.

59

Organismic Funding

It is in relation to the quality of meaning acquisition that Becker's normative position receives its most specific formulation. As the organism encounters objects, attains symbols, and registers responses and feelings, it gradually becomes a 'funded reservoir of meanings'. The world is gradually built into the organism so that at any given time there is a fund of symbol-action-feeling potential which describes the organism's state of tension and readiness to move forward. This readiness varies from individual to individual, depending mainly on the developmental balance between two broad types of experience: 'doing' and 'undergoing'. These phases describe respectively the active-testing and passive-integrating aspects of organism-object interaction. In the doing phase, the organism stretches itself out toward the object, probing, penetrating, exercising its powers in an attempt to clarify the difference between 'me' and 'it'. In the undergoing phase, the organism reverts back upon itself, assessing the effect of the world on its own characteristics and consolidating experience into new structures for future action.

The normative basis for human action can thus be related to a 'better' or 'poorer' developmental process of organismic funding. The positive side of the evaluative continuum goes in the direction of a proper, ongoing balance between doing and undergoing, while the negative side develops in relation to an over-emphasis *in the one or the other* mode of experience. A 'richly funded' organism is one which has grown through a balanced process of outgoing, experimental action and incoming, integrating reflection. The testing out of self-powers on objects renders a deep sense of organismic competence at the same time that the periods of passive integration allow for the consolidation of a complex structure of stored, functional symbols. The organism moves forward with a growing repertoire of action-symbol possibilities and an increasingly complex understanding of the totalistic setting of its personal well-being. A strong sense of identity and a warm feeling of self-regard become the individual's most vital resources in a world for which he is otherwise instinctively barren.

On the negative side of development, we find excesses in either doing or undergoing. If the organism acts too easily in relation to its environment, if it doesn't get the chance to test out its powers in difficult but surmountable confrontations, there will then arise a situation where action possibilities are numerous and widespread in relation to a large number of objects, but where the symbol repertoire is extremely narrow and invested with a poverty of feeling. Unless organismic action is periodically confronted by the limits of self-powers, there will be no need to 'fall back and regroup', no phases of undergoing, and no variation in the symbol-action structure. All actions will be imbued with the constricting symbolical-emotional content which happens to accompany the peculiar ends of the **primary socializing agent**. Becker associates this particular form of deficient funding with such mental problems as psychosis and depression.

The other negative extreme in organismic development is the situation where the organism is systematically hindered in action; where the exercise of self-powers is either constantly frustrated or not allowed at all; and where the self is forced to withdraw more and more into a saving world of internal symbols. Instead of getting overly easy action with poor feed-back for funding, the organism which undergoes too much gets practically *no* self-initiated-and-carried-out action and does not, therefore, build up a differentiated sense of organismic powers. At the worst extreme, this can lead to a total severance of the symbolic from the organismic (as in infant autism), but at best it implies a mode of passive resignation and powerlessness; a retreat to the internal world of fantasy and symbolic 'action'. In general, Becker associates this type of excessive undergoing with the difficult and controversial syndrome of schizophrenia.

In sum, an excess of doing tends to empty experience of its content while an excess of undergoing tends to undermine power. The desirable is a balance between the two whereby the organism achieves 'both a richness of experience and a flexibility in action'.[11]

Abstraction and Intervention

The idea of organismic funding also presents interesting and relevant perspectives on the individual's ability to abstract from, and intervene in, social processes. 'To abstract', for Becker, is 'to refer an object to one's own intended use'. Such intentions always arise from, and are connected back to, initial object-organism interactions. We saw above that these interactions, or 'fundings', are always characterized by three elements: (1) the dyad of object qualities and organismic powers, i.e., the 'object-as-action possibility', (2) organismic feeling along the anxiety/self-esteem continuum, and (3) the symbol (or cognitive structure) by which the organism stores the above two aspects for future action. We saw further that all initial interactions are unique in regard to the countless combinations of characteristics which can emerge from the contingent fusion of these three elements. This means that when the organism begins to group initial interactions in broader classes for the facilitation of action, these broader classes will be affected by the quality of the initial funding. In other words, *distortions in the balance of organismic funding become permeated by class-specific peculiarities in the mode of object response*. The ability to abstract and theorize are thus *in general* either constricted or enhanced in line with the quality and balance of organismic funding.

It is from this perspective that Becker speaks of 'behavioral stupidity' and relates the problems of neurosis and alienation to deficiencies in *cognition*. If my ability to abstract is hampered as a result of constrictions in organismic funding, it is clear that the entire world of objects falls under the peculiar rules of my own self-esteem maintenance. This means, in turn, that my ability *to intervene* in the world for my own well-being is systematically distorted so as to work back *against* me, instead of *for* me. The individual that is poorly funded lacks the ability to act boldly and integrate broadly within an ever-increasing scope of meaning. An excess of doing results in a shallow and poorly integrated symbolic structure, such that abstractions do not render an adequate sense of extended

61

causality. The 'overdoer' is blindly unaware of the ramifications of his actions, both for his own basic well-being, as well as for that of others. An excess of undergoing, on the other hand, produces abstractions that are not solidly based in reaction potential, such that the notion of causality is at best diffuse and at worst totally misconceived. Intervention for the undergoer is usually such a frightening and nonsuccessful experience that the regress to symbolic 'action' becomes the major mode of self-esteem maintenance.

Individual and Community

A final relevant perspective from Becker's work is that on the relationship between the individual and the community. The key to understanding this relationship is the vital principle of *symbolic self-esteem maintenance.* Man needs a mothering-one as both a primary object for self definition and as an intermediator between other objects and self. Full humanization takes place only when the infant has replaced physical interaction with the mothering-one with symbolic interaction. The organism is propelled forward by the need to avoid anxiety and attain a positive feeling of self-regard, and its object world becomes infused with the symbol-feeling tonus necessary to this end. The mothering-one uses biological dependence to gradually entice the organism into a mode of behavior which is in line with the mothering-one's own needs and desires, and which can be manipulated at a distance through symbols. In the first instance, therefore, the individual's relation to the community is established as a set of parental rules for the attainment of self-esteem through organismic action.

It is not long, however, before the organism is forced to perform and bargain in a wider context of symbolic demands. The various agencies of secondary socialization take over as the child is gradually brought into contact with an increasingly complex set of rules for self-esteem maintenance. Already at this stage it is possible to judge the quality of primary funding in relation to secondary demands, but the process remains an ongoing and emergent one with the potential for countless combinations of either change or reinforcement. This process of secondary socialization continues until death, at which point the final act itself is incorporated in a set of rules which may or may not aid the bereaved in their own continuing self-esteem projects. The death of a hero in charging an enemy 'pillbox' is, after all, received in a manner considerably different from a self-incurred death from a box of pills.

The example is fitting for the whole problem since, as Becker points out in a brilliant analogy, it is the business of being a 'hero' which seems to be at the very core of human motivation. Whether as seen from the perspective of the infant doing its utmost to please mom and dad, or from the perspective of the child trying to succeed in school, or of the worker struggling to advance on the job: all are *at least* characterized by one and the same motive, i.e., *the need to be an object of primary value in a world of meaningful action.* The languages of primary and secondary socialization are thus nothing more – nor *less* – than the equipment and ground rules for the game of heroism.

The analogy between human striving and heroism is extremely important because it directs attention to the fact that man's highest aspirations and lowliest defeats are all part of a fictive cultural plot. Culture-systems are hero-systems which provide the symbolic roles and statuses necessary for the transcendence of human instinctual deficiencies. The culture-system thus corresponds on the societal level to the linguistic self-system on the individual level. Both are integrated sets of meaning which provide the action-symbol-feeling combinations necessary to keep both biography and history moving forward. Both call out for attention and action specific objects which become invested with specific symbol-feeling characteristics in the pursuit of specific forms of heroism. Not only are they similar systems, however, but, more importantly, they are *integrated* systems. Personal languages of self-esteem maintenance are a reflection of parental self-esteem needs, which in turn are a reflection of societal self-esteem demands. Individual plots for heroism invariably become channelled into distinct structure-role patterns, which in general take on the character of rigid typecasting.

It is the rigidity of hero-systems and the extremely poor distribution of true heroic roles that calls for a clear understanding of the relationship between individual and community. In the first place, the cultural plot will lack *conviction* if each player does not do his best to sustain the fiction. Without conviction, the symbolic animal has no true basis for action, no touchstone of 'reality', and no *reason* to keep moving forward. Whether they are conscious of it or not, therefore, all individuals 'participate' in maintaining *some* form of hero-system.

Secondly, the rigidities of specific modes of organismic funding can be loosened up only through new and different funding experiences. The quasi automatic determinism which we associate with the idea of 'the unconscious' is in reality the constricting set of rules for interaction with objects which was laid down in the interests of both organismic and parental self-esteem. The rules, and their object-action-emotion referents, are 'unconscious' because the organism had no real say-so in the humanization contract. Due to the functional integration of society (in the service of specific self-esteem interests), these unconscious rules are usually reinforced in the course of organismic development such that personality and culture dovetail in the service of common themes. *The only way to unravel rules from objects, therefore, is to press for a reactivization of the funding process through current action in contemporary settings.* Man must either act as an adult on the objects and rules that determine him; or die as a child. To turn one's efforts toward the community meaning system and its rules of maintenance is thus to confront both the limits and potentiality of personal identity. To highlight the nature of this confrontation, Becker offers a provocative formula for testing out the funding characteristics of any given situation. He suggests two simple but penetrating questions: (1) Why do I not feel that I have the *right* to my own meanings? and (2) Why do I not have the *strength* to sustain that right?[12]

Finally, a third aspect of the individual-community relationship is the problem of ultimate meaning and ultimate transcendence. If all hero-systems are characterized by relativity and an unequal role allocation, the vital question arises as to whether or not a hero-system can be devised which offers *both* conviction and equal opportunities for heroism. Becker's answer is that, if such a system is to be attained, it will have to be characterized by a *maximization of individuality within a maximization of community*. This implies that a maximization of organismic growth requires a maximization of action possibilities within a rich and diversified cultural scheme.

Such a possibility is, as Becker points out, actually a paradox, since individual freedom cannot be expanded without, initially at least, threatening community solidarity. This is not seen as a problem, however, since an ideal *should* be paradoxical if it is to stimulate the imagination in a critical direction and serve as a yardstick on progress. The core idea of Becker's principle here is that the individual requires a rich meaning system to grow and that the attainment of this system is a community project. When carried to its logical limit within Becker's framework, it can be seen that this project is ultimately one of total cooperation within a nonmanipulative communication system, since anything less implies that some individuals are stunting the growth of others, *as well as their own growth,* by hindering a maximum of action-object-symbol development. It is necessary to stress the fact that the individual's basic well-being is dependent on the role *others* play in the joint heroic epic, not only because of the need for conviction mentioned above, but more importantly because it is only through a total knowledge of 'the other' that the individual can know the depths and limits of his own action-symbol possibilities.

Such knowledge is necessary, since to be properly funded from a transcendental perspective is to possess a symbol system which incorporates *all* objects in a framework of self-enhancing action readiness. Given the fact that the most unpredictable of these objects is man himself, the individual's funding in this regard can never be complete, due to the realization that man is, as Sartre puts it, the creature who in essence can always say 'no'. 'No', that is, to being defined as an object in another's self-esteem project. Once the core of freedom is established as the right to a self-defined identity, the ethical basis will be laid for nonsadistic communication within a common emancipatory project. The good society from Becker's point of view is thus a society characterized by a democratization of man's *only* essential need: the need to name and claim the material world as a stage for heroic transcendence. The categorical imperative for such a society is not only 'do unto others as you would have others do unto you,' but also 'fund others as you yourself *must* be funded to attain full humanity'.

4. Action and Participation

It now remains to spell out some of the implications of Becker's ideas for the problem of participation and democracy.

Each individual life project can be seen as being carried out within a variety of action settings. These settings vary widely in their degrees of institutionalization, i.e., in the degree to which action is structured in terms of articulated, sanctioned, and shared role specifications. From the point of view of organismic funding, these role specifications provide the individual with: (a) a set of *symbols* (rights, duties, rules) in relation to (b) a set of *objects* (things, people, tasks) which, when taken in combination, provide (c) a certain *status* (prestige, self-esteem). Each action setting is thus a re-enactment of the basic funding process whereby the individual strives to maintain and enhance self-esteem by taking symbolic cues from his environment for the facilitation of forward-moving action. If we follow the emphasis of Pateman, Bachrach, and others on *decision making* as the focal point of participation, we can then say that we are interested here in decisions relevant to the above three role elements. Who decides which symbols will characterize the action-object-status characteristics of a given action setting?

A major advantage of Becker's approach is that it enables us to discuss the general characteristics of an action setting in relation to funding characteristics, at the same time that the 'demands' of these characteristics direct attention to the most essential decision-making areas. It is also possible to talk about different *types* of decision making, since it is now clear that action settings are composed of several interrelated elements, *any one of which* is open to manipulation and change. Management can, for example, restructure a job setting by altering spheres of duty, by taking away or supplementing objects, by changing status hierarchies, or by denying access to the action setting altogether. By focusing attention on these possibilities through the model of organismic growth, it should be possible to sensitize actors to their overall self-esteem needs and to guide their participatory efforts toward those decisions which have the most direct funding consequences. *The model of participation in funding settings is thus both an explanatory tool and an exhortation to critical consciousness.* As such, it provides at least one set of answers to the questions raised above in relation to Pateman's approach.

(1) *Why are people happy when they participate?*

Pateman cites a large number of studies showing that in nearly every instance where participation is increased there is a rise in feelings of self-esteem and well-being. Quoting from Blumberg's comprehensive survey of experiments in industrial democracy, she says that 'there is hardly a study in the entire literature which fails to demonstrate that satisfaction in work is enhanced or that other generally acknowledged beneficial consequences accrue from a genuine increase in workers' decision-making power'.[13] These results are, of course, one of the major supports for her argument, but she is nonetheless somewhat surprised since, as she points out, most of the participatory schemes thus far employed are actually cases of pseudo or, at best, partial participation.[14] She concludes that even the semblance of participation seems to have positive psychological effects, but she does so rather nervously, since she seems to realize that this might be interpreted as proof for the argument that token democracy is actually sufficient.

The model of organismic funding here provides a clearer perspective on the matter, especially since Pateman never really spells out exactly what the 'psychological effect' of greater participation consists of. From what was presented above, it is possible to view each action setting as providing opportunities for either balanced or imbalanced organismic growth. By definition, an individual will be most happy in a balanced setting which allows for the development of self-powers freely in relation to a wide and varying scope of objects. The cognitive-symbolic structure developed in this type of setting should be of such an expansive nature as to constantly bring the individual into direct contact with whatever it is that seems, at a given moment, to be hindering further action integrations. It is at these points of decision making that, theoretically, the demand for participation both should and will arise spontaneously. Well-being in general derives from the feeling that the individual is himself creating a meaningful existence by associating new symbols and emotions with the exercise of self-powers in difficult but challenging situations, and that the feeling of mastery is growing in both space and time.

The opportunity for such balanced organismic funding is, at present, mainly an idealistic goal rather than a common event. Most action settings are characterized by one or the other form of imbalance, and the problem for participation is to correct the balance in the direction of better funding opportunities. Still, the ideal type provides an understanding for why, *under certain conditions,* only token participation can result in greater personal satisfaction. Since most action settings are extremely out of balance – marriage and wage labor, for example – the slightest change can have enormous significance in allowing the individual to alter either actions or symbols in a more self-fulfilling direction. Providing it is not too late, that is; providing, in other words, that the individual has not already cut off his sense of action or sense of meaning in the face of overwhelming self-esteem demands. In such cases, token participation along *any* dimension will in all probability be neither registered nor exploited.

(2) *What happens when people do not participate?*

The inability of people to take advantage of preferred participation possibilities is one of the clearest results of a lack of *true* participation. For the vast majority of citizens in industrialized, democratic polities, political participation has long since taken on the function of ritualized mass 'undergoing'. Sporadic electoral participation in the political system and nonparticipation and manipulation in the industrial system have left the average citizen basically unfunded in relation to both the means of power and the means of production. Politics has become, in Murray Edelman's term, 'symbolic action', with the average citizen discussing more and more and doing less and less. Political apathy is not, therefore, part of an understandably weak human nature in the age of affluence, but rather part of a weak history of organismic developement in the age of passivization. In pursuing the rewards of materialist, alienated hero-systems, modern political man has sold his birthright to his own self-determined identity and retreated to the world of periodic political circuses. Instead of confronting his object world in his own name – and *naming process* – he has accepted the mediating definitions of 'representatives' and entrusted his 'interests' to corporate political poker.

In short, people who do not participate in the action settings which determine their identities and self-esteem are bound to become alienated from both their societies and themselves. In general, the major problem at present seems to be in the direction of excessive undergoing, where the individual is strongly limited in objects-as-action-possibilities. How meaningful can a world really be, in terms of a wide range of potential actions and symbols, when the major part of one's daily action is devoted to monotonous interaction with a single mechanical object? The beauty of Becker's scheme, however, is that it is not limited to the classical case of industrial alienation, but applies to any action setting where one or the other element of the funding process is deficient. We might be led to believe, for example – as both Pateman and Bachrach apparently do – that the powerful in society are *really* the 'participators' who, because of their control over their own life situations, are in positions with maximum self-esteem potential.

Becker's demand for organismic balance warns against such a mistake. Power and the freedom of action over outcome may give the impression of well-being which we associate with decision-making in The Achieving Society, but if the underlying mode of funding is a result of excessive doing, there is little cause to envy the narrow and fragile meaning base upon which the psychological structure rests. The loss of only *half* a fortune has frequently been enough to send the over-achieving hero plummeting from a tenth-story window to the utter bafflement of the 'man in the street'. It is extremely important, therefore, to be clear over the 'how' of participation, as well as the 'where' and 'what', so as to avoid the rather common dialectic of moving from one mode of funding imbalance to another.

(3) *What actually is the educative effect?'*

A more specific answer is required for this question, since Pateman's educative effect is apparently derived from a rather simplistic learning theory, which implies that participation *per se* leads to greater participation and a better political awareness, much in the same way as the learning of physics makes better handymen of us all. Well maybe it does and maybe it doesn't, *depending on the qualitative nature of the participatory learning going on*. Increases in participation can be structured as increases in doing, increases in undergoing, or increases in balanced organismic development. Action settings can be structured so that actors: (a) do more within the same narrow symbol-feeling framework, (b) do the same or less within an artificially expanded symbol-feeling framework, or (c) increase coincidentally *both* action-object possibilities and the richness and scope of symbol-feeling structures. Only the latter qualifies as true participation from the perspective of organismic growth, and only the latter will have the ultimate positive effects on the community as a whole.

If the educative effect is to have any substance at all, it must be an effect which changes the individual in the direction of a deeper understanding of the forces determining his personal well-being and life chances. If action settings, such as the workplace, bias funding in one or the other directions of imbalance, the individual will lack qualities of both initiative and abstraction so that it is virtually impossible for him to know where he should intervene in the system of causality which surrounds and oppresses him. He is 'behaviorally stupid', in that he lacks the symbols and actions necessary for self-enhancing change. Political consciousness can only be developed through an awareness of funding limitations and funding needs as these are tested out, threatened, and enhanced in concrete action settings.

The core of the educative effect is, therefore, not that participation in one setting leads to participation in another setting, but rather that *true* participation in one setting is the catalyst for understanding the relationship *between* settings. By insisting on an expanding scope of meaning (object-action-symbol-feeling possibilities) to micro levels, the individual gradually extends his range of understanding to include those macro processes which form the context of his various institutionalized projects. This enables him to comprehend 'distant' political decisions in terms of his own growth needs, at the same time that he is able to initiate actions in the direction of self-enhancing structural change. Participation in terms of balanced organismic funding thus becomes a program for uniting theory and praxis in the service of a transcendental life project.

5. The Languages of Action

Summing up, it is possible to demonstrate the relevance of Becker's ideas for a social-psychology of participation in terms of four 'languages' of action. Each language refers to the set of symbols, rules, or gestures which guide individual action by means of anxiety/self-esteem overtones through the object worlds of various behaviour settings.

(1) *The language of primary socialization,* by which the organism receives its original funding and develops a basic personality mode in the course of being humanized. The relationship between rules, objects, and emotions acquired here serves as a fundamental perceptual and behavioral structure through which subsequent funding experiences must be filtered for testing, reinforcement, and change.

(2) *The language of secondary socialization,* by which the individual gradually, but with increasing intensity, enters into the arena of the cultural hero-system. The self-esteem demands of institutional roles take over the guiding function of the facilitation of action and make their own, more general, contribution to the developing fund of meaning.

(3) *The language of situational motivation,* which in any contemporary action setting provides demands on the languages of primary and secondary socialization at the same time that it offers the potential of new funding experiences. The motivation of current action settings is always one of tension between 'unconscious' rule-following in the service of previous self-esteem demands and the primary need of transcendent organismic growth.

(4) *The language of transcendent growth,* which is the language of Becker's

ethical position interwoven with his empirically based synthetic model. It is a language constructed from the idea of what it is to be human for the sake of measuring deviations from *man's* potential. It is both a guideline for comparing existing hero-systems and a program for ultimate heroism. Its key premise is the existence of only a single basic human need: the need to integrate space and time in ever-widening cognitive structures for the facilitation of emancipatory action.

These four languages are not separate phenomena, but integrated aspects of human development in specific historical and socio-economic settings. Every individual life cycle begins in relation to mothering-ones who have themselves been affected by the dynamics of the other four languages. Ultimately, therefore, the individual's desire and capacity for participation in society are dependent upon extremely complex patterns of motivational themes in relation to social objects and groups. Each individual will judge his participation chances and needs in terms of a personal knowledge of 'social reality', which is a result of both a structural position (i.e., a conglomerate of interlocking institutional roles) and a personal biography. Such a situation demands a theory of participation which views isolated personal preferences skeptically; structural consistencies critically; and human striving ethically. Becker's perspective forces us to acknowledge that the relationship between participation and democracy is not one which can be established by fiat from classical theorists nor built up empirically from 'present reality'. It is a relationship which must be constantly redefined in terms of emerging social reality and rewon in the face of recurrent social reification.

NOTES

1. Carole Pateman, *Participation and Democratic Theory* (Cambridge: The University Press. 1970). For a useful short summary of the debate with a good bibliography see Herbert McClosky, 'Political Participation', in the *International Encyclopedia of the Social Sciences* (New York: The Macmillan Co. and Free Press, 1968), Vol. 12, pp. 252–265.

2. Numerous contributions have already been made to both sides of the issue since the appearance of Pateman's book. Among the most relevant for the present discussion are Robert Dahl, *After the Revolution? Authority in a Good Society* (New Haven and London: Yale University Press, 1970); Daniel C. Kramer. *Participatory Democracy; Developing Ideals of the Political Left* (Cambridge, Mass.: Schenkman Co., 1972); Campbell Balfour, *Participation in Industry* (London: The Free Press, revised edition, 1971); and John Plamenatz, *Democracy and Illusion: An Examination of Certain Aspects of Modern Democratic Theory* (London: Longmanns, 1973).

3. Cf., J. A. Schumpeter, *Capitalism. Socialism and Democracy* (London: George Allen & Unwin, 1943).

4. Pateman, p. 27.

5. *Ibid.*, p. 37.

6. *Ibid.*, pp. 42–43.

7. *Ibid.*, p. 108.

8. P. Bachrach, *The Theory of Democratic Elitism: A Critique* (Boston: Little, Brown & Co., 1967).

9. Ernest Becker, *The Birth and Death of Meaning* (New York: The Free Press, Revised edition, 1971); *The Revolution in Psychiatry: The New Understanding of Man* (New York: The Free Press, 1964); and *The Structure of Evil: An Essay on the Unification of the Science of Man* (New York: George Braziller, 1968).

10. A short summary of many of Becker's major ideas is to be found in his article 'Mills'

Social Psychology and the Great Historical Convergence on the Problem of Alienation,' in Irving Louis Horowitz (ed.), *The New Sociology* (New York: Oxford University Press, 1964), pp. 108–133.

11. Becker, *The Revolution in Psychiatry*, p. 42.
12. Becker, *The Structure of Evil*, p. 258.
13. Pateman, p. 66.
14. Pateman's differentiation between 'pseudo', 'partial', and 'full' participation is a vital one, and one that is often overlooked in the participation debate. Here too, however, the lack of a more specific social-psychology leaves a number of questions unresolved. See Pateman, pp. 67–72.

[9]

Participation Behavior and Personal Growth

Bernhard Wilpert

PROBLEM CONTEXT

Participation, as a concept and as a practice, has been a long and hotly contested notion. Less than 20 years ago an eminent German social critic deemed it synonymous with "the new name of the future" (Dirks, 1969). At around the same time a Dutch organizational scientist called participation the most vital organization problem of our time and expressed his astonishment at the fact that so little and theoretically so meager research had been conducted on the issue (Mulder, 1971). And after 35 years of statutorily regulated participation (co-determination) in German enterprises, a well-known industrialist flatly claims: "Co-determination was an error" (Mohn, *Die Zeit*, 4 April 1986).

Undoubtedly, such contradictions are partly due to differences in a priori value orientations. But in part they seem to be due to the wide gamut of semantic connotations of the very term "participation" itself. For some participation denotes nothing more than personal involvement, such as when economists speak of "labor market participation." For others it means the personal, usually informal, opportunity to influence directly the immediate environment of one's living and working conditions; for still others it refers to the statutorily regulated rights of employees or their elected representatives to information access, to develop their own initiatives, and to influence or co-determine decision outcomes in social, personnel, organizational, and economic matters of their work organization. The latter understanding of the term participation also includes the representation of employees in management or governing boards of their companies.

Finally, for still others, participation means the representation of workers' interests in economic, social, and infrastructural domains on a level above individual plants or companies.

Whatever one's value position and whatever one's definitional preference, the social–scientific discussion of participation will always find itself in a force field of contradictory intentions, political aspirations, and terminological conceptions. While a growing number of recent empirical studies have begun to close the research gap lamented by Mulder, the deficit in the underpinning of participation research with psychological theorizing continues. This is particularly surprising in view of the tradition of conjecturing about participation and its consequences which should long ago have given the concept of participation a special place in psychological theory. For instance:

- In following the work of Meissner (1971) and Hacker (1976), Ulich (1978) sees activities of individual or collective self-regulation in work as playing a significant role in processes of cognitive and social learning. This view appears to be intimately linked to implicit notions about human nature which provide the requisite criteria to evaluate what must and can be considered conducive for personal growth (Dachler and Wilpert, 1978, 1980).
- Managers and organization researchers frequently consider participation as an appropriate social technology to enhance group cohesion and employee commitment and satisfaction in the interest of increased productivity and organizational goal achievement. The implicit value orientation here seems to be effectiveness and efficiency.
- Finally, the consequences of participation for society as a whole are indicated by Pateman (1970, p. 42) thus: "The existence of representative institutions at national level is not sufficient for democracy, ... for democracy must take place in other spheres in order that the necessary individual attitudes and psychological qualities can be developed. This development takes place through the process of participation itself." Participation is seen in this case as an educational means for democratizing society, as an educational process counteracting hetero-determination.

The context, then, in which the social scientific discourse on participation takes place is characterized, on the one hand, by a high degree of contentiousness in terms of social policies and its intrinsic value-ladenness. On the other hand, we note far-reaching psychologically impaired assumptions about the consequences of participation on the individual, organizational, and societal level.

DEFINING PARTICIPATION

Before going into the possible psychological bases of participation, let us, for the purposes of this chapter, attempt a definition through the use of a mapping sentence:

Participation is
the totality of *forms*
i.e. direct (immediate, personal) or indirect (via representatives or institutional
  means)
and *intensities*
ranging from negligible to comprehensive
through which *individuals, groups, collectives*
ensure their *interests*
through self-determined *choices* of possible *actions*.

The distinction of direct and indirect forms of participation follows the seminal paper of Lammers (1967). It is particularly important, because both forms can be assumed to have differential social and psychological consequences of as yet largely unknown characteristics. The pursuit of interest implies that with reference to participation we speak of goal-oriented actions and not of any incidentally occurring behavior or interaction. The point of goal directedness is further strengthened by the notion of chosen actions, the actors being individuals or social entities. Finally, the gradation of intensities through which actors aim to safeguard their interests corresponds to the general experience that actors are able to control the outcome of their actions only to a varying extent.

The function of participation in its most general sense, then, is to realign decisions and their outcome to the interests and needs of those who are affected (cf. Kirsch, Scholl, and Paul, 1984). In the subsequent parts of this chapter we try to show that a person's self-determined choices, in choosing from action alternatives that control his/her environment, are fundamental for personal growth and self-realization. A psychological theory of participation, however, will have to take into account the interaction of individual prerequisites and the situational factors impacting on the consequences of participation.

TOWARDS A PSYCHOLOGICAL THEORY OF PARTICIPATION

Let us first pursue the question regarding the individual psychodynamic principles that appear to contribute to the emergence of participatory behavior and its assumed consequences.

G. W. Allport may be considered a forerunner in psychological theorizing on participation (1945). Starting with a reflection on the preoccupation of American psychology with motor activities and respective research findings, he points out "that people have to be active in order to learn, . . . to build voluntary control" (p. 121). He continues by making a distinction between mere *activity* as such and "true, personal *participation*." Accordingly, the critical characteristic of participation would be ego-involvement which is fed by a "dynamic factor": the individual's desire for prestige, self-respect, autonomy, or self-regard. This ego-involvement in various life-spheres expresses itself through the individual's active participation in influencing these spheres and is for Allport a necessary condition for personal self-realization and democratic development of society as a whole: *"unless [a person] is in some areas ego-engaged and participant his life is crippled and his existence a blemish on democracy"* (Allport's emphasis), and: *"unless we try deliberately and persistently to affect our destinies at certain points . . . we are not democratic personalities, we have not balance as wholeness, and society undergoes proportionate stultification"* (Allport 1945, p. 127). By his passionate concern with the democratic condition of society Allport's position may strike the reader today as more programmatic than analytic, but he heralds already at that early date all the themes to be developed later on.

A more comprehensive attempt to establish participation as an essential constitutive element of individual and social development was made by Becker (1968, 1971) and Lafferty (1975, 1979). With reference to John Dewey's normative behaviorism Becker develops a philosophical–anthropological position which ascribes an overriding importance to social action domains when one considers the development or obstruction of an individual's acquisition ("funding") of competences. Learning and "organismic growth" take place in the context of these social action domains. Personal well-being, individual action potential, and meaningfulness of human existence are necessarily linked to participation in designing social systems. Participation is an existential necessity. Lafferty (1979, p. 10) attempts to transform Becker's approach into a social–psychological theory of "normative–symbolic interaction":

Participation is a basic human well-being. It is basic because not to participate in the decisions which affect my funding possibilities is to give up that which is *most* essential to expand my control over object–action–symbol possibilities. To not participate in decisions which symbolically control the emotional value (status, legality, worth, etc.) of my action world is quite simply, to choose a lesser degree of humanism (actually a form of organismic sickness) for both myself and my community.

Becker's and Lafferty's theorizing remains very much at a philosophical, speculative level. Not so Robert W. White (1959) in his important reanalysis and reintegration of hitherto developed motivation theories. In a critical analysis of the motivation theories of Freud and Hull and their followers, he demonstrates that instinct and drive concepts are insufficient to explain such phenomena as exploratory behavior, playful manipulation, attention, environmental mastery. The more comprehensive and more appropriate explanatory concept is for White a universal need for competence, its motivational component being "affectance." Affectance motives emerge from all effective interactions of an organism with its environment. Such interactions mediate the positively valued feeling of efficacy. In passing, it may be pointed out that this approach overcomes the traditional reluctance of psychologists to study the interaction of the individual and his/her environment, the interaction with the world of things (Graumann, 1974, 1979).

White's reflections were to have consequences that are of immediate importance for our context. Referring to White it was Deci (1975) who postulated that intrinsically motivated behavior is generated from an innate, ever-present need for competent and self-determined interaction with the environment. It is this very need which makes people look for environmental challenges, which correspond to their competences, in order to master them. It appears that Deci's concept of competent action might usefully be complemented by a distinction made by Bandura (1977): the expectancy or conviction that one can successfully carry out the problem-solving action (self-efficacy), as against the expectancy that a certain behavior will lead to certain consequences (outcome expectancy). A similarly useful distinction is offered by Staw (1982) between the link of a person's expectations regarding the *control of outcomes* (similar to efficacy) and the accuracy of *predicting outcomes* (e.g. rewards in a tightly controlled organization). The different expectations are assumed to lead to different behavior. From here to Deci's more recent theorizing about a psychology of self-determination (Deci, 1980; Deci and Ryan, 1985) is but a short distance. "Control" theory is an individual's experience of having the possibility to choose among different action options, that is, the experience of internal causation (locus of causality). The concept of "locus of causality" or "personal causation" (Heider, 1958; DeCharms, 1968) is not identical with Rotter's notion of "locus of control" (1966). The central issue for Rotter is whether events are perceived to be contingent results of one's own behavior. For Deci the question is what is perceived to be the source of initiating or regulating behavior.

As a preliminary answer to our initial question regarding the psychodynamic principles underlying participatory behavior we may now formulate, with reference to White and Deci, that it is a general motivational disposition to self-determined (self-chosen) and competent (effective) action. In order to be able to describe and explain participation in real life settings it is necessary to expand this proposition with various additional theoretical notions.

SOME ELABORATIONS

The first elaboration concerns the consequences of frustrating the self-determination need. Similar to White and Deci, Brehm (1966, p. 9) assumes for his reactance theory that it is crucial for individuals to experience themselves as sole directors of their behavior. In cases where an individual experiences his/her freedom of action (choice of options) as threatened or lost, reactance will develop, that is, "a state of motivation which activates a person to do everything possible to maintain or regain the threatened or lost freedom of action" (Keller, 1981, p. 365). Subjective salience of the threatened freedom of action seems to be an important moderator variable for the ensuing reactance. The reactance theory has been linked by Wortmann and Brehm (1975) to Seligman's (1975) concept of learned helplessness. Both approaches were integrated in a model in which expectancies regarding control possibilities/loss and the degree of helplessness training represent the critical parameters. In other words, it seems possible to understand both reactance and helplessness as specific consequences of frustrated self-determination and competent interaction (Sauer and Müller, 1980) with one's environment in Deci's sense.

A second elaboration of the basic theory of participation concerns the subjective salience of intended events, which constitutes an important element in the integrated model of reactance and learned helplessness, although not, however, in Deci's theory of self-determination. Wortmann's and Brehm's models share here the well-known weakness of all process-oriented motivation theories, which usually indicate only inadequately the conditions under which subjective salience develops. Without being able to offer a perfect solution to the problem we would like to suggest that a psychology of property (as yet to be developed) might possibly offer at least partial answers. The idea may be surprising. However, we can go back almost a century to draw on an argument developed by William James (1890): property objects, whether material or immaterial ones (e.g. ideas), are essential for the development of the self. Continuous utilization and familiarization with objects leads to an integration of these objects into the individual self-concept because of the "law of mental association of contiguity." The process is further advanced by social valuation processes (cf. Beaglehole, 1932, p. 298). Furby (1978), in her studies of the ontogenesis of property feelings and the ensuing behavior of young children, has identified object control as an additional characteristic: in all groups of children studied the control of objects was consistently found to be the most important element of property sentiments (cf. Stanjek, 1980). In short, the experience of property of an object results from spatio-temporal contiguities and constitutes a context (in the gestalt psychological sense) between individual and object which manifests itself in effective object control (without necessarily being identical with legal property titles: Wilpert, 1983; Thie, 1985). Hence the hypothesis: Subjective salience is a corollary of psychological property titles. They legitimate action in terms of object control and induce reaction in cases where control is threatened.

THE SOCIAL DIMENSION

So far we have only discussed intraindividual dynamics of participation behavior. Mulder (1977) has developed one of the few social–psychological theories of participation as an exercise of power in hierarchical structures. The basic assumption in his "power-distance-reduction-theory" is that the mere exercise of power (defined as determination of other's behavior) is intrinsically satisfying, and therefore individuals strive to expand their power. Up to this point Mulder's approach is easily reconcilable with Deci's notions. But Mulder attempts to show empirically that people in hierarchical relations always strive to reduce the power distance to the next more powerful level while people on that level strive to maintain the power distance to the next lower level. From the intrinsically hedonistic aspects of power it follows that *power is addictive*. On the other hand, if the power distance between two actors increases too much, the striving for power distance reduction decreases due to cost–benefit considerations, and low-power individuals may become apathetic. The hopelessly powerless have, at best, only the chance to develop solidarity with other powerless individuals and/or revert to obstruction.

Mulder's theory presents an organization-centered perspective in spite of its individual psychological premises. His reflections on the individual consequences of exercising power come more as a sketchy afterthought than an important part of his theory (1977, p. 87). These reflections relate to learning processes of an individual, which he describes in terms of a circle: exercise of power → power distance reduction → acquisition of relevant abilities → exercise of power. This notion could easily be related to Dewey's pragmatism and its elaboration by Allport and Becker described above, which would show its significance for the relationship between exercising power (a term which for purposes of this chapter we have used as a synonym for participation) and individual development.

Social psychology has so far also failed to provide a better understanding of the psychodynamic characteristics of representative, indirect participation. This is so much the more deplorable because in our industrialized societies this form of participation is of critical importance. The types of problems which a theory of representative participation would have to tackle are, for instance,

- what are the conditions and criteria for effective interest representation (ratio of representatives: clientele, terms of office, communication structures, etc.)?
- which conditions ensure/obstruct systems loyalty, create identifiction/alienation among constituencies/clienteles?
- what are the individual preconditions for and consequences of being a representative?

From a strictly theoretical perspective we may conclude from what has been said so far that a psychological theory of participation can be considered to provide an important contribution to the understanding of individual and social action in physical and social contexts. Deci's theory of self-determination might serve as a useful beginning, if expanded and complemented by certain concepts of control expectancies, attribution theoretical concepts, aspects of psychological property theory, and social psychology of power and representative relations.

The following concluding section points to some of the most relevant research evidence and the more important lacunae of our knowledge about the connection between participation and personal development.

ACTUAL RESEARCH EVIDENCE AND RESEARCH GAPS

From the point of view of *personality psychology* we may go back once more to Deci's cognitive evaluative theory of self-determination and ask how personal characteristics influence a person's participation behavior. Corresponding to given dominant causality orientations (internal, external, impersonal), Deci (1980) developed a typology of personalities. His typology shows a certain parallelism to Rotter's (1966) internal–external control orientations, which have also frequently been described in the literature as relatively stable personality dimensions (Hohner, 1984). The intriguing question for the present context is whether and how a given personality type moderates the relationship between the energetic principle for participation (need for competent self-determination) and demonstrated participation behavior. Hoff (1982a, 1982b) and Hohner (1984) have warned against a conception of a person–environment relationship that is too rigid and monodeterministic and have expanded the control concept in the direction of a more interactive and variable (in terms of different situations and life cyclical positions) conceptualization. Deci (1980) and Deci and Ryan (1985) have also maintained that their personality classification should not be taken too categorically but rather be seen as basic and dominant (relatively enduring) orientations. They present, however, a large variety of evidence showing that participatory self-determining activities covary with the characteristics of different basic orientations.

The other aspect of the central psychological question regarding participation concerns its consequences. More precisely, from the point of view of *developmental and educational psychology*, what is the relationship between life-span socialization and the experience with participation on the one hand and a desire for participation and the acquisition of participatory competence on the other? Deci (1980) assumes that personality development in terms of establishing dominant causality orientations is largely accomplished by the age of 12. The question raised here is whether it is possible for people to acquire participatory competence beyond that age.

Research on socialization through work suggests that this is indeed possible (Baitsch and Frei, 1980; Hoff, Lappe, and Lempert, 1985). Mulder's (1977) circular model of participatory learning also assumes such learning processes. A more elaborate model, which is quite compatible with Mulder's, was developed by Kissler (1978, 1980). It is characterized by a double helix of interconnected learning processes resulting in professional autonomy. The first helix presents the interaction between biography (career) and participation. It results in participation learning which leads to professional autonomy as the first helix mixes with the second one composed of the combination of factual knowledge with participatory competence (cf. Kissler, 1980).

It is unfortunate that both Mulder and Kissler remain rather formalistic or processual; virtually nothing is said about the content and nature of acquired competences. One of the few longitudinal studies among workers gives the first hints about the resulting competence characteristics (Baitsch, 1985): increase in professional competence and abilities to articulate and enforce one's preferences, more balanced and realistic self-concept, and higher levels of differentiation and integration of cognitive structures.

Greif and his collaborators (Greif and Falrup, 1981) go one step further in their attempt to teach participatory competences to work counselors and employee representatives through role play and simulation of real-life settings where worker representatives negotiate with management. Using an action theoretical framework they try to elicit the cognitive representations that worker representatives have formed through their own experiences. Feedback and discussion are expected to increase the adequacy of these representations in the interest of improving the efficacy of participation of worker representatives. Systematic and comprehensive evaluations of the effectiveness of these training programs have, however, not yet been published.

Mulder's and Kissler's models of participatory learning suggest that we are faced with spiraling effect between the experience with participation and the aspiration level for participation. We could show in our own research that such a dynamic seems indeed to prevail (Wilpert and Rayley, 1983): personal participation in organizational decision-making processes correlates with the desire for further increased participation ($r = 0.35$). Similar results were obtained in other national studies (Gardell, 1977; Koopman-Iwema, 1977).

The most convincing demonstration of the universal occurrence of the dynamic interplay between participation and heightened participatory aspiration levels is found in the results of the hitherto largest international comparative study on participation conducted in twelve countries by the Industrial Democracy in Europe International Research Team (IDE, 1981). Based on research in 134 matching companies and on close to 9,000 respondents, the correlations between actual participation and desired participation ranged from $r = 0.40$ to $r = 0.74$. Gardell (1983) has pointed out that the experience of direct personal participation not only increases the desire for more personal participation but also the desire of employees that their representatives become more involved in more complex organizational decisions which affect the work organization as a whole. Participation and participatory aspiration levels apparently are linked to each other in a dynamic relationship which can be explained by existing theoretical notions. We are dealing here with cognitive and conative consequences of participation that have as yet to be systematically integrated into theories of adult socialization and development.

In a similar· vein we might consider the often postulated and studied relationship between participation and evaluative cognitions such as satisfaction. Although research shows that there usually exists a positive relationship between the two aspects (Wall and Lischeron 1977), the relationship is usually not strikingly strong. Evidently other factors must be taken into account which moderate their connection.

One of the—at first sight surprising—results of the IDE-study was connected with the satisfaction of employees from different countries with their respective national normative and institutional systems of participation. It was hypothesized that the existing freedom of participatory action for representatives would be positively related to employee satisfaction with the given system. This was in fact found to be unequivocally true only for Yugoslav workers. However, what correlated positively with system satisfaction was the degree of *legally* possible action for representatives, even when that freedom was de facto not necessarily used (IDE, 1981, pp. 260ff.). In other words, satisfaction with a given representative (legal/normative) system is not so much connected with the de facto intensity of representative participation but with the degree representatives *could* legally participate! With reference to Deci's cognitive evaluative theory of self-determination, we might hypothesize: In countries with relatively far-reaching participatory norms (e.g. Yugoslavia, Federal Republic of Germany) employees perceive a relatively wide range of action options for their representatives, which, in itself, is positively valued. In countries with relatively restricted action options for representatives these options are perceived as limited and, in themselves, valued less positively even if the de facto level of representative participation matches that in the former countries.

Since participation in work organizations always takes place within given (national) normative frameworks the example shows that in considering participation and its individual consequences (here, cognitive-evaluative ones) one must be aware of this system's imbeddedness, a postulate that is rarely realized in current theorizing about personal development. Dachler (1986) has recently drawn attention to this need for a more systemic consideration of participation by vehemently criticizing the individualistic myopia of traditional participation research and by pointing out that decision processes in organizations are in the first place processes of social construction of reality. Recent approaches in conceptualizing and describing the development of cognitive interpretive patterns in participatory processes may serve as starting points to get a grip on this problem (Staehle and Osterloh, 1985). These considerations already lead from the narrower focus of individual cognitive-evaluative consequences of participation and enter more consciously the often neglected field of the psychology of industrial relations. The by now classical participation study of Koch and French (1948) attempted to prove the conflict-minimizing function of participation. Research evidence today points to a somewhat different direction: that is, the relationship seems again to be more complex: conflicts tend to increase with higher levels of participation and increasing power balance among hierarchical levels (DIO, 1979; IDE, 1981; Heller, Drenth, Koopman, and Rus, 1987). In particular, the higher the influence of employee representatives, the greater the level of conflict in decision-making processes. A partial explanation of these findings could be found in drawing on reactance theory as an integral element of a psychological theory of participation: high levels of participation imply a widened range of options to act which is experienced as a threat to given managerial propositions and, thus, induces reactance which shows in increased conflictuality. This should not be surprising in view of the fact that the main function of participation can be seen in the alignment of decisions to the interests and needs of those affected. Participation is, therefore, always connected with the articulation of possibly contradictory preferences. And it is possibly here that we can identify one of the most critical participatory competences for efficacious participation: the ability to articulate interests and needs in negotiations. Hence, the often-voiced fear of increased conflictuality as a social consequence of participation dwindles to the question of how one is to evaluate such conflicts: as uneconomical, costly disturbances, or as catalysts in the mobilization of resources for solutions to problems and the development of commitment among the partners in conflict to a found consensus.

At this point we must widen our scope to the domain of yet another psychological subdiscipline. A psychology of participation becomes in its widest sense part of political psychology (Allport, 1945, Krampen, 1986), which deals, theoretically and practically, with the equally important problem of the psychological conditions and consequences of acting largely through anonymous mass organizations (parties, unions, churches, social movements). They are, almost by definition, organizations where the principle of interest articulation through representatives is usually the only viable means of interest articulation. The construct of party identification (Streiffeler, 1975) as a mechanism for reduction of complexity, or the notion of trust in experts or of eclectic participation in only a few social spheres (Allport, 1945), are, after all, tantamount to an abrogation of the concept of personal causality. This is where we enter a realm where ground is still to be broken by systematic psychological research and theorizing in order to show under what conditions participation can be an effective means of control for widening or maintaining options for goal-oriented action.

Participation, as a form of self-generated goal-oriented effective action upon one's social and physical environment, may thus be conceived of as a crucial link to personal growth and self-realization. This conception rests on the consequences of participation for an individual's learning and his/her acquisition of ever-increasing participatory competencies through the process of participation itself, competencies that consist of the capability to formulate and realize self-set goals. Personal growth and self-realization, in that sense, are understood as the acquisition of broadened options for choice as a widened and increased differentation of a person's life and action space.

REFERENCES

Allport, G. W. 1945. The psychology of participation. *Psychological Review*, 52: 117–132.

Baitsch, Chr. 1985. *Kompetenzentwicklung und partizipative Arbeitsgestaltung* Vol. 162. Bern/Frankfurt/New York: Europaische Hochschulschriften: Reihe 6, Psychologie.

Baitsch, Chr., and Frei, F. 1980. *Qualifizierung in der Arbeitstätigkeit.* Bern/ Stuttgart/Vienna: Hans Huber.

Bandura, A. 1977. Self-efficacy: Toward a unifying theory of behavioral change. *Psychological Review*, 84: 191–215.

Beaglehole, E. 1932. *Property: A Study in Social Psychology.* New York: McMillan.

Becker, E. 1968. *The Structure of Evil.* New York: George Braziller.

Becker, E. 1971. *The Birth and Death of Meaning.* New York: Free Press.

Brehm, J. W. A. 1966. *Theory of Psychological Reactance.* New York/London: Academic Press.

Dachler, H. P. 1986. Toward a systemic perspective of participation and industrial democracy. *21st International Congress of Applied Psychology, Jerusalem, July 1986.*

Dachler, H. P., and Wilpert, B. 1978. Conceptual dimensions and boundaries of participation in organizations: A critical evaluation. *Administrative Science Quarterly*, 23: 1–39.

Dachler, H. P., and Wilpert, B. 1980. Dimensionen der Partizipation: Zu einem organisationswissenshaftlichen Analyserahmen. In W. Grunwald and H.-G. Lilge (Eds.), *Partizipative Führung*. Bern: Paul Haupt, pp. 80–98.

DeCharms, R. C. 1968. *Personal Causation.* New York: Academic Press.

Deci, E. L. 1975. *Intrinsic Motivation.* New York/London: Plenum Press.

Deci, E. L. 1980. *The Psychology of Self-Determination.* New York: Lexington.

Deci, E. L., and Ryan, R. M. 1985. *Intrinsic Motivation and Self-Determination in Human Behavior.* New York/London: Plenum Press.

DIO. 1979. [Decisions in Organizations—Research Group.] Participative decision making: A comparative study. *Industrial Relations*, 18: 295–309.

Dirks, W. 1969. Der neue Name der Zukunft ist Mitbestimmung. *Gewerkschaftliche Monatshefte*, 20: 385–389.

Furby, L. 1978. Possessions: Toward a theory of their meaning and function throughout the life cycle. In P. B. Baltes (Ed.), *Life Span Development and Behavior*. Vol. 1. New York/London: Academic Press.

Gardell, B. 1977. Autonomy and participation at work. *Human Relations*, 30: 515–533.

Gardell, B. 1983. Worker participation and autonomy: A multi-level approach to democracy at the work place. In C. Crouch and F. A. Heller (Eds.), *International Yearbook of Organizational Democracy*, Vol. 1. Chichester: John Wiley, pp. 353–387.

Graumann, C. F. 1974. Psychology and the world of things. *Journal of Phenomenological Psychology*, 4: 389–404.

Graumann, C. F. 1979. Die Scheu des Psychologen vor der Interaktion. Ein Schisma und seine Geschichte. *Zeitschrift für Sozialpsychologie*, 10: 284–304.

Greif, S., and Flarup, J. 1981. Training social competences for workers councils. *Economic and Industrial Democracy*, 2(3): 395–398.

Hacker, W. 1976. Zu Wechselbeziehungen zwischen Arbeitsbedingungen und der Persönlichkeitsentwicklung. *Pädagogik, Beiheft*, 1(31): 28–34.

Heider, F. 1958. *The Psychology of Interpersonal Relations*. New York: Wiley.

Heller, F. A., Drenth, P. J. D., Koopman, P., and Rus, V. 1987. *Decisions in Organizations: A Three Country Longitudinal Study*. London: Sage.

Hoff, E. H. 1982a. Formen des Kontrollbewusstseins. In S. Peiser (Ed.), *Kognitive und emotionale Aspekte politischen Engagements: Fortschritte der politischen Psychologie*, Vol. 2. Weinheim: Beltz.

Hoff, E. H. 1982b. Kontrollbewusstsein: Grundvorstellungen zur eigenen Person und Umwelt. *Kölner Zeitschrift für Soziologie und Sozialpsychologie*, 34: 316–339.

Hoff, E. H., Lappe, L., and Lempert, W. (Eds.). 1985. *Arbeitsbiographie und Persönlichkeitsentwicklung*. Bern: Hans Huber.

Hohner, H. U. (1984). *Kontrollbewusstsein und berufliche Restriktivität*. Berlin: Max-Planck-Institut für Bildungsforschung.

IDE. 1981. [Industrial Democracy in Europe—International Research Group.] *Industrial Democracy in Europe*. London: Oxford University Press.

James, W. 1890. *Principles of Psychology*, Vol. 1 & 2. New York: Dover (1950).

Keller, J. A. 1981. *Grundlagen der Motivation*. München: Urban & Schwarzenberg.

Kirsch, W., Scholl, W., and Paul, G. 1984. *Mitbestimmung in der Unternehmenspraxis*, Vol. 39. München: Planungs- und Organisationswissenschaftliche Schriften.

Kissler, L. 1978. *Politische Sozialisation*. Baden-Baden: Nosmos.

Kissler, L. 1980. *Partizipation als Lernprozess*. Frankfurt/New York: Campus.

Koch, L., and French, J. R. P. 1948. Overcoming resistance to change. *Human Relations*, 1(4): 512–532.

Koopman-Iwema, A. M. 1977. *Participation and Power Distance Reduction*. 2nd International Conference on Participation, Worker's Control and Self-Management, Paris.

Krampen, G. 1986. Politische Psychologie: Geschichte, Defizite, Perspektiven. *Psychologische Rundschau*, 37: 138–150.

Lafferty, W. M. 1975. Participation and democratic theory: Reworking the premises for a participatory society. *Scandinavian Political Studies*, 10: 53–70.

Lafferty, W. M. 1979, *Participation, Personal Choice, and Responsibility*. Conference Paper, Dubrovnik, January 16–18, 1979.

Lammers, C. J. 1967. Power and participation in decision making in formal organizations. *American Journal of Sociology*, 74: 201–217.

Meissner, M. 1971. The long arm of the job: A study of work and leisure. *Industrial Relations*, 10: 239–260.

Mulder, M. 1971. Power equalization through participation? *Administrative Science Quarterly*, 16: 31–38.

Mulder, M. 1977. *The Daily Power Game*. Leiden: Martinus Nijhoff.

Pateman, C. 1970. *Participation and Democratic Theory*. London: Cambridge University Press.

Rotter, J. B. 1966. Generalized expectancies for internal versus external control of reinforcement. *Psychological Monographs*, 80: 1–28.

Sauer, Cl., and Müller, M. 1980. Die Theorie der gelernten Hilflosigkeit: Eine hilfreiche Theorie? *Zeitschrift für Sozialpsychologie*, 11: 2–24.

Seligman, M. E. 1975. *Helplessness*. San Francisco: W. H. Freeman.

Staehle, W., and Osterloh, M. 1985. Wie, wann und warum informieren deutsche Manager ihre Betriebsräte? In W. Ballwieser and K. H. Berger (Eds.), *Information und Wirtschaftlichkeit*. Wiesbaden: Gabler.

Stanjek, K. 1980. *Die Entwicklung des menschlichen Besitzverhaltens*. Berlin: Max-Planck-Institut für Bildungsforschung.

Straw, B. M. 1982. Motivation in organizations: Toward synthesis and redirection. In B. M. Staw and G. R. Salancik, *New Directions in Organizational Behavior*. Malabar, Fla.: Krieger, pp. 55–95.

Streiffeler, F. 1975. *Politische Psychologie*. Hamburg: Hoffmann & Campe.

Thie, H. 1985. *Zur Psychologie des Eigentums*. Berlin: Technische Universität, Diplomarbeit.

Ulich, E. 1978. Über mögliche Zusammenhänge zwischen Arbeitstätigkeit und Persönlichkeit. *Psychosozial*, 1: 44–63.

Wall, T. D., and Lischeron, J. A. 1977. *Worker Participation: A Critique of the Literature and Some Fresh Evidence*. London: McGraw-Hill.

White, R. W. 1959. Motivation reconsidered: The concept of competence. *Psychological Review*, 5: 297–333.

Wilpert, B. 1983. *Psychological and Legal Property Titles and the Future of Industrial Democracy*. Conference Contribution, Dubrovnik, Oct. 2–7, 1983.

Wilpert, B. and Rayley, J. 1983. *Anspruch und Wirklichkeit der Mitbestimmung*. Frankfurt/New York: Campus.

Wortmann, C. B., and Brehm, J. W. 1975. Responses to uncontrollable outcomes: An integration of reactance theory and the learned helplessness model. In L. Berkowitz (Ed.), *Advances in Experimental Social Psychology*, Vol. 8. New York/London: Academic Press, pp. 227–336.

Part II
The Top Management Decision Making Programme (TMDM)

Overview Part II

The first essay by Frank Heller (Chapter 10) presents the theory and procedure of a method of field research called Group Feedback Analysis (GFA) which combines quantitative and ethnographic field material and validates the emerging data. With variations it was used by at least one research team, in two of the three research programmes (TMDM and DIO). Chapters 34 and 35 in Part IV describe applications of GFA to cross-sectional as well as longitudinal designs.

Chapter 11 by Frank Heller draws on experience in two South American countries during the 1960s where the then prevalent universalistic styles of decision-making – for instance, those used in the extensive University of Michigan studies of Rensis Likert and colleagues, do not fit the prevailing patterns of behaviour. As a consequence, a five-level contingency model of alternative leadership styles is developed and tested on two senior levels of management. The same model is then applied to a sample of senior American managers. The essay by Heller and Yukl (Chapter 12) further develops the contingency model of decision-making by demonstrating significant different styles used by student leaders and three levels of management. Furthermore, descriptions of leadership behaviour varied significantly with different situations. Chapter 13 then draws on previous experience with the contingency model and uses two interlocking senior levels of management in British and German companies. Heller and Wilpert show that managers in both countries consistently use a variety of styles in tackling different task situations. There is no universal best style.

In Chapter 14 the essay by Heller develops, extends and refines the theoretical model of participative decision-making as a flow process over time. Decision-making between individuals at the micro-level is seen as influenced by a series of meso- and macro-level variables ordered by their assumed degree of immediacy and psychological proximity to the decision-makers. In the evolving model, a particularly important place is given to skills, abilities and the motivating effect that their utilization has on the behaviour of people at all levels of the organization. Data derived from Group Feedback Analysis with senior managers is presented to support some aspects of the model.

The final essay by Heller and Wilpert (Chapter 15) describes an application of the contingency model to assess the distribution of influence and power among senior managers in eight countries. Differences between countries – the 'culturological' explanation – have to be seen in relation to other, equally important contingencies – for instance, the industrial sector in which the managers work. In all countries skill is an important factor in explaining the variation of centralized or participative decision-making. The policy implications of variations of leadership competence in the decision-making process are also discussed.

The TMDM programme took place in large successful companies in eight countries. Overall, the results clearly demonstrate the weakness of the global generalization about a uniformity of a leadership decision-making style which is appropriate in all or most situations. Leadership adjusts itself to contingencies, the nature of the task being one of the most important. In our samples in all eight countries, personality was less decisive than situational variables, including industrial sector and competence. Influence is unequally distributed even at senior management levels, and the belief system which underpins these differences is also an important determinant of behaviour.

Further Reading

Heller, Frank and Wilpert, Bernhard (with P. Docherty, J.M. Foucarde, P. Fokking, R. Mays, B. Roig, T. Weinshall, W. t'Hooft) (1981), *Competence and Power in Managerial Decision Making*, Chichester: John Wiley and Sons.

[10]

Psychological Bulletin
1969, Vol. 72, No. 2, 108–117

GROUP FEEDBACK ANALYSIS:

A METHOD OF FIELD RESEARCH

FRANK A. HELLER [1]

University of California, Berkeley

The increasing complexity and subtlety of problems investigated in field research puts a strain on our standard research techniques, particularly the mailed questionnaire, while interview results do not usually lend themselves to multivariate statistical analysis. "Group feedback analysis" combines a number of features from nomothetic and idiographic methods, thus overcoming some of the limitations of the mailed questionnaire. Certain advantages are described by reference to a number of research problems. Group feedback analysis has three interrelated stages: (*a*) Individual research instruments are administered to a group of subjects; (*b*) some, or all, of the results from Stage 1 are fed back to the group as means and deviations; (*c*) a discussion based on feedback of results is stimulated, recorded, and later content analyzed. Moving from unstructured to focused questioning, the investigator obtains a varied amount of information which acts both as a check and extension of the results obtained from Stage 1.

The behavioral sciences are working on problems that are becoming more complex every year, and this imposes a great strain on the relatively small number of research methods which are available to investigate them. In applied and field research, the duopoly of the interview and the self-administered questionnaire has remained relatively undisturbed for many decades (Selltiz, Jahoda, Deutsch, & Cook, 1959). Furthermore, one observes deep-rooted divisions between the few alternative research strategies. In personality assessment, for instance, there is a traditional opposition between the clinical interview approach and a battery of multidimensional tests; in field research on organizations there is a similar division between observational case studies and survey questionnaire methods (Scott, 1965). Other areas of controversy on methodology erupt frequently and often with considerable vehemence (Price, 1968a; Starbuck, 1968). At times, conflict between methodologies seems to lead to polarization and an uneasy state of isolation for a whole school of thought.[2]

The antagonism between the methods has not led to any very intensive search for alternatives, except possibly for the recent advocacy of nonreactive research (Webb, Campbell, Schwartz, & Sechrest, 1966) and adaptations of Kelly's Repertory Grid (Bannister & Mair, 1968). Nor is there much evidence that the middle ground between the major protagonists has been carefully explored. The field worker is often painfully aware of the practical limitations imposed on him by the tools he has available for doing his job (Rubenstein & Haberstroh, 1966, Section 1); the survey questionnaire method is now very extensively used, but this popularity owes more to its easy administration than to its perfection as a tool of investigation. Speak (1967) has recently produced a brief summary of some common problems involving questionnaires, starting with Muscio's (1916) famous paper which showed how different grammatical construction of sentences can change the response to questions. Later research confirmed these

[1] The author wishes to express his appreciation to Edwin Ghiselli, Raymond Miles, Arthur Kohnhauser, Karlene Roberts, George Strauss, and Leslie Wilkins for helpful comments on earlier drafts.

Requests for reprints should be sent to Frank A. Heller, Human Resources Center, Tavistock Institute of Human Relations, Belsize Lane, London N.W.3, England.

[2] This seems to have happened in the case of the anthropological direct observation method which has adherents in the United States (William Foote Whyte and his followers) as well as in England (Tom Lupton; W. H. Scott).

problems of interpretation and added others (Payne, 1951). The average person's knowledge of commonly used words was seen to be very much more restricted than questionnaire users had assumed (Thorndike & Gallup, 1944). Even more important for most empirical research is the finding that people interpret the same question according to widely different frames of reference (Campbell, 1945). Speak (1967), from her own experience, adds a serious warning against the assumption that "pilot surveys" discover all the problems of questionnaire design. She reports that respondents frequently answer meaningless questions with complete confidence (Speak, 1967, p. 178). Similarly, Dean (1958) shows that questionnaire answers on whether or not respondents had attended union meetings were false when compared with the findings of a research colleague who had personally observed the same union meetings and measured attendance.

Discussion on alternative methodologies tends to raise issues in the chiaroscuro of what Churchman (1968, p. 136) has recently called *hard* versus *soft* science. For instance, the controversy over the reliability and validity of personnel selection through questionnaire or interview methods has a long and acrimonious history (Ghiselli, 1966; Tiffin & McCormick, 1965). Hard scientists usually prefer the questionnaire, although serious problems concerning the interpretations of questions continue to be well documented (Crutchfield & Gordon, 1947; Weitz, 1950; Wells, 1963). Advocates of the interview are similarly divided into those who prefer the easily measurable structured questions over the open-ended interview (Lazarsfeld, 1944). One observer has suggested that the choice of research tool is at least as much related to the personality of the research worker as to any of the scientific reasons he adduces for the choice of his method (Schwab, 1960).

There seem to be three key problems in the various methodological controversies: One is the division between those who insist on precisely stated hypotheses, and a minority, like Skinner, who openly defend an opportunist empiricism (Bixenstine, 1966). Second, there is the problem of the choice of a particular technique which may be *hard* or *soft*. Third, one notices a reluctance to embrace eclecticism, as if it were immoral like polygamy.

However, eclecticism seems to be making some progress; several famous experiments have successfully combined different research methods in the same project (Lawrence, 1958; Sherif, 1956; White & Lippitt, 1968), and open advocacy of multiple methods is not unusual (Bray & Grant, 1966; Cook & Selltiz, 1964; Taft, 1959; Webb & Roberts, 1969; Webb & Salancik, in press). Even a self-styled *one method man* is now pleading for a broader methodological training of future generations of students (White, 1963).

The research method described in this paper has some relation with each of the three key methodological controversies. "Group feedback analysis" is a multiple approach to the measurement of attitudes; the first part uses questionnaires for which rigorous, *hard* statistical techniques of analysis are available, based (if required) on precise hypotheses. Multivariate analysis as advocated by Price (1968b) and others is, therefore, possible. The second stage feeds back results obtained from the questionnaires. The third stage uses discussion and is opportunistically empirical and *soft*. The objective of the second and third stages is, inter alia, to act as a check on the meaningfulness of the results from the questionnaire inquiry. In the feedback part of the method, semistructured and motivationally more powerful methods can be used to explore attitudes within the same research framework. The three stages are not independent of each other in the way that many projects use interviews *and* questionnaires as *alternative* methods of obtaining information. The third stage is entirely *integrated* with the first stage, amplifying and checking on selected aspects of the interim results.

Ideally, any variation of existing methods should be tested against the alternative from which it was developed. In practice, this is rarely possible. The critical incident technique, for instance, was put forward as an imaginative combination of a number of previously existing methods, but no attempt was made to prove its superiority over other methods (Flanagan, 1954). The same is true of the well-known focussed interview (Merton & Kendall, 1946). One reason for lack of experimental evidence is that a new approach is usually developed to do something different and not simply to improve on the reliability or validity of a variable in the previous research design.

Group methods of gathering data are not new. Consumer panels, for instance, have been found useful in obtaining information on customer attitudes. More recently, television cameras have helped in analyzing expressive bodily movement in interpersonal situations, and video tapes are beginning to be used extensively as a way of obtaining an extra dimension of information from groups, as well as providing a powerful feedback mechanism. Group feedback analysis has its own characteristics, and the next section of this article briefly describes the method. This is followed by a claim of possible advantages with examples from recent research projects. The method was developed over a period of over 15 years, having started as a teaching technique designed to stimulate interest by feeding back the results of simple student-centered inquiries. As has been found elsewhere (Bass, 1967; Leavitt & Mueller, 1951), teaching exercises can turn up very useful research material. The strength of feedback as a motivator also accounts for the use of similar methods as change agents in action research (Mann, 1957). In recent years, group feedback analysis has been found to be economical in its combined use as a teaching-based change agent, as well as a research tool (Heller, 1968a), but this article will deal with the method only from the point of view of research.[3]

DESCRIPTION OF THE METHOD

Most of the description that follows is based on a recent field research that investigated managerial attitudes and perceptions of decision-making behavior of two senior levels of management in 20 large California companies (Heller, 1968b). The research was car-

[3] When group feedback analysis is used only as a research method, it carefully avoids the possibility of contamination with the role of change agent.

ried out with groups of 5–25 people seated around a table. There is no magic in the numbers; 5 is possibly the smallest group for which a useful *average* result can be fed back in Stage 2 of the method to be described later. Larger groups than 25 could be handled if more than one person is available to carry out the administration of the investigation. Group feedback analysis is based on three interrelated steps. However, details of the design are flexible and can be adapted to meet a number of research demands.

Step 1

After the research objectives were briefly explained to the group and their cooperation enlisted, each person filled in a number of research instruments in the presence of the researcher or his assistant. In the California research, a battery of 22 questionnaires was used, one-half were on a single page, 4 had two pages, and 1 used five pages. A tape recorder was used to give the basic instructions, thereby reinforcing the written explanations printed on each form. The sessions lasted 1 hour.

Step 2

A selected part of the results from the 22 questionnaires was statistically analyzed, giving group averages and simple measures of variance. If a desk calculator and secretary were available, the results could be worked out in less than 1 hour, and it was therefore possible to have the feedback session following an interval for lunch.

The selection of the material to be fed back depends on the hypotheses of the study. For instance, in one study, the objective was to discover (*a*) current requirements in senior management skills, (*b*) changes in these requirements over time, and (*c*) differences in skills between manufacturing and nonmanufacturing industry, and in different job specializations. A second objective was to see whether skill priorities differed in the same industry from one country to another. In this case, the feedback information was supplemented by the results obtained from other groups in other industries, other job specializations, and other countries. Where appropriate, each individual was given his own results (in confidence) as well as the average results of his group. This encouraged people to make comparisons and to bring out points relevant to the hypothesis under investigation.

Step 3

A discussion of the feedback results was stimulated. Depending on the amount of time available, it was usually appropriate to introduce as little structure as possible into the early part of the discussion. The tape recorder which gave the standardized instructions in Step 1 was then used (after permission was obtained) to record the proceedings. Semistructured, prepared questions were then introduced to guide the discussion and probe into the areas relevant to the research objectives. For instance, the group was asked to talk about any shift in managerial skills over the *past* 10 years. Later, they were asked whether they would expect any changes in skill requirements in their particular businesses during the *next* 10 years.

When a research question was concerned with participatory styles of decision making, the respondents were encouraged to give examples of what they had in mind when they had previously answered the questionnaire on this topic.

There is no doubt that this part of the method produced extremely interesting information and probed into deeper layers of meaning than the statistical results which were available from Step 1. The more complicated and controversial a questionnaire the more useful was Step 3, both as a check on what was found and on the logic of the hypothesis which produced the research design.

Participation, for instance, is a topic on which it is increasingly difficult to do research by written questions alone. Almost any way of asking questions on this topic may evoke a series of preset attitudes based on attendance of courses or reading of the voluminous literature. This is one of the main conclusions of the recent international study of managerial attitudes in 14 countries (Haire, Ghiselli, & Porter, 1966). In the feedback discussion, it was possible to draw from each group some very useful material on (*a*) their

own company policy in relation to participation, (*b*) their exposure to specific participatory influences, (*c*) their *real group attitudes* to a *group subject* like participation, and (*d*) examples of what they meant by participation in their own businesses. The crisscross of interaction in group discussion produced results that were different and, in some ways, more specific and meaningful than the previous questionnaire responses. The analysis of Step 3 was usually done by content analysis of the tape transcript. The choice of content-analysis procedures is increasing very rapidly, and these procedures vary from simple to highly sophisticated (Gerbner, 1969).

In the California research, all three stages of the field project were completed in 2 hours (not counting the computation of the simple statistical results).

ADVANTAGES OF THE METHOD

At this point, it may be most helpful to simply list the favorable points that can be claimed for group feedback analysis. This is intended to provoke researchers into making their own critical evaluation.

1. *Hard statistical data plus soft insights.* The method combines some of the advantages of self-administered questionnaires, particularly quantification, with some of the flexibility and depth available through the interview. The research on managerial skills used ranking and rating questionnaires which were subjected to a variety of techniques of multivariate analysis, including factor analysis, regressions, and analysis of variance. The clinical information giving insight is produced quite independently.

Example of insight: Questionnaire 1 in the battery requires a simple ranking of skills in order of their importance. One of these skills is "rapid decision making." A group of 12 executives in a public utility company ranked this skill substantially lower than previous groups of comparable managers. During the feedback stage, the group discussed their ranking of executive skills. Most of the points made during the discussion related to the technology of the product and the methods by which it was distributed. It was claimed that, given these technological considerations, rapid decision making was inappropriate. These "explanations" can, of course, be "excuses" and they must be further tested. In this case, other public utility companies were still to be investigated in the chosen sample, and the new hypothesis could be tested (see Point 3 below for a similar procedure).

A second illustration with the same variable, rapid decision making, can be cited. Content analysis of the discussion of a sample of British and South American managers showed that the trigger word "rapid" had quite different connotations for these two national groups. The British group felt that the adverb "rapid" was undesirable though probably unavoidable in the context. The South Americans, however, associated the word with prestige, since only very few highly placed executives are given the authority to make "rapid decisions." The explanation threw new light on the statistical results (Heller, 1968c).

2. Stimulus equality versus receptor inequality. The essential scientific bases for interpreting questionnaire results, unless they are used as a projective test, is that each question evokes the same meaning in every subject. While this aim is not easily achieved, researchers attempt to minimize difficulties by a careful pretesting of the questionnaires. There are two problems to overcome. First, the question itself must be tested to make sure that the *stimulus* it transmits is exactly what the researcher intends it to be. Second, the reception of the stimulus in the subject should vary only in respect of the conditions that are being tested. For instance, if old people answer questionnaires, we would expect the replies to be affected by whatever receptor conditions are associated with age (let us say slow reading for the sake of the example).

Stimulus equality is more easily achieved in questionnaires than in interviews where intonation, gesture, and exact wording cannot be repeated with accuracy from subject to subject. *Receptor equality,* however, is complex, particularly with mailed questionnaires. A given stimulus may conjure up a variety of different associations even where the stimulus words are identical. There are two main reasons for receptor inequality: One

is due to the variety of mind states (motives, attitudes, prejudices) which receive the stimulus,[4] while the other relates to the environmental setting within which the question is received and answered (quiet and leisurely versus noisy and hectic environment, etc.).

Pretesting only enables us to get a very general notion of the broad interpretation of a question. Like testing, it has two control objectives: reliability and validity. The first is easier to check than the second, but it may have nothing to do with stimulus equality among different members of the test population. Validity tests are always in search of suitable criteria and, in practice, one is often thrown back on construct validities. Construct validity, however, measures the stimulus and not the receptor impact. The more complicated a question is (the more it involves attitudes and judgments of controversial issues, rather than simple factual information) the more difficult it is to reduce receptor inequality to manageable proportions. Let me give one example from a choice of many.

Example: The paired-comparison test item "security in your work" had not given rise to any problem for several years. Suddenly, in 1966, a group was tested which was on the point of changing to a new comprehensive pension scheme in 12 months. Should the managers answer the questions as of today or next year? A decision on this point had to be made, taking into account the specific research objectives.

Another, almost completely neglected, problem, concerning receptor inequality, relates to the physical and mental condition under which questionnaires are usually answered. The researcher rarely has any control over these circumstances and does not know what they are. Let us suppose that a man fills in one-quarter of a long questionnaire in his office; he then goes home to a house of lively children who go to his room every few minutes with some innocent interruption until they are put to bed. The final part of the

---

[4] Subjects vary in their tolerance of ambiguity, their use of extreme judgments on measuring scales, their hostility to a given research topic or to certain questions, etc.

FRANK A. HELLER

questionnaire is completed in relative solitude —in the company of his wife who interrupts from time to time to cover the more dramatic stories of the day, and a television screen which attracts his interest unequally but reaches a peak during the sports coverage of the news. What is the effect on the final answers? It is surprising that so little work has been done on this problem. One reason for the lack of interest in this kind of research is likely to be the virtual impossibility of estimating the nature and intensity of receptor inequality in the case of each questionnaire. The captive audience in group feedback analysis minimizes many of these problems.

3. *Reevaluation of hypotheses.* A working hypothesis is a "belief pertaining to the course of inquiry but not necessarily pertaining to its ultimate destination (Kaplan, 1964)." Even a test hypothesis leaves a considerable margin of uncertainty, and several alternative hypotheses may explain a high correlation between two sets of variables. Which is *the* correct hypothesis? In the behavioral sciences, we frequently have no satisfactory means of choosing between alternative hypotheses. This is highly unsatisfactory, since it tends to lull us into a false sense of security; for a long time, for instance, we believed that work groups with high morale had high productivity. Under favorable circumstances, group feedback analysis enables one to check on the appropriateness of a given hypothesis.

Example: It was anticipated that "technical managerial skills" would be more important to managers in underdeveloped than in highly industrialized countries. A pair of interlocking hypotheses for such a relationship was put forward by two social scientists familiar with the situation and the relevant literature. The results validated the hypotheses by finding significant differences between the means of the two groups of countries (Heller, 1964). This led to the question whether the hypotheses exhausted the possible explanations for the statistical findings. In the feedback discussion, which was tape recorded, subjects had volunteered explanations for the findings. These explanations took the form of post facto hypotheses, four of which came up spontaneously in 65% of the meetings. At

TABLE 1

HYPOTHESIS VERSUS CONTENT ANALYSIS AND VERBAL RANKING ON THE IMPORTANCE OF "TECHNICAL ABILITY" AMONG MANAGERS IN DEVELOPING COUNTRIES—ARGENTINA AND CHILE

A	B	C
Ranking of hypotheses to explain research: by two social scientists	Content analysis of specific explanations (Weighted Frequency × Duration of Comment)	Verbal ranking of stated preferences
1. Low level of technology	1. Lack of technical specialists (234)	1. Lack of technical specialists
2. Low level of technical education (in Argentina and Chile)[a]	2. Lack of trust (182)	2. Low level of technology gives scope
	3. Low level of technology gives scope (98)	3. We decide purchases of technology
	4. We decide purchases of technology (85)	4. Lack of trust
	5. Belief this accounts for superiority of the west (57)	
	. . . .	
	9. Low level of technical education (11)	

Note.—Figures in parentheses represent frequencies weighted by duration of comment.

[a] This hypothesis related exclusively to the schooling system and is not the same as Point 1 in Columns B and C. The major source of technical specialists comes from South Americans trained abroad. This training has prestige and is preferred to local training. A second source is the hiring or loan of foreign specialists, particularly in companies with overseas shareholdings. A third source is through bilateral or multilateral technical assistance.

the end of each meeting, individuals were asked to rank the four post facto hypotheses in order of their importance. The results are summarized in Table 1. It will be seen that the first of the original hypotheses (Column A) also came high in the explanations measured by content analysis (Column B) and high in the verbal ranking (Column C). However, the second original hypothesis came ninth in the priority of content analysis. More important still is the fact that a new hypothesis, that is, "lack of technical specialists" came first both by content analysis and ranking.

It was now possible to devise methods to test the new hypothesis further.

4. *Superior handling of complex questions.* The group-administered research instruments can handle psychologically complex material with greater confidence than mailed questionnaires. In a way, this point is obvious, and some of the reasons for the claimed superiority were discussed in relation to receptor inequalities under Point 2 above. However, it is difficult to realize how many different and quite unexpected problems can arise unless some checks are used at various stages after pretesting the questionnaire. The group method assures a measure of continuous surveillance.

Example: The point can be illustrated by looking at Figure 1. The problem was to define five alternative styles of leadership, so that the exact meaning of each style would be clearly understood by each subject and related to his own work. The following procedure was adopted: All five definitions were presented on a single sheet of paper separate from the questionnaire (Figure 1). My experience with a pilot survey led to the adoption of the following additional precautions: (*a*) The definitions were distributed first, and the whole group was given time to read through them carefully before the questionnaire was distributed. (It had been found that some managers glanced at the definitions briefly and then immediately started to answer the questions, while others read through the definitions carefully.) (*b*) The essence of each style of decision was summarized in the heading, as in the example below, on each of the 16 items of the questionnaire. (*c*) The group was asked to place the loose sheet of definitions next to the questionnaire and to refer to it, when necessary.

The precautions were fully justified, and most of the managers were seen to consult the list of definitions as they were giving their answers. Even so, some questions were not correctly understood. This was revealed in the discussion. In a few instances, managers had not noticed the implication of the last sentence in the following definition:

OWN DECISION *without* detailed explanation:
These are decisions made by you without previous discussion or consultation with subordinates and no special meeting or memorandum is used to explain the decision. *This method includes decisions made after consulting with managers at the same level or superior.*

This problem was considerably reduced, but not completely eliminated, by underlining the last lines in the definition.

The example demonstrates that, while all inquiries are subject to some error, elaborate precautions to minimize them are fully justifiable. This is, of course, particularly important when the size of the sample is small; however, even in large samples one cannot be absolutely sure that errors of the kind described will be eliminated through randomiza-

---

Methods of Making Decisions

OWN DECISION *without* detailed explanation:
These are decisions made by *you* without previous discussion or consultation with subordinates and no special meeting or memorandum is used to explain the decision. *This method includes decisions made after consulting with managers at the same level or superiors.*

OWN DECISION *with* detailed explanation:
The same as above, but afterwards you explain the problem and the reasons for your choice in a memo or in a special meeting.

PRIOR CONSULTATION with subordinate:
Before the decision is taken, you explain the problem to your subordinate and ask for his advice and help. You then make the decision by yourself.

Your final choice may, or may not, reflect your subordinate's influence.

JOINT DECISION MAKING with subordinate:
You and your subordinate(s) together analyze the problem and come to a decision. The subordinate(s) usually has as much influence over the final choice as you. Where there are more than two in the discussion, the decision of the majority is accepted more often than not.

DELEGATION of decision to subordinate:
You ask your subordinate to make the decision regarding a particular subject. You may or may not request him to report his decision to you. You seldom veto his decision.

FIG. 1. Definition of styles of decision making.

tion; the error gradient may be systematic and cumulative.

The additional precautions that can be built into group feedback analysis make it particularly suitable for cross-cultural research; it is not only a question of the correct translation of stimulus words, but, as Triandis (1967, p. 30) has pointed out, there is the problem of dealing with unknown cultural expectations.

5. *Insight into situational variables.* The investigator frequently obtains clues that arise from the group's behavior during the administration of the research. While this information is impressionistic, some of it lends itself to quantification by unobtrusive measures along the lines described by Webb et al. (1966). In any case, the additional information gives one a much broader and deeper understanding of the sample's composition.

Example: Groups of senior managers in two different retailing organizations were being studied by group feedback analysis. Organization A's managers appeared quiet, unimaginative in response to questions, slow to react to each other and to the researcher, and clearly under the influence of their chief executive. By contrast, managers in Firm B bristled with wit and ideas, obviously got along well with each other, showed independence of thought and quick interpersonal reactions.

Both firms were retailing similar merchandise in the same city, but for some reason had attracted quite different kinds of managers. While it may have been possible to devise psychological tests to bring out many of these personality differences, this would have required an additional investigation.

6. *Completeness of data.* Questionnaires distributed by mail or similar methods are known to have a more or less limited response rate (varying from 30% to 80%). This introduces many problems of interpretation. Equally important is the fact that a percentage of the replies are incomplete or spoiled. The longer and more complex the questionnaire the more likely that the percentage of incompleteness increases.

The captive audience of the group feedback analysis helps to avoid most, though not all, of these problems. In the present research, each of the 22 short questionnaires was collected and checked while the next one was being handed out and completed; this reduced errors and omissions to a minimum.

7. *Efficiency considerations.* Once a group has agreed to spend a certain amount of time with the investigator, the amount of work that can be done is considerable. "Questionnaire fatigue" and flagging interest can be handled through the intervention of the investigator and is minimized by seeing the rest of the group at work. Consequently, the quality of the response toward the tail end of a long series of questions is likely to be greater than with self-administered instruments.

Furthermore, where the alternative is the individual interview, an organization may find it easier to set up a group procedure involving 10 or 20 people than the same number of separate appointments. There is, of course, a similar economy in the investigator's time.

DISCUSSION

For many research workers, the major disadvantage of the method is the apparent *contamination* of results obtained from Stage 3. At this point, answers are given by individuals in a group; when the discussion becomes animated, the interplay between personalities and attitudes increases, and the information is contaminated by the interaction process and the group setting in which it takes place. Some individuals will be inhibited, other spurned; there may be a *conformity* effect, and, where groups vary in size, this itself will lead to differences in the amount of contribution each participant can make.

These difficulties have to be carefully evaluated in the case of each research project, and it has to be remembered that uncontaminated answers relating to the same hypothesis or problems are in any case available from Stage 1. The objective is to derive benefits from the results of *both* research data. Careful consideration should also be given to the possibility that there are a number of research questions for which *group answers* or answers in a group setting are meaningful, because these circumstances correctly simulate the real life parameters that are being tested.

It is also necessary to briefly consider the *cost* of group feedback analysis. Starbuck

GROUP FEEDBACK ANALYSIS 116

(1968) has said that the "choices of what data to collect and what analytic methods to employ form an optimization problem in which the objective is to maximize the usefulness of the research study, subject to constraints on available resources [p. 135]." While it is certain that simpler methods, like mailed questionnaires, take up less resources, there is some evidence to suggest that differences in cost are smaller than had been suspected. One very rough cost comparison exists. This investigator's research in California, using group feedback analysis, was carried out with 260 managers in 15 companies, using 22 questionnaires. It was completed in 6 months of part-time work with the help of a part-time research assistant. In moderately comparable conditions, a colleague, working on a similar research problem, used a questionnaire distributed by management through six divisions of a large company. The colleague's sample was slightly larger, and it took 5 months to collect. An almost 100% rate of return was achieved with both methods, but it is likely that with the self-administered questionnaire a smaller percentage of the senior researcher's time was taken up. Accurate comparisons cannot be made between different projects unless this comparison were itself undertaken as a research. However, it seems reasonable to say that group feedback analysis is not prohibitively expensive.

The case for group feedback analysis rests on the probability that the complexity and subtlety of problems in which behavioral scientists are currently interested has frequently outstripped the methods available for investigating them. In nonlaboratory investigations, we still rely on a very small number of methods of collecting data; in fact, mainly on self-administered questionnaires *or* interviews.[5] Group feedback analysis is put forward for consideration on the strength of a number of claims that are briefly described in this article. The main characteristic of the approach is its capacity to integrate some of the advantages from two usually opposed

methodological camps. On the one hand are the advocates of the hypothetico-deductive method, strictly controlled conditions, carefully tested instruments, large samples, and complex statistical designs. On the other extreme are those who prefer to explore small populations in depth by using fairly flexible, often informal, clinical methods which rarely lend themselves to systematic evaluation and even less to a testing of alternative hypotheses. Gordon Allport described a similar dichotomy by the terms nomothetic and idiographic, his own preference inclining toward the latter (Hall & Lindzey, 1957). Group feedback analysis leans toward the nomothetic approach, but obtains valuable data that are normally only available by using small-group research and idiographic methods.

REFERENCES

BANNISTER, D., & MAIR, J. M. M. *The evaluation of personal constructs.* London: Academic Press, 1968.

BASS, B. Program of exercises for management and organizational psychology. (Instructor's manual, Rev. ed) University of Pittsburgh, Management Research Center Graduate School of Business, 1967.

BIXENSTINE, E. Empiricism in latter-day behavioral science. In A. Rubenstein & C. Haberstroh (Eds.), *Some theories of organization.* Homewood, Ill.: Dorsey Press, 1966.

BRAY, D. W., & GRANT, D. L. The assessment center in the measurement of potential for business management. *Psychological Monographs,* 1966, 80(17, Whole No. 625).

CAMPBELL, A. A. Two problems in the use of the open question. *Journal of Abnormal and Social Psychology,* 1945, 40, 340–343.

CHURCHMAN, W. C. *Challenge to reason.* New York: McGraw-Hill, 1968.

COOK, S. W., & SELLTIZ, C. A multiple approach to attitude measurement. *Psychological Bulletin,* 1964, 62, 36–55.

CRUTCHFIELD, R. S., & GORDON, D. A. Variations in respondents interpretations of an opinion-pool question. *International Journal of Opinion and Attitude Research,* 1947, 1(3), 1–12.

DEAN, L. R. Interaction reported and observed: The case of one local union. *Human Organization,* 1958, 17(3), 36–44.

FLANAGAN, J. C. The critical incident technique. *Psychological Bulletin,* 1954, 51, 327–358.

GERBNER, G. (Ed.) *Proceedings of the University of Pennsylvania national conference on content analysis.* Philadelphia: University of Pennsylvania, Annenberg School of Communications, 1969.

GHISELLI, E. The validity of the personnel interview. *Personnel Psychology,* 1966, 19, 389–394.

---

[5] Social survey techniques use both questionnaires and interviews, but the material included in the questionnaire is usually of a simple nature.

HAIRE, M., GHISELLI, E., & PORTER, L. *Managerial thinking: An international study.* New York: Wiley, 1966.

HALL, C. S., & LINDZEY, G. Theories of personality. New York: Wiley, 1957.

HELLER, F. A. *Desarrollo de Ejecutivos.* Cuadernos Tecnicos No. 9, 1964, Buenos Aires, Centro de Productividad de la Argentina.

HELLER, F. A. Group feedback-analysis. University of California, Berkeley, 1968. (Mimeo) (a)

HELLER, F. A. A research on managerial skills, perceptions and decision-making: Interim report. University of California, Berkeley, School of Business, 1968. (Mimeo) (b)

HELLER, F. A. The role of management in economic development. *Management International Review,* 1968, 8(6), 63–75. (c)

KAPLAN, A. *The conduct of enquiry: A methodology for behavioral science.* San Francisco: Chandler, 1964.

LAWRENCE, P. *The changing of organizational behavior Patterns.* Boston: Harvard University, Graduate School of Business Administration, 1958.

LAZARSFELD, P. F. The controversy over detailed interviews: An offer for negotiation. *Public Opinion Quarterly,* 1944, 8, 38–60.

LEAVITT, H. J., & MUELLER, R. A. H. Some effects of feed-back on communication. *Human Relations,* 1951, 4, 401–410. (Republished: In E. A. Fleishman, Ed., *Studies in personnel and industrial psychology.* Homewood, Ill.: Dorsey Press, 1967.)

MANN, F. Studying and creating change: A means to understanding social organization. In C. Arensberg et al. (Eds.), *Research in industrial human relations.* New York: Harper & Row, 1957. (Reprinted: In T. W. Costello & S. S. Zalkind, Eds., *Psychology in administration.* Englewood Cliffs, N. J.: Prentice-Hall, 1963.)

MERTON, R. K., & KENDALL, P. L. The focused interview. *American Journal of Sociology,* 1946, 51, 541–557.

MUSCIO, B. The influence of the form of a question. *British Journal of Psychology,* 1916, 8, 351–386.

PAYNE, S. L. *The art of asking questions.* Princeton: Princeton University Press, 1951.

PRICE, J. L. Design of proof in organizational research. *Administrative Science Quarterly,* 1968, 13, 121–134. (a)

PRICE, J. L. *Organizational effectiveness.* Homewood, Ill.: Irwin, 1968. (b)

RUBENSTEIN, A., & HABERSTROH, C. (Eds.) *Some theories of organization.* (Rev. ed.) Homewood, Ill.: Irwin, 1966.

SCHWAB, J. J. What do scientists do? *Behavioral Science,* 1960, 5, 1–27.

SCOTT, W. R. Field methods in the study of organizations. In J. G. March (Ed.), *Handbook of organizations.* Chicago: Rand McNally, 1965.

SELLTIZ, C., JAHODA, M., DEUTSCH, M., & COOK, S. *Research methods in social relations.* (Rev. ed.) New York: Holt, 1959.

SHERIF, M. Experiments in group conflict. *Scientific American,* 1956, 195, 54–58. (Reprinted: In H. Leavitt, Ed., *Readings in managerial psychology.* Chicago: University of Chicago Press, 1964.)

SPEAK, M. Communication failure in questioning: Errors, misinterpretations and personal frames of reference. *Occupational Psychology,* 1967, 41, 169–179.

STARBUCK, W. H. Some comments, observations and objections stimulated by "Design of proof in organizational research." *Administrative Science Quarterly,* 1968, 13, 135–161.

TAFT, R. Multiple methods of personality assessment. *Psychological Bulletin,* 1959, 56, 333–352.

THORNDIKE, R. L., & GALLUP, G. H. Verbal intelligence in the American adult. *Journal of General Psychology,* 1944, 30, 75–85.

TIFFIN, J., & McCORMICK, E. *Industrial psychology.* Englewood Cliffs, N. J.: Prentice-Hall, 1965.

TRIANDIS, H. C. Interpersonal relations in international organizations. *Organizational Behavior and Human Performance,* 1967, 2(1), 26–55.

WEBB, E. J., CAMPBELL, D. T., SCHWARTZ, R. D., & SECHREST, L. *Unobtrusive measures: Nonreactive research in the social sciences.* Chicago: Rand McNally, 1966.

WEBB, E. J., & ROBERTS, K. H. Content analysis and reference systems. In G. Gerbner (Ed.), *Proceedings of the University of Pennsylvania national conference on content analysis.* Philadelphia: University of Pennsylvania, Annenberg School of Communication, 1969.

WEBB, E. J., & SALANCIK, J. R. Supplementing the self report in attitude research. In E. Sommers (Ed.), *Handbook of research on attitudes.* Chicago: Rand McNally, in press.

WEITZ, J. Verbal and pictorial questionnaires in market research. *Journal of Applied Psychology,* 1950, 34, 363–366.

WELLS, W. D. How chronic overclaimers distort survey findings. *Journal of Advertising Research,* 1963, 3(2), 8–18.

WHITE, R., & LIPPITT, R. Leader behavior and member reaction in three "social climates." In D. Cartwright & A. Zander (Eds.), *Group dynamics.* New York: Harper & Row, 1968.

WHITE, W. F. Towards an integrated approach for research in organizational behavior. (Presidential address) *In, Proceedings of the 16th Annual meeting of the Industrial Relations Research Association,* Boston, 1963. (Reprint No. 155, Cornell University, New York State School of Industrial and Labor Relations.)

(Received September 4, 1968)

Reprinted from INDUSTRIAL RELATIONS, Vol. 12, No. 2, May 1973

FRANK A. HELLER*

Leadership, Decision Making, and Contingency Theory

"How DO MANAGERS make decisions in a variety of different circumstances?" This broad question underlies a continuing research project on leadership styles begun at the University of California, Berkeley, in 1967.[1] Although this question seems simple enough, it is nevertheless different from those usually asked in behavioral research on leadership and decision making. This article, therefore, explains the circumstances leading to the conception of this research and describes a socio-technical contingency model used in its undertaking. The model is supported with data obtained from a sample of 360 senior managers in 20 British firms (compared, in some analyses, with similar previously published data on 260 managers from 12 U.S. companies).[2] The overall conclusion is that leadership and decision-making behavior must be analyzed from a contingency rather than a universalistic perspective.

Background

During the sixties, I worked in several South American countries as a United Nations adviser on the use of behavioral sciences, particularly in the areas of management development and leadership. Both then and today the dominant trend in the academic literature on management and

---

* Senior Staff Member, Tavistock Institute of Human Relations.

[1] Initial research support was provided by various grants from the Committee of Research at Berkeley. The continuation of this research in England is supported by grants from the Social Science Research Council.

[2] Results of this project have been fully published for the U.S. portion of the sample in F. A. Heller, *Managerial Decision-making: A Study of Leadership Styles and Power-sharing among Senior Managers* (London: Tavistock Publications, 1971). Partial results have been published for England in F. A. Heller, "The Decision Process: An Analysis of Power-sharing at Senior Organizational Levels," TIHR Doc. No. SFP 2337, 1972, to be published in R. Dubin, ed., *Handbook of Work, Organization and Society* (New York: Rand McNally, forthcoming), and Germany in B. Wilpert and F. A. Heller, "Power-sharing and Perceived Skill Reservoirs at Senior Management Levels," International Institute of Management, West Berlin, 1972. Work is still proceeding in Holland, Sweden, France, Spain, Japan, and Israel.

184 / FRANK A. HELLER

leadership can be summed up in the word "participation." Claims were that both productive efficiency and human relations sensitivity could be combined in an effective participative management program. And, further, it was argued that participative management methods, developed mostly in the United States,[3] could be exported to many other industrial nations of the world.

South America is a particularly interesting region in which to introduce managers to participative techniques because there is little doubt that many organizations in this area are administered quite autocratically. I started several pilot projects using as the primary research instrument questionnaires of the kind developed by the University of Michigan's Institute of Social Research. These questionnaires included very general items about such organizational variables as leadership, responsibility, communications, etc. and asked managers to describe their organizations on a scale ranging from favorable to unfavorable alternatives.[4] Results were then fed back to managers for discussion.[5] These feedback discussions were popular, led to a considerable amount of managerial self-analysis, and to persistent criticism of certain characteristics of the method of inquiry. Criticisms centered around two main points: (1) questionnaire items were too general and led to oversimplified answers, and (2) many managers felt that they had to specify the situation to which their answers applied. Regarding the latter criticism, for example, the use of upward or downward communication had to be different, managers argued, depending on whether they were handling production schedules or finance. This was due in part to the turbulent economic conditions so typical of underdeveloped countries: exchange rates fluctuated wildly, foreign currencies were scarce, government regulations changed unpredictably, and astronomical rates of inflation were experienced from time to time. It was argued that in such circumstances it was unrealistic for communication or decision processes to be the same for different tasks—even the apparently simple matter of buying a typewriter, which could normally be handled by a supervisor, might become a senior management concern if foreign currency was involved.

After the first 17 months of my stay in South America, I was definitely moved by the force of these arguments. By that time I had worked in many organizations, learned the language, and become fairly familiar with what

---

[3] See, for example, Rensis Likert, *New Patterns of Management* (New York: McGraw-Hill, 1961) and Rensis Likert, *The Human Organization* (New York: McGraw-Hill, 1967), or Robert Blake and Jane Mouton, *The Managerial Grid* (Houston, Texas: Gulf Publishing Co., 1964).

[4] Likert, *New Patterns of Management.*

[5] See Floyd C. Mann, "Studying and Creating Change: A Means to Understanding Social Organization," *Research in Industrial Human Relations* (Madison, Wisc.: Industrial Relations Research Association, 1957).

one could loosely call the local "culture." Clearly, it seemed that global advocacy of participatory methods was in conflict in some countries with prevailing values concerning interpersonal relations, the roles of older people, the role of the church, the father in his family, and so on. If they were to be effective, therefore, participatory techniques would have to be modified to meet the particular needs of different groups of managers.

The purpose of participation. Various interpretations of what participation means in practice are in part a consequence of the assumptions one makes about people and the theoretical framework within which these assumptions are made. Miles has described a "Human Relations Model" in which key relationships appear as follows: Participation ➤ Improved Satisfaction ➤ Improved Compliance with Authority.[6] This model seems to lend itself to manipulation. In order to achieve "compliance with formal authority," managers may be tempted to consult people *after* a decision has already been made or when there is little likelihood of advice being accepted. Satisfaction, the middle variable in the chain, is not easily assessed, since subordinates are not likely to tell their superiors that they see through the "manipulation."

A different sort of participatory situation occurs in Miles' "Human Resources Model," where similar variables are related as follows: Participation ➤ Improved Decision Making ➤ Improved Satisfaction (there is a feedback loop from satisfaction back to improved decision making). Managers working with this model gain no advantage from feigning participative styles; presumably their reason for using this model is that they *want to make better decisions.* In any event, improved satisfaction and productivity are viewed as *by-products* of the better use of people rather than of a managerial style.

We can anticipate one of our findings at this point by showing that when managers in industrialized countries are asked why they use participation, they consistently vote for "better decisions" as their first choice and "increased satisfaction" as their second, third, or fourth choice (see Table 1). The evidence from South America was not collected as systematically, but comes to the same conclusion—that is, it supports the Human Resources Model.

The Human Resources Model makes a great deal of sense in developing countries where experience and skills are, almost by definition, scarce. People who are conscious of this scarcity and have gone to the trouble to acquire knowledge and skills become resentful if they are not allowed to use them.

---

[6] Raymond E. Miles, "Human Relations or Human Resources?", *Harvard Business Review*, XLIII (July-August, 1965), 148–163.

186 / FRANK A. HELLER

Also, countries which spend their scarce resources on advanced education and training can ill afford to see them underutilized. However, the Human Resources Model (as does the Human Relations Model) assumes that the postulated relationship among variables operates in all situations; that is, the nature of the decision and the socio-technical circumstances which surround it are irrelevant. For example, there is no suggestion that a partici-

TABLE 1
REASONS FOR USING PARTICIPATION AS RANKED BY
AMERICAN AND BRITISH MANAGERS

	US (1967) n = 260		UK (1970) n = 360	
	L.1[a]	L.2[a]	L.1[a]	L.2[a]
To increase satisfaction	2	3	3	4.5
To improve the technical quality of decisions	1	1	1	1
To train subordinates	4	4	4	3
To improve communication	3	2	2	2
To facilitate change	5	5	5	4.5

SOURCE:
[a] L.1 = senior management level. L.2 = senior middle management level (i.e., L.1's immediate subordinates).
NOTE: For the sake of simplicity, approximate average ranks rather than mean ranks are given.

pative leadership style is less appropriate in cases where there are few skills and little experience in the subordinate group than when there is a considerable amount of both. Should a leader use the same method in both situations?

Universalism versus relativism. So-called "situational" or "contingency" models of management and leadership are few. Some have dealt with broad managerial or organizational systems,[7] but contingency models dealing with superior-subordinate relations are rare. A tentative contingency view of leadership has been described by Tannenbaum and Schmidt,[8] but Fiedler is undoubtedly the best known proponent of this view.[9] The model described here, however, differs from that of Fiedler in several important respects:

1. Fiedler measures leadership style with a leader's description of his "least preferred co-worker" (LPC), a fairly basic attribute of an individual

[7] F. E. Emery and E. L. Trist, "Socio-technical Systems," in C. W. Churchman and Michel Verhulst, eds., *Management Sciences, Models, and Techniques*, Vol. 2 (Oxford: Pergamon Press, 1960); T. Burns and G. M. Stalker, *The Management of Innovation* (London: Tavistock Publications, 1961); J. Woodward, *Industrial Organization: Theory and Practice* (London: Oxford University Press, 1965); J. Thompson, *Organizations in Action* (New York: McGraw-Hill, 1967); C. Perrow, "A Framework for the Comparative Analysis of Organizations," *American Sociological Review*, XXXII (April, 1967), 194–208; P. R. Lawrence and J. W. Lorsch, *Organization and Environment: Managing Differentiation and Integration* (Boston: Harvard Business School, 1967); F. A. Heller and G. Yukl, "Participation and Managerial Decision-making as a Function of Situational Variables," *Organizational Behavior and Human Performance*, IV (August, 1969), 227–241; J. C. Wofford, "Managerial Behavior, Situational Factors and Productivity and Morale," *Administrative Science Quarterly*, XVI (March, 1971), 10–17.
[8] Robert Tannenbaum and Warren Schmidt, "How to Choose a Leadership Pattern," *Harvard Business Review*, XXXVI (March-April, 1958), 95–101.
[9] Fred E. Fiedler, *A Theory of Leadership Effectiveness* (New York: McGraw-Hill, 1967).

which does not change easily. Certainly this style does not change in relation to different situations in which a leader may find himself. Consequently, the managerial task is to match people who have a certain amount of LPC to tasks and situations for which they are most suited.

2. The model does not appear to offer useful insights in cases where a leader's job has (over the years) components of several quite different (a) task structures, (b) leader-member relations, and (c) leader position power (Fiedler's three central situational factors). In other words, leadership style does not adjust to these changing situations.

3. Fiedler's situational factors are confined to the three categories mentioned above and to eight permutations based on them. There is, however, no reason to suppose that these three characteristics exhaust the range of important contingency factors (see Table 3 later).

While the contingency model and the findings reported in this paper differ from Fiedler's model on all of these points, there is little doubt that his extensive research has produced strong evidence for treating leadership in situational terms. The difficulties I encountered in attempting to apply participative leadership methods in South America further support this contention.

After my experiences in South America, I came to the United States to develop and test a situational model of leadership. This project has subsequently been extended to a wide variety of other countries, and data collection and analysis are still proceeding.

Broad Outline of the Model

Leadership style, decision making, and participation are closely intertwined variables. In a critical review of the literature on participation, Strauss notes that if one wishes to analyze the decision-making process within and among various hierarchical levels of management, then interpersonal leadership methods—including participation—cover only some of the alternatives.[10] There is a continuum of perhaps seven or eight alternative "decision-making styles," ranging from the solitary decision of the "lonely man at the top" to complete delegation by a superior to a subordinate with no provision for short-term review.

A more complete framework for analyzing decision-making style, which uses five clearly defined alternatives, has been developed (see Table 2). These five methods form what is called an "Influence-Power Continuum (IPC)."[11]

---

[10] George Strauss, "Some Notes on Power Equalization," in H. J. Leavitt, ed., *The Social Science of Organizations* (Englewood Cliffs, N.J.: Prentice-Hall, 1963).

[11] For a fuller description of the terms and their relation to the organizational decision process, see Heller, *Managerial Decision-making. . . .*

188 / FRANK A. HELLER

The relationship of the IPC to what is usually called decision making requires a brief explanation. First, it can be seen from the introductory definition in Table 2 that we have stretched the meaning of the word "decision" to include the process of giving advice and recommendations in certain circumstances. Second, the IPC is designed to analyze *how* decisions are made in terms of the distribution of power and not *what* decisions are made.

TABLE 2
METHODS OF MAKING DECISIONS (THE INFLUENCE-POWER CONTINUUM)

The five methods are defined for each manager as follows:
"In this form we are concerned with the management skill called 'decision-making'. This term includes the process leading up to the final decision, and advice or recommendations which are usually accepted also count as decisions for the purposes of this research. Many alternative methods of decision-making exist, among them those described below. All have been shown to be widely used and effective."

1. *Own decision without* detailed explanation.
   Decisions are made by managers without previous discussion or consultation with subordinates. No special meeting or memorandum is used to explain the decision.
2. *Own decision with* detailed explanation.
   Same as above, but afterwards managers explain the problem and the reasons for their choice in a memo or in a special meeting.
3. *Prior consultation* with subordinate.
   Before the decision is made, the manager explains the problem to his subordinate and asks his advice and help. The manager then makes the decision by himself. His final choice may, or may not, reflect his subordinate's influence.
4. *Joint decision-making* with subordinate.
   Managers and their subordinates together analyze the problem and come to a decision. The subordinates usually have as much influence over the final choice as the managers. Where there are more than two individuals in the discussion, the decision of the majority is accepted more often than not.
5. *Delegation* of decision to subordinate.
   A manager asks his subordinate to make the decision regarding a particular problem. He may or may not request the subordinate to report the decision to him. The manager seldom vetoes the subordinate's decisions.

Third, certain aspects of the *content* of decision making are used as contingency variables; that is, we use groupings of decisions by content and by the management function which carries them out as measures of the *situation*. It is believed that these contingent situations influence the choice of method as described by the IPC.

Delegation. The five IPC alternatives cover a wider range of behavior and reflect a broader concept of leadership than that used by Likert and his colleagues and other investigators. This extension is primarily due to including "delegation" as one means of making decisions. Delegation appears to have been avoided in the past because it was felt that leadership styles range from authoritarian methods which avoid interpersonal influence to democratic methods which require a group situation. The IPC, however, is concerned with measuring the distribution of power in relation to decision making and in this context delegation clearly plays a part.[12] Furthermore, the psychological and organizational advantages usually claimed for democratic decision procedures would appear to apply equally to methods 3, 4, and 5 of the IPC.

There are at least three reasons for extending the range of decision-making styles beyond what is usually called participation:

1. Participative methods are said to motivate and they enable people to self-actualize. Participation is also said to increase a person's range of freedom for making decisions relative to his work. Similar motivational claims have been made for semi-autonomous work groups.[13] Delegation can be viewed as a further step towards increased autonomy on work tasks.

2. According to the Human Resources Model, participation enables people to use their abilities and helps them to acquire new skills. The more influence a person has (assuming he has relevant experience and skill), the better his resources will be utilized. The same arguments apply to delegation.

3. Finally, there is the undeniable existence of delegation as a form of managerial behavior. Delegation is a choice available to many leaders; some use it extensively, others do not. There is also a connection between delegation at one level and the choice of leadership styles available to the next lower level. If an L.1 manager delegates the decision for the purchase of a piece of equipment to his L.2 subordinate, then the latter manager may use methods 1, 2, 3, or 4 with his own subordinates. If L.1 had *not* used method 5, this choice of style would not have been open to L.2.

Subordinate influences on decision making. In any complete model of organizational decision making, it is also necessary to include situations where influence-power interactions are initiated by subordinates. Inverse participation and delegation upward are certainly factors in the decision process in the British Civil Service.[14] In Japan, the well-known *ringi* system of "bottom-up management" is said to rely on subordinates consulting superiors and gradually getting decisions accepted by higher levels up to the chief executive.[15]

---

[12] For this reason, I have recently extended the range to cover two methods of delegation. Method 5 now involves a short time span at the end of which the superior reviews the decision, while Method 6 describes a long time span and no review or evaluation for a considerable period of time. The extension to Method 6 is not incorporated in the analyses here.

[13] See A. K. Rice, *Productivity and Social Organization* (London: Tavistock Publications, 1958), and E. J. Miller and A. K. Rice, *Systems of Organization* (London: Tavistock Publications, 1967).

[14] F. A. Heller, "The Administrative Process in Government Departments: Decision-making and Related Factors, A Preliminary Study," TIHR Doc., 1971.

[15] The *ringi* system is considerably more complex and varied than the literature suggests. I recently spent six weeks in Japan studying this system. So far, we must rely on anecdotal evidence and the personal experience of a limited sample of managers, but interviews reveal wide disagreement between academics and Japanese managers concerning the *ringi* method.

FIGURE 1

RELATIONSHIPS BETWEEN DECISION STYLE AND CONTINGENCY VARIABLES

The influence-power continuum

1. Own decision without explanation

2. Own decision with explanation

3. Prior consultation

4. Joint decision making

5. Delegation

Groups of contingency variables

Alpha — Various characteristics of the manager: age, experience, skill, attitudes, values.

Beta — Situational variables close to the decision maker: technology of the managerial job, job function, nature of the decision (to whom it is important, etc.), organizational level.

Gamma — Micro-structural variables: span of control, number of authority levels, size of department, policy and control procedures, centralization.

Delta — Macro-structural variables: size of organization, relationships with other departments, workflow technology.

Omega — Ecological variables: the influence of the socio-political and cultural environment of a geographic area, turbulence of environment, state of economic development, degree of competition, educational system variables.

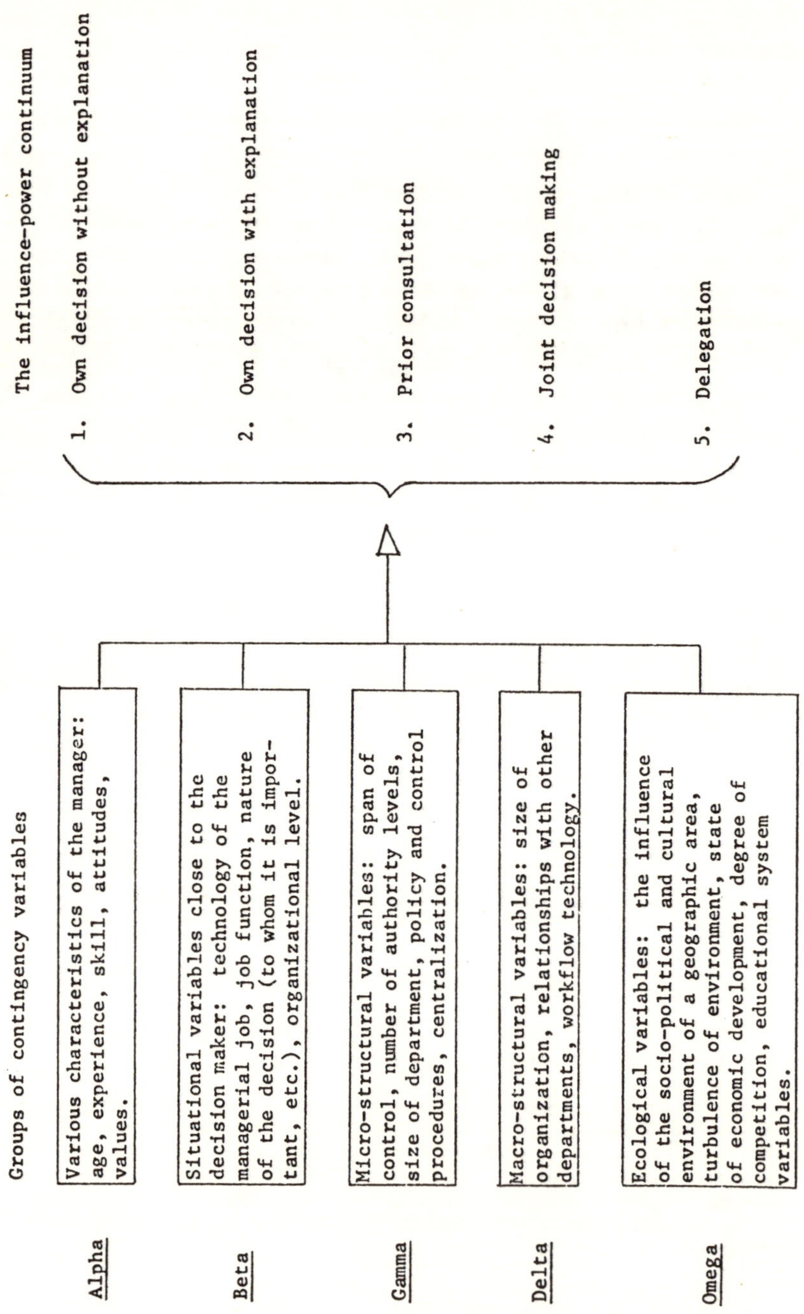

Symposium: Cross-national Research / 191

Value-free definitions. All five of the decision methods shown in Table 2 have been defined in terms which are as neutral as possible so that managers can report their behavior without fear of appearing "unprogressive."[16] The apparent lack of neutrality in a number of existing research instruments[17] may be responsible for some of the uniformity in findings based on these instruments.

A Contingency Model of Leadership and Decision Making

The present model has two main parts. The first focuses upon the interaction between (1) various characteristics of the manager and the situation in which he carries out his work, and (2) the alternative decision styles used by managers. The second part of the model deals with relationships among decision style, skill utilization, managerial satisfaction, and organizational effectiveness.

Part 1 of the model is shown in Figure 1. Contingency variables are listed separately in five groups called Alpha, Beta, Gamma, Delta, and Omega. Each group of variables has a certain theoretical homogeneity in that they form a system of relationships (e.g., Alpha variables relate to the individual while Omega variables are macro-economic and macro-sociological). Elsewhere, I have indicated that international research on decision making and power equalization has evolved to the point where nearly all of the variables shown in Figure 2 (with the exception of the Omega group) have now been at least roughly measured. The present discussion, however, is concerned with making a plausible argument in favor of a contingency analysis of decision style. This objective can be met by looking at any one of these groups of variables, and, therefore, attention is directed at the Beta group.

We can also briefly consider the second part of the model, although no supporting evidence will be presented here. Figure 2 illustrates hypothesized relationships among:

1. the five alternative decision styles
2. their impact on the utilization of skills and experiences currently available among the various groups of managers
3. managerial satisfactions, and
4. measures of organizational effectiveness.

Rudimentary ways of measuring these variables are included in the re-

---

[16] In the field research, this neutrality is stressed both in questionnaires and in verbal instructions accompanying them.

[17] Likert, *New Patterns of Management* and *The Human Organization;* C. G. Smith and A. N. Ari, "Organizational Control Structure and Member Consensus," *American Journal of Sociology,* LXIX (May, 1964), 623–638; A. Tannenbaum, "Control and Effectiveness in a Voluntary Organization," *American Journal of Sociology,* LXVII (July, 1961), 33–46.

192 / FRANK A. HELLER

FIGURE 2

RELATIONSHIPS AMONG DECISION STYLE, SKILL UTILIZATION, MANAGERIAL
SATISFACTION, AND ORGANIZATIONAL EFFECTIVENESS

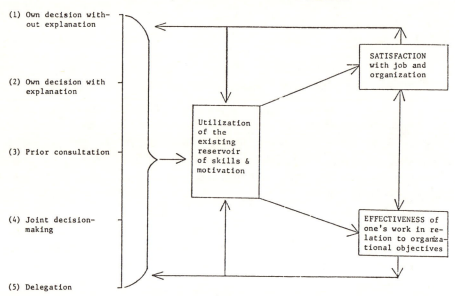

search design, but more and better ways of assessing these factors may have
to be devised before their interaction can be adequately tested. In the meantime, the assumption is that power sharing methods 3, 4, and 5 (prior consultation, joint decision making, and delegation) will harness more of the
existing reservoir of skills[18] and that such improved utilization produces
increased motivation and satisfaction. At the same time, it is postulated
that better use of skills and increased motivation improve work effectiveness.
Feedback loops reinforce skill utilization, and, via improvements in work
effectiveness, lead to greater managerial confidence in the use of power-
sharing decision methods. If greater satisfaction is achieved, various feedback loops increase work effectiveness and lead to a greater use of skills
and power sharing.

Parts one and two of the contingency model can be seen as a series of
open interacting systems of variables. Their hypothesized interaction can
be tested by multivariate statistical methods; the objective of such analyses
can be described in two stages. Part one of the model attempts to identify
those contingencies which lead to significant variations in decision style. A
number of hypotheses have been put forward which concern these con-

---

[18] For a fuller description of the skill reservoir model, see Heller, *Managerial Decision-making*,
and Heller, "Social and Technical Aspects of Manpower Utilization," *Management Education and
Development,* I (1971), 111–123.

tingencies and the evidence to support them is moderately strong.[19] Information along these lines should lead to a different and more analytical as well as flexible approach to management development and organizational design than currently exists.

Part two of the model—which links individual and situational factors to broader organizational processes—explores the possibility of increasing the input of skills, experience, and motivation already available in the organizational system, but which for various reasons is left unused. Power-sharing decision methods are seen as *one* way of liberating pent-up skill-motivation resources, but they have to be used situationally rather than universally.[20] Judgments of when and how to use power-sharing methods derive from the evidence relating to part one of the model.

Findings

Data obtained from managerial samples throughout the world are gradually giving shape to the contingency model described above (the model is now in its third metamorphosis). Throughout its various phases, this framework provides a means for measuring the *intersituational* variability of leadership style with regard to decision making in addition to the more usual *interpersonal* variability. Among the questions for which the model is designed to facilitate answers are the following:

1. Do individuals use different degrees of power sharing in a variety of specified circumstances?

2. Do all managers vary their leadership style or is this variability confined to a minority of individuals?

3. In making a variety of different decisions, do individuals use the full range of alternative leadership styles or do they restrict themselves to a small range of styles?

4. What are the socio-technical circumstances that exert strong influence on the variability of leadership styles?

If the answer to the first question is negative, then there is no point in asking any of the others. Evidence shown in Figure 3 indicates that U.S. managers do in fact use leadership styles that are contingent upon their awareness of different situations. Where decisions are important to the organization but not particularly important to subordinates (Curve C), managers use methods 1 and 2 predominantly, while decisions which are

---

[19] Heller, *Managerial Decision-making . . .*, and "The Decision Process. . . ."

[20] Other obstacles to the use of available human resources obviously exist, but are not part of the discussion here. See Heller, "The Managerial Role in the Effective Use of Resources," *Journal of Management Studies*, VI (February, 1969), 1–14.

194 / FRANK A. HELLER

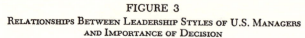

FIGURE 3

RELATIONSHIPS BETWEEN LEADERSHIP STYLES OF U.S. MANAGERS
AND IMPORTANCE OF DECISION

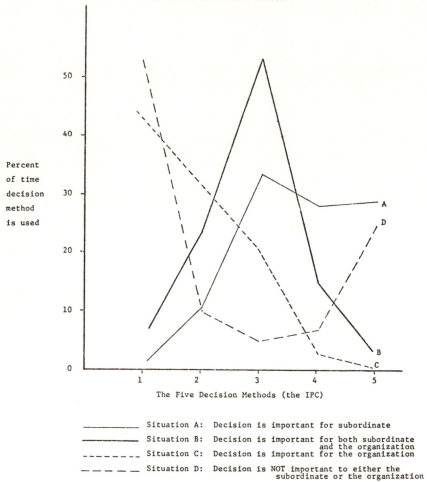

The Five Decision Methods (the IPC)

	Situation A:	Decision is important for subordinate
	Situation B:	Decision is important for both subordinate and the organization
	Situation C:	Decision is important for the organization
	Situation D:	Decision is NOT important to either the subordinate or the organization

important for the subordinate, but not particularly so for the organization,
lead to a predominance of methods 3, 4, and 5 (Curve A).

In other words, managers use highly *autocratic* leadership styles in one
type of situation, but *democratic* styles in another. Where the decision is
not particularly important for either the organization or the individual manager (Curve D in Figure 3), *both* autocratic and democratic leadership
styles seem to be used. This finding suggests the possibility that managers
are aware that relatively unimportant decisions can be made by using decision methods which demand *little time*. Method 1 (making decisions one-

Symposium: Cross-national Research / 195

self) and Method 5 (delegation) use considerably less time than "prior consultation" or "joint decision making." Such a finding clearly supports a contingency model of leadership.

The second question above asks: do all managers vary their leadership style or is this variability confined to a minority of individuals? Data for the Level 1 managerial portion of the U.K. sample appear in Table 3. Column 2

TABLE 3
How Senior British Managers
Describe Their Leadership Methods

	Frequency with which the styles are used	
Column 1 Managers who use:	2 Description of L.1 managers (n = 143)	3 Description of L.2 managers (n = 143)
All 5 methods	41	52
4 methods	62	58
3 methods	29	28
2 methods	9	5
1 method	2	0

shows the judgments of Level 1 managers regarding their own decision behavior, column 3 the perceptions of Level 2 managers (Level 1 managers' immediate subordinates). As indicated, both levels agree to a remarkable extent on the average frequency with which Level 1 managers use the

TABLE 4
Frequency Distribution of Leadership Styles
Among British Managers

Column 1 Method	2 Per cent of time used as seen by L.1 managers (n = 143)	3 Per cent of time used as seen by L.2 managers (n = 143)
1	62.4	72.0
2	88.5	76.2
3	96.5	93.0
4	86.0	91.6
5	59.5	76.2

various leadership styles. Between 41 and 52 out of 143 senior British managers use all five decision styles in relation to 12 specific decisions which senior managers in all industries tend to make.[21] Approximately 60 of the 143 managers use four of the five decision styles and 28–29 managers use three styles. Fewer than 10 out of the 143 managers use only two methods and almost no one uses only one method.

Data showing the frequency with which Level 1 British managers use each of the five decision styles are shown in Table 4. According to Level 1

---

[21] These 12 decisions and the questionnaire format are described in Heller, *Managerial Decision-making . . .*, pp. 121–124.

196 / FRANK A. HELLER

managers, none of the styles is used less than 60 per cent of the time, with a high of nearly 97 per cent for Method 3 (prior consultation). Their immediate subordinates see each of the alternative methods being used even more extensively (from 72 per cent for "own decision without explanation" to 93 per cent for "prior consultation"). Although the published findings from the American sample are not presented for Tables 3 and 4, the results show a very similar distribution to that of British managers.

In sum, the majority of senior British and American managers vary their styles of leadership according to specific decision situations, and they make extensive use of all five alternative styles.

Socio-technical Factors

Given these variations, what socio-technical circumstances may account for them? This is the final question to which we will attempt to give at least a partial answer here. In the American sample, there was a significant association between types of decisions made and the decision style used. The 12 decisions can be broken down into three categories:

SUB decisions relate to issues that are confined to the boss and his immediate subordinate (e.g., "The decision to change an operating procedure followed by your subordinate").

TABLE 5

THE USE OF DECISION STYLES FOR DIFFERENT TYPES OF
DECISIONS AMONG SENIOR BRITISH MANAGERS

Decision style	SUB	EMP	DEPT
1	18.8%	4.9%	14.8%
2	30.8	9.5	23.8
3	32.9	39.3	40.2
4	15.3	35.2	16.8
5	2.2	11.1	4.4

SUB = decisions between L.1 managers and their immediate subordinates.
EMP = decisions by L.1 managers relating to employees two levels down in the hierarchy.
DEPT = decisions by L.1 managers relating to the entire department.
n = 172

EMP decisions are made by a manager in relation to problems that concern employees two levels lower on the organization chart than himself (e.g., "The decision to discharge one of your subordinate's staff").

DEPT is a description of decisions that concern the whole department (e.g., "The decision relating to the purchase of a piece of equipment for your department at a cost within your budgetary discretion").

American managers use different decision styles when making SUB, EMP, or DEPT type decisions.[22] A similar pattern is apparent in the British sample (see Table 5). Decisions relating to immediate subordinates (SUB) are made

---

[22] See *ibid.*, pp. 83–84.

Symposium: Cross-national Research / 197

much more autocratically (Methods 1 and 2) than decisions relating to employees two levels further down in the hierarchy (EMP). Decisions on purely departmental matters (DEPT) are closer to SUB than to EMP type decisions in terms of styles used. The highest degree of delegation is used with EMP decisions (11 per cent compared with 2 per cent and 4 per cent with SUB and DEPT decisions, respectively). Type of decision is, therefore, a critical factor and is associated with significant variations in leadership style among British as well as American senior managers.

A second contingency factor is the technology of the managerial task. The nature of accounting work, for instance, is clearly different from that of personnel or marketing work. Until precise socio-technical dimensions of these managerial tasks are available, a comparison between job functions

FIGURE 4

VARIATIONS IN DECISION STYLE AMONG U.S. MANAGERS
IN SIX DIFFERENT JOB FUNCTIONS

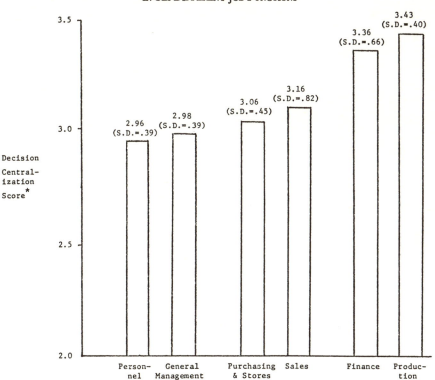

*Low score = power sharing
High score = unilateral decision making
n = 130

198 / FRANK A. HELLER

may serve as an approximation of the socio-technical differences. In the American sample, three groups of job functions were isolated on an empirical basis and found to differ significantly from each other (Figure 4). Personnel and unspecialized managerial jobs showed the lowest decision centralization score,[23] purchasing and sales were intermediate, and finance and production showed the highest decision centralization. The British data follow a different distribution and the reason for this has not yet been fully analyzed, but again, job function shows a statistically significant variation with decision style.

Discussion and Conclusions

All findings reported here and elsewhere of this ongoing research project reveal the limitations of the universalistic approach to leadership and decision making. Although the evidence is only now beginning to build up, it clearly suggests that the best current cross-national approach to organizational leadership, participation, and power sharing is via a contingency model. Methods for measuring managerial decision-making behavior presented in this article are more adequate than previous efforts. However, the assessment of situational and other contingency variables made here is relatively primitive and is unlikely to cover all of the influences affecting managerial decision behavior.

The contingency approach receives strong support from recent work by Vroom and Yelton.[24] Their research, which is both detailed and sophisticated, dealt with problems and hypotheses similar to the research described here and resulted in similar conclusions. Their finding that most managers use four out of five alternative decision styles is almost identical with my own, and they argue that "the decision process . . . was influenced much more by the properties of the situation . . . than . . . by [the leader's] average style."[25] They go on to conclude that "the results clearly establish the importance of the situation as a determinant of autocratic or participative behavior."[26] It will be recalled that Vroom had previously found that the effectiveness or acceptability of authoritarian leadership methods varied with the authoritarianism among subordinates.[27] More recently, Crowe, Bochner, and Clark have demonstrated in a laboratory situation that man-

[23] Decision centralization is a way of summarizing the distribution of the five decision styles in a single score. The higher the score, the more autocratic is the decision style.
[24] V. Vroom and P. Yelton, "Some Descriptive Studies of Participation in Decision-making," Carnegie-Mellon University, Pittsburgh, 1972 (mimeographed).
[25] *Ibid.*
[26] *Ibid.*
[27] V. Vroom, *Some Personality Determinants and the Effects of Participation* (Englewood Cliffs, N.J.: Prentice-Hall, 1960).

Symposium: Cross-national Research / 199

agers change their preferred style of leadership in response to their subordinates' behavior.[28]

Findings such as those described in this article do not diminish the importance of participation to the management of modern organizations. On the contrary, as we learn more about the various psychological and sociotechnical circumstances under which power-sharing decision methods are most appropriate, we improve the theory as well as the practice of organization design and development.

---

[28] B. J. Crowe, S. Bochner, and A. W. Clark, "The Effects of Subordinates' Behaviour on Managerial Style," *Human Relations*, XXV (July, 1972), 215–237.

[12]

Reprinted from Organizational Behavior and Human Performance, Vol. 4, No. 3, Aug. 1969

Organizational behavior and human performance 4, 227–241 (1969)

Participation, Managerial Decision-Making, and Situational Variables[1]

Frank A. Heller

University of California at Berkeley

AND

Gary Yukl

Sacramento State College

Two hundred and three senior managers, first and second-line supervisors and student leaders from 16 organizations reported on their decision behavior. The research has three distinct features: a) it presents a five-fold typology of decision behavior on a continuum of subordinate influence which can vary from delegation at one end of the scale, to decisions made by the leader without explanation to his subordinate, at the other end; b) the measuring scales use realistic organizational problems for the purpose of assessing decision-making and participation; c) the decision-making preferences of different groups of leaders are compared and related to situational variables. Significant relationships were found between decision behavior and six of the seven situational variables. The implication of these findings for the literature on participation is discussed.

Over the last ten years, the literature on management and administration has reflected a growing interest in the subject of managerial decision-making. A number of frequently appearing terms such as "participation," "power equalization," and "democratic leadership" refer to an important and controversial aspect of managerial decision-making, namely the extent to which it is shared by the manager's subordinates. There are a number of different decision-making procedures that managers, or for that matter, any formal leader, can use. Some procedures involve a great deal of subordinate influence, and others exclude the subordinate altogether from the decision-making process. Although there is no widely accepted typology or model for classifying the decision behavior of managers, there does appear to be wide acceptance of the

[1] The authors wish to express their appreciation to Professors Selwyn Becker, Vaughn Blankenship, and Lyman Porter for helpful comments on an earlier draft of this paper.

general concept of a continuum of subordinate influence along which various decision procedures can be ordered.

Probably the most influential decision-making typology was introduced in the pioneering study by Lewin, Lippitt, and White (1939) who described three leadership styles: "democratic," "authoritarian," and "laissez faire." Authoritarian leaders made nearly all of the decisions themselves, whereas laissez faire leaders allowed the subordinates to make all the decisions (a style not appropriate for business organizations). Democratic leaders made their decision jointly with their subordinates. In retrospect, this categorization, which clearly reflects the influence of political theory, may have been an unfortunate one. In subsequent research there was a tendency to focus upon democratic and autocratic styles, when in fact, other equally important decision styles are also used by managers. This tendency to conceptualize managerial decision-making in terms of two widely divergent styles is still evident today (Sales, 1966; Davies, 1967; Lowin, 1968), despite appeals for more differentiated and well-defined theory (Leavitt, 1962; Strauss, 1963; Argyris, 1964).

Various other social scientists have also proposed systems for classifying managerial decision-making or for describing the amount of subordinate influence. March and Simon (1958, p. 54) suggested a continuum of supervisory styles ranging from "decisions made by the supervisor and communicated to the worker without prior consultation" to "decisions made on the basis of free and equal discussion." In the same year, Tannenbaum and Schmidt (1958) described a scale of leader behavior with seven differentiated styles of decision-making. Likert (1961 and 1967) has elaborated four styles of managerial decision-making, each corresponding to one of his four theoretical approaches to organizational management. In addition, Likert (1961, p. 242) mentioned a twelve point scale for describing the amount of subordinate participation that occurs when organizational change is introduced. Blake and Mouton (1961) have proposed a system for evaluating the amount of weight an individual exerts on a decision made by himself and a subordinate, measured on a "power spectrum." Strauss (1963) has differentiated between decisions made by managers alone, decisions made jointly by managers and subordinates, and decisions which the manager permits the subordinate to make on his own. Blankenship and Miles (1968) have developed a questionnaire which takes into account three stages in the process of making organizational decisions and attempts to find the organizational locus for each of these three stages.[2] Finally, other

[2] Scale B to be described later was influenced by the business decision categories used in the Blankenship and Miles (1968) questionnaire.

writers, including Argyris (1964) and Tannenbaum (1962) have proposed systems for describing the amount and distribution of influence and control in the organization as a whole.

Despite the basic agreement that various decision styles represent different degrees of subordinate influence and participation, there has been little attempt to develop and apply measures based on a complex typology of decision procedures. The measures that have been used in field research to date are simple rating scales indicating the degree of overall subordinate influence as computed by some averaging procedure. While this type of participation index is useful, the exact pattern of decision procedure used by a leader may be more meaningful. A further weakness of most previous measures is the failure to assess managerial decision behavior in relation to specific, typical organizational decisions. Finally, although there has been much discussion in the literature of the constraints and demands placed on the leader by his situation (e.g., Tannenbaum and Massarik, 1961) a systematic investigation of the relation between situational variables and leader decision-making has not been undertaken. The small number of studies that have related situational variables to decision-making (surveyed briefly by Bass, 1967) strongly support the proposition that a leader's situation substantially limits and shapes his decision behavior, but further research is clearly needed.[3]

In view of these various omissions from the research literature, the purpose of this article is threefold. The first objective is to present a meaningful model of decision procedures that incorporates the best features of earlier systems for classifying managerial decision-making along a continuum of subordinate influence. The second objective is to describe a method of measuring (by self report) how often a leader uses each of these decision procedures to make typical leadership decisions and, in general, how much subordinate participation is allowed. The final objective is to analyze the responses to these questionnaires by a variety of different leaders in order to identify the influence of various situational variables on the leader's use of the decision procedures. The situational variables include the following: authority level in the organization, span of control, job function, staff-line position, length of time in present position, and type of decision.

[3] On a broader front, but excluding decision-making, Porter and Lawler (1965) have reviewed studies supporting the relation of structural variables to attitudes and job performance in business organizations. In Europe, there have been several sociologically oriented studies on the effect of structural variables (Woodward, 1965; Pugh, Hickson, Hinings, and Turner, 1968); and sociotechnical systems (Trist, Higgins, Murray, and Pollock, 1963). These studies also exclude decision-making at the plant level.

THE DECISION BEHAVIOR MODEL

The amount of subordinate influence in decision-making within a formal unit of the organization can be viewed as a continuum ranging from no subordinate influence to complete subordinate influence. Figure 1 shows the hypothesized relationship between the influence continuum

LOW SUBORDINATE INFLUENCE			HIGH SUBORDINATE INFLUENCE	
Own decision without explanation	Own decision with explanation	Consultation	Joint decision making	Delegation

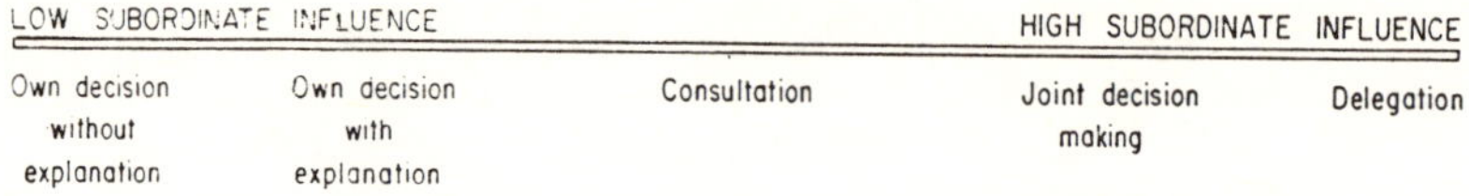

FIG. 1. Relation of decision styles to the influence continuum.

and five decision procedures that have been found to be relatively clear and meaningful for managers. These decision procedures were defined in behavioral terms and can be briefly summarized as follows.

Own Decision without Explanation refers to decisions made by a manager without any prior consultation with his subordinates (consultation with persons at a higher or equal authority level in the organization is not excluded).

Own Decision with Explanation refers to decisions made without prior subordinate consultation but adds a formal post-decision explanation of the reasons for the decision; this may induce the manager to take into account any known subordinate preference before he makes the decision (Bass, 1967).

Prior Consultation refers to decisions made only after consultation with one or more subordinates. The manager makes the decision himself, but his decisions will usually reflect some subordinate influence.

Joint Decision-making is a process of consensus formation in which one or more subordinates participate and some determination of the majority position is made. Although the manager may occasionally overrule the majority, more often than not the majority view is accepted.

Delegation refers to decisions that the manager allows subordinates to make on their own. A report on the decision may or may not be requested, and although the manager can veto the subordinate decision, he seldom does so.[4]

Until more sophisticated scaling methods can be applied, the precise

---

[4] Several of the decision procedures could be further subdivided within the range of the continuum. In particular, different degrees of delegation are possible in terms of the time span of a manager's review and the probability of revoking any given decision. There is a slight and possibly superficial resemblance between *delegation* and *laissez faire* leadership. However, delegation does not represent passive leadership and, although subordinates are given some freedom, the area of choice is usually delineated and constrained.

location of the five decision procedures on the influence continuum is not possible. The two scoring procedures that were used on the present scale will be described in the section on methodology.

METHODOLOGY

The leaders used in the research included 82 senior managers in 15 large West Coast companies, 28 first-line supervisors and 72 second-line supervisors from three of these companies, and 21 student leaders from a large university. The student leaders were elected and appointed officials of traditional student organizations. Information was obtained from the senior managers by a combined questionnaire and discussion approach (Heller, 1968). Information from the rest of the sample was obtained by means of mailed questionnaires; the average response rate for the survey was 90 percent.

Leader decision-making behavior was measured by three similar questionnaires, which will be referred to as Forms A, B, and C. Form A was a one-item questionnaire requiring the leader to indicate what percentage of his decisions was made with each of the five decision procedures.

Form B had eleven decision items involving specific decisions which are appropriate for senior managers. If a manager was not usually responsible for making one of the decisions he was asked to indicate that it was not applicable and to go on to the next item. Otherwise, he was to indicate what percentage of the time each of the five decision procedures was used by him to make that kind of decision. Of course, if a manager used only one procedure to make a given decision, then he could put 100 percent next to that style; if he used more than one of the procedures, the percentages could be distributed to reflect the relative frequency of use for the five styles.

The eleven items in Form B can be subdivided into two classes of decisions, EMP and SUB. The term EMP refers to decisions that in some way involve the employees of the manager's subordinates. An example of an EMP decision is: "The decision to give a merit pay increase to one of your subordinate's employees." SUB decisions involved only the immediate subordinate himself. An example of a SUB decision is: "The decision regarding what targets or quotas should be set for your subordinate(s)." This SUB-EMP classification did not stand out in the wording of the questions.

Form C had eighteen decision items consisting of decisions that most leaders must make. For each decision item, the leader was required to select which of the five decision procedures he was most likely to use to make that particular kind of decision. The eighteen items in Form C can be divided into two categories of decisions. The categories cor-

respond to the distinction that is often made between task and maintenance functions of leaders. Task decisions are those that involve planning and execution of the group task. An example of a task decision is
the following: "The decision how to schedule the various tasks that need
to be performed." Maintenance decisions involve personnel matters (e.g.,
promotion, pay), discipline, and preservation of subordinate satisfaction and cohesiveness. An example of a maintenance decision is: "The
decision as to which subordinate to recommend for promotion or appoint-
ment to a position outside of your group."[5]

Relative frequency scores for the five decision procedures were obtained from Forms A and B but not from Form C. In the case of Form B,
the average percentage score for each decision procedure was calculated
using the percentage scores (for that procedure) from the eleven decision
items. Average percentage scores were also calculated separately for the
EMP and SUB decision categories. An index of the average relative degree of leader and subordinate influence was obtained from all three
forms. This index, referred to as Decision-centralization, enabled leaders
to be ordered with respect to how much influence they allow subordinates. In order to facilitate the computation of Decision-centralization,
the five decision procedures were assumed to be separated by equal
intervals on the influence continuum, and scale scores of 1, 2, 3, 4, and 5
were assigned (Delegation = 1, etc.). With Form C, each item was
scored in terms of the scale value of the decision procedure selected
by the leader. The mean of the eighteen items provided an index ranging from 1 to 5 (high Decision-centralization means low subordinate
influence). A comparable index was obtained from Forms A and B by
multiplying the average frequency scores by the scale values (1 to 5),
summing these products and dividing the sum by 100.

Only a moderate amount of internal consistency was expected for
Forms B and C, since a variety of different types of decisions was pur-
posely included in these questionnaires. Item-total correlations were calculated for Form C, and of the eighteen items, seventeen had an item-
total correlation of .40 ($P < .01$) or better. Although all three forms were
not administered to every leader, there was some overlap of method in
order to test for method comparability. Decision-centralization scores
for Form A correlated .55 ($P < .01$) with Decision-centralization scores
for Form C. For Forms A and B, Decision-centralization scores correlated .71 ($P < .01$). Re-test reliability for Form B with an interval of
seven weeks was .82 ($P < .01$).

---

[5] Copies of the various scales can be obtained from the authors.

Information regarding the situational variables other than type of decision was obtained from straightforward questionnaire items and from organization records. The term *situational* is used, for want of a better term, to describe a mixed group of variables. Two of them, namely, authority level and span of control are usually called structural variables.

In interpreting the results in the next section, certain limitations in the design of the study should be borne in mind. Perhaps the most important limitation is that in a correlational study of this nature, no conclusions about causality can be made. A second limitation is that three different questionnaires were used on four samples of leaders; while the questionnaires were found to be reasonably well intercorrelated, the design makes it impossible to present exactly the same information for all four samples. Thirdly, Forms A and B were used to obtain Decision-centralization scores (Tables 1 and 2) as well as percentage scores distributed over the influence continuum (Figure 1, Tables 3, 4, and 5). Percentage scores probably simulate very accurately the real managerial choice situation, but the scale is limited by the fact that the choices must add up to 100. As a consequence, the correlations between situational variables and the five decision styles are not entirely independent of each other. This is not likely to be a major problem, however, if conclusions are based on the overall trends rather than on individual correlations or *t*-tests. Finally in the present study, the effect of the intercorrelations between the situational variables is not eliminated. However, the intercorrelations are generally small.

RESULTS

1. The means and standard deviations of the Decision-centralization scores for the four groups of leaders are presented in Table 1. An analysis of variance indicated that there were significant differences

TABLE 1
DECISION-CENTRALIZATION MEANS AND STANDARD DEVIATIONS
FOR FOUR TYPES OF LEADERS[a]

Type of leader:	Mean	S.D.	N
Student leaders	2.98	.42	21
Senior managers	3.14	.52	82
Second-line supervisors	3.26	.37	72
First-line supervisors	3.66	.53	29
$F = 8.73, p < .01$			

[a] Note: Data is from Questionnaire B and C.
High scores imply decision-centralization.

234   HELLER AND YUKL

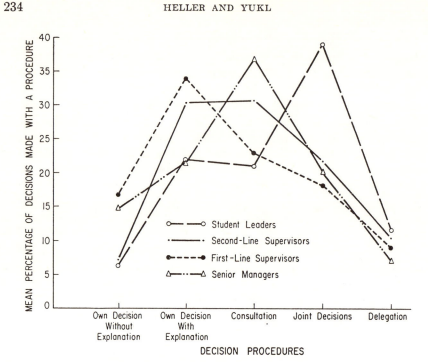

FIG. 2. Pattern of decision making for four groups of leaders.

among groups with respect to Decision-centralization ($F = 8.73$, $P < .01$). For the three groups of industrial leaders, the higher the leader was in the authority hierarchy, the less centralized was his decision-making. Student leaders tended to be more permissive in their decision-making than the industrial leaders. The difference between the four groups can be seen more clearly in Figure 2. The most preferred decision style among student leaders was Joint Decision-making. Senior managers used Prior Consultation most frequently. Second-line supervisors used Prior Consultation and Own Decision with Explanation more often than the other three styles. First-line supervisors used Own Decision with Explanation most frequently. This pattern of results is not surprising considering the differences between the leadership roles for the four groups of leaders. Blankenship and Miles (1968, p. 119) have recently reported the finding that senior levels in a hierarchy involve their subordinates in decision making more than managers at lower levels. Factors such as the nature of their subordinates' task, the capacity of the subordinates to contribute to the decision process, and expectations regarding the proper amount of subordinate influence probably all contribute to the tendency of leaders at higher authority levels to allow greater subordinate influence.

DECISION-MAKING   **235**

TABLE 2
DECISION-CENTRALIZATION MEANS AND STANDARD DEVIATIONS
FOR SIX MANAGEMENT FUNCTIONS[a]

	Function:	M	S.D.	N
High Centralization group	Production	3.43	.40	15
	Finance	3.36	.66	11
Medium Centralization group	Sales	3.16	.82	8
	Purchasing	3.06	.45	7
Low Centralization group	General	2.98	.39	17
	Personnel	2.96	.39	8

F for the three functional groups = 3.84, $p < .05$
[a] Note: Data is from Questionnaire B.
High scores imply decision-centralization.

2. Functional specialization is also related to the style of decision-making that will be selected. The sample of senior managers could be divided into six managerial functions: production, finance, sales, purchasing, personnel, and nonspecialized "general" management.[6] Table 2 presents the mean and standard deviation of the Decision-centralization scores for these six groups of managers. The six functions appear to form three clusters. Production and finance managers tended to use centralized decision styles, whereas nonspecialized "general" managers and personnel managers tended to be the most permissive. Managers of purchasing and sales units occupied an intermediate position on the influence continuum. An analysis of variance indicated that the mean Decision-centralization scores for these three clusters of managers were significantly different ($F = 3.84$; $P < .05$).[7] The differences in decision styles are most likely related to the nature of the task performed by the manager's department. The degrees of freedom available to managers in the tasks performed in the finance and production departments are probably fewer than in the case of the relatively unprogrammed jobs in the personnel and "general" management fields. Also, there is evidence that production divisions are under greater pressure than non-production divisions (Fleishman, Harris, and Burtt, 1955, pp. 98–99).[8] The extent to

[6] General management is not usually considered to be a separate function. In the present sample, the term nonspecialized "general" management was used to describe all managerial positions in control of divisions or sections which do not have specialized functional responsibility. These managers were at the same level of seniority as the functional managers.

[7] The F-test for the six separate functions was not significant.

[8] Heller in a 1968 study now being analyzed, used a scale of job constraints. Preliminary analysis suggests that the degrees of freedom available to managers differ with their task function in a way comparable to the findings of Fleishman *et al.* (1955, p. 98).

which programmed jobs restrict the meaningful possibilities of participation, has been pointed out in the literature, but particularly in relation to low level jobs (Leavitt, 1965, p. 1166; Strauss, 1963, p. 71). The present finding would suggest that the concept may also operate at very senior levels (see also Lefton *et al.*, 1966).

3. The distinction between line and staff is another way of classifying managers by function. Although many of the senior managers could not be clearly classified as line or staff managers, it was possible to differentiate 26 managers whose primary function was to implement and control managerial policy (line) from 16 managers whose major function was to advise and recommend on policy matters. The mean and standard deviation of the Decision-centralization scores for line managers were 3.18 and .55 respectively. The mean and standard deviation of the Decision-centralization scores for staff managers were 2.93 and .32 respectively. Although the line managers were expected to be less permissive in their decision-making, the difference between means was not significant ($t = 1.61$).[9]

4. Information about span of control was available for all of the industrial leaders, but first line supervisors were omitted since their subordinates were workers rather than supervisors and the variance in their span of control was extremely small. Span of control ranged from 2–16 subordinates for second-line supervisors and from 1–14 subordinates for senior managers. The relation between decision-making behavior and span of control for these two groups of leaders can be found in Table 3. When group size or span of control increases, decision procedures such as Consultation and Joint Decision-making become less feasible since they require considerable time-consuming interaction and communication between group members. These time pressures could lead us to expect three alternative approaches to decision-making when span of control is large. The leader could make the decisions by himself; he could decentralize; or he could centralize some decisions and decentralize others. Table 3 shows that both senior managers and second-line supervisors tended to centralize their decisions when the span of control was large. However, only senior managers used delegation as a second time saving procedure, thereby demonstrating greater flexibility.

5. The relation between a leader's decision-making behavior and the amount of time that he has occupied his leadership position is shown in Table 4. The correlations in this table are consistent with the differ-

[9] Since the direction of relation between the situational variables and the dependent variable was not always clearly specified beforehand, the significance tests of all product-moment correlations and "Student's" *t*-tests, are two tailed.

DECISION-MAKING   **237**

TABLE 3

CORRELATION BETWEEN SPAN OF CONTROL AND THE USE OF FIVE DECISION
PROCEDURES BY MANAGERS AND SECOND-LINE SUPERVISORS[a]

Decision procedure:	Span of Control:	
	Senior manager	Second-line supervisors
Own decision without explanation	.33[c]	.00
Own decision with explanation	−.09	.34[c]
Consultation	−.20	−.14
Joint decision-making	−.10	−.10
Delegation	.22[b]	−.12
	$N = 82$	$N = 72$

[a] Note: Data is from Questionnaire A and B.
[b] $p < .05$.
[c] $p < .01$.

The five correlations for each sample are not independent because ipsative scoring was employed.

ences in decision behavior found for the three authority levels (see Table 1). The longer they have been in their job, the greater is the tendency for first and second-line supervisors to shift from permissive to directive decision procedures. In contrast, the senior managers tend to use more delegation as their length of tenure increases. It would appear that the better the lower level leaders get to know their job and

TABLE 4

CORRELATION BETWEEN A LEADER'S TIME IN PRESENT POSITION AND HIS
USE OF FIVE DECISION PROCEDURES[a]

Decision procedure:	Leader's time in present position		
	First-line supervisor	Second-line supervisor	Senior manager
Own decision without explanation	.45[b]	.38[c]	.08
Own decision with explanation	.06	−.01	−.07
Consultation	−.16	−.10	−.12
Joint decision-making	−.22	−.04	−.03
Delegation	−.19	−.17	.39[c]
	$N = 29$	$N = 72$	$N = 82$

[a] Note: Data is from Questionnaire A and B.
[b] $p < .05$.
[c] $p < .01$.

The five correlations for each sample are not independent since ipsative scoring was employed.

subordinates, the less inclined they are to share decision-making, perhaps because there is a real or felt difference in skills between the lower level leader and his subordinates. On the other hand, as the senior managers get to know their subordinates better, some of the decision-making responsibility is handed over to them completely. This would suggest that the managers gain confidence in their subordinates' ability, or that they have been able to train them to carry out a wider range of tasks.

6. The nature of the problem requiring a decision also appears to be related to the leader's decision-making behavior. The findings presented in Table 5 suggest that leaders vary their decision behavior

TABLE 5

COMPARISON OF DECISION PROCEDURE FOR TWO TYPES OF DECISIONS
N = 82[a]

Senior managers decision procedure:		Percentage of time the procedure is used		
		Mean percentage	S.D.	t
Own decision without explanation	EMP	7.1	16.1	4.58 $p < .001$
	SUB	20.9	24.1	
Own decision with explanation	EMP	12.2	17.9	3.70 $p < .001$
	SUB	30.7	24.0	
Consultation	EMP	41.4	31.7	−3.18 $p < .01$
	SUB	30.4	21.2	
Joint decision-making	EMP	27.1	27.3	−6.27 $p < .001$
	SUB	16.0	21.9	
Delegation	EMP	12.0	19.5	−5.39 $p < .001$
	SUB	2.1	5.3	

[a] Note: Data is from Questionnaire B. EMP = Decisions concerning employees working under the subordinate of the leader. SUB = Decisions concerning the immediate subordinate of the leader.

The five *t*-tests are influenced by the ipsative nature of the scale which adds up to 100%; however, they indicate trends.

according to the hierarchical locus of the problem. The two centralized decision styles are used more frequently when the problem relates to their immediate subordinates (SUB decisions). On the other hand, leaders tend to use one of the three influence-sharing methods when the problem to be decided involves persons two levels down the authority hierarchy (EMP decisions). The difference in the choice of style between EMP–SUB problems is highly significant. This finding is consistent with the notion that the authority structure represents functional specialization and delegation of responsibility. A manager would not need lower level supervisors if he had to make *their* decisions for them. On the other hand, the figures in Table 5 indicate that most managers continue to play an important part in the making of EMP decisions.

7. For first and second-line supervisors, a different kind of distinction was made with respect to the nature of the problem. Decision-making dealing with task problems was compared to decision-making dealing with group maintenance problems by the use of Form C. The mean and standard deviation of Decision-centralization scores for the task decisions were 3.05 and .53, respectively. The mean and standard deviation for the maintenance decisions were3.62 and .36, respectively. A t-test indicated that the means were significantly different ($t = 9.20$, $P < .01$). Apparently the supervisors were more willing to allow subordinate participation in making task decisions than in making maintenance decisions. Perhaps this is because many maintenance decisions, especially those involving personnel matters or discipline problems, do not lend themselves easily to decentralization, even though some discussion with subordinates will often be necessary.

DISCUSSION AND CONCLUSIONS

The results of the present study support the thesis that the amount of influence a leader allows his subordinates changes with six of the seven situational variables studied in this research. More specifically, the results show that sharing of decision-making with subordinates was greatest under the following conditions:

—When the leader was a senior manager rather than a supervisor or foreman.
—When the leader was an elected or appointed student leader rather than an industrial leader.
—When the leader was a personnel manager or a general manager, as opposed to managers of sales, purchasing, production, or finance divisions.
—When the leader had a small span of control.
—When a first or second-line supervisor was newly appointed to his position.
—When a senior manager had been in his position for a considerable amount of time.
—When the decision involved persons more than one level down in the authority hierarchy.
—When the decisions were concerned with task matters rather than with personnel matters, discipline, or morale.

As has been pointed out earlier, recent reviews of the literature on participation (Sales, 1966; Lowin, 1968) show clearly that the majority of previous studies have been concerned with broad overall relations between participatory behavior and other variables. In their view, this research has been indecisive. There are probably three reasons for this. Firstly, previous investigators have not taken into account the variety of decision styles commonly used by managers. Secondly, specific decisions of the kind typically confronting leaders have not been used in scales measuring decision behavior. Finally, "the mediating conditions which shape the effect of participatory decision making" have been largely ignored (Lowin, 1968, p. 99).

The five point decision continuum and the measuring scales which were used in this research appear to lend themselves to a study of how leaders adapt their decision-making to the needs of the situation. These questionnaires could also be used to investigate the relation between leader decision-making and group performance. Furthermore, the situational variables found to be related to leader decision-making in this study are potential mediators of the relation between participation and group performance. These situational variables and others like them will be useful for determining the parameters of feasibility for participation in different kinds of organizations.

REFERENCES

Argyris, C. *Integrating the Individual and the Organization.* New York: Wiley, 1964.

Bass, B. Some effects on a group of whether and when the head reveals his opinion. *Organizational Behavior and Human Performances,* 1967, **2**, 375–382.

Blankenship, V., and Miles, R. Organization structure and managerial decision behavior. *Administrative Science Quarterly,* 1968, **13**, 106–120.

Blake, R., and Mouton, J. *Group Dynamics: Key to Decision Making.* Houston, Texas: Gulf Publishing Company, 1961.

Davies, B. Some thoughts on organizational democracy. *Journal of Management Studies,* 1967, **4**, 270–281.

Fleishman, E., Harris, E., and Burtt, H. Leadership and supervision in industry. Ohio State University Studies, Bureau of Educational Research Monographs No. 33. Ohio State University, Columbus, Ohio, 1955.

Heller, F. Group feed-back analysis: A method of applied research. Paper presented at Western Psychological Association meeting. San Diego, March 1968. Mimeographed, University of California, Berkeley. To be published *Psychological Bulletin* 1969.

Leavitt, H. Unhuman organization. *Harvard Business Review,* 1962, July–August, 90–98.

Leavitt, H. Applied organizational change in industry: structural, technological and humanistic approaches. In J. March (Ed.) *Handbook of Organizations.* Chicago: Rand McNally, 1965.

Lefton, M., Dinitz, S., and Pasamanick, B. Decision making in a mental hospital: real, perceived and ideal. In Rubenstein, A. R., and Haberstroh, C. (Eds.) *Some*

DECISION-MAKING   241

Theories of Organization. Homewood, Illinois: Dorsey Press, Revised Edition, 1966.

LEWIN, K., LIPPITT, R., AND WHITE, R. Patterns of aggressive behavior in experimentally created "social climates." *Journal of Social Psychology,* 1939, **10**, 271–299.

LIKERT, R. *New Patterns of Management.* New York: McGraw-Hill, 1961.

LIKERT, R. *The Human Organization.* New York: McGraw-Hill, 1967.

LOWIN, A. Participative decision-making: a model, literature, critique and prescription for research. *Organizational Behavior and Human Performance,* 1968, **3**, 68–106.

MARCH, J. G., AND SIMON, H. A. *Organizations.* New York: Wiley, 1958.

PUGH, D., HICKSON, D., HININGS, C., AND TURNER, C. Dimensions of organization structure. *Administrative Science Quarterly,* 1968, **13**, 65–105.

SALES, S. Supervisory style and productivity: a review. *Personnel Psychology,* 1966, **19**, 275–286.

STRAUSS, G. Some notes on power-equalization. In H. Levitt (Ed.). *The Social Science of Organizations.* New York: Prentice-Hall, 1963.

TANNENBAUM, A. Control in organizations: industrial adjustment and organizational performance. *Administrative Science Quarterly,* 1962, **7**, 236–257.

TANNENBAUM, R., AND MASSARIK, F. Participation by subordinates. In Tannenbaum *et al.* (Eds.). *Leadership and Organizations.* New York: McGraw-Hill, 1961.

TANNENBAUM, R., AND SCHMIDT, W. How to choose a leadership pattern. *Harvard Business Review,* 1958, **36**, 95–101.

TRIST, E., HIGGINS, G., MURRAY, H., AND POLLOCK, A. *Organizational Choice.* London: Tavistock Publications, 1963.

WOODWARD, J. *Industrial Organization: Theory and Practice.* London: Oxford University Press, 1965.

RECEIVED: August 16, 1968

[13]

Limits to participative leadership: Task, structure and skill as contingencies - a German-British comparison*

FRANK A. HELLER

Tavistock Institute of Human Relations, London

BERNHARD WILPERT

International Institute of Management, Berlin

Abstract

The research investigated the relationship between managerial decision-making and a set of specified contingent situational factors: decision type, perceived skill requirements and objective skill inputs. The study was based on 663 German and British managers in two interlocking senior management levels of 37 large enterprises. The data were collected by means of Group Feedback Analysis as part of a large study of managerial decision-making in eight countries.

The results show a significant (p = < .05) relationship between the choice of decision styles and the postulated contingency variables. Only 1 % of 615 senior managers consistently use a single decision style, more than two-thirds use four or five different styles. Very large variations occur as a function of different decision tasks, perceived skill requirements and objective skill availability.

There are differences between the relatively well matched samples of German and British managers, but they are less significant than the broadly similar way in which both samples respond to the particular contingencies under investigation.

The results are interpreted in the context of an open systems contingency framework. Their action implications are seen to suggest a link with socio-technical theory on job design and wider issues of organisational and social policy.

* The European research was initially financed by the Social Science Research Council (Britain), who have supported it with two grants. It was later cofinanced by the International Institute of Management. The research described in this paper was made possible as the result of funding from these two bodies.

Eur. J. soc. Psychol. 7 (1), pp. 61-84

62　　*Frank A. Heller and Bernhard Wilpert*

The research objective

The research was stimulated by the difficulty of applying well-established findings on leadership styles (Likert 1961, 1967) to two Latin American countries. Was there a fundamental difference in culture or were there other factors which made a universalist approach to participative decision-making ineffective (Williams, Whyte and Green, 1966; Heller, 1969a, 1973)?

There are a number of alternative strategies one can use in attempting to answer such a question. One very stringent scientific approach is well described by Triandis (1972) who supports Strodtbeck (1964) in the view that the nature of culture itself must be the objective of the 'experimental treatment'. In such a methodological approach, an essential task is to develop cross-culturally equivalent variables and to standardise and/or control the research situation within very narrow limits. Such a methodology is not only costly and time intensive, it is also unlikely to obtain the necessary conditions of control (Triandis, 1972:53-55) where organisations as well as individual respondents have to sanction access to information.

Among the alternative possibilities, the one adopted for the present research uses a multivariate contingency framework. Instead of using one major dimension for comparative purposes – for instance culture – we use more than a score of variables and include among them national groupings.[1] Our major research question is as follows: which of the variables in our research design accounts for a significant variation in participative behaviour? Eventually we will want to rank order the impact of the various contingency measures on the core phenomenon under investigation.

Open systems and contingencies

The basic concepts in our theory are (i) open systems of interacting variables, and (ii) the notion of contingencies as sources of variance.[2] The approach to open systems follows Emery (1969) but extends it to factors *inside* organisations. Emery believes 'that it has been shown that living systems whether individuals

1. A national group is more easily defined for our purpose than culture. The major problem is the representativeness of our sample and we do not pretend to have solved this issue.
2. The variances are between peripheral and core variables. We use these terms, instead of the more usual terms independent and dependent variables, to stress that the model does not require assumptions of causality. In this respect it differs from Emery and Trist (1965).

or populations, have to be analysed as "open systems", i.e. as open to matter-energy exchanges with an environment. Human organisations are living systems and should be analysed accordingly. The fact that it faces us with the task of analysing forbiddingly complex environmental interactions gives us no more of an excuse to isolate organisations conceptually than the proverbial drunk had when searching for his lost watch under the street lamp because there was plenty of light when he knew he had lost it in the dark alley.'

The variables used in this research are arranged in a hierarchy of systems, from influences close to the person to the more distant effects of the environment (Heller, 1971, 1972). The model is deliberately labelled transitional to show that we expect to modify our system boundaries and their hierarchical arrangement as a result of our findings. Nor do we exclude the need to introduce further systems of variables in future research designs.[3]

Social scientists, and particularly psychologists, have always been aware of the potential importance of situational factors like heat, lighting, noise, task structure, but the effort to develop general laws of human behaviour has often taken precedence over the more careful examination of the relative impact of these situational variables. The parallel development in management theory and management science has also been in the direction of establishing universal laws in the possibly mistaken belief that this is the best way in which academic work can help the practitioner in the field.

Technology was one of the first contingency variables to impose itself on the slowly developing study of behaviour in organisations and, with varying interpretations of what technology is, it has remained a critical factor. The pioneering work can be associated with the studies of coal mining under the direction of Trist (Trist and Bamforth, 1951; Trist, Higgin, Murry and Pollock, 1963) from which has evolved the socio-technical systems approach. The technical component in this theory was at first conceived in terms of machines and their interaction with people at the lowest level of the organisation. More recently the theory has been used to describe various technical, physical and ecological constraints in interaction with psychological and social variables (Emery and Trist, 1960, 1973).

Other schools of social science have found it necessary to adopt analogous formulations or to consider other multivariate extensions to their theory. McGregor, for instance (1967), used an elaboration of Lewin's (1951) famous formula

---

3. The present model does not include interorganisational analysis. Consequently we do not, at the moment, assess the influence of other organisations, competitors, suppliers, banks, etc. as part of the environment.

(B = f (Person, Environment)) to arrive at a comprehensive statement of the interaction between a group's behaviour and various task-environmental contingencies:

$$B_{group} = f(M\ a, b, c, \ldots T\ f, g, h \ldots O\ l, m, n \ldots L\ q, r, s \ldots E\ u, w, x)$$

where M = attitudes, knowledge, skills capabilities, etc. of members

T = the nature of the job and variables related to the primary task

O = structure and internal controls of the subsystem

L = the skills, capabilities, and other characteristics of the leader

E = environmental variables in the larger organisational system and society

In recent years a number of contingency theories have been developed and others like March and Simon (1958) and Burns and Stalker (1961) have been interpreted as belonging to this group (Terry, 1973). Various field and experimental studies have shown the significant relationship between situational factors and the choice of certain supervisory and corrective techniques in the interaction with subordinates (Kipnis and Consentino, 1969; Goodstadt and Kipnis, 1970; Kipnis, 1972). Such factors are considered to be: positional influence in terms of control over resources, type and complexity of the problem to be solved, experience on the job, span of control. At least four major organisation theorists have used technology as a contingency (Woodward, 1958, 1965; Thompson, 1967; Lawrence and Lorsch, 1967; Perrow, 1967 and 1970). If task and task structure can be considered as part of technology, then we have to include several others, for instance: Shaw (1962); Shaw and Blum (1966); Fiedler (1963, 1967); and Heller and Yukl (1969).

While technology and the uncertainties of the environment have so far attracted the major share of attention, at least in leadership studies, other situational variables have been considered important recently.

Sadler, Webb, and Lansley (1973) in a study of 50 companies, half in Printing and half in Building industry, find that the decision style of managers has to be considered together with structural measures of organisation before reasonable performance prediction becomes possible. Furthermore, the results coming from the 25 companies in each industrial sector are really substantially different and this could be due to differences in technology. Vroom and Yetton (1973) have developed a very sophisticated situational model of leader decision-making in which contingencies like time constraints, quality of problem-solving, adequacy of information, trust in subordinates, expected conflict among subordinates and acceptance of decisions by others, are measured. They find that information is a particularly important situational variable. When managers said they had sufficient information, they were less participative, and when they thought that subordinates had additional information, they were more participative. The availability of information could of course be a function of the technology surrounding the managerial job, but it was not possible to investigate this.

In reviewing this literature, the question has to be asked whether socio-technical theory is related to the more recent situational and contingency theories, or should be treated separately. The greatest success of socio-technical thinking has so far been achieved in applications at or near the shop floor level, but this could simply be an accident of history (Hill, 1972; Davis and Taylor, 1972).

The answer to our question will to some extent depend on one's definition of technology. Joan Woodward, for instance, found that her original classification was imperfect for a number of reasons. One was that the technology of the major product was not a determining factor in accounting for the behaviour of people who were not physically close to the production process. Her interest therefore moved to an analysis of control and control systems in organisations (Woodward, 1970).

The structure of administrative-managerial jobs has never been adequately analysed, certainly not in terms of technological components. It is therefore possible that an extension of socio-technical thinking to higher levels of organisation still waits for a suitable classificatory theory of the critical environmental dimensions of administrative jobs. In the meantime what we call a contingency framework in this research may be considered as a step in this direction.

The research

The research has been described elsewhere (Heller, 1971; Wilpert and Heller, 1973, 1974). It will therefore be possible to be brief. This study analyses organisational decision-making at two senior-management levels in 17 German and 20 British companies. A total of 663 managers from both countries participated in the research. Some of the statistical analyses are based on smaller subsamples.

Apart from certain explorative, descriptive purposes about the nature of decision-making among German and British managers, the research was to test some hypotheses that were formulated in the context of our contingency framework. Its basic contention is that people vary their behaviour according to circumstances or situations. With reference to our core variable – decision-making – we formulated the following hypotheses:

Hypothesis 1
Managers will use different decision methods in different decision-task situations.

66   *Frank A. Heller and Bernhard Wilpert*

Hypothesis 2

The choice of specific decision-making methods will vary with the reference point of the decision: subordinates, lower-level employees, department as a whole. More specifically: the decision method of superiors (L1) will be more centralised (i.e., less participative) if the decision directly concerns their immediate subordinates (SUB or Level 2) than if it concerns L2's subordinates (EMP). Decisions concerning the senior manager's department as a whole (DEPT) will be in between SUB and EMP decisions.

Hypothesis 3

Differences in perceived skill requirements of the respective jobs in Level 1 and Level 2 will be associated with differences in the choice of decision-making methods; the more demanding an L1-manager perceives his work to be in comparison to his subordinate's job, the more centralised will be his decision-making.

Hypothesis 4

Differences in 'objective' skill inputs will be associated with differences in decision centralisation: higher qualifications in education will be associated with more participative decision-making.

The data collection took place between 1970-1974 and was based on a method of field research called Group Feedback Analysis (Heller, 1969b). The German and British samples of companies were fairly successfully matched for size, managerial progressiveness, industrial sector, technology and level of organisational hierarchy.[4]

The average age and experience of the sample is shown in Table 1.

---

4. The matching procedure for the European sample of companies was carefully planned between the scientists in each of the national research centres, but certain problems and difficulties inevitably arose and had to be dealt with on an ad hoc basis. A full description of the procedures used and difficulties encountered will be published with the multinational research report next year. The German-British matching was reasonably satisfactory, with the following exceptions:

(a) one sector (oil technology R & D) could not be matched.

(b) The L1-sample is almost 100 % of the L1-level in British but approximately 80 % of German L1.

(c) The German sample is more heavily represented on the manufacturing and engineering function and has fewer 'general' nonspecialist managers than the British sample.

Table 1. *Age and experience of German and British managers (International Management Decision-Making Research – abbreviated IMDMR)*

| | Level 1 [a] | | Level 2 [b] | |
	German	British	German	British
Age	45.4	48.6	42.6	44.1
How long in present post [c]	5.9	4.4	4.9	4.7
How long in company [c]	15.6	20.2	14.5	17.6
Number in sample	106	177	147	185

a. Level 1 are senior managers who report directly to a chief executive.
b. Level 2 managers are senior subordi-nates of L1.
c. In years.

Instruments

The reliability and validity of the 14 research instruments used in the comprehensive research are discussed by Wilpert and Heller (1974). Only 3 instruments are relevant for the purpose of this report:

(1) *Form 5 – Specific Decisions Questionnaire (see Appendix)*
It defines five different decision-making methods on a hypothetical continuum of influence and power-sharing. L1-managers are asked to report on a cumulative percentage scale how frequently they chose different methods in making the 12 different decisions. L2-managers report how they see their superiors making the decisions.

(2) *Form 2 – Skill Requirements Questionnaire*
L1-managers were asked to describe as objectively as possible the skill requirements of their own job in comparison to the requirement of their immediate subordinate's job on a 5-point scale (see Table 7). These job descriptions had to be related to 12 specific managerial skills and qualities. Each L2-manager similarly compared his own job with that of his immediate superior. By use of factor analysis (Wilpert and Heller, 1974), we reduced the 12 items to 3 composite variables: technical competence, interpersonal competence, entrepreneurial competence.

(3) *From 11 – Objective Skill Questionnaire*
This form asks managers to describe their formal skills in terms of levels of education, the amount of work-related reading they do, the professional

68   *Frank A. Heller and Bernhard Wilpert*

associations they belong to, and the courses they have attended inside and outside their industry.

The research is part of a larger multinational project which started in the United States in 1967 and has been extended and considerably refined in Europe during 1970-1974. In addition to Germany, Britain and USA; France, Israel, Netherlands, Spain and Sweden have participated.[5] Most of the data is now available. It will cover approximately 120 companies and over 1500 senior managers. This is a substantial sample if it is considered that each of the companies was visited at least twice and managers were interviewed in groups of 3 to 15.

Findings

Managers use more than one style

Table 2 shows the frequency with which German and British managers at both levels describe the use of a single decision method in 12 managerial situations. Only 1 % of our total sample of 615 managers appear to use one single method consistently. There are no significant variations for levels or national grouping.

Table 2. *How often do managers use single rather than multiple styles of desicion-making? (Form 5 IMDMR)*

Level 1[a] As senior managers describe their behaviour		Level 2[b] As subordinates see the behaviour	
Germany	Britain	Germany	Britain
1 out of 106 .0094	2 out of 177 .0113	2 out of 149 .0134	2 out of 186 .0107

a. As senior managers describe their behaviour.

b. As subordinates see the behaviour.

5. The following research institutes were in charge of the national research project: International Institute of Management (Germany); Tavistock Institute of Human Relations (Britain); University of California, Berkeley (USA); Institut Supérieur des Affaires (France); The Leon Recanati Graduate School of Business Administration (Israel); Erasmus University (Netherlands); Instituto de Estudios Superiores de la Empresa (Spain); and Economic Research Institute of the Stockholm School of Economics (Sweden).

The majority of managers use either four or all five alternative methods. This can be seen from Table 3.

Table 3. *Variations in leadership methods used by senior managers: German and British samples (Form 5 IMDMR)*

Use of methods	British L1 and L2 as %	German L1 and L2 as %
All 5 methods	29	19
4 out of 5	43	39
2 or 3 out of 5	26	41
Only 1	1	1
Size of sample	286	255

Note. In this research L1-managers describe their own leadership method in relation to 12 specific decision situations relevant to their job. Level 2 managers (their immediate subordinates) describe their superior's leadership method in the same 12 situations. For the purpose of this table, the L1 and L2 descriptions of decision-making are pooled.

72 % of the British sample and 58 % of the German managers use four or five methods. For the purpose of this comparison the self-report of L1 and the description of L2 have been merged, and it can be seen that German managers appear to use a smaller variety of the available five methods than British managers. Since both national groups describe the same 12 decision situations, this comparison is of some interest.

Decision task as contingency

However, even more significant than the variation between our national samples is the variation within each national group. These variations are clearly based on the nature of the tasks. The results for one of the national groups can be seen in Table 4.

To illustrate the difference, it is only necessary to compare the answers to Question 1 with Question 3.[6] In relation to Question 1, 97 % of senior managers describe their decision behaviour as highly centralised and their subordinates perceive it similarly (95 %). The same managers report only 12 % of centralised decision-making for the situations described by Question 3 and again subordinates agree (11.4 %). These differences can be seen more easily in Figure 1. These findings support

6. The 12 different situations are described in the appendix.

70　*Frank A. Heller and Bernhard Wilpert*

Table 4. *How two interlocking levels of senior British management see the senior level make decisions in 12 distinct decision areas (UK sample: L1 = 177; L2 = 185)*

FORM 5

Decision style												
Level 1												
1	52.0	5.5	3.9	12.8	13.2	4.4	6.1	14.9	3.5	7.2	8.6	6.8
2	45.3	11.0	8.0	6.6	20.7	8.5	10.5	27.7	9.9	13.7	38.2	27.7
3	2.7	52.5	27.6	18.6	41.7	47.3	33.8	41.4	39.9	42.2	42.5	44.4
4	0.0	28.4	40.7	6.4	17.1	32.5	37.3	15.9	35.9	28.6	10.7	20.9
5	0.0	2.6	19.7	55.6	7.3	7.4	13.0	0.1	10.8	8.3	0.0	0.2
Level 2												
1	62.0	3.5	5.6	9.1	22.1	2.5	5.8	1.8	3.7	1.4	5.9	3.4
2	32.8	5.9	5.8	5.9	7.9	6.8	6.0	27.3	6.3	6.7	27.8	17.2
3	3.7	32.4	16.7	7.7	23.9	25.0	31.3	26.3	32.2	32.0	47.1	31.3
4	1.0	50.0	32.6	12.8	30.6	45.7	40.4	22.6	37.8	31.6	17.0	39.6
5	0.5	8.3	39.3	64.5	15.5	15.0	16.5	2.0	20.0	28.3	2.2	8.5

Note. Level 1 describes his own decision behaviour, Level 2 describes the behaviour he attributes to his boss. For a description of the five decision styles, see Form 5 (Appendix).

hypothesis 1: (Managers will use different decision methods in different decision-task situations).

Organisational distance as a contingency

The 12 questions on Form 5 were designed to describe a range of tasks which senior managers in almost all industrial and service organisations carry out at least once a year and usually more often.

The decisions fall into three categories, each category relating to one of three organisational levels of an average department or group of managers. The man in charge of the group is L1, his immediate subordinates (abbreviated SUB) form the second level. Other, lower-level employees (abbreviated EMP) are at least two levels below L1. Finally, some decisions apply to the department as a whole (abbreviated DEPT) and therefore affect the senior level, his immediate subordinates and other employees.

Decisions focussing on the tasks related to SUB, EMP and DEPT can be ordered in terms of their 'organisational distance' from the senior-level manager.

Limits to participative leadership   71

Figure 1. *Decision-method variations according to the nature of the task*

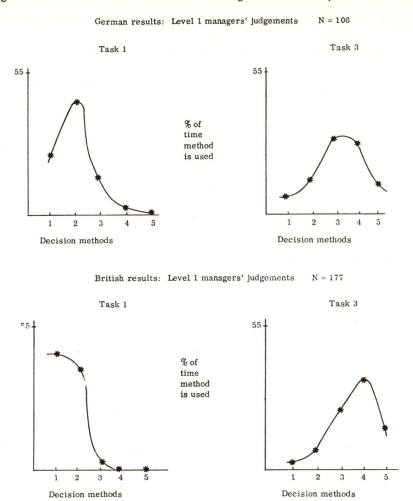

German results: Level 1 managers' judgements   N = 106

Task 1   Task 3

% of
time
method
is used

Decision methods   Decision methods

British results: Level 1 managers' judgements   N = 177

Task 1   Task 3

% of
time
method
is used

Decision methods   Decision methods

SUB decisions are those between L1 and managers who report to him directly; here the organisational distance is short (Distance A). DEPT decisions are made about tasks that affect his immediate subordinate (SUB) as well as other employees at lower levels of the department (EMP). This group of decisions tasks is more distanced from L1 than SUB decisions (Distance B). Finally, decisions

72 *Frank A. Heller and Bernhard Wilpert*

that affect lower levels of employees are organisationally further from L1 than DEPT type decisions (Distance C).

Figure 2. *Departmental organisation and the organisational distance of the different types of decisions*

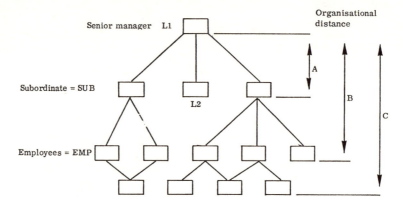

Organisational distances:

A corresponds to SUB type decision
B corresponds to DEPT type decision
C corresponds to EMP type decision

Our hypothesis (H2: decision centralisation will covary with the reference point of the decision-subordinate, lower-level employees, department) has been confirmed by findings from the German and British samples (see Tables 5 and 6). From Table 5 it can be seen that method 1 where a manager makes his own decision without even communicating the outcome or the reasons for making the decision, is taken most readily in SUB-type situations and least in EMP decisions. DEPT falls between the two. At the other end of the range of alternatives, method 5 (delegation) is used progressively more as we move from SUB to DEPT to EMP. Table 5 combines the results from both levels but shows the pattern of decision styles over the five methods. Table 6 shows the judgements of the two managerial levels separately but the decision-method alternatives are summarised in a single score called DCS (Decision Centralisation Score). It expresses the general tendency of decision-makers: the higher the score the more centralised the method of decision-making.

Table 5. *Decision method as a function of decision type and organisational distance: German and British managers at Levels 1 and 2 combined (Form 5 IMDMR)*

Method of decision-making	Decisions with immediate subordinates		Decisions on departmental issues		Decisions relating to employees below immediate subordinate	
	SUB		DEPT		EMP	
	German %	British %	German %	British %	German %	British %
1	14.30	18.43	8.17	18.01	5.51	4.45
2	22.09	26.00	11.69	20.74	8.73	7.74
3	34.63	29.90	37.08	33.20	34.29	34.20
4	23.35	18.84	35.33	21.74	42.00	38.20
5	5.61	6.06	7.70	6.26	9.39	15.39

Totals approximate to 100%   German sample = 253   British sample = 362.

Note. For a description of the five decision methods, see Form 5 (Appendix).

Table 6. *Decision method as a function of decision type and organisational distance: German and British managers at Levels 1 and 2 (Form 5 IMDMR)*

	Decisions with immediate subordinate		Decisions on departmental issues		Decisions relating to employees below immediate subordinate	
	SUB		DEPT		EMP	
	German	British	German	British	German	British
DCS as seen by L1	3.42	3.5	3.01	3.28	2.83	2.63
DCS as seen by L2	2.97	3.15	2.60	3.17	2.42	2.33

Note. A high DCS (Decision Centralisation Score) signifies centralised nonparticipatory methods. The highest possible score is 5; the lowest 1.

74   *Frank A. Heller and Bernhard Wilpert*

It can be seen that the hypothesis is supported at both levels and for German as well as British managers.[7]

Perceived skill difference as a contingency

The results on perceived skill requirements and their relation to decision-making are shown in Table 7. Two findings emerge from this tabulation. Firstly there is considerable agreement between German and British managers at both levels. Secondly, as expected, there is a considerable amount of disagreement about skill requirements as judged by the two levels of management; both levels describe their own job as requiring more skill than the other level! The scores in Table 7 are averages but there are considerable variations around the average.

Table 7. *Perceived skill difference of two interlooking levels of management (Form 2 IMDMR)*

Skills	Level 1		Level 2	
	Mean scores			
	German	British	German	British
1. Knowledge of technical matters	2.8	2.8	3.6	3.5
2. Technical competence factor	2.4	2.2	3.2	3.2
3. Interpersonal competence factor	2.4	2.4	3.3	3.4
4. Entrepreneurship factor	1.8	1.9	2.8	2.8
5. Average score of 12 items	2.2	2.2	3.1	3.1
Number in sample	106	177	147	185

Note: 1. Items 2, 3 and 4 are composites based on factor analyses.

2. The scores in the table are means based on a 5-point scale:

For Level 1

1	2	3	4	5
much more	about the same		somewhat less	much less

For Level 2

5	4	3	2	1
much more	somewhat less	about the same	more	much less

The findings from both German and British managers support the prediction of hypothesis 3: High differences in perceived skill requirements at L1-level are associated with centralised decision-making of L1 (Table 8).

Senior managers who judge the skill requirements at their own level to be much greater than those at the level of their immediate subordinate are also inclined

7. There is one exception. British L2-managers judging their boss's behaviour on DEPT decisions show a slightly higher score (3.17) than their judgements of SUB decisions (3.15).

Table 8. *Relationship between the senior manager's judgement of skill require-ments and his method of decision-making (Forms 2 and 5 IMDMR)*

Managerial skills: requirements at L1 and L2	Decision centralisation (DCS)	
	British manager L1	German manager L1
1. Knowledge of technical matters	—19*	—19
2. Technical competence factor [a]	—28**	—19
3. Interpersonal competence factor [a]	—13	—31**
4. Entrepreneurship factor [a]	—25**	—11
5. Average score	—30**	—25*
Number in sample	177	106

** $p = < .01$
* $p = < .05$
a. These variables are based on factor analysis of 12 specific skills.
Note: A negative correlation indicates that senior managers who judge their own jobs to require more skill than their subordinates' jobs, also use more centralised decision methods (less power-sharing).

to use more centralised (nonparticipatory) decision methods (Table 8). Similarly, when subordinates describe their own jobs as being more challenging than their superior's, they also see him use power-sharing (participatory) methods (see Table 9).

Table 9. *Relationship between the subordinate manager's judgement of skill requirements and his description of how his superior makes decisions: German and British subordinate managers (Forms 2 and 5 IMDMR)*

Managerial skill requirements at L1 and L2	Decision centralisation (DCS)	
	British managers L2	German managers L2
1. Knowledge of technical matters	—10	—33**
2. Technical competence factor [a]	—03	—30**
3. Interpersonal competence factor [a]	—17	—32**
4. Entrepreneurship factor [a]	—15*	—21*
5. Average score	—14	—33**
Number in sample	185	147

** $p = < .01$
* $p = < .05$
a. These variables are based on factor analysis of 12 specific skills.
Note: A negative correlation indicates that when subordinate managers judge their own jobs to require as much or more skills than their superiors, they describe their superiors' decision method as power-sharing.

76   *Frank A. Heller and Bernhard Wilpert*

The judgements and perception at both levels are quite consistent; managers seem to see a connection between the use of participation and the availability of skill. Where skill is lacking, participation seems less appropriate.

Objective skill as a contingency

The skill assessment just described (based on Form 2) is semi-objective, semi-subjective. Managers at both levels are asked to describe *the jobs* not the people, but their ego involvement is unlikely to make them neutral judges in their job description. This expected perceptual distortion is confirmed by the results: One's own job seems always more demanding than one's subordinate's/superior's (Table 7).

However, the research attempted to provide also a more objective means of describing the available skills at both levels. This task is very difficult, but it seems to have been solved adequately for our purpose. The results in Table 10 have considerable face validity. In general we found that L1-managers who are older and have been in their company longer than their subordinates, also have higher scores on formal skills. They belong to more scientific and professional institutions, take and read more work-related journals and are more highly educated. This pattern is identical for German and British managers.

Table 10. *Formal skill qualifications of two senior levels of German and British management (Form 11 IMDMR)*

Categories of experience and skill	Level 1		Level 2	
	German	British	German	British
1. Number of scientific and professional associations	0.61	1.22	0.35	0.79
2. Number of journals taken	3.98	3.84	3.48	3.45
3. Number of journals read (Scale 1 - 7)	5.08	5.46	4.54	5.28
4. Educational level (1 = low, 4 = high)	2.21	1.07	1.60	0.95
5. Number of courses outside industry	1.22	1.27	1.03	1.36
6. Number of courses inside industry	0.95	1.19	0.82	1.42
Number in sample	106	177	147	185

When it comes to postexperience education, the results are more complex. German L1-managers attend more courses outside their own work place as well as inside their companies than their subordinates. In contrast to this, British-L2 managers attend more outside and inside courses than their next higher level. This could be a reflection of different management development strategies with

German companies paying more attention to higher rather than middle levels of management, while British companies concentrate on slightly lower levels. Our samples are too small to draw any firm conclusion at this stage.

The research set out to test the hypothesis (H4) that higher education qualifications are associated with more participative behaviour.[8]

Table 11. *Relationship between formal educational qualifications and power-sharing among German and British managers (Forms 5 and 11 IMDMR)*

	Formal educational qualification Senior level	
Average of 12 specific decision situations (Decision centralisation score)	German sample N = 147 —34**	British sample N = 185 —29**

** $p = < .01$

Note: A negative correlation means that senior managers with lower educational qualifications are more inclined to use centralised styles, while managers with higher formal qualifications use more participative methods.

This hypothesis receives support from the results for both German and British senior managers (Table 11). The average decision style used in 12 specific situations correlates significantly with formal educational qualifications; the higher the qualifications the more power-sharing.

Discussion

We started the paper by drawing attention to the limitation of a universalistic approach to participation and followed it up by describing an open-system contingency research on decision-making styles in two countries.

The findings show that senior, experienced and presumably successful managers do not use the same decision method in all circumstances.[9] A manager will use a 'democratic' method on one occasion and an 'autocratic' one on another. The terms democratic and autocratic are really inapplicable because they pretend to describe *personality* whereas our findings suggest that the *situation* or *task* is

8. Previously it had been shown that there was a straight progression of more participative behaviour from first line to second line supervisors to senior managers to university students (Heller and Yukl, 1969:233).

9. The companies were selected by impartial judges in part because they were 'progressive' and successful. Similar findings have been reported by Vroom and Yetton, 1973, and Bass and Valenzi, 1973.

the real differentiator. Vroom and Yetton come to the same conclusion.

Their work and ours was pursued quite independently, neither knowing of the others' existence for a while. In some respects our methods and hypotheses are similar, in others they are different, but we have certainly worked with quite distinct samples of managers. The congruence of many of our findings is therefore encouraging. Vroom and Yetton (1973:120) say that: 'in the literature on participation, ... leaders have been typed as autocratic, consultative or participative ... the findings seriously question the explanatory power of either the type or the trait concept ... each manager studied indicated that he would use at least four of the five leadership methods ... The manager's choice of decision process was influenced much more by the properties of the situation depicted than it was by his average style.'

Our findings here, as well as previously with American data, fully support these conclusions (Heller and Yukl, 1969; Heller 1971, 1973).

It would be untrue to say that all psychological work in the area of leadership and decision-making had in the past ignored contingency factors. Some of the best theorists and experimenters had for a long time mentioned situational factors in leadership but mainly as afterthoughts or footnotes rather than as major structures in the framework of analysis. As long ago as 1948, Stogdill came to the conclusion that personality factors alone do not satisfactorily account for leadership behaviour, and in 1956 he successfully tested the hypothesis that leadership performance was contingent on the organisational position of actors. Wispe and Lloyd (1955), studying life insurance representatives, found a significant tendency for persons who perceived little threat in their environment to prefer permissive decision styles in group situations.

The main problem remained, in spite of extensive critical prodding (Gibb, 1947; Hemphill, 1949; Etzioni, 1965), and was well described by Koreman (1966:355: 'What is needed however in future concurrent (and predictive) studies is not just recognition of this factor of "situational determinants" but rather a systematic conceptualisation of situational variance as it might relate to leadership behaviour'.

The research from which the German-British findings reported here derive, was started in 1967 with the objective described by Koreman. It was felt that a considerable number of psychological, social, technical and structural contingencies would have to be examined step by step since the number of variables involved was too great for a single project. The early results with data from American managers fully supported a few contingency hypotheses (Heller, 1971), and the present report on German and British samples extends and confirms the conclusions.

A great deal more work remains to be done, both conceptually and in terms of methodological refinements. It is most unlikely that a complex process like decision-making will yield simple analytical solutions. We would not expect to be able to account for more than a certain percentage of the variance of leader behaviour, but it should be possible to identify meaningful and consistent patterns of the more powerful contingencies supporting or opposing a variety of decision styles. The findings already show that psychological as well as nonpsychological factors set limits to the exercise of influence-sharing processes in organisations.

We live in an era where more and more people, institutions and even political organisations are committed to policies for increasing the scope for autonomous decision procedures and participative practices. Up to now the major psychological contribution towards achieving such ends has been through a variety of training schemes designed to make people use more participative styles irrespective, or largely irrespective of the situations in which they find themselves. If our findings are correct, it would follow that we must expect considerable inconsistencies, strain and possibly deception in the attempt to fulfil global prescriptions for more participation. A similar point has been made by Mulder (1971). Apart from the necessary motivation to participate in the decision-making about subjectively salient issues, Mulder stresses expertness in the decision area as a necessary condition for effective participation. Our findings on the connection between objective skill input and decision centralisation supports this perspective.

Is it likely that the variations in decision styles discovered in recent research can be 'ironed out' by training? Or are there limits set by the socio-technical interaction between the variables? These issues require further exploration and link our area of research with the field of job design and the experiments with semi-autonomous work groups which are now developing very rapidly in a number of countries (Davis and Taylor, 1972; SSRC 1974).

Psychologists interested in this developing field of enquiry may also find it requisite to consider the relationship between managerial decision practices and the attitudes of trade unions (van Beinum, 1972; Hughes and Gregory, 1974), as well as the implications of the wider social polity (Thorsrud, 1972; Emery and Trist, 1973).

80   *Frank A. Heller and Bernhard Wilpert*

Appendix

Form 5 – Specific Decisions Questionnaire

The five methods of the Influence-Power-Continuum
The five methods are defined for each manager as follows: 'In this form we are concerned with the management skill called "decision-making". This term includes the process leading up to the final decision, and advice or recommendations which are usually accepted also count as decisions for the purposes of this research. Many alternative methods of decision-making exist, among them those described below. All have been shown to be widely used and effective.'

1. Own decision without detailed explanation
   Decisions are made by managers without previous discussion or consultation with subordinates. No special meeting or memorandum is used to explain the decision.

2. Own decision with detailed explanation
   Same as above, but afterwards managers explain the problem and the reasons for their choice in a memo or in a special meeting.

3. Prior consultation with subordinate
   Before the decision is made, the manager explains the problem to his subordinate and asks his advice and help. The manager then makes the decision by himself. His final choice may, or may not, reflect his subordinate's influence.

4. Joint decision-making with subordinate
   Managers and their subordinates together analyse the problem and come to a decision. The subordinates usually have as much influence over the final choice as the managers. Where there are more than two individuals in the discussion, the decision of the majority is accepted more often than not.

5. Delegation of decision to subordinate
   A manager asks his subordinate to make the decision regarding a particular problem. He may or may not request the subordinate to report the decision to him. The manager seldom vetoes the subordinate's decisions.

The twelve specific decisions are as follows:
(The following wording is for the L1-manager. The L2-manager answers the same questions, but referring to his end of the same decision process – i.e., he reports how he sees his superior making decisions.)

1. To increase the salary of your direct subordinate.
2. To increase the number of employees working for your subordinate.

3. To hire one of several applicants to work for your subordinate.

4. To change the extension number of your subordinate's telephone. (In Germany: To change the format of official letters).

5. To purchase for your department a necessary piece of equipment costing over a stated amount.

6. To promote one of the employees working for your subordinate.

7. To give a merit pay increase to one of your subordinate's employees.

8. To increase the financial allocation for your department during the preparation of the organisational budget.

9. To fire one of your subordinate's employees.

10. To change an operating procedure followed by your subordinate.

11. To assign your subordinate to a different job (on same salary).

12. The decision regarding what targets or quotas should be set for your subordinate.

REFERENCES

Bass, B., and Valenzi, E. (1973). Contingency aspects of effective management styles. Management Research Centre. Technical Report 67: May.

Beinum, H. von (1972). The relations between the role of the trade union in modern society and the attitudes of workers. In Davis and Taylor (Eds.), *Design of jobs.* Penguin Modern Management Readings.

Burns, T., and Stalker, G. M. (1961). *The management of innovation.* London: Tavistock.

Davis, L., and Taylor, J., Eds. (1972). *Design of jobs.* Penguin Books.

Emery, F. E., Ed. (1969). *System thinking.* Penguin Modern Management Readings.

— and Trist, E. L. (1960). Socio-technical systems. In Churchman and Verhulst (Eds.), *Management sciences: Models and techniques,* Vol. 2. Oxford: Pergamon Press.

— and Trist, E. L. (1965). The causal texture of organisational environments. *Hum. Rela.,* 18: 21-31.

— and Trist, E.L. (1973). *Towards a social ecology.* London: Plenum Press.

Etzioni, A. (1965). Dual leadership in complex organisations. *Amer. soc. Rev.,* 30: 688-98.

Fiedler, F. E. (1963). A contingency model for the prediction of leadership effectiveness. Urbana, Ill.: University of Illinois. Mimeo.

— (1967). *A theory of leadership effectiveness.* New York: McGraw-Hill.

Gibb, C. A. (1947). The principles and traits of leadership. *J. abn. soc. Psychol.,* 42: 267-84.

Goodstadt, B., and Kipnis, D. (1970). Situational influences on the use of power. *J. appl. Psychol.,* 54(3):201-207.

Heller, F. A. (1969a). *Management's contribution to economic development.* Michigan State University. Business Topics, Winter: 37-43.

— (1969b). Group feed-back analysis: A method of field research. *Psychol. Bull.,* 72(1):8-117.

— (1971). *Managerial decision-making: A study of leadership styles and power-sharing among senior managers.* London: Tavistock.

82	*Frank A. Heller and Bernhard Wilpert*

— (1972). The decision process: An analysis of power-sharing at senior organisational levels. Tavistock Institute of Human Relations. Mimeo SFP2337. (Also as chapter in the *Handbook of work organisation and society*. Ed. R. Dubin, Rand McNally, 1976).

— (1973). Leadership, decision-making and contingency theory. *Industr. Rela.,* 12: 183-199.

— and Yukl, G. (1969). Participation and managerial decision-making as a function of situational variables. *Org. Beh. hum. Perform.,* 4, 227-241.

Hemphill, J. K. (1950). Relations between the size of the group and the behavior of 'superior' leaders. *J. soc. Psychol.,* 32: 11-22.

— (1960). Dimensions of executive positions: A study of the basic characteristics of the position of 93 business executives. Ohio State University. Bureau of Business Research Monograph No. 98.

Hill, P. (1972). *Towards a new philosophy of management.* London: Gower Press.

Hughes, J., and Gregory, D. (1974). Work organisation: Some issues of practice and concept. *SSRC.*

Kipnis, D. (1972). Does power corrupt? *J. Pers. soc. Psychol.,* (1):33-41.

— and Cosentino, J. (1969). Use of leadership powers in industry. *J. appl. Psychol.,* 53 (6):460-466.

Koreman, A. K. (1966). Consideration, initiating structure and organisational criteria: A review. *Personnel Psychol.,* 19:349-361.

Lawrence, P., and Lorsch, J. W. (1967). Differentiation and integration in complex organizations. *Admin. Sc. Qua.,* 12:1-47.

Lewin, K. (1951). *Field theory in social science.* New York: Harper.

Likert, L. (1967). *The human organization.* New York: McGraw-Hill.

March, J. G., and Simon, H. A. (1958). *Organizations.* New York: Wiley.

McGregor, D. (1967). *The professional manager.* New York: McGraw-Hill.

Mulder, M. (1971). Power equalization through participation? *Admin. Sc. Qu.,*

16 (1):31-38.

Perrow, C. (1967). A framework for the comparative analysis of organisations. *Amer. soc. Rev.,* 32:194-208.

— (1970). *Organisational analysis.* London: Tavistock.

Sadler, P., Webb, T., and Lansley, P. (1973). Management style and organisation structure in the smaller enterprise. Ashridge Management Research Unit. Final Report to the Social Science Research Council: April. Mimeo.

Shaw, M. E. (1962). *Annual technical report.* Gainesville, Fl.: University of Florida.

— and Blum, J. M. (1966). Effects of leadership style upon group performance as a function of task structure. *J. Pers. soc. Psychol.,* 3:238-241.

Social Science Research Council (1974). Recent changes in work organisation in Sweden. Papers of the Anglo-Swedish Conference held in London: March. (To be published in bookform 1978).

Stogdill, R. M. (1948). Personal factors associated with leadership: A survey of the literature. *J. Psychol.,* 25:35-71.

— and Sharfle, C., and Associates (1956). Patterns of administrative performance. Ohio Studies of Personnel Research Monograph No. 81.

Strodtbeck, F. L. (1964). Consideration of metamethod in cross-cultural studies. *Amer. Anthr.,* 66:223-229.

Terry, P. T. (1973). The contingency theory of organisation: Its development and application. University of Loughborough. Master's Thesis. August.

Thompson, J. (1967). *Organizations in action.* New York: McGraw-Hill.

Thorsrud, E. (1972). Job design in the wider context. In Davis and Taylor (Eds.), *Design of jobs.* Penguin Modern Management Readings.

Triandis, H. (1972). *The analysis of subjective culture.* New York: Wiley.

Trist, E. L., and Bamforth, K. W. (1951). Some social and psychological consequences of the Longwall-method of coal-getting. *Hum. Rela.,* 4:3-38.

— Higgin, G. W., Murry, H., and Pollock,

A. B. (1963). *Organisational choice*. London: Tavistock.

Vroom, V., and Yetton, P. (1973). *Leadership and decision-making*. Pittsburgh, Pa.: University of Pittsburgh Press.

Williams, L. K., Whyte, W. F., and Green, C. S. (1966). Do cultural differences affect workers' attitudes? *Industr. Rela.*, 5(3):105-117. May.

Wilpert, B., and Heller, F. A. (1973). Power-sharing at senior management levels. *Omega*, 1:451-464.

— and Heller, F. A. (1974). Decision-making in German and British companies. Paper to the 18th International Congress of Applied Psychology, Montreal. August.

Wispe, L. G., and Lloyd, K. E. (1955). Some situational and psychological determinants of the desire for structured interpersonal relations. *J. abn. soc. Psychol.*, 51:57-60.

Woodward, J. (1958). *Management and technology*. Her Majesty's Stationery Office.

— (1965). *Industrial organisation theory and practice*. London: Oxford University Press.

— (1970) *Industrial - organisation: Behaviour and control*. London: Oxford University Press.

Résumé

La présente étude a pour objet d'examiner le rapport existant entre le pouvoir décisionnel des cadres et un ensemble de facteurs spécifiés, aléatoires et situationnels tels que: le type de décision, les exigences de compétence perçues et les investissements de compétence objectifs. Cette étude a été réalisée sur 663 cadres allemands et anglais à deux niveaux de gestion supérieure interdépendants dans 37 grandes entreprises. Les données ont été rassemblées à l'aide de la Group Feedback Analysis et faisaient partie d'une vaste étude effectuée sur le pouvoir décisionnel des cadres dans huit pays. Les résultats démontrent un rapport sensible ($p = < .05$) entre le choix des styles de décision et les variables aléatoires postulées. Sur 615 cadres supérieurs, seul 1 % adopte systématiquement un style unique de décision, plus des deux tiers choisissent 4 ou 5 styles différents. On constate de très grandes variations résultant des différentes tâches décisionnelles, des exigences de compétences perçues et de la disponibilité de compétences objective. Il existe des différences entre les échantillons relativement bien appariés des cadres allemands et anglais mais elles s'avèrent moins significatives que la manière plus ou

Zusammenfassung

Das vorliegende Forschungsprojekt untersuchte die Beziehung zwischen Entscheidungen im Managementbereich und einer Reihe bestimmter kontingenter situationaler Faktoren: Entscheidungstyp, wahrgenommene Kenntnisanforderungen und objektiver Kenntnis Input. Die Untersuchung beruhte auf Daten von 663 deutschen und britischen Geschäftsleuten in zwei ineinandergreifenden höheren Managementebenen 37 großer Unternehmen. Die Daten wurden mittels einer Gruppen Feedback Analyse gewonnen und waren Bestandteil einer größeren, in acht Ländern durchgeführten Studie über Entscheidungen im Managementbereich. Die Ergebnisse zeigen eine signifikante ($p = < .05$) Beziehung zwischen der Wahl von Entscheidungsstilen und den postulierten Kontingenzvariablen. Nur 1 % von 615 Geschäftsleuten in höheren Positionen verwenden durchweg einen einzigen Entscheidungsstil, mehr als zwei Drittel verwenden vier oder fünf verschiedene Stile. Sehr große Variationen treten in Abhängigkeit von verschiedenen Entscheidungsaufgaben, wahrgenommenen Kenntnisanforderungen und objektiver Verwendbarkeit von Fachkenntnissen auf. Es gibt zwar Unterschiede zwischen den relativ gut

84　*Frank A. Heller and Bernhard Wilpert*

moins similaire dont ces deux types d'échantillons réagissent aux contingences particulières analysées. Les résultats sont interprétés dans le contexte d'un cadre ouvert de contingence des systèmes. Les implications de ces actions semblent révéler un lien avec la théorie socio-technique relative au modèle des professions et avec des problèmes plus vastes portant sur la politique organisationnelle et sociale.

zusammengesetzten Stichproben deutscher und englischer Geschäftsleute, doch sind sie weniger signifikant, als die weitgehend ähnliche Art und Weise, in der beide Stichproben auf die untersuchten Kontingenzen antworten. Die Ergebnisse werden im Rahmen einer Theorie der Kontingenz in offenen Systemen interpretiert. Ihre praktischen Implikationen verweisen auf eine Verbindung mit der soziotechnischen Theorie über 'job design' und weitreichenderen Fragen organisatorischer und sozialer Politik.

[14]

Decision Processes:
An Analysis of Power-Sharing at
Senior Organizational Levels

FRANK A. HELLER

The Tavistock Institute of Human Relations

PART I: TOWARDS A MODEL OF DECISION-MAKING

Our understanding of decision-making in organizations has improved as a result of important theoretical and research contributions from diverse sources during the last fifty years. Nevertheless, it is still an underdeveloped subject and much in need of further theoretical refinement and subsequent validation. While such a sweeping statement could be made about many areas of business activity, not least about the oldest specialized discipline, economics, it may justify particular attention in this case. It may be asked whether the *act* of making a decision, defined in the manner described by the greater part of the literature on this subject, is really an important, recognizable managerial activity in modern organizations. The question is of some importance since the activity called decision-making has been endowed with a considerable amount of prestige and there has been a tendency to describe administration or management (particularly at senior levels) in terms of making decisions.

This chapter has two objectives. One is to present a theoretical framework for the discussion and evaluation of the decision-making process in organizations. It is an open system, multivariate approach and it stresses the *relative* rather than the *universal* importance of variables which contribute to the understanding of decision-making. For this reason the model will be called a contingency model to fit in with currently used terminology.

The second objective is to present some findings from field research at senior management levels to validate important aspects of this model. As a result of the gradually accumulating data, the model has been changed and, it is hoped, improved. The research, too, has expanded and it now covers seven

The following colleagues have read parts of the manuscript and made valuable comments: John Child, Robert Dubin, William Starbuck, George Strauss, Cecil Gibb, Cornelius Lammers and Eliezer Rosenstein. The many remaining inadequacies are due to the writer.

countries and will eventually draw on a multinational pool of results from several more. An important aspect of the presentation of the currently available results is to describe a relatively new method of research which has certain advantages for the model used here and for multivariate and multinational comparisons. The method enables one to collect simultaneously highly quantifiable data as well as in-depth qualitative information.

We have said that the activity called decision-making has been endowed with special importance and prestige. This is in part due to its close association with the concept of power and this has had an important effect on the description of organizational typologies such as line and staff functions. It is possible that the often rigid differentiation between giving orders and giving advice, which is so widespread in the classical description of organizations, is based on a misunderstanding of what happens when people say that a decision is being made. What really matters when a person gives an order or makes a recommendation is whether the substance of the order or advice is acted upon. In this sense, advice which is usually accepted is closer to decision-making than orders which are implemented after considerable delay and extensive changes. Accountants or Industrial Engineers may be staff specialists in theory, but if the Accountant's system of apportioning overheads and the Industrial Engineer's suggestions on preventive maintenance are acted on, they are indistinguishable from other decisions made by line managers. It can even be argued that line managers, particularly at senior levels, often *endorse* decisions which were really made much lower down in the organization.

This chapter will start with a theoretical analysis of the decision-making process and its relation to concepts such as influence and power, as well as to other dimensions of the environment surrounding the people who contribute to this process. Having developed the theoretical model we will describe the recent research project which sets out to test some of the assumptions of the model and which appears to validate them.

Some Important Contributions

Probably the most important contribution to our understanding of decision-making (DM) comes to us as a derivative of economic theory and is based on the work of Simon and his colleagues at the Carnegie-Mellon University. Simon (1957) successfully challenged two major assumptions made by traditional economics with its long history of building normative and deductive models of analysis. One is that DM is based on perfect knowledge, and the other is that man attempts to maximize his utilities or satisfactions. Simon's arguments go much further than simply reducing some of the over-rigorous elements of the normative model; he argues as a psychological realist to the effect that man's mind could *never* store and digest the complex information available. Man's rationality is not only bounded, it is also distorted by subjective processes which make him see *his reality* in a special perspective. Furthermore, man's search for alternatives is hampered by these perceptual and knowledge limitations as well as by his limited motivational stamina. Typically, man stops looking for alternatives when some minimum set of priorities is met fairly adequately. By chance, a particular choice could represent optimum conditions, but more usually *he is satisfied* with far less and looks no further. The model used by Simon and his followers stresses the need for empirical work to check on the formulated hypotheses, but like other economic models it is based on charting DM as a process of choice based on objective or subjective probabilities of outcomes. The new emphasis on subjective choices forged a fruitful alliance between statisticians working with Bayesian theories and psychologists exploring the phenomenon of thinking.

A second major contribution to this field, particularly to the analysis of power and its relation to DM comes from sociological theory and especially from the work of Weber (1947) and those who followed a structural-functional analysis of organizations. One can call this the institutional model, which like that of the classical economists, produced a logical and normative framework for explaining bureaucratic processes. Weber, however, centered his analysis around deliberately isolated logical categories called "ideal" types which were chosen to represent a selection of certain elements of reality, while at the same time avoiding the de facto reality of an empirical investigation.

Weber was interested in describing conditions which enabled the decision process to become operative and effective and he saw three major alternative forces at work: (1) rational beliefs based on a legal framework and effective bureaucratic machinery, (2) the force of traditionalism and the predictive stability it provided and (3) the forcefulness and exceptional qualities of leadership which enable some few people to impose their personal authority on the decision process. The orderly development of the bureaucratic process was seen to be helped by the existence of widely diffused values and by the recognition of self-interest in the legitimated decision procedure. Such a conceptual schema gets quite close to certain aspects of modern organization theory. Sociologists, however, usually avoid psychological explanations as carefully as psychologists avoid considering the impact of social structure and institutions on their preferred unit of analysis.[1]

Weber's analysis of bureaucracy and power has had a considerable impact on sociological and political thinking and fits in very well with the somewhat formal, legalistic and structural design of the European system of industrial relations. While Britain remains an exception, the European approach to DM has legitimated a formal division of influence and power which finds its apogee in the German legal code of co-determination based on a series of laws starting in 1951.

The third major impetus to the work on DM and power-sharing comes from the interpersonal analysis of social psychologists. Rensis Likert and many of his colleagues at the University of Michigan have worked on several different approaches in the late 1940s with investigations into supervisory styles of clerical work in insurance companies and manual work on the railways.

The long series of investigations have been summarized in a number of books (Likert, 1961, 1967; Tannenbaum, 1968) and the more experimental orientation of interpersonal DM and power-sharing was carefully reviewed by Cartwright (1965) and from a broader perspective by Vroom (1970). Most of this work is based on the view that decision styles can be adequately described

---

[1] Weber was not quite as doctrinaire in this respect as some sociologists who preceded and followed him. He did not see social structures or social institutions as collective wholes but insisted on looking for molecular explanations at the level of social interaction between industrial actors. The sociological schools that followed him usually failed to develop this eclectic trend.

690　Frank A. Heller

by two modal categories, authoritarianism and participation (Lowin, 1968). As in the case of the economic and sociological models, the theoretical formulations concentrated on a universalistic position; that is to say, they tested propositions that would apply in most or all circumstances and conditions. Occasionally, exceptions were found and explanations to account for them were put forward (Likert, 1961; Fleishman, et al., 1955), but the view that decision styles are a function of known predictor variables related to the situation, technical factor, organization structure, etc. has been put forward only very recently (Fiedler, 1964; Heller and Yukl, 1969; Lawrence and Lorsch, 1967a; Wofford, 1971).

The three modes of DM analysis stemming from model-building in economics, sociology and interpersonal behavior have developed on autonomous lines and, with the notable exception of the Carnegie-Mellon work of March, Simon and Cyert have contributed little to each other. However, there are now signs that this isolation may soon break down under the influence of open systems thinking. The model to be described in this chapter certainly owes a great deal to a wide spectrum of work.

Our model started from the perspective of an interpersonal analysis of influence and power-sharing between dyads of senior managers. From the beginning, and in contrast with the bulk of the interpersonal work just mentioned, the model was designed to explore the effect of potential moderator and contingency conditions. The question was: How do these contingency variables affect each other and how do they relate to DM methods (the dependent variables)? The model was designed to make few explicit causal assumptions and to begin by studying independent variables that were thought to be psychologically and spatially close to the decision-makers.

Before describing our model and some examples of the supportive research evidence, it is necessary to take a close look at decision-making, which can be treated either as an event, a series of connected events, or as a flow process.

DM as a Series of Events

Most descriptions and definitions of DM concentrate on the modal point where a final *choice* is made (Vroom, 1964:19; Taylor, 1965:48; Applewhite, 1965:53; Brown, 1960:23; Tiffin and McCormick, 1942:500–502). This is particularly clear in all models using decision trees although in that case a number of modal points with a "go-no go" alternative describe a series of steps until the final outcome is reached. This concentration on *choice* based on a careful consideration of alternative utilities can no doubt be justified with many examples and it has certainly facilitated the building of mathematical models in which binary conditions are easily accommodated. Choice is an adequate description of DM when we focus on the activity of one person or on a group of people, such as committees making decisions in a limited time-span. However, organizational DM can only be described by a choice model if one makes a number of unrealistic assumptions and ignores the complex input of advice, recommendations and preferences which make up what eventually emerges as a decision.

The lack of reality is due to the assumption that, at the point where a person takes an action, he had a number of realistic alternatives from which to choose. As we shall show later, this is usually not the case. Nor does action in relation to alternatives require a decision; it often leads to an endorsement of someone else's decision or, more frequently, to a recommendation to be added to other recommendations that eventually lead to an outcome, such as the purchase of a machine.

The complexities of organizational DM have now been carefully documented in a number of case studies (Cyert, Simon and Trow, 1956; Dufty and Taylor, 1962; Cyert and March, 1963; Pettigrew, 1973). It is useful to draw a distinction between routine decisions, for which a computer program can be devised, and nonprogramed decisions which resemble one-off productions of prototypes with novel and unstructured variations. We will be concerned entirely with nonprogramed DM and with the *pattern of influence* which describes *how* decisions are made rather than *what* the decision is. This separation between the process and the content is somewhat artificial, since the former influences the latter and the nature of content also reacts on the process. Eventually, both aspects of DM will have to be described by means of a single model.[2]

In the meantime, we recognize the great value of case studies, since they make it possible to describe the process and content all at once, as well as to give some indication of the pattern of influence. This versatility of the case method is apparent in a well-known and detailed description of selecting a computer and EDP system (Cyert, et al., 1956). However, when the authors come to summarize what they call the "anatomy of the decision" within the constraints of a search-choice model they leave out all considerations of interpersonal relations and influence. This omission would make it very difficult for the model to predict outcomes, even where the decision content remained the same. The authors recognize this difficulty and try to deal with it intuitively by drawing an analogy with an engineering model transmitting and filtering information. Subordinates are said to be "information filters" who can secure a considerable amount of influence over a decision which is eventually made by their boss. The research to be described here measures information filtering in the sense used by Cyert, et al. (1956, 1963), but without using the engineering communication model.

Recommending Decisions or Deciding on Recommendations

Before we can explain our model, we must produce a realistic description of what a typical organizational decision is like. It is worth bearing in mind that when researchers have described what managers actually do during the course of an ordinary work day, they have rarely observed anything resembling the activity of making a decision. Carlson, the pioneer of managerial activity studies, actually concluded that in the judgment of most senior managers "they did not take part in so very many decisions and it was seldom that they gave orders" (Carlson, 1951:49). Most of the senior managers' time was taken up with advising other people and giving them explanations. Many other studies of managerial activities do not even mention decision-making (Stogdill, et al., 1956; Stewart, 1970; Marples, 1967). This strange contrast between one group of researchers who see DM as the truly major managerial activity and another

---

[2] We start by concentrating on the process, but since we are working with a contingency model, we are able to show how different types of content affect the process.

group who find very little trace of DM in the daily work diaries of managers has not yet been adequately explained. Different conceptual models and terminology are undoubtedly one aspect of this puzzling contrast, but there is also something more important. In our research, the main DM questionnaire consists of twelve decisions which were selected from a wide range of alternatives because they were typical of situations which most senior executives had to handle in their businesses. It soon became clear, however, that executives often "made" these decisions only very indirectly. Firstly, they "shared" the activity with various people: their subordinates, colleagues and their superiors. Secondly, it emerged that while they made *a* decision, the final authority could lie with somebody else and it was not always clear where the final decision emerged.

Thirdly, managers were often conscious that although they had the authority to make a final decision, they were in most cases unable and unwilling to reject the recommendations which had come to them. This situation of the decision-maker as the *endorser* of other people's recommendations has not often emerged in the literature, but has been eloquently described by Galbraith, who maintains that even presidents of large organizations such as General Motors "exercise only modest power over substantive decisions" (Galbraith, 1967:67–70). A similar situation of relative powerlessness at the top of the pyramid is noticed by Wilkins (1967) in the legal process. There is very little difference between a "decision" which could be countermanded at a later stage of the process and a "recommendation" which is almost invariably accepted.

DM as a Flow Process

The picture that emerges from these considerations is of a broad and lengthy process meandering its way up a pyramidal structure as in Figure 1. At various points in the DM process people search for facts, make suggestions, recommendations, write reports and make decisions. At a certain stage (called D/E on the diagram) a final resolution of the problem emerges. This can be either in the form of a final decision or an endorsement of recommendations which could have emerged from quite low levels of the pyramid (Blankenship and Miles, 1968).

An alternative way of describing the flow process is to describe a series of events as they relate to a business problem (Figure 2). Let us consider the problem of choosing a new manager for an important position. The process starts with a job description by person A, the previous manager of that job, who has just been promoted to another position. Person B, a relatively junior clerk in the personnel department, drafts the advertisement and suggests where it should be inserted. Person C, a senior member of the personnel department, revises the draft and slightly amends the list of advertising media (after consulting with G, the man who will be the new manager's superior). A short list of ten candidates is drawn up by D, the head of the personnel department and E, the adviser on management development. An outside consultant, F, has devised tests and the interview procedure through which he and D make the decisions on a short list of three candidates, one of whom is particularly highly commended. These three are interviewed by G, the senior manager, who decides on one of them.

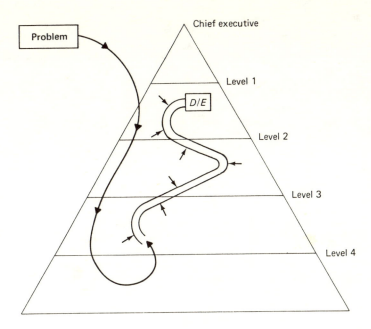

Figure 1. The decision process in a pyramidal structure.

Note: D/E = Decision or Endorsement.

In Figure 2 seven stages have been identified in the DM process in this particular and fairly simple problem. Although G appears to have made the final decision, there are clearly several other stages in the process at which important decisions were made. Only at Stage 7 does DM look like the classical tree choice situation, but in many important respects, G has less influence over who joins the company than several other people who contributed to the earlier stages. The usual questions: "Who made this decision?" "Who is responsible for it?" "Who has contributed most to the final outcome?" are all fairly meaningless. In order to improve the final outcome, namely the selection of the best possible candidate, a more useful question would be: "At which stage of the decision procedure should there be a change of time and money resources to improve the final outcome?" When the question is put in this way, several alternatives emerge which could lead to greater or reduced investment at any one of the seven stages. Just to make a discussion point, one could envisage a situation where the most junior of the eight contributors to the selection DM, namely the clerk, could be responsible for the most critical aspect of the whole process, namely the recommendation where and how to advertise. If substantially better candidates could be attracted at stages 2 and 3, then the subsequent stages of the process are affected by this change, and it is conceivable that none of the final trio who were selected at point 6 would have been sent forward to manager G. By treating DM as a flow process with various inputs of suggestions, choices and recommendations, the sobering conclusion emerges

694   FRANK A. HELLER

Stages

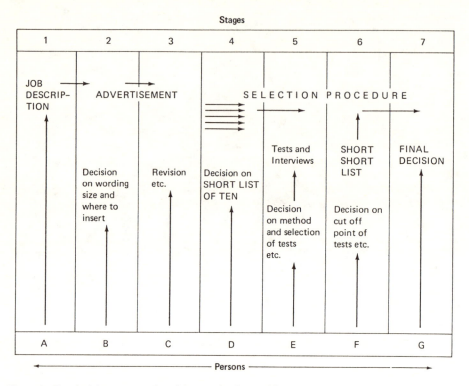

Figure 2. The decision process describing a selection problem.

that every stage of the DM process before the final "go-no go" choice may be more important than the final decision itself.

This example also shows why it is important to consider how much influence and authority (power) is exerted at each stage of the DM process. If we think that stages 2 and 3 are critical in this particular series of events, then we have to know how much influence B, C, and G have on the wording, size and location of advertisements. How do these three people interact in making their decision?

This brings us to a subject which textbooks describe as leadership and the styles of management and it is necessary to make an evaluation of its contribution to DM.

A Neutral Model of "Decision Styles"

The literature on decision styles and leadership methods is full of value assumptions which are so obtrusive that they are likely to influence the results. For instance, the standard research instrument developed by the Institute for Social Research of the University of Michigan uses a series of 4-point scales which are often headed by terms like "exploitive authoritative," "benevolent authoritative" (Likert, 1961:223). Even when these terms are replaced with more neutral terms such as System 1 and System 2 (Likert, 1967:4) the de-

scriptions for each of the points on the scale are quite unequivocally positive
or negative. For instance, "Have no confidence and trust in subordinates" as
against "Complete confidence and trust in all matters" (Likert, 1967:4). Measurements on such a scale can be anticipated to produce results which will reflect people's values more than the actuality of the organization they are describing. When people are asked to describe on such a scale how they see the
situation now and how they would like it to be later, the invariable result is
a shift towards what are seen to be more positive or acceptable values (Likert,
1961:28).

There is therefore a need for a more realistic and neutral model of alternative decision methods. By this I mean a range of alternatives which are sufficiently well balanced to enable researchers to observe the empirical distribution of behavior without inviting response bias, resulting from a person's guess
of what the "correct" or "desirable" response would be. The absence of such
a neutral model is probably responsible for a fair proportion of the generalizations in the current leadership literature.

A neutral model of alternatives will enable us to collect evidence on the
decision methods used by administrators in a variety of organizations and
under a *range of different conditions.* We can then discover whether leadership
styles are univariate or, alternatively, whether they vary in relation to predictable circumstances.

Research: The Influence-Power-Continuum

In our research model, the core variable is the DM process and this is obviously a very complex phenomenon. We have simplified our task by concentrating on how a decision is made rather than on the decision content.[3] Decisions
are described in terms of the influence or power which a person or persons
exert. We define these terms as follows.

Influence.   This is assumed to exist when a person has access to the decision process. Influence is legitimized when this access is formally recognized
by the organization within which influence is exerted. As a result of this access,
a person or group can make a contribution to decision-making with various
degrees of impact. When the impact leads to acceptance of the contribution in
the final outcome, it is called power.

Power.   This concept is defined as influence which has been incorporated
in the decision process. When we talk about degrees of power, we attempt to
assess or measure the relationship of a particular input to the total determination of all the other elements in the process of arriving at a decision.

Because we have conceptualized DM as a flow process with multiple inputs
(as in Figures 1 and 2), we asked our managers to stretch the term *Decision
to include advice-giving and recommendations,* as long as there is a high probability that the advice is accepted.[4]

---

[3] It must be repeated that we are aware that content and method are interrelated; we
check on this, but concentrate on the latter.

[4] It would be preferable to use another word for DM described in this way, but so far
no suitable term has come to mind.

696   FRANK A. HELLER

Six positions can be identified on what is called an Influence-Power Continuum (IPC). Figure 3 describes the relationship graphically.[5]

- *Method 1: Manager's own decision without detailed explanation.* These are decisions made by *you* without previous discussion or consultation with other people in the organization. There are situations where the decision or recommendation communicates itself without special procedures.
- *Method 2: Manager's own decision with detailed explanation.* The same as above, but afterwards you explain the problem and the reasons for your choice in a memo or in a special meeting, etc.
- *Method 3: Prior consultation.* Before the decision is taken, you explain the problem to the other person(s) and ask for advice and help. You then make the decision by yourself. Your final choice may, or may not, reflect other people's influence.
- *Method 4: Joint Decision-making.* You and the other person(s) together analyze the problem and come to a decision. The other person(s) usually exerts as much influence as you. Where there are more than two in the discussion the decision of the majority is accepted more often than not.
- *Method 5: Delegation (short span).* You ask a subordinate or colleague to make the decision regarding a particular subject. You make it clear that you want to be kept informed on this matter, and that within a fairly short period you expect to review this decision with him.
- *Method 6: Delegation (long span).*[6] As above, but you do not ask to be kept informed and there is no short-term review. It is understood that even if you did not like the other person's decision, you would intervene only in exceptional circumstances. Some review or evaluation does take place in the long run. The time span will depend on a number of circumstances, such as role expectation, but principally on the nature of the work process and the budget review period.

The Concept of Power in Relation to DM

The concept of power occupies a very important place in the literature of sociology and political science. It is occasionally used in the description of organizational life (March and Simon, 1958; Simon, 1957; Whyte, 1969) and plays an important role through the use of related or overlapping concepts such as authority, control and participation. We have seen that purely organizational terms like *line* and *staff* rely heavily on an analysis of power and this is true of other terms such as *hierarchy* and *leadership*.

Definitions.   It is possible that the word "power" is *not* very widely used in the management literature because of its close association with politics on

---

[5] The IPC methods described here apply the DM process to subordinates, colleagues and superiors. The wording can be changed slightly if we want to study boss-subordinate interaction only as in our research project.

[6] In previous descriptions of the IPC, I used only one method of delegation and therefore only five points on the scale (Heller, 1971a:27–28). The research to be described here is also based on a five-point IPC. The advisability of introducing two modes of delegation arose from discussions during the feed-back stage of the research. The difference between positions 5 and 6 can be seen in time span of responsibility terms (Jaques, 1956).

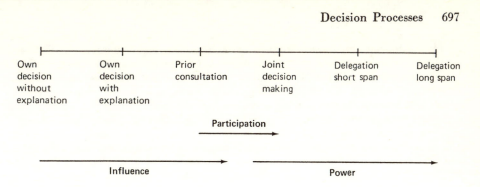

Figure 3. Influence power continuum.

the one hand and an almost medieval stereotype of dominant-submissive relationships, on the other. Terms like *line* and *staff*, *authority* and *control* appear
less tainted and do not offend current values with their emphasis on equality.
Against this background, it may be thought inept or at least unnecessary to
describe six alternative decision methods in terms of a distribution of power.
It can also be argued that if a term like power is used, then it should follow the
most widely accepted definitions, such as those of Weber or Dahl (1968). These
are weighty arguments and we must explain why we have not accepted
them.

The first reason for not accepting the standard definition of power is that
if the six alternatives in Figure 3 correspond to the reality of the DM process
in organizations, and if we want to describe them as a continuum under a
single concept, then power or some synonym becomes the obvious choice. As has
already been said, most previous investigations have avoided this problem by
concentrating on a smaller range of methods, *excluding* delegation. This has
led to the possibility of seeing the range of alternatives in terms of authoritarian versus group-sharing methods and in this context *participation* is the
term most widely used. Faced with the necessity to choose the term power or
a less aggressive sounding synonym, it was thought that two considerations became relevant. One is the increasing tendency to draw on a wide range of social
sciences for the purposes of organizational analysis. Sociology, political science
and social anthropology have already made substantial contributions and use
the concept power in their analysis. Secondly, it is a question of whether the
realities of organizational life should be seen in sharp or soft focus either from
the point of view of a better understanding or in relation to democratic values.
It was decided that a sharp focus was more appropriate for descriptive as well
as normative purposes.

The need for our definition of influence and power is more easily justified.
Almost all current definitions concentrate on the relationship between individuals, or between groups of individuals, or between individuals and groups. Our
own definitions *relate* the contribution of *people to a process*. In contrast,
French and Raven (1959) say that their "theory of social influence and power
is limited to influence on the person." Similarly, Dahl in his well-known article
on power (1968:407) states the case quite categorically: "...power terms in
the social sciences exclude relations with inanimate or even nonhuman objects."
Elsewhere, he defines power as determining the behavior of one social unit by

698   Frank A. Heller

another. Alternatively he sees what he calls "agents" exerting influences, whether they are "individuals, groups, roles, offices, governments, nation-states or other human aggregates" (Dahl, 1957). It is possible, but not necessary, to see the decision process as a human aggregate; in many situations, in government bureaucracies, for instance, the process is best described and identified in relation to a file or set of papers that move from office to office for comment, endorsement or decision.

Weber has been the most influential person in this field and chose to conceptualize power in a classical but aggressive form. It is "the chance of a man or of a number of men to realize their own will in a communal action even against the resistance of others who are participating in the action" (Gerth and Mills, 1947:180). More briefly, he sees power as the "possibility of imposing one's will upon the behavior of other persons" (Bendix, 1960:294). The use of unequivocal German words like *Macht* and *Herrschaft* served to underline the coercive aspect of power which many writers have since followed.

Another important influence on the conceptualization of power is the possibility of relating it to causality (Dahl, 1957, 1968) or even more radically, of treating it as a special instance of causality (March, 1955; Simon, 1957). Our own model avoids causal conclusions and is even opposed to them.

Finally, there is the much debated question surrounding the *fixed* or *elastic* nature of power. The simpler and historically much more important view is to see it as fixed so that if one person obtains more of it, somebody else loses a corresponding amount. Parsons, however, has argued strongly against the dominant and erroneous "tendency in the literature that there is a fixed quantity of power in any relational system" (Parsons, 1963). Tannenbaum has taken the same position; he has operationalized a measure of *control* (Tannenbaum, 1957) and has shown that, by his definition, it is not a fixed amount so that one group of people can substantially increase the amount of control they have (or feel they have) without diminishing the amount held by other people in the same organization. In our description of the IPC (Figure 3), we probably approach zero sum game conditions at the two extremes of the continuum while Tannenbaum's definition applies to the middle ranges (to Methods 3 and 4).

These are the various reasons which have inclined us to define influence and power in an organizational rather than an interpersonal context. The particular organizational anchorage we have chosen is the decision process (Figure 1). Various gateways provide access to DM (our definition of influence) or beyond that, they facilitate incorporation (our definition of power). It must be emphasized that the organizational focus on power does not prevent it from being used in interpersonal power situations, as long as they relate to organizational variables. In our case the organizational variable is DM. For instance, interpersonal promotion and conflict problems may be analyzed as a part of the decision process and the definitions of influence and power given above apply.

A Contingency Model of DM

The next stage in the theoretical analysis of DM is to relate the IPC to a minimum number of variables which can be assumed to influence the styles of decision-making in organizations. From the very large number of conditions that could conceivably correlate with the IPC we have selected a number from the available evidence in the literature and from our previous research.[7] The contingency model on which the present research is based is expected to give way to a succession of simpler and empirically more accurate models under the guidance of the research findings; we will therefore talk of *transitional* models to stress our deliberate policy of revision.

Transitional models. The first transitional model (Heller, 1971a:xiii) is made up of systems of variables which are ordered by their assumed degree of immediacy and psychological proximity to DM (see Figure 4). The *alpha* system level is composed of variables of the person: age, experience, skill, attitudes, values, personal characteristics.

The *beta* system level describes situational variables close to the people making the decision, technology of the managerial job, job function, nature-of the decision (to whom it is important), decision level (on whom does it act), job constraints.[8]

Micro structural variables surrounding the DM make up the *gamma* system level: span of control, number of authority levels, size of department, organizational constraints, policy and control procedures, centralization.

The *delta* system level includes the larger structural conditions: size of organization, relationship with other units, degree of competition in sector, turbulence of the immediate environment, technology of organizational workflow.

Finally, to complete the schema, one could consider the possible influence of the sociopolitical and cultural ecology of a geographic area where a business unit is located. The *omega* variables include: the trade union system, social class structure, education, political system and the economic policy emanating from it, state of economic development of the region or country, turbulence of the wider environment.[9]

One reason for expecting several transitional models is the uncertainty concerning the boundaries between the postulated system of variables. These boundaries are conceptual rather than empirical. Since our model is designed to measure patterns of interaction rather than cause and effect relationships, we do not expect that "boundary disputes" will seriously affect our work.[10]

---

[7] The 1967 US research used a number of variables which showed very little correlation with DM and were dropped in 1968. After pretesting, we added further variables in 1968 and again in 1970 and 1971. Some of the instruments were found to be very useful but could not be fitted into the two-hour maximum available for the field research. They will, however, be used for the "in-depth" studies which follow the broader field work. The identification of the various levels of the contingency model has been influenced by the sociotechnical systems approach (Trist, et al., 1951; Emery and Trist, 1960), by the conceptual scheme of Pugh, et al. (1963) and to some extent by Lawrence and Lorsch (1967b).

[8] We also measure how one level of management perceives the behavior or the requirements of another level. To identify such variables we could use terms like alpha-meta, beta-meta variables, etc. Meta is used here in its zoological meaning, signifying subsequent and more developed (shorter Oxford English Dictionary).

[9] Many omega system variables cannot easily be measured at this point of time, but it is important to consider these factors in the case of comparative organization research. Ajiferuke and Boddewyn (1970) have shown that eight indicators of socio-cultural, political and economic dimensions can be measured and correlated with attitudinal data (as the dependent variable).

[10] At the same time, various organization research projects will help to test our assumption. The work of Pugh and his co-workers has established a very carefully documented relationship between contextual variables and organization structure (Pugh, et al., 1963). These two groups of variables correspond fairly closely to our delta and beta levels of analysis.

700   FRANK A. HELLER

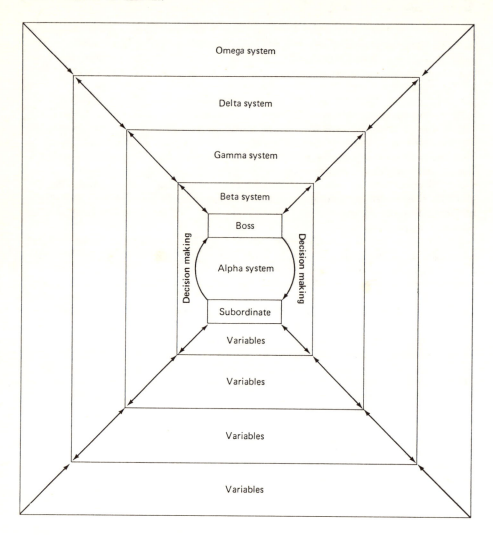

Figure 4. Transitional model: variables affecting decision-making.

It should not be thought, however, that in *any given situation* alpha variables will have a stronger effect on behavior than beta variables and beta variables more than delta variables. The assumption is simply that alpha variables will *normally* impinge on the DM process more continuously and possibly more directly than systems or variables that are at a greater sociopsychological distance from DM.

It will probably be argued that the five-level framework is too broad and complex to be handled in a single research project by means of existing statistical procedures. The purpose of the model, however, is long-term and is intended to achieve two objectives. One is to introduce the necessary amount of reality into the conceptualization so that, unlike the classical model of economic man, potentially critical variables are not left out even if they cannot all be measured at any one time. Secondly, it is expected that by successive stages and approximations, many variables will be eliminated because they are seen to make a small contribution to the problem under investigation, while other variables will be seen to be related to each other and together make a significant impact on our core variable.

The emergent theoretical model will almost certainly turn out to be very different from Figure 4 and may resemble a group of clusters as in Figure 5. Some clusters (for instance C_1) may be seen to make an independent impact on the core variables; others will have a certain amount of overlap (C_2 and C_3, C_4 and C_5).

In this way, the DM process will be described by a series of transitional models of increasing parsimony, measuring the major components which exert influence on the process in defined circumstances. For instance, it is hypothesized that the variable "tranquillity-turbulence" will be associated with low and high power centralization, but only at the extreme ends of the turbulence continuum, while the system of variables describing technical differences in tasks and the perceived existence of skills are expected to emerge as a cluster correlating with the Influence-Power Continuum at several points. It is conceivable that some of the clusters in Figure 5 will be made up mainly from variables described as belonging to one of the five levels in the first transitional model, while others will be made up of highly correlated items from several levels. The distance of each of the clusters of peripheral variables from the core variable is intended to describe the statistical contribution each makes to the total variability in the DM process. The specific hypothesis of interaction between DM and some of the variables in our model has been described in detail elsewhere (Heller, 1971a).

Vroom and Yetton have recently carried out a major research project on leadership styles which adopts contingency assumptions very similar to those reported here (Vroom and Yetton, 1973).[11] They use the term *situational variables* to cover the important circumstances which make leaders use different leadership styles and these styles are roughly comparable to the first four or five alternatives on our Influence-Power Continuum. A central hypothesis in their work is that no single leader-style (we would say decision method) is applicable to all situations and that the best way of testing this assumption is to look at the way managers solve particular problems.

While Vroom and Yetton use a different method of data gathering and different situational variables, their findings, like our own, clearly support the contingency framework and will be referred to later in this chapter.

Leadership Styles and Organizational Effectiveness

Discussion of leadership behavior has always looked for tangible criteria of effectiveness so that different leader methods could be judged by them. As

---

[11] The Vroom-Yetton research had been far advanced when our first report was published in 1969 and they were already writing up results when the first full report was published by Heller in 1971. Nevertheless, it has been possible to compare results. Many are sufficiently similar to strengthen the conclusions from both studies.

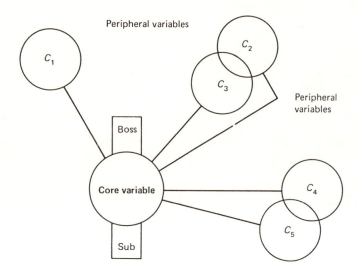

Figure 5. Second transitional model: clusters of variables accounting for observed variations in decision behavior.

the first flush of enthusiasm gave way to disappointment when personality factors did not predict leader behavior (Stogdill, 1948), mediating factors such as attitudes, motives and job satisfactions, were interposed between leader styles on the one side and effectiveness on the other. In recent years, this approach to leadership received a great deal of attention, and most models claimed causal relationships between the so-called styles of leadership and organizational effectiveness. Usually there was no provision for feedback loops or contingency conditions postulating that different circumstances would substantially affect the leader style. These models are now in some danger of following the demise of the earlier personality-behavior model. The difficulty is that the causal links are unreliable and have not been tested under a sufficient variety of conditions.[12] We still do not know what leader style makes for greater production or efficiency.

At one time it was thought that the critical link was the improved satisfaction of people who worked under the preferred (democratic) leader. This thinking has been incorporated into what can be called the Human Relations Model (Miles, 1965). It is illustrated in Figure 6.

The assumptions underlying this model turned out to be quite unreliable; sometimes they did predict correctly, sometimes they did not. The great debate since 1936, following on the Hawthorne studies, has never resolved the leader-

---

[12] As we shall show later, there must also be a serious doubt surrounding the global value-laden questions which serve as measuring devices in most current research on leader style (Likert, 1967; Marrow, et al., 1967; Blake and Mouton, 1964; Reddin, 1970).

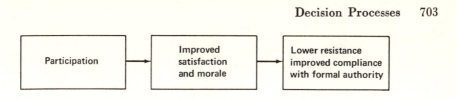

Figure 6. Human relations model (After Miles, 1965).

ship question. What was responsible for the steady improvement in output of the relay assembly girls between 1927 and 1932? Was it a new style of supervision, the size of the groups, the incentive system, the special conditions of the room, or the famous Hawthorne effect itself?[13] The Human Relations school of thought tended to look for simple, causal relations and universalistic association between independent and dependent variables. With hindsight, it could be argued that a contingency model would have led to less consternation on the part of the Hawthorne investigators as they were faced with one surprise after another when the introduction of new independent variables and a return to previous conditions failed to affect the steady climb of the output curve.

The major blow to the simplicity of the Human Relations thinking came with the famous review studies of Brayfield and Crockett (1955), Herzberg, et al. (1957) and Miller and Form (1964), which noted very irregular relations between morale and output. So-called "good" leadership practices did not always lead to high morale, and morale could certainly not be relied upon to correlate with high output. It then became necessary to look for some new or additional factors. Likert has come to believe that more time is needed to allow a new leadership style (participation) to affect output. He estimates that if we measured all variables at least over three, and preferably over five years, we would stop getting inconsistent results (Likert, 1967:79–95). This may be so, but it is a difficult proposition to test.

An alternative idea, associated with the views of Likert, McGregor, Haire and others, has been well argued by Miles, who has called it the Human Resources Model (Miles, 1964, 1965). It is based on two assumptions which sharply differentiate it from the Human Relations school. One is the set of attitudes and beliefs which McGregor called Theory Y and which attribute positive qualities such as initiative, responsibility, self-direction and self-control to most people. A consequence of holding Theory Y beliefs is that you trust people.

The second characteristic of the new model is its stress on the hidden resources of skill which participative practices may evoke. Under the Human Relations Model, people might use participation simply to improve communications or to make people "feel" better (improve their morale). Apart from being relatively ineffective, at least with a sophisticated staff, it leaves the field wide open for manipulation and make-believe.

---

[13] By this is usually meant the effect of having a special extraneous factor such as an experiment or the feeling of the subjects that they are important enough to receive the "new" attention. There have been many interpretations and reinterpretations since 1949 when "Management and the worker" was published. One recent reinterpretation of the complete Relay Assembly study up to 1932 uses participative decision-making as the major explanation of the fluctuations in output (Blumberg, 1968).

704   FRANK A. HELLER

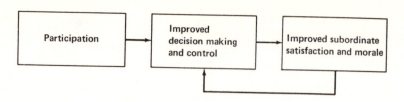

Figure 7. Human resources model (After Miles, 1965).

The contrast between the two models can be seen by comparing Figure 6 with Figure 7. In the Human Resources Model, participation is used because it is thought that better decisions would be made. The improved contribution to DM leads to improved satisfaction and morale and this in turn feeds back to the greater willingness to work and to take part in the decision process. Evidence from field research is now beginning to support this model (Ritchie and Miles, 1970; Miles, et al., 1968).[14]

It will not have escaped the reader's attention that we have recently started to use the popular term, "participation" when talking about leadership methods, while the previous discussion managed to do without this term. After this brief excursion into a description of the work of a very important school of thought, we will now return to our terms influence and power, because, in recent years, the term participation has become ambiguous and emotive.[15] It is also felt that the terms influence and power as defined for the purpose of the IPC enable us to make a very important extension to the participative model by including delegation. Delegation has been deliberately excluded from the Human Resources Model by Likert and his followers because they see a special virtue in group interaction which they cannot extend to a relatively solitary activity. However, it is difficult to reconcile this view with the Human Resources Model's stress on making the best use of a subordinate's opportunities and skills (Strauss, 1968). In this context, delegation is surely a potent alternative to consensus DM.[16] Delegation enables subordinates to show whether they have skill resources that can be used. Similarly, it is difficult to see why consensus and joint DM should be the optimum point on the Likert scale when that school of thought holds Maslow's self-actualization need and autonomy as major human goals. Both can be achieved at least as easily by handing over areas of power to subordinates (giving them an extended amount of autonomy) as by insisting on casting the very labor intensive interaction methods as the major stars of the model. For these reasons,

---

[14] As will be seen later (Figure 9) our own model allows for the interrelationship between effectiveness, satisfaction, DM and other variables. It must be admitted, however, that objective indeces of managerial effectiveness are not available at the present moment, at least at senior levels. This unsatisfactory position can change at any moment and we are therefore justified in including effectiveness in the model, although the research to be described later does not measure this factor.

[15] Furthermore, it is a difficult term to translate into some foreign languages. For a review of alternative approaches, see Walker (1974).

[16] Strauss (1963:58) was probably the first to treat delegation as an integral part of participation.

and a few others we will mention in a moment, we have found it necessary to produce an alternative Human Resources Model.

On the Lookout for Skills

Work in underdeveloped countries, where skilled people are irreplaceable, draws our attention to problems which industrialized countries have been able to overlook for a long time. One problem is the absence of any mechanism for identifying resources or capital other than land, machines, buildings or money. This is exacerbated by time-honored accounting procedures invented at a time when people were cheap and all other resources scarce. The lack of flexibility in the conventional accounting methods has been identified as an important obstacle to the better use of skills (Heller, 1964:1–2). These shortcomings have recently received very careful attention (Likert, 1967:Chapter 9; Pyle, 1970) and have been found to be as important in the highly industrialized United States as they were in underdeveloped areas (Heller, 1969a).

A second difficulty that showed up very clearly in underdeveloped countries was the absence of a concept such as *infrastructures* in organization theory. The term infrastructure is used by economists to draw attention to the differences between trees in the middle of a jungle and wood ready for shipment. Roads, airports, harbors, etc., are essential structural requirements for transforming potential resources into economic wealth.

Such a concept is as necessary in organization theory as it is in economics. The term organizational infrastructure has consequently been used to draw attention to the presence or absence of mechanisms, procedures, technologies and sociopsychological conditions which *facilitate* the use of existing human skills (Heller, 1969a). Several examples of business infrastructures have been given, from the communication system operating at board level to the method of training building workers. In each case, it was possible to show a connection between the wastage of human skills and the absence of certain infrastructure conditions. This extension to the Human Resources Model is illustrated in Figure 8. It describes relationships between an input of skill resources and motives at the upper end of a hopper and the various infrastructure conditions which facilitate their output or obstruct their passage. The hopper analogy enables us to describe a provision for storage since it would be quite unrealistic to assume that *all* available skill and motivational resources could or should be released into the operating system, that is to say, the work-place. Even if we restrict input to those skills which are related to work, we can presume that at least two conditions would result in *some* permanent storage or lack of output. One is the need for any two related dynamic systems, like the water supply to a city and that city's requirements for water, to keep a quantity in reserve. Secondly, one could assume that there would be some loss of effectiveness on the way through the hopper and the infrastructures. The more complex the structures, the more the loss of resources.

A second feature of the Infrastructure Model is its focus of attention on the *nature of the facilitating* or obstructing *quality* of the various channels which connect the hopper to the work system. These channels can describe technical, social or psychological factors. The communications procedure which made the board meetings in some companies more effective than in others was a technical procedure. A combination of dysfunctional status and a certain

706   FRANK A. HELLER

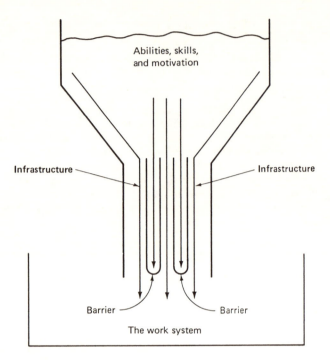

Figure 8. Infrastructure human resources model.

Note: Barrier is a negative infrastructure. An infrastructure is described as a facilitator of skill throughout, while a barrier prevents skills from entering the work system.

technique of writing, wasted the skill of highly trained secretaries (an example of a sociotechnical obstacle). The Theory Y attitudes described by McGregor (1960) are psychological facilitators because they give people a chance to show what they have in their skill hopper that could be applied at work (Heller, 1969a, 1971b). However, the Theory Y *Weltanschauung* is too wide and universalistic to fit into our contingency model; many real life situations do not permit the luxury of implementing managerial practices derived from a rigid adherence to Theory Y. In practice, the infrastructure model operates in relation to specified environmental circumstances (Figure 4) and this enables us to study *which* psychological beliefs, social and technical factors *are* facilitators in a given real situation.

One group of facilitators are of particular importance to our model; they are the various combinations of *influence* and *power* described in the IPC (Figure 3). It will be remembered that influence was defined as having access to the process of decision-making. Access can be thought of as a series of channels merging into the DM flow (as illustrated in Figure 1). The *sources of access* are very numerous and will not be discussed in detail here; they include the five bases of power described by French and Raven (1959), namely reward, coercion, legitimacy, identification and expertness. They also include the control a person may exercise over his environment in order to gain access to power and the Lewinian concept of social gatekeepers who control the access channels through which change may be accomplished.

In organizational terms, we can think of devices like committees and the numerous procedures or customs which decide who shall be members of such committees. Let us think of an organization which has a series of committees which shape policy and some that evaluate and control the ongoing work process. A subcommittee of the board shapes investment policies for the next three years and a lower level committee evaluates departmental cost performance against budgeted standards. When cost performance is off target, they recommend how to achieve a return to a desirable equilibrium. In company *A* the membership of these committees is based largely on seniority, in company *B* there is a deliberate policy of rotation and an emphasis on bringing in a proportion of younger people. It is clear that company *B* has more varied access channels and a greater spread of influence. Over a period of time one can see that, in terms of the model described in Figure 8, company *A* will have more barriers and company *B* more infrastructures.

Let us assume that in both organizations there are many people with knowledge, experience and innovative ideas on investment possibilities and the many factors that influence cost performance; we can then predict that the committee procedure of company *B* will make better use of existing skills, which in turn is likely to produce a higher level of motivation for a greater number of executives than in company *A*.

In the imaginary examples of company *A* and company *B* we have so far described two alternative arrangements relating to the *composition* of the committees.[17] The next step is to consider how each member of the committee relates to his subordinates and colleagues. Does he use methods 1, 2, 3 or 4? In this particular example, the committee members are not free to use delegation (methods 5 and 6) but they may consult or introduce joint procedures which would enable them to feed into the respective committee the opinions and experiences of noncommittee members or even consensus recommendations.

For the sake of the example, let us make the further assumption that committee members in company *B* will, on the average, use more influence-sharing methods with their subordinates and colleagues than company *A* managers. This would extend still further the range of infrastructure channels which tap available skill resources. If the people who are brought into the DM process by these means have skills to contribute, then it is reasonable to assume that the quality of the recommendations of the various committees in company *B* will be higher than in company *A*.

It follows that the analysis of DM methods and the various degrees of influence and power used by managers in solving work problems is an important ingredient of the "hopper" model. While our schema accepts the possibility that in *many* large organizations methods 1 and 2 (where the boss makes the decision on his own, see page 696, this chapter) will be used and may be appropriate in some circumstances, *these methods do not facilitate* the use of subordinates' or colleagues' skills. While these methods should not be condemned, as Likert condemns them, it is necessary to study (a) the extent to

---

[17] To simplify the description we have ommitted considering the method of DM inside the committees themselves and the role of the chairman, that is to say, his leadership methods.

708   FRANK A. HELLER

which they are used, and (b) the sociotechnical circumstances which might legitimize them.[18] To make this point graphically; any business that, for whatever reason, were to use exclusively decision methods 1 and 2, would close many of the infrastructure channels in Figure 8 and this would lead to slow learning and poor quality DM.[19]

Skill Utilization as a Motivator

We may speculate for a moment on the relationship between skills, motives, infrastructures and organizational effectiveness. Economic infrastructures bring about a change from *potential* to actual physical resources and the same process of change can be studied with manpower resources. There is, of course, one important difference. Inanimate resources, such as machines and raw materials, do not *feel* underutilized; people do. Consequently, any scheme for using manpower resources must take account of the effect on people's satisfaction.

The behavioral science literature on satisfactions at work is very extensive and inconclusive but in relation to managerial satisfactions there has been a convergence of view between some major schools of thought (marred slightly by a bitter controversy over methodology). Maslow's famous hierarchy has at its peak a need called *self-actualization*, by which he means to "become more and more what one is, to become everything that one is capable of becoming" (Maslow, 1943). McGregor did not develop a formal theory of motivation, but in later life he became convinced that the major obstacle to man achieving satisfaction is the underestimation of other people's potential (McGregor, 1967:98). Various questionnaire studies on large samples of managers have obtained a rough corroboration of the self-actualization view[20] (Porter, 1964; Haire, Ghiselli and Porter, 1966; Heller and Porter, 1966). Alderfer reformulated Maslow's theory into three major groups of motives, one of which, *growth*, was described as satisfaction from utilizing one's capacity to the fullest extent. Alderfer claims that his ERG theory stands up very well to a preliminary empirical test (Alderfer, 1969:171, 1974).[20a] Moving away from the problems associated with covering large samples by distributed questionnaires, Herzberg asked people to describe critical work incidents during which their feelings about their jobs were either rated very high or low. *Achievement* feelings related to their work and receiving some *recognition* for what they had done always rank very high among positive elements and, of course, achievement and recognition are related, "they satisfy the individual's need for self-

---

[18] Legitimize in the sense of being formally acceptable to the people in the work system. We have, for instance, found many occasions when subordinates welcome centralized DM methods and complain when superiors resort to excessively time-consuming ways of consultation and group activity (Heller, 1971a:95–97). In this context one must strive to assess individual and role expectations. Expectations are subtle but powerful forces; they change over time and they are influenced by a variety of sociotechnical circumstances, including the research literature in our field.

[19] This is true unless we are to assume that subordinates and colleagues have no relevant experience and information to offer. But this would be quite an indictment of an organization.

[20] A recent factor analytic study of Maslow type questionnaires gives only moderate support to his *a priori* categories, but finds strong support for factors that can be called growth and recognition (Roberts, et al., 1971).

[20a] ERG stands for three components of motivation; needs of Existence, Relatedness and Growth.

actualization" (Herzberg, et al., 1959:114). While Herzberg has been severely criticized for an aspect of his theory, namely his claim to have isolated two orthogonal factors, this is not an issue that concerns us here, since we are interested only in the priority given to satisfactions.[21] More relevant to our argument is the circumstance that under-utilization of worker skill emerges as a major finding when Herzberg-type job enrichment schemes are applied in industry (Scott, 1964; Paul and Robertson, 1970). People can do more than they were previously expected to do and they like doing it. Furthermore, the findings on the possibility of redesigning jobs to make them fit in better with both technical and social requirements had been anticipated and substantiated by work at the Tavistock Institute of Human Relations (Trist and Bamforth, 1951; Emery, 1959; Herbst, 1962) and by Davis (1957).

The importance of having a large measure of autonomy in jobs, particularly managerial jobs, has been emphasized time and again, particularly in the evidence from questionnaire surveys. Some of this work has been done multinationally and the similarity in the motivational profiles in different national groups is surprising (Haire, Ghiselli and Porter, 1966; Sirota and Greenwood, 1971).[22] The need for autonomy and self-actualization was ranked highest in all fourteen countries studied (Haire, et al., 1966:100). A similar high priority for having considerable freedom to adopt their own approach to the job and to have work from which one gets a personal sense of accomplishment emerges from a recent research project with 13,000 managers and staff in one large, multinational corporation. The managers came from forty-six countries; the opportunity for training to improve skills, job challenge and job autonomy are ranked first, second and third (out of fourteen job goals) in this sample of salesmen, technical personnel and service staff (Sirota and Greenwood, 1971).

Taken together, the evidence, though inconclusive, supports the suggestion that *underutilization* of a person's *skill* could lead to two negative consequences. The first is identical to the loss sustained by underutilizing a machine or land: one simply fails to harness the available capacity. The second consequence arises only with human resources. It seems that people who have experience and skill feel dissatisfied when it is not used. This dissatisfaction could lead to further negative consequences such as low morale, high labor turnover or reduced efficiency. These tertiary dysfunctional consequences have not been established, they are simply a suitable subject for speculation and enquiry. However, even the primary and secondary effects of underutilization justify us in paying attention to the various infrastructure channels in our skill "hopper". One of these infrastructures, as we have seen, is the process of DM and the distribution of influence and power in the work system.

The model which contains the various components which we have described in the first part of this chapter is illustrated in Figure 9. Reading the model from left to right, we see that DM methods are influenced by various ecological variables surrounding the work. If, for whatever reason,

---

[21] See the critical reviews by Dunnette, et al., (1967) and Viteles (1969). Other criticisms could be more damaging (Vroom, 1964:127–129; Schneider and Locke, 1971).

[22] The similarity could be a sign of methodological weakness. It has been alleged that, although managers are assured anonymity, they still give the kind of answers they feel they ought to give.

710   FRANK A. HELLER

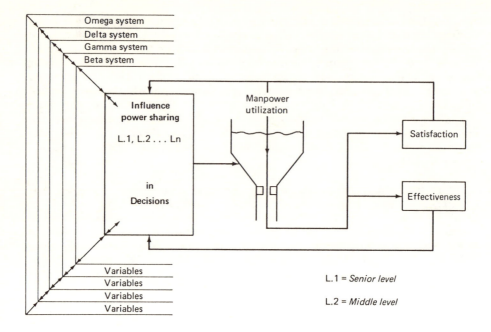

Figure 9. Contingency model of the decision process.

the DM methods are consistently low on the IPC, that is to say, if they fail to share influence and power with subordinates and colleagues, then they lead to an underutilization of the reservoir of available skills. This will tend to reduce satisfaction and to lower the quality or quantity of work. Various feedback loops are set up which reinforce, or moderate, the DM methods, contingency variables and manpower utilization.

Sociotechnical Remedies

One characteristic of the contingency model is to point to more than one possible remedy for a problem of skills wastage. Let us assume that high centralization of decision-making correlates with certain variables from the alpha to delta system, for instance, with the span of control. In such a situation, a change in the gamma system variable (span) might lead to less centralized decision behavior. This way of looking at the contingency model opens up the possibility that a change in organization structure could affect interpersonal relations.[23,24]

---

[23] This suggestion is not new, for instance, it is similar to that put forward by Fiedler (1967), although his theoretical and research approach are quite different. For a discussion on this, see Heller (1973:186–7).

[24] When structure is considered in relation to sociopsychological variables on a broad front, we can be said to have used an extension of the sociotechnical model. Structure becomes the equivalent of technology. We can postulate the need for a joint optimization of structure and sociopsychological variables.

The other alternative is the one which most current Organizational Development schemes champion, namely an attempt to change people's leadership values and decision-making styles directly by means of various organizational training and change agent procedures. We will not pursue this discussion further, since it has been well documented (Argyris, 1970; Heller, 1970, 1975).

In the second part of this chapter, we will present some preliminary evidence in support of a part of our contingency model. This evidence comes from a field research on fifteen large and progressive American companies and 260 senior managers. Supplementary evidence will be cited from a more recent study of a closely matched sample of British companies and over 300 British managers.

PART II: RESEARCH METHODS AND FINDINGS

From Theory to Field Research

While the model is multivariate in so far as it attempts to establish relationships between a considerable number of organizational and people-generated variables, it *starts* with people in interaction and then moves outward by stages to include more and more relevant ecological conditions. Other schemas start at the organization level and gradually move towards an inclusion of sociopsychological variables. Whether the movement is from micro to macro factors or vice versa is not important. However, there is an important distinction between open system multivariate models of this kind and the more self-contained research models which are preoccupied exclusively with variables within one level of conceptualization, be this psychological, sociological or ecological (Argyris, 1972).

While the ecological open systems approach claims advantages over simpler research designs, it must be admitted that it is, in practice, very difficult to implement. The difficulties are practical as well as conceptual; one needs a considerable amount of resources in time and staff to develop the research instruments, to test them and to obtain the willing cooperation of a reasonable sample of industry. Moreover, it is doubtful whether a single method of data gathering and data analysis is sufficient for a complex interactional approach of this kind. Data gathering must be differentiated from analysis. It is usual for data obtained from questionnaires to be analysed by a series of statistical procedures.[25] It is less usual for several different data gathering methods to be used on the same basic hypotheses and population.

In relation to the contingency model described in Part I of this chapter, it was thought advisable to rely on several kinds of data collection as well as on several statistical and qualitative procedures of data evaluation. These preferences were incorporated even at the micro stage of the research, that is to say, when the emphasis was chiefly on assessing sociopsychological variables. They have proved valuable and have been retained through the various extensions covering alpha, beta, gamma and delta system variables.

The main research method has been called Group Feedback Analysis (GFA). It is a multiple data gathering approach and will be described below.

---

[25] The analyses, however, tend to be either parametric *or* nonparametric, rather than a combination of both.

Other methods have since been added. There is, for instance, an extended interview with a chief executive to obtain more objective information on delta system variables, including what have been called contextual and structural variables (Pugh, et al., 1963) and turbulence of the environment (Emery and Trist, 1965). Unobtrusive measures (Webb, et al., 1966) are sometimes obtained and will be used for detailed case descriptions of individual companies. Finally an attempt is being made to use the Delphi method of convergent expert judgments (Dalkey and Helmer, 1963; Campbell and Hitchin, 1968). This method attempts to obtain an independent evaluation of measures of uncertainty and the rate of change facing different industrial sectors in the sample of companies represented in this research project. We want to see whether evaluation from the Delphi method coincides with the *felt* turbulence experienced by managers inside the organization.

Group Feedback Analysis for Gathering Field Data

While the method has been described elsewhere (Heller, 1969b, 1971a), it is convenient to summarize briefly the three main stages and to mention some of the reasons why Group Feedback Analysis (GFA) may be particularly appropriate for handling sensitive psychological and sociological data.

As the name suggests, the method is applied to a group of people who meet in an informal setting to produce the required data. In this particular case, the groups are managers and they are selected for their level and homogeneity. The senior level is made up of all the managers reporting directly to the chief executive of an organization. There are usually five to twelve in number, though larger groups are possible. At a later date, the same procedure is applied to an equal number of their immediate subordinates. Typically, the managers under observation are seated around a boardroom table. The three stages of the method are as follows:

Stage one. The research is introduced by means of a very brief statement by the researcher who also explains that the purpose of the tape recorder on the table is *in part* to standardize instructions for all the groups visited by the researcher. The tape recorder is then used to give a slightly more detailed explanation of the research objectives, including the feedback of results stage. It then gives the instructions for Form 1. The essence of the instructions is repeated on the form itself and, in the case of the more complex instruments, some verbal reinforcement is also given by the researcher. Each questionnaire is short (a maximum of three pages). At the beginning of each new instrument, the tape recorder gives a brief explanation and instructions; the time is used to collect the previous forms from the participants. While the group fills in the second form, the first one is checked for completeness or error. This stage lasts one hour.

Stage two. Some of the forms used in Stage one are submitted to a simple statistical analysis (means and an indication of variance). With the aid of a desk calculator, this takes about thirty to sixty minutes depending on the size of the group. These results are then fed back to the group from which they were taken. This feedback session sometimes takes place on the same day, after an interval for lunch, or anytime within one week.

Stage three.   The purpose of the feedback session is—in part—to obtain the group's own interpretation of the results in the light of their knowledge of the situation. A group discussion based on the feedback information is stimulated. It starts off by being virtually unstructured; the researcher's question might be: "Well, these are *your* results, what do you make of them?" Later, more specific questions gradually structure the situation to give more quantifiable form to the discussion.

The tape recorder is on the table in the same position as before and again is used to give one part of the introduction to Stage three. Then, following the feedback, the group is asked whether it has any objection to the tape recorder to save the researcher the trouble of making elaborate notes on their replies. There has never been any opposition. Most of the ensuing discussions are then recorded; if the subject matter strays far afield, the machine can be switched off. The researcher uses the clock counter of the tape recorder to make very brief summary notes on the content of the discussion. This will save time in the subsequent content analysis.

The purpose of the third stage of this method is threefold: (a) to get a "group response" to questions that have previously been put to each individual in questionnaires, (b) to check on the validity of the hypotheses which form the basis of the inquiry, and (c) to deepen the understanding of the subject under inquiry beyond the specific questions asked in the research instruments during Stage one.

The method just described is a relatively novel approach to field research, although the particular ingredients it uses are all well known. Group Feedback Analysis claims to have a number of advantages over the widely used alternatives, namely the interview and particularly the self-administered questionnaire.

In essence, GFA uses the informants twice, for different objectives. During Stage one, we collect the usual questionnaire information, though it can be claimed that the reliability and validity of the results from the group setting are considerably greater than those from a distributed questionnaire. The main advantage is a uniform, undisturbed environment at which the speed of completing answers is controlled.

In Stage three. we use the same informants, and their experience in relation to the variables under discussion, as *interpreters* of the results. The group then analyzes the finer meanings of the research material and explains why the uniformity or heterogeneity has occurred and what specific organizational circumstances must be understood to explain the particular constellation of answers. Stage three is full of rich, often unsuspected depth, similar to the information one obtains from collecting case material. However, unlike case material, the base of the information consists of hard statistical data which can be analyzed by sophisticated multivariate procedures, if this is considered useful.

The Group Feedback Analysis method attempts to bridge the often very considerable gap between the so-called *hard* and *soft* scientific methods (Churchman, 1968) and to add their respective advantages without incurring any special penalty. It will be realized, for instance, that the standardized questionnaire answers are collected *before* the interpretative discussion and therefore remain unaffected by it. It is also worth pointing out that GFA is quite different from the often practiced combination of questionnaire and interview as separate methods of working on the same problem. It is not only

714   FRANK A. HELLER

that the methods remain separate, but by contrast with GFA they are usually carried out on different parts of the total sample and do not use the subjects to *interpret and enlarge on their own group responses.* The value of having a group interpret its own averages and frequency distribution can be considerable when the subject under discussion is a group or organizational phenomenon. This will be illustrated by the examples given later.

Variables, Measurements and Samples

The research was carried out at two senior levels. The most senior was made up of a group reporting directly to the chief executive and will be abbreviated: L.1. The other level was made up of their direct subordinates and will be abbreviated L.2. In America, the managers in the L.1 group were most usually called vice presidents. The American sample consisted of 260 managers from fifteen large and progressive companies.[26]

The *core variable* in Figure 5 and Figure 9 is the method of decision-making described by five alternative positions on the Influence-Power Continuum. The *Specific Decision Questionnaire* (Form 5) uses twelve decision situations which were selected so that most senior (L.1) managers in a considerable variety of business and industrial undertakings would be able to answer the questions based on their personal experience. In other words, each decision situation was of such a nature that the managers would be involved in it at least occasionally. The twelve decisions were:

1. To increase the salary of your direct subordinate.
2. To increase the number of employees working for your subordinate.
3. To hire one of several applicants to work for your subordinate.
4. To change the extension number of your subordinate's telephone.
5. To purchase for your department a necessary piece of equipment costing over an X amount of dollars.
6. To promote one of the employees working for your subordinate.
7. To give a merit pay increase to one of your subordinate's employees.
8. To increase the dollar allocation for your department during the preparation of the organizational budget.
9. To fire one of your subordinate's employees.
10. To change an operating procedure followed by your subordinate.
11. To assign your subordinate to a different job (on same salary).
12. The decision regarding what targets or quotas should be set for your subordinate.[27]

The items were selected after an extensive pilot survey and full use was made of items from an instrument that had previously been validated (Blankenship and Miles, 1968).

The answer to each question was given on a five stage cumulative percentage scale; each point represented one decision style:

1. Own decision without detailed explanation   _____%
2. Own decision with detailed explanation   _____%

---

[26] Where comparisons are made with the British research, they will be based on a sample matched firm by firm for industrial sector, technology, level, size and "progressiveness." Similar matched samples have been collected in five European countries.

[27] The following description is taken from Heller, 1971a.

3. Prior consultation with subordinate   _____%
4. Joint decision-making with subordinate   _____%
5. Delegation of decision to subordinate   _____%

These five decision styles were carefully defined on a separate sheet of paper. There are two main methods of scoring the Specific Decision Questionnaire. The first makes full use of the five alternative styles, aggregating and averaging them across all respondents and producing an average frequency distribution of the preferred styles in each sample or subsample. The resulting percentage scale requires a forced choice, since high scores on one end necessarily require low scores on the other. This leads to a difficulty in interpreting the precise level of significance of correlation coefficients associated with the five-point scale. The second scoring method, which avoids this problem to some extent, produces an index called *decision centralization*. For this purpose the five decision styles are assumed to be separated by equal intervals on the IPC and scale scores of 5, 4, 3, 2 and 1 were assigned from left to right (delegation = 1). The frequency score, multiplied by the scale values divided by 100 gives the decision centralization index. The advantage of the index, for certain purposes, is that a single score summarizes the point on the IPC characteristic of a person's leadership style. A high score implies that a leader allows his subordinate little influence.

The same form was given to the subordinate managers who used it to describe their chief's decision behavior. Both levels described the *same decision behavior* and it was therefore possible to measure the *perceptual congruence* of matched pairs of boss-subordinates on this important variable.

Of the several *Alpha System* variables (Figure 5) two will be described here. The first measures skill requirements at two different levels and is called the *Skill Difference Questionnaire* (Form 2). The second assesses the time required for subordinates to reach the minimum skill requirements necessary for carrying out the senior job, and it is called the *Skill Acquisition Time Questionnaire* (Form 3). In both forms the questions revolve round the same twelve skills, abilities and personal characteristics:

1. Knowledge of technical matters   7. Decisiveness
2. Closer contact with people   8. Tact
3. Knowledge of human nature   9. Adaptability
4. Imagination   10. Forcefulness
5. Self-confidence   11. Intelligence
6. Responsibility   12. Initiative

These twelve items were chosen from a considerably longer list, for a variety of motives. One was to cover a range of frequently used job-description categories. Secondly, some of the "skills" had to be of a kind that made it reasonable to suppose that L.2 could require as much as, or more than, L.1. Thirdly, they had to be items that applied to all kinds of senior management jobs and were not specialized by function or type of industry. Several lists had previously been developed; six of the items came from Porter (Porter and Henry, 1964), four came from Heller (Heller and Porter, 1966), and two came from Miles (1964).

The Skill Difference Questionnaire asks for an assessment of the requirements of one's own job, compared with that of the other level. Most of the questions are worded as follows: "Does your own job require more or less knowledge of technical matters?" The answers are marked on a five-point scale from "very

716   FRANK A. HELLER

much more" to "much less." When L.1 managers answer the questions, they compare their job with their subordinates'; when the latter answer, they compare the job requirements at their level with the L.1 job. As a consequence of this arrangement, it is possible to measure the difference in job skills as seen by each level as well as to assess the difference in judgement between the two levels.

The *Skill Acquisition Time Questionnaire* asks the following question at the L.1:

> If you were promoted to another job today and your (named) subordinate were to step into your shoes tomorrow, how much time—if any —would he need to acquire the necessary skill?

The answers can be marked on a ten-point scale:

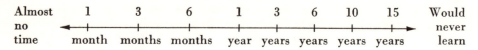

Almost	1	3	6	1	3	6	10	15	Would
no									never
time	month	months	months	year	years	years	years	years	learn

The subordinate is given a similar form but asked to consider how long he would take to acquire the "skills" necessary at the level of his immediate superior. The twelve skills, abilities, and personal qualities are the same as in the Skill Difference Questionnaire.

The *Beta System* is represented (Figure 5) by several variables: decision level, nature of the decision and job function. Only job function will be used in the present description; nine alternative categories are provided, using the standard alternatives from accountancy to personnel management.

The *Gamma System* is also included with several variables, of which span of control and size of department will be used in this chapter.

Some Basic Assumptions

In the original research formulation, twelve hypotheses were put forward and ten were supported by the statistical findings (Heller, 1971a). The present chapter is more concerned with the description of a theoretical model than with the analysis of research data. We will therefore present only sufficient findings to make out a case for the contingency multivariate model. This can be done by discussing seven assumptions which will be numbered in the same way as the original hypotheses:

H1.   Both levels of management believe that more skills are necessary in their own jobs than in those of the other level.

H2.   When L.1 and L.2 managers estimate the amount of time L.2 managers need to acquire the skills and qualities required at L.1, the senior manager's estimate will be larger than the subordinate's.

H3.   Subordinate managers see themselves as having more influence and power in relation to L.1 managers' decisions than L.1 managers believe to be the case.

H4.   Senior managers (L.1) who perceive a substantial gap between their own skill requirements and those relating to L.2 will use more centralized decision procedures than if the perceptual gap is small.

H5.   A large span of control (that is to say, the need to deal with a large

number of people in one's department) will be associated with decision methods that save time (i.e., highly centralized or decentralized).

H6. Occupants of jobs that have a small degree of freedom (whose job
environment exercises constraints on them) will use a centralized
style of decision-making.

H9. Where decisions are more important to the business as a whole and
to L.1 than to L.2, then centralized decision procedures will be used
by L.1. Where the decision is more important to L.2, his superior
will use more power-sharing styles.

These contingency hypotheses are supported by the American findings,
and, where the same evidence was collected in the British research, the same
trends emerge, sometimes with even greater statistical significance[28]

How Managers Evaluate Skills: Results

When managers judge the requirements of skills at their own level compared
with that of the subordinate level, they attribute higher requirements to their
own level. This would seem natural and probably accurate in view of the promotion and reward systems operating in most organizations. The twelve skills,
however, were chosen so that some of them do not depend so much on rank,
level or experience as on the nature of the task, and others could be more
necessary at the subordinate level. The results as shown in Table 1 reflect these
realities to some extent. Many managers at L.1 judged that their subordinate
needed at least as much or more "technical knowledge" and this is reflected
in the average shown in Table 1. By contrast, few managers doubted that the
senior job required more or very much more "responsibility." The other judgments fell in between these two extremes.

A substantially different picture emerges when we look at the results for L.2
in Table 1 which describe how the subordinates describe the requirements at
their own level compared with those of the senior level. The differences between the judgments of the two levels are substantial and in ten cases out of
twelve are statistically significant. To interpret these results, it is important
to know that the average age of the senior manager was 45.7 and that of the
subordinate was 41 years. The L.1 manager had 9.3 years of experience in his
company, the L.2 manager 7.2 years. In the British research, the age and experience differences were similar, but the difference in skill judgments was more
extreme between levels.

Table 2 describes the results of the Skill Acquisition Time Questionnaire.
It is worth remembering that the instructions ask both levels to estimate the
amount of time the subordinate would need to acquire the minimum skills
necessary to operate effectively at the senior level. The differences in judgement between the two levels are statistically very significant.[29] While the broad
pattern in Tables 1 and 2 is similar, the divergence between the senior and

---

[28] An exception in the British sample relates to H9 which does not show the same trend
as the American finding. In the British sample we collected other information bearing on this
hypothesis which has not yet been analyzed.

[29] The reader should be aware that the subordinates were chosen by the senior level as
being the most experienced and senior and this objective was probably achieved in most cases
in assemblying the L.2 sample. However, this does *not* mean that the subordinates were chosen
for their likelihood of succeeding the senior manager. In many organizations, successors would
not necessarily be chosen from the subordinate group.

718   Frank A. Heller

TABLE 1
SKILL DIFFERENCE QUESTIONNAIRE
US SAMPLE

Skills, abilities and job requirements	Means from a five-point scale*		
	Average L.1	Average L.2	Significance of difference
Knowledge of technical matters	3.1	3.4	NS
Close contact with people	2.9	3.5	.01
Knowledge of human nature	2.3	3.1	.01
Imagination	2.0	3.0	.01
Self-confidence	2.1	2.9	.01
Responsibility	1.6	2.1	.01
Decisiveness	2.0	2.8	.01
Tact	2.3	3.1	.01
Adaptability	2.4	3.3	.01
Forcefulness	2.2	2.8	.01
Intelligence	2.7	2.7	NS
Initiative	2.2	3.2	.01
Average Age	45.7	41.0	
Average Number of Years in Company	9.3	7.2	
Average Number of Years in Job	4.9	3.6	

Note: L.1 refers to level 1, the senior level of management immediately below the chief executive. L.2 is the level immediately subordinate to L.1.
* Scores below 3 indicate a judgement that the skill is more important for L.1 than for L.2. Scores above 3 indicate the reverse.

subordinate is considerably more pronounced in Table 2. The British results show even greater differences in judgments; the average for L.1 was 21.0 months and for L.2, 5.6 months.

During the feedback session, the average results from both these skill questionnaires and the frequency distribution are fed back to each group for discussion, but they receive only their own results, not those from the other level. Nevertheless, the discussions reveal a distinct feeling of unease as far as the L.1 managers are concerned. When they see the pattern of their results the majority of senior managers wonder whether they have not exaggerated the position. What seems to happen is that the managers whose own judgments have been less extreme than the average challenge their colleagues to say why subordinates should need so much time to prepare themselves for the senior

TABLE 2
SKILL PROMOTION QUESTIONNAIRE*
US SAMPLE

	Answer in months			
	Mean	SD		
Leader L.1	11.93	14.19	t = 3.88⁵	p < .001
Subordinate L.2	4.93	8.08	df = 76	

* Question Form: "If you were promoted today and your (named) immediate subordinate were to step into your shoes tomorrow, how much time—if any—would he need to acquire the necessary skill?"
(This is the L.1 version.)

job. "Did *we* have as much time as all that?" is a question often asked. In response to this kind of challenge, other managers admit that the results suggest that their management succession problems appear serious. Sometimes they suggest that their judgments may have been unduly hard.

The implications of these results for the contingency model will be discussed later; the first two hypotheses (H1 and H2) are confirmed.

How Managers Share Influence

The phenomenon of influence and power-sharing is difficult to measure since no objective visual indices are available. In group discussions involving problem-solving tasks in laboratory situations, an independent observer may make his own judgments, but there is no evidence that these estimates are more accurate than the judgments of the participants. In any case, real-life processes do not lend themselves to the outside observer method. Both for this reason and to introduce some element of control, we asked *both* levels to describe the behavior of the senior level on the given twelve decisions.

The average distribution of influence is shown in Figure 10. There is a highly significant difference in the way senior and subordinate managers de-

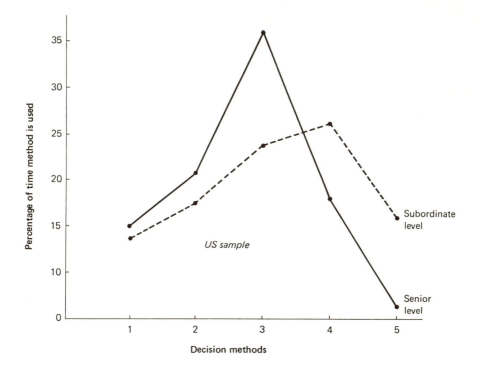

Figure 10. The style of decision-making as seen at two senior levels of management.

Note: The decision methods are those described in Figure 3 of the preceding section (Part I).

scribe the same behavior. The L.1 manager says that he uses "Prior consultation" over 35% of the time and that he delegates very little. The subordinate manager sees his boss using very much more "delegation" and "joint decision-making" and correspondingly less of the other methods. This result would appear to go against common sense. When one asks senior managers how they expect the subordinates to describe the senior's decision-making, they always guess that the shape of the curve would be displaced towards the more autocratic end of the continuum. Since the opposite is the case, it is important to report that the British results follow exactly the same curves and that German results also support this finding.[30]

Some Explanations. We cannot be sure what these results mean. At the moment, three explanations seem possible. One is in terms of the subordinates' wish-fulfillment and presupposes a high degree of motivation to exercise more power. It suggests that the motive leads to perceptual distortion. The second explanation also assumes that the subordinate is motivated to use more power, but that, in fact, he exerts more influence than his boss is aware of. Such an explanation makes sense if we accept the description of the decision process as a flow of events (as in Figures 1 and 2) rather than as a series of discrete choices on a decision tree. In such a situation uncertainties about the real extent of one's contribution or influence can arise. A decision is not a "go" or "no-go" act but a probability that a given piece of advice or other action is incorporated into the flow of events and influences it in some measure. In any case, both explanations of the perceptual gap presuppose the existence of motivations of which the senior managers appear not to be aware. This energy is an important ingredient in our skill "hopper" model (Figure 8). Together with the findings that senior managers have a lower estimation of their subordinates' skills and readiness to take on senior responsibilities, the present finding lends strong support to the possibility that the available human resources are not fully used. A third explanation suggests that the difference is due to a "positional perspective and somewhat comparable to the well studied phenomenon of perceptual illusion" (Wilpert and Heller, 1973).[31]

With the possibility of skill underutilization in mind we will now look at the relationship between a manager's perception of skills at the lower level

---

[30] The German results are reported in a paper by Wilpert and Heller (1973) and Heller and Wilpert (1974).

[31] Vroom and Yetton report a finding they consider to be inconsistent with ours (Vroom and Yetton, 1973:79). Managers were asked to rank order the frequency with which they employed the various decision methods. They were also asked to give the frequency with which these methods were used by their superiors. They report that "managers' superiors were typically seen as using much more autocratic styles than the managers themselves used." Vroom puts forward various explanations; we accept one and add another. In this part of his research, Vroom asked a *general* question about participation in all kinds of situations while we asked twelve questions describing specific decisions. The more specific the question, the less likely that stereotyped views of the *value* of participation will intrude in the judgments. Secondly, our research was carried out inside organizations and both levels knew that we would obtain data from the other. Anonymity was guaranteed, but the knowledge that both levels were to describe the same situation might have acted as a further limitation on the influence of value judgements. Vroom's finding is more in line with general common sense expectations. On the other hand, ours has now been obtained in four different samples (US, UK, Germany and a UK study in four government departments not yet reported). Further research is necessary to solve this issue.

TABLE 3
PERCEPTION OF SKILL RELATED TO
DECISION METHOD
US SAMPLE

METHOD OF DECISION-MAKING	How differently does L.1 see sub. skill from own skill:	significance level
1 Own decision without explanation	−.31	<.01
2 Own decision with explanation	−.17	NS
3 Prior consultation	.03	NS
4 Joint decision-making	.24	<.02
5 Delegation	.26	<.02

Note: A correlation in this table indicates a relationship between the following variables:
    (a) L.1's judgement of the differences in job skills between his own level and that of the subordinate level.
    (b) The frequency of L.1 using a certain decision style (frequency expressed as a percentage distributed over the five styles).

and his decision style (Hypothesis [H4.]). Table 3 produces some support for the assumption that managers who see less skill in their subordinates will use more centralized decision methods than managers who make more positive skill judgements.[32] The British and German results replicate these findings (Heller and Wilpert, 1974). Vroom and Yetton, using different methods and samples, arrive at the same conclusion (1973:83). This evidence can be interpreted in two ways. Either the senior manager's judgement of his subordinate's skill is correct, in which case his adjustment of decision style is logical. There is, after all, little point in spending time and effort on consultation or joint decision-making if the subordinate lacks the skill or qualities to make a real contribution to the process. Alternatively, if the senior's judgement is incorrect, and the subordinate has skills, etc., more nearly in line with his self-estimate, then the more centralized decision style could be a major factor in the under-utilization of managerial resources.

The Influence of Contingencies on Decision-Making

Hypotheses H5, H6 and H9 select three variables from the Beta and Gamma systems to test their predicted interaction with the decision process. To begin with, let us look at the interaction between a manager's span of control and his decision method. It is assumed that if a large number of subordinates act as a contingency variable, then they should influence decision-making by leading to methods which would save the senior man's time. A manager can save time by using either extreme of the decision continuum, that is to say, methods 1, 2 or 5. The other methods would seem to be more difficult to handle with many subordinates. Table 4 shows the results supporting this hypothesis. The result from the British research also supports this hypothesis.[33]

In the second place, it was thought that the technology of the managerial

---

  [32] For further support, see Heller (1971a:78).

  [33] The British results show a different pattern, the significant correlations showing that the tendency is to keep away from "prior consultation" and to lean slightly towards decentralization.

722   FRANK A. HELLER

TABLE 4
RELATION BETWEEN SPAN OF
CONTROL AND METHOD OF DECISION-MAKING:
LEVEL 1

Methods	Correlation with span of control* Significance level
1 Own decision without explanation	<.01
2 Own decision with explanation	NS
3 Prior consultation	NS
4 Joint decision-making	NS
5 Delegation	<.05

* The larger the span, the more likely that Methods 1 or 5 will be used.

job would vary with the function of the work. Job function was therefore taken as a contingency factor and Figure 11 shows the relationship between six functions and the degree of decision centralization. The results show a clear relationship and an analysis or variance between the pairs of functions is statistically significant, confirming Hypothesis H6.[34]

The third contingency hypothesis postulated a relationship between the nature of the decision, for instance, its importance to the company, as a major

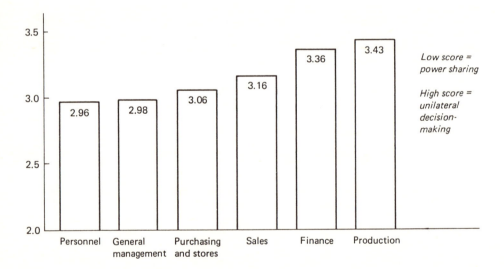

Figure 11. The relation of decision method to job function (US sample).

Note: The means are scores of Decision Centralization.

_____

[34] The British results do not follow the same pattern and we have to await the results from further samples before reaching a conclusion.

influence on the decision method. Four different alternatives were envisaged:
1. Where the decision is of great importance for the subordinate.
2. Where the decision is about equally important for the company and the subordinate.
3. Where the decision is particularly important for the company.
4. Where neither the company nor the subordinate have a special interest in the decision.

The distribution of influence and power sharing on these four contingencies follows the curves of Figure 12. It can be seen that managers have no difficulty in differentiating the alternatives. Where the decisions are particularly important for the subordinate, the senior manager is prepared to give him a considerable amount of power. In sharp contrast, he retains most of the available decision power in his own hands when the company is the major interested party. When both parties are equally concerned, the power distribution approximates to a normal curve. When decisions are of relatively little importance to either, then the main preference is to avoid time-consuming procedures and to go straight for extreme "autocracy" or delegation.[35]

An Evaluation of Participation as a Style of Management

We have said earlier that we prefer to avoid the term "participation." It seems that in a large part of the literature on the subject, this term has become associated with various values which range all the way from the purely political to the sales talk of consultants who offer ready made packages of "how to do it" kits. In between these unsatisfactory extremes, participation is a term used by psychologists and sociologists to describe an organizational or inter-personal phenomenon based on power or influence. For this reason, it seems preferable to keep to an influence-power description and to avoid the emotional and usually vague term, participation. Throughout the research described up to now and in the definition of the five alternative decision methods, we have upheld this preference. A further reason for avoiding the term participation is that it does not lend itself to a description of the various types of delegation (see Figure 3). Delegation is, of course, a particularly important aspect of distributing power throughout an organization. If power were not "delegated" to various appropriate levels, there would be little genuine participation at lower echelons (that is to say, consultation, joint decision-making and consensus methods of various kinds). In the absence of a distribution of delegated power one would be left with "manipulative participation" which can be defined as a process that gives the appearance of distributing influence when no such influence is available. One is concerned here with the facts of the situation, not the reasons for them. Influence may not be available because the real decision has already been taken or because the key person in the process has no intention of allowing himself to be influenced, irrespective of the value of the contribution. We have said earlier that the reason why the major schools of thought on participative decision-making omit delegation from their range of alternatives is that they attach a particular value to group

---

35 We put the term "autocracy" in quotation marks to signify that no negative implications should be attributed to the term; it is simply descriptive of a logical and possible appropriate alternative.

724   Frank A. Heller

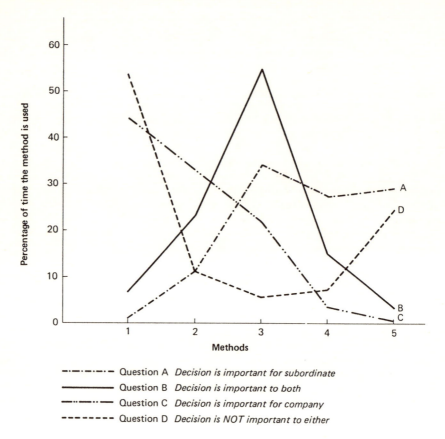

Figure 12. Decision method varies with importance of decision (US sample).

Note: For a description of the five decision methods, see Figure 3 and preceding section (Part I).

and interpersonal processes and that this somewhat doctrinaire position prevents them from including delegation.

Despite our preference, it must be recognized that practising managers in nearly all parts of the world have become accustomed to the term participation (Haire, Ghiselli and Porter, 1966). For this reason, we included this word on one of the fourteen questionnaires used in the present research. During the last ten minutes of the feedback discussion, we asked our group what managerial pay-off they expected from the use of the influence and power-sharing process which, in the literature, is often called "participation." The importance attributed to the various alternatives is scored and the results are shown in Table 5.[36]

The results are almost the same for both levels and show that managers

_____

[36] In the first phase of the American research, the scoring was based on a method of content analysis of the tape recordings (Heller, 1971a). Later, a simple questionnaire was used, leading to a ranking of the five most important reasons.

Decision Processes   725

TABLE 5
WHY MANAGERS USE
"PARTICIPATIVE" DECISION METHODS:
RESULTS FROM TWO SENIOR LEVELS

Reasons	Ranking L.1	L.2
To improve the technical quality of decisions	1	1
To increase satisfaction	2	3
To improve communication (understanding of problems)	3	2
To train subordinates	4	4
To facilitate change	5	5

Note: L.1 refers to Level 1, the senior level of management immediately below the chief executive. L.2 is the level immediately subordinate to L.1.

expect "participative" methods to be of most benefit in improving the quality of decision-making; secondly, in improving communication; thirdly, in increasing satisfaction and fourthly, in training subordinates. While behavioral scientists are particularly interested in "participation" as a powerful method of facilitating the introduction of change, managers give relatively little importance to it. The British results are identical to the American findings.

Finally a note about "management styles" and "democratic" management. As in the case of the word participation, these terms have strong emotive connotations and for the sake of accuracy and as a way of arriving at a description of organizational reality, it is best to avoid them. Instead of "styles," one can use the more neutral term "method;" this avoids the evocation that a certain "style" is fashionable or unfashionable, good or bad. Democratic management is a particularly inappropriate term since it has clear value implications.

However, beyond terminological preferences there is a very real question of how much influence and power is shared by different levels of management and how much of the senior man's influence is *seen* to be shared by his subordinates. We have two sources of evidence. One comes from the statistical summary of decision methods as seen by L.1 and L.2; this result is presented in two alternative ways in Table 6. In the first assumption, we define influence and power sharing by including "prior consultation." In the second, we include only the most powerful methods, 4 and 5. On the first assumption, both senior and subordinate see the distribution of power in roughly the same way, and over 60% report that Methods 3, 4 and 5 are used in their company. In making the more stringent assumption, differences of judgement between the two levels appear. The senior level reports 27% and the subordinate level 42% of power-sharing. Even this amount is considerable if we remember that several of the decision situations do not lend themselves to joint decision-making or delegation; it will be remembered, for instance, that Question 1 asks how L.1 decides about increases in the subordinate's salary.

If one relied on the statistical picture alone, one could well conclude that the average distribution of influence and power in this sample was very considerable. We will now look at other evidence.

A Reevaluation Based on Feedback Analysis

There are several reasons why the results from questionnaire enquiries alone may be inadequate, even if the research instruments have been carefully tested

726   Frank A. Heller

TABLE 6
TWO INTERPRETATIONS OF
INFLUENCE AND POWER-SHARING
AS SEEN BY TWO SENIOR LEVELS

	As seen by L.1	As seen by L.2
INTERPRETATION 1		
Methods 1 & 2	36.2	33.6
Methods 3, 4 & 5	63.8	66.4
	100%	100%
INTERPRETATION 2		
Methods 1, 2 & 3	73.0	58.1
Methods 4 & 5	27.0	41.9
	100%	100%

Note: L.1 refers to Level 1, the senior level immediately below the chief executive. L.2 is the level immediately subordinate to L.1.

(Heller, 1969b). One problem relates to the bias due to expectations on a popular topic like participation or styles of management. Even if one avoids these value terms there is, at least in America, a constant stream of articles, books and public speeches which hammer home the point that certain styles of managerial behavior are better than others. Since the contingency framework has not yet gained much ground, the credo of "democratic" management in all circumstances has had no substantial opposition.[37] People take sides even before they think carefully. As a result of reading or attending courses, they have come to consider themselves as being a certain person, using a particular method of leadership and being judged as "avant-garde" rather than "old fashioned." This is, of course, a major reason for not using emotive trigger words. Thoughts like this lead one to question the value of enquiries which ask two questions: firstly, how much participation people experience now and secondly, how much they would like to have. Given that the stimulus word relates to a desirable experience, the answer to the second question is hardly in doubt, and tells us more about the nature of the response set than about the variable in question.

One of the major objectives of Stage three in Group Feedback Analysis (GFA) used as a method of field research is to delve into the real meaning of the statistical findings, to motivate managers to interpret their meaning and to reevaluate the results where necessary. The details of these reinterpretations and the content analysis used are described elsewhere (Heller, 1971a:59–68, 91–99); here we will describe only the main conclusions.

There is strong evidence that, as a result of the feedback discussion, one becomes conscious of two distortions in the statistical results. One is due to a substantial element of what we have called manipulative participation, particularly where managers have described themselves as using prior consultation. What typically happens in an L.1 feedback discussion is this:

---

[37] In the footnotes of the vast literature on this subject there are of course many caveats and the cumulative contribution of the work of Fiedler (1967), Woodward (1965), Burns and Stalker (1961), Lawrence and Lorsch (1967a), Trist, et al. (1963) is beginning to have an effect. For a review of these arguments, see Heller (1971a).

One manager has described himself as using prior consultation in 48% of his decisions, while others in the same group have put down figures varying between 20% and 35%. No names appear next to the results but every manager can recognize his own. A member of the group challenges the plausibility of 48% in the circumstances of their company. Two other managers identify themselves as having used much lower percentages. There is silence. Then Mr. Jones says that he "believes" he probably put down 48% but he would like to explain that he includes under that heading all the occasions when he meets his subordinate on a Monday morning to discuss performance against budgets for the previous week and the production plan for the following week. There is a pause and more silence. Then several colleagues challenge this interpretation; they point out that the budget targets are fixed a long time before and cannot be changed, and that the Monday morning meetings are almost entirely informational, since the plans have been hammered out between themselves (that is to say, the L.1 group) in the weekly review on Friday afternoon. Mr. Jones argues a bit about the possible interpretation of prior consultation; he says that he presents the plans as if they were for discussion, because his people like it that way. They refer to the written definition again and it is then agreed that only 25% or thereabouts was really appropriate under that heading; the remaining 23% should be divided between Methods 1 and 2.

This is an extreme case but the general trend of the re-evaluation is always in that direction. Unfortunately, there is usually not enough time to produce precise results as in the example above; the discussion tends to be in much vaguer terms and no worthwhile statistical readjustment of the original questionnaire results is practical.[38]

The second major distortion occurs in relation to Method 4, Joint Decision-Making. In discussion after discussion, it becomes clear that, in spite of the carefully prepared definition and verbal reinforcement by the researcher, a proportion of managers interpret Joint Decision-Making as describing situations that are more appropriate to Method 3 or to a point on the continuum close to Method 3. This seems to be due to the difficulty managers have in visualizing genuine consensus power-sharing situations in *specific circumstances*. They may be willing to talk about it in *general terms*, but when in the feedback discussion they are pinned down to actual examples, they readily admit that the formal definition of Method 4, where the "subordinate(s) usually has as much influence over the final choice" as the senior manager, is not feasible in the majority of cases.

We come back to the point that subjects like leadership, power-sharing or the pervasive "participation" cannot be described with complete objectivity. To a large extent *the reality of the behavior is the belief and the interpretation* of the parties concerned. One is therefore entitled to use judgments based on neutrally worded questions describing specific managerial behavior, backed up by careful definitions. This we do and the consequent results are probably as accurate as the questionnaire method alone permits. Group Feedback Analysis enables us to submit these results to further scrutiny but in the time available during the research described here, the conclusion must be put very tentatively. We estimate that in the American sample of senior managers, Methods 4 and 5

---

[38] If more time were available, and the number of questionnaires restricted, GFA could be used for a statistical reappraisal of results.

are used between 15%–20% of the time and Method 3 between 20%–30%. This would leave at least half the total decision behavior and possibly 65% to be described by Methods 1 and 2.

CURRENT RESEARCH EXTENSIONS IN EUROPEAN COUNTRIES

Following the American work, a British research with twenty large companies was carried out. Fifteen of these companies were carefully matched to the American companies in type of industry, technology, size and managerial level.[39] Between 1972 and the end of 1974, six other countries joined the project, five of them European.[40] The research now covers over 1600 managers in 100 companies.

The European work was an extension rather than a replication of the American research. In addition to the questionnaires used in the United States, nine further instruments were developed and validated. They were based on variables conceptualized in the alpha to omega hierarchy of contingencies (Figures 4 and 9) and will be briefly described.

- *Pressures and constraints questionnaire*—Form 4
  An assessment of the effect of constraints surrounding the managerial task. For instance, pressures and the amount of formal authority invested in a job limit a manager's choice of alternatives. A gamma level variable.
- *Lateral decision-making questionnaire*—Form 6
  Extended the IPC from the superior-subordinate level to an assessment of influence-power sharing among colleagues (an extension of the core variable).
- *Skill utilization measure*—Form 8
  A simple and very preliminary attempt to obtain a rough assessment of the perception of *underutilization* of skill at the two levels of management (skill hopper model Figures 8 and 9).
- *Turbulence and uncertainty questionnaire*—Form 9
  This is an attempt to measure a part of the theoretical concept of complexity and turbulence, discussed by Emery and Trist (1965). A variety of environmental variables which fall within the gamma and delta systems are included.
- *Expectation of change questionnaire*—Form 10
  While the turbulence questionnaire measures current conditions, here we assess expectation of the rate of change during the next five to ten years (delta system).
- *Formal skill qualification questionnaire*—Form 11
  This is the first attempt within the present research to obtain an ob-

---

[39] This work was done by the Tavistock Institute of Human Relations in London and supported by two grants from the Social Science Research Council (of Great Britain), including the European extension.

[40] The following European research centers are involved: The Erasmus University of Rotterdam supported by the Dutch Productivity Centre; The International Institute of Management, West Berlin; Centre d'Enseignement Superieur des Affaires, France; Economic Research Institute, Stockholm School of Economics; Instituto de Estudios Superiores de la Empresa, Barcelona; and the Leon Recanati Graduate School of Business Administration.

jective measure of the available skills of senior management at the
two levels represented. It is designed to measure skills in the hopper
model (Figures 8 and 9).
*   *Work satisfaction measure*—Form 14
    A simple questionnaire to measure the satisfaction and motivation vari-
    ables described in Figure 9.
Finally, there are some organizational measures obtained through an interview with the chief executive of each company in the sample:
*   *Aston measures of organization structure and context* as defined by
    Pugh, et al. (1963) and measured in a short scale (Inkson, et al., 1970).
    We have made slight adaptations to this scale and have included a
    simple assessment of organization effectiveness. This is part of the delta
    system of variables.

Further Assessments of Organizational Turbulence

Two similar measurements were attempted; first by interviewing the chief executive in each company and secondly by obtaining a panel of expert judges
who knew the industrial sectors of our sample and who judged the relative
degree of turbulence surrounding each of them. A form of "Delphi method"
was used.[41]

Preliminary Results from Some European Research[42]

All field work was completed by the end of 1974 and most countries had
analyzed a part of their results at that time. The following summary of some
preliminary findings is based mainly on the British and German data.[43]
One of the simplest, but in terms of the contingency model very important,
findings relates to the diversity of power-sharing methods used by senior man-

---

[41] The Aston and second stage turbulence measures were used only in the British sample.

[42] The statistical methodology for data analysis will not be described in detail since this
falls outside the objective of this chapter. The basic outline will be mentioned to enable the
reader to form a judgment about the eventual empirical validity in support of the contingency
model. Each of the main variables described in this chapter has been factor analyzed to form
composites of the dimensions in the model (Wilpert and Heller, 1974). The multivariate
analysis was based on parametric methods in the first place (intercorrelation matrix of variables
and composites; t-tests and one-way analysis of variance of noncontinuous variables such as
comparisons between levels of management, industrial sectors and countries). Multiple regression analysis and cannonical correlations were used to test the interaction between our peripheral and core variables. In the second stage the same data was treated nonparametrically.
Contingency tables were constructed to test the main hypotheses; Kendall's tau and chi square
tests were applied to three by three tables based on a high, medium and low trichotomization
of all continuous variables. Multidimensional scaling was used on the British skill perception
variables to compare with the factor analysis. Since many variables are not normally distributed,
the main findings will be those that are confirmed by parametric as well as nonparametric
methods. Finally, the tape recordings from the feedback discussions are being content analyzed
in each country. It was agreed that the methods of content analysis would not be standardized
since an idiographic rather than nomothetic result is aimed at.

[43] The West Berlin-based International Institute of Management has taken a leading part
in the European research and its financial support. Dr. Wilpert, the chief German investigator,
co-authored two papers with Dr. Heller presented at international research meetings in Canada
during the summer of 1974. These papers are drawn on for the summary of results.

agers. There are two main trends in the leadership literature. The older approach, referred to earlier, was to see participatory or autocratic leadership methods as a function of *personality*. More recently, organizational psychologists have argued in favor of participatory methods in terms of a *normative* model. The norm became an organizational objective and managers were expected to converge to that norm irrespective of their personality.

It now seems that neither personality nor norm in fact decides the methods of decision-making used.[44] Managers change their method in relation to different *situations*. Both in Germany and Britain only one out of a hundred managers uses a single method of decision-making. 20% of the German managers and 30% of British managers use all five methods of the IPC on the twelve decisions described earlier in this chapter. Between 40% and 50% use four out of the five methods. This finding has considerable validity since the descriptions of both levels of managers agree and both levels describe the same behavior (Heller, 1973; Heller and Wilpert, 1974). The multiple use of styles by the same leaders is fully confirmed by Vroom and Yetton (1973), Bass and Valenzi (1973) and Hill (1973). The potential importance of situationally determined leadership has been discussed for a considerable time (Stogdill, 1948. 1956; Hemphill, 1950; Seeman, 1953; Wispe and Lloyd, 1955; Gibb, 1958; Argyris, 1964; Koreman, 1966), but it is only now that we are beginning to understand the nature of the specific contingencies which account for variations in leadership behavior (Fiedler, 1967; Lawrence and Lorsch, 1967; Heller and Yukl, 1969; Heller, 1971a; Vroom and Yetton, 1973; Bass and Valenzi, 1973; Hill and Hughes, 1974).

The major situational factors accounting for variations in managerial decision-making methods in the European research appear to be *task* and *skill*. Both come from the alpha and beta system of contingency variables. Task has been variously described as technology of the managerial job, job function and the nature of the decision. It is this last variable, measured by the twelve decisions described earlier in this chapter, which accounts for the greatest variance in decision method (Heller and Wilpert, 1974).

One particular way of differentiating task is to choose some decisions which apply to a whole group of people and compare them with decisions made only between a manager and one of his immediate subordinates. This difference is highly significant in the American, British and German samples (Heller and Wilpert, 1974).[45]

The second major contingency variable is measured by three indicators of skill. Two are attitudinal and judgmental, while the third presents the actual formal qualifications and skills of each manager (Form 11). The American results on the attitudinal measures have already been given (Tables 2, 3 and 4). The British and German results support these findings. On the basis of a sample of fifty companies and nearly 600 managers, it is now possible to argue as follows.

Managers who perceive a substantial difference between their own jobs and the jobs of their subordinates and/or between themselves and their subordinates (these are different judgments) tend to use centralized decision meth-

---

[44] A recent controlled laboratory research study confirms the relatively small contribution of personality factors in DM (Taylor and Dunnette, 1974).

[45] For other significant task dimensions, see Figures 11 and 12 (pages 722, 724).

ods. Small perceptual gaps on these dimensions are associated with participatory decision-making.

We cannot be sure that these perceptions of skill differences correspond to actual differences in every case, but the subordinate's judgments follow the same pattern.

An even stronger support for the hypothesis that skills and decision-making methods interrelate, comes from the measures of formal educational qualifications. British and German senior managers with high educational qualifications use participative decision methods. Those with lower qualifications use more autocratic methods (Heller and Wilpert, 1974).

The last specific finding to be mentioned here relates to the effect on decision-making of a complex and uncertain environment. In the present research, Form 9 is an attempt to operationalize Emery and Trist's (1965) ideas on turbulence of the environment.[46]

The hypothesis that a highly complex and turbulent environment is associated with decentralized decision-making is supported at both senior levels. The preliminary analysis suggests, however, that the relationship is weaker and less consistent than with the alpha, beta and gamma variables. If this turned out to be the case, it would support the hierarchical contingency assumptions. It will be remembered that turbulence was thought to be relatively peripheral to the decision act at these particular levels of management and was classified as a delta level variable (Figure 9).

It must be emphasized that this finding is very tentative since turbulence had not been explored in the earlier American research. A relatively low impact value of environmental turbulence would have to be reconciled with a considerable recent emphasis on the importance of this variable (Starbuck, 1972).[47]

PART III: A TENTATIVE OVERVIEW

Our main objective was to put forward a theoretical framework for an analysis of power relationships between decision-makers in organizations. There are three parts to the framework: infrastructures, flow process and contingencies. Some data were presented to provide a preliminary test of the dimensions incorporated in the theoretical framework. Other data are available in the literature referred to.[48]

---

[46] The instrument has nine closed and one open question. Repeat reliability and internal consistency are satisfactory. Construct validity is achieved by reasonable correlations with Form 4 (Pressures and constraints) and Form 10 (Expectation of change). Factor analysis yields two factors accounting for 44% of the variance, three factors 55%. The intercorrelations between perceived turbulence at the two levels are high and consistent.

[47] One argument which anticipates the possibility of low impact of environmental factors has been put forward by Child (1972). Child says that managers have a wide range of choices which are unlikely to be decisively constrained by a factor like turbulence. At the same time, we fully endorse Child's view that subjectively perceived turbulence is at least as important as objective measures. Since "coping with turbulence" rather than the uncertainty itself is likely to be the critical factor (Crozier, 1964; Hickson, et al., 1971), it is worth mentioning that the instructions used in our research instruments elicit judgments on the environmental impact on the here-and-now-work-situation. There is evidence that responses were in terms of "coping."

[48] For further examples of recent literature relevant to a flow analysis of DM, see Friend and Jessop (1969), Sadler and Barry (1970), Braybrooke (1974).

732   FRANK A. HELLER

Decision Analysis

The flow process model of decision-making (Figures 1 and 2) departs from traditional approaches in several respects. The literature on decision-making tends to concentrate on solutions as choice between known alternatives. The decision process is usually thought of as going on in the mind of a single person and the objective is to work out an optimal solution within a set of constraints and a criterion of output. Much less attention has been paid to the dynamic interaction between people in arriving at a solution. In real life, this second situation is much more usual. Quite often, the constraints and alternative choices emerge only in the social interaction between people who represent different roles and positions of power.

In the area of industrial relations the inapplicability of the classic decision model is particularly clear. The outcome and the process of people-interaction are inextricably intertwined. The medium is the message and the outcome is the process, be it a strike or a compromise solution.

The present research on decision-making has concentrated on the people-interaction aspect and has left the question of alternative solutions to one side. Ultimately, these two branches of research will have to merge. For the time being, the area we are investigating and reporting on has been much less carefully developed than the other. This imbalance of knowledge about the socio-psychological compared with the cognitive side of decision-making has to be redressed before an integration of the two disciplines is possible.

Contingencies and Infrastructures

The second departure from tradition is the multivariate, multilevel contingency model which has been adequately described earlier. It developed gradually since about 1965, when work in the socioeconomic setting of South America demonstrated the difficulty of applying the then dominant theories of managerial leadership (Heller, 1973; Heller and Yukl, 1969). While there have been many additions and changes, it will be noticed that the term "transitional model" is still used and will continue under a new program of research currently in its early stages. The point to be underlined here is the deliberate provision for evolution and choice within the model itself.

The provision of choice among defined alternatives is also a feature of the contingency framework compared with an assumption of finality. A similar way of thinking about organizations has recently been described as the "equifinality principle." It is based on the finding that various dimensions of bureaucracy can be put together in several different arrangements which "appear to be equally viable strategies for the various sample organizations" (Reiman, 1973:402). By analogy with the bureaucracy example, one could say that different contingencies lead to decentralized power. According to our model, a devolution of influence and power could be a legitimate organizational objective since one of its outcomes is a higher utilization of skills. In such a case, the model would highlight a number of *alternative choices* for achieving the objective.

A possible disadvantage of such a model is the difficulty of reconciling its tentativeness and lack of finality with a change agent's demand for a normative theory. We recognize the apparent dilemma but wish to make two points. First, it could be argued that the premature, normative theories of the 1950s and 1960s may have been responsible for an ossification in managerial thinking about the subject of participation and "ideal" styles of leadership. We are still trying to recover from this in the 1970s.[49]

Second, we would not agree that a normative model is necessary for the practical purposes of helping organizations, their subunits or individual pairs of managers to improve their decision methods. A normative model may be useful for teaching or training purposes, but is not a requirement for action research.[50]

We can complete the description of the theoretical framework by pointing out that it differs from manpower models by its claim that the utilization of skill is a motivator. The infrastructure model (Figure 8) directs attention to various conditions which facilitate or inhibit the free flow of available skill resources.

The Macro-Micro Interface

The present application of the model focuses on individuals and small groups. That is to say, the micro level of organization. Even so, the micro level is assumed to interact with technical, structural policy and external sociopolitical events. In a sense, the model is designed to act as a bridge between micro and macro levels of analysis. It is rightly felt by some that this interface is one of the most neglected areas of theory and empirical study (Pugh and Phesey, 1968; Phesey, et al., 1971; Reiman, 1973; Leavitt, et al., 1974). Moreover, it seems likely that the transitional model can be adapted to work in other areas of organizational analysis, with a focus on organizational units or subunits instead of individuals. It can also be used for longitudinal studies of organizational processes.[51]

We should be aware of the limitations of narrow and specialized models and methodologies in a field of study as complex and controversial as power.[52] At a general level, this argument has been put very forcefully by Argyris, who

---

[49] A partial exception to our doubts about normative models is the recent and very sophisticated research of Vroom and Yetton (1973). They have produced a normative model which is a clear improvement on the theories of Likert (1967) and the training packages of Blake and Mouton (1964), Reddin (1970) and Kepner and Tregoe (1965). Even so, it is evident that the eight particular contingencies incorporated in the Vroom and Yetton model cannot claim to be the only or the major determining factors of leadership in the future. For instance, our own contingencies overlap with theirs only minimally, but both produce highly significant interaction patterns and account for a reasonable percentage of the total variance in behavior.

[50] While there is a wide range of different methods of introducing organizational change, we have argued elsewhere that "action research" should pay much more attention to the *research* part of the method than is usually the case (Heller, 1975). The search or research part of the change process benefits from having a flexible theoretical framework. A strictly normative model may mean that some predetermined "best solution" is the change agent's first and last choice. Very similar points have been made by Chris Argyris in his various writings (see, for instance, Argyris, 1970).

[51] The cross-sectional study reported in this chapter is now being followed up by a flow process analysis of decision-making and participation in Holland, Yugoslavia and Britain. The new study will pay special attention to the longitudinal interrelations between power and the use of skills. While the field methodology will be different, the basic structure of the transitional model is being used, at least to begin with.

[52] It must be remembered that as recently as 1964 Crozier drew our attention to the need to make power the central problem in studying bureaucratic organizations (Crozier, 1964: Chapter 6). Since that time there has been an enormous increase of research in this field (Participation and Self-Management, 1972–73).

734   FRANK A. HELLER

criticizes sociological work on organizations for its neglect of the individual (Argyris, 1972). Curiously enough, this neglect is less clear in the special case of power which, since Weber, has usually been defined in terms of individual actors. This excessive psychological emphasis has been criticized by Perrow (1970). There is now some danger that we might overcompensate by depersonalizing power altogether. Argyris could also extend his strictures of subject specialization by pointing to his more traditional colleagues in industrial psychology who have striven hard to avoid many relevant and real issues because they fall outside the framework of interpersonal analysis.

EVALUATION

While it may seem natural that this chapter has stressed the more positive aspects of the model and research findings, there are important limitations and weaknesses. Most of the findings on both dependent and independent variables were collected at one moment of time and from only two levels of management. The one hundred organizations spread over eight countries and are not representative of the total population of companies, although they are fairly adequately matched to each other. While we went to a great deal of trouble to standardize the research administration in the various countries, differences have inevitably emerged.

More importantly, perhaps, we are very much aware that our resources and conceptual framework are not capable of dealing with all the subtle complexities of power and decision-making in organizations. We have not assessed most of the important omega level variables, nor what can be called meta power. Meta power is a description for various forms of control which limit the exercise of power at any one place and time (Buckley & Burns, 1974). Meta power is usually exercised one or more levels above the level which is constrained, although power cliques can exercise a similar effect by limiting the influence of their colleagues in a horizontal direction. The constraining influence of organizations on each other (banks on businesses; suppliers on manufacturers; professional associations or trade unions on businesses of various kinds) is an example of environmental turbulence but also, in many cases, of meta power. Other researchers have begun to work in these critical areas (for example Hickson, et al., 1971; Hinings, et al., 1974; Rus, 1974; Salancik and Pfeffer, 1974; Abell, 1975).

Finally, it must be said that we are aware of the limitation of findings derived from formal responses to formal questions. Even if one could produce an atmosphere in which respondents felt free to express their real views, one could not be sure that they accurately reflected their behavior (Argyris, 1965, 1976). The limitations of the stimulus-response method of enquiry led to the use of Group Feedback Analysis (GFA) which was described earlier. This method enables one to make some spot checks on the veridity of the statistical findings. As we saw, distortions occurred and we can make some rough allowance for them in our conclusions. However, we do not have a method for correcting statistical data for distortion of this kind.

Several of the problems we have described are too large to be tackled immediately. Others are due to the severe limitation imposed by studies that take a single "snapshot" and extrapolate from it to resemble real life. Snapshot research is economical and fully justified at certain stages of exploration, but we feel that a point has been reached when an understanding of power based on the contingency model described here (particularly Figures 1 and 2) requires studies in depth and over time. The challenge is to devise methods which will enable one to carry out longitudinal studies with reasonable objectivity.[53]

DISCUSSION AND CONCLUSIONS

We are moving into an era of hectic discussion of the case for and against "democracy" at the place of work. In Europe, this term is usually applied to power sharing with lower levels of organization, while in America, under the term "participation," it applies a little more to power-sharing at junior, middle and senior managerial levels. In Europe, the trend has been to underpin the movement by legislation, while in America, the emphasis has been on training in interpersonal skills.[54] The European structuralist and the American socio-psychological approach are beginning to merge in some Scandinavian countries.[55] These rapid increases in the application of power-sharing in different parts of the world throw up a number of questions:

- Can influence and power be shared in all circumstances?
- Which of the various methods of power-sharing are most effective?
- Are there limits to the distribution of influence and power?
- Is it possible to provide a feeling of participation without actually sharing power?
- What are the consequences of simulating power-sharing?
- Do people want to participate in most decisions or only in some?
- Can power-sharing be effectively used at only one level of a multilevel organization?
- Is democratic decision-making a function of personality, role, or situation?

Our research and the literature we have cited deals with a few of these issues but many more remain unanswered. Past experience suggests that the answers will depend substantially on the theoretical model used for the research. The choice of model is therefore important.

Udy (1965) has suggested that the search for *principles* of organizations can be contrasted with a *contingency* approch. The former is a search for constants and it seems that mary writers who have followed this line have over-

---

[53] A pilot study for this new phase of research is currently under way in Britain and Holland supported by the Social Science Research Council (in Britain) and the Science Foundation (in Holland).

[54] For a guide to the very extensive literature on this subject see, for instance, Blumberg (1968), Participation and Self-Management (1972–73) and Walker (1974).

[55] Social scientists were at first very sceptical of mixing legal and sociopsychological remedies (Emery and Trist, 1960). It seems, however, that political and trade union pressures have coincided with a great shortage of skilled and semi-skilled labor. Workers have shown themselves unwilling to take on repetitive short cycle jobs. These factors have led to a great deal of experimentation with the redesign of jobs based on "democratic" decision-making procedures. The famous examples of Hunsfos, Saab and Volvo are based on sociotechnical theory (Trist and Bamforth, 1951; Emery and Trist, 1960; Davis and Taylor, 1972) and work through semi-autonomous groups. In addition, but more recently, the Norwegian and Swedish governments have legislated for worker participation at various levels, including the board of directors. Elsewhere, and particularly in America, more emphasis is placed on theories of motivation, job enrichment based on expert advice, and job satisfactions (Dowling, 1973).

structured and over-simplified the evidence to a point where it seriously departs from organizational reality. The opposite view is equally misleading; managers and critics of the behavioral sciences often argue that all situations are unique. This is the "it all depends" argument taken to an extreme. A contingency framework does not exclude the existence of organizational constants. It sets out to test the assumption very severely by assuming that these constants operate over a *limited area* of the phenomenon under investigation. The research is therefore directed towards an exploration of the limits within which a generalization applies. For instance, our investigation follows the assumptions made by previous research that power-sharing leadership styles can produce increased satisfaction and organizational effectiveness, but it tests power-sharing under a series of specified conditions. This enables us to conclude that power-sharing is limited by factors such as the size of the working group, the constraints imposed by the nature of the job, the importance of the decision, the available managerial experience and skill, etc. These and other contingency assumptions have now been supported by data from our samples in three countries.

There are some modern protagonists of power-sharing who hold the view that ethically correct procedures will always be effective. At the beginning of the century, management scientists took a different and more cynical view; procedures that could be shown to be effective were thought to be ethically correct. The second proposition is now widely discredited but the first is difficult to sustain.[56]

The approach we have used in this chapter and the evidence that has accumulated so far suggests an alternative position. We assume that participation and power-sharing are ethically and normatively acceptable to most people. According to our model, power-sharing methods are preferable to autocracy, "other things being equal." But why are power-sharing methods preferred? The answer (within the limits of our model) is that they lead to a better utilization of skills and there is some evidence that people like to use their skills. However, circumstances are not always equal. This is where the contingencies come in. In what circumstances is power-sharing not appropriate? As an example one can give the finding, also well substantiated by laboratory studies (Mulder and Wilke, 1970; Mulder, 1971), that a large difference in skill between people is associated with centralized methods of decision-making. What is an appropriate personal or organizational response to this situation? There seem to be at least four:

1. One can accept the position as it is and put up with the existence of differential power as a concomitant of differential skills.
2. One could try to rearrange the organization to produce a better match between boss-subordinate groups.
3. One can carry on as if this finding did not exist or did not matter. This is probably what actually happens in the majority of cases today. It explains the considerable amount of pseudo or manipulative participation one finds in real life and in the feedback discussions during our research (see our evidence above and Heller, 1971:97–98).
4. The organization, or individuals, could take deliberate steps to narrow the skill gap. One method of doing this "on the job" is by a more ex-

---

[56] A subtle analysis of the difficulty of reconciling some existing evidence on power sharing and efficiency is put forward by Lammers (1973).

tensive use of consultation, joint decision-making and delegation. In other words, power-sharing decision methods could be used as a means of increasing subordinate's experience and skill. Once this was achieved, power-sharing would make sense for a different reason; namely to use available resources.

Among the four alternatives mentioned, the last one is likely to be most acceptable from a humanistic point of view. It is also a realistic and practical solution from an organizational perspective. Our research has some data to test whether such a view receives any backing in present circumstances. Unfortunately, the answer is no. We have described the results of Table 5. Respondents were asked to say why participation was important. What were the consequences or results they expected? According to our respondents, "Training of subordinates" received a very low score, coming fourth out of five reasons. The results from equivalent groups of British and German managers gave the same low ranking. In all cases, "The improvement of the technical quality of decision" was given first rank.

This finding is not inimical to the use of participation since it shows that managers value the specific skill contribution subordinates can make. Moreover, they value participation for reasons that are "genuine" rather than "pseudo." Nevertheless we are left with the problem of a considerable skill gap. Senior and subordinate managers make significantly different judgments about their skills; this is likely to lead to unnecessarily centralized decision-making and to an under-utilization of skill resources.

Can anything be done about this? We believe that our research findings based on a contingency model, may facilitate the introduction of change in organizations. The existence of organizational choice (based on contingency thinking) should facilitate the task of organizational design (Clark, 1972; Kingdon, 1973) or redesign based on action research. Action research has two complementary objectives: one is to make new discoveries (or at least to obtain valid information) and the second is to use the discovered data to make a practical contribution to the solution of problems. If the conflictual perception of skill differences stands in the way of a more democratic pattern of leadership and a better use of skill, we have a problem. The nature of the problem can be explored by means of the data we have described. There is evidence that the use of suitable methods of feeding this information back to our respondents encourages a reexamination which usually leads to a shift in perception and eventually to a change in behavior (Heller 1970, 1975).

REFERENCES

Abell, P. (ed.)
   1975 "Organizations as bargaining and influence systems." Mimeographed. Imperial College of Science and Technology, London (To be published).
Ajiferuke, M. and J. Boddewyn
   1970 "Socioeconomic indicators in comparative management." Administrative Science Quarterly (15):453–458.
Alderfer, C.P.
   1969 "An empirical test of a new theory of human needs." Organizational Behavior and Performance (4):142–175.

738   Frank A. Heller

1974 "The effect of variations in relatedness need satisfaction on relatedness desires." Administrative Science Quarterly (19):507–532.
Applewhite, P.
1965 Organizational Behavior. Englewood Cliffs, New Jersey: Prentice-Hall.
Argyris, C.
1964 Integrating the Individual and the Organization. New York: Wiley.
1965 Organization and Innovation. Homewood, Illinois: Irwin.
1970 Intervention Theory and Method: A Behavioral Science View. Reading, Mass.: Addison-Wesley.
1972 The Applicability of Organizational Sociology. London: Cambridge University Press.
1976 "Problems and new directions in industrial psychology," in M.D. Dunnette (ed.), Handbook of Industrial and Organizational Psychology. Chicago: Rand McNally College Publishing Co.
Bass, B. and E. Valenzi
1973 "Contingency aspects of effective management styles." Technical Report 67. Management Research Centre, May.
Bendix, R.
1960 Max Weber: An Intellectual Portrait. London: Heinemann.
Blake, R. and J. Mouton
1964 The Managerial Grid. Houston, Texas: The Gulf Publishing Co.
Blankenship, L.V. and R.E. Miles
1968 "Organizational structure and managerial decision behavior." Administrative Science Quarterly (13):106–120.
Blumberg, P.
1968 Industrial Democracy. London: Constable.
Braybrooke, D.
1974 Traffic Congestion Goes Through the Issue Machine. London and Boston: Routledge and Kegan Paul.
Brayfield, A.H. and W.H. Crockett
1955 "Employee attitudes and employee performance." Psychological Bulletin (52):396–424.
Brown, W.
1960 Explorations in Management. London: Heinemann.
Buckley, W. and T.R. Burns
1974 "Power and meta power." Paper prepared for the 8th World Congress of Sociology, Toronto, August.
Burns, T. and G.M. Stalker
1961 The Management of Innovation. London: Tavistock Publications.
Campbell, R.M. and D. Hitchin
1968 "The Delphi technique: implementation in the corporate environment." Management Services (November–December):37–42.
Carlson, S.
1951 Executive Behavior: A Study of the Work Load and Working Methods of Managing Directors. Stockholm: Strombergs.
Cartwright, D.
1965 "Influence, leadership, control," in J.G. March (ed.), Handbook of Organizations. Chicago: Rand McNally.

Child, J.
  1972 "Organizational structure, environment and performance: the role of strategic choice." Sociology (6) :1–22.
Churchman, W.C.
  1968 Challenge to Reason. New York: McGraw-Hill.
Clark, P.
  1972 Organizational Design. London: Tavistock Publications.
Crozier, M.
  1964 The Bureaucratic Phenomenon. London: Tavistock Publications.
Cyert, R.M. and J.G. March
  1963 A Behavioral Theory of the Firm. Englewood Cliffs, New Jersey: Prentice-Hall.
Cyert, R.M., H.A. Simon and D.B. Trow
  1956 "Observation of a business decision." Journal of Business (29) :237–248.
Dahl, R.A.
  1957 "The concept of power." Behavioral Science (2) :201–215.
  1968 Power. International Encyclopedia of Social Science. New York: Macmillan.
Dalkey, N. and O. Helmer
  1963 "An experimental application of the Delphi method to the use of experts." Management Science (9) :458–467.
Davis, L.
  1957 "Job design and productivity: a new approach." Personnel (33) :418–430.
Davis, L. and J. Taylor (eds.)
  1972 Design of Jobs. Harmondsworth, Middlesex, England: Penguin.
Dowling, W.
  1973 "Job redesign on the assembly line." Organizational Dynamics 51–67.
Dufty, N.F. and P.M. Taylor
  1962 "Implementation of a decision." Administrative Science Quarterly (7) :110–119.
Dunnette, M.D., J. Campbell and M. Hakel
  1967 "Factors contributing to job satisfaction and job dissatisfaction in six occupational groups." Organizational Behavior and Human Performance (2) :143–174.
Emery, F.E.
  1959 "Characteristics of sociotechnical systems." Unpublished. Tavistock Institute of Human Relations, Document Number HRC 527.
Emery, F.E. and E.L. Trist
  1960 "Sociotechnical systems," in C.W. Churchman and M. Verhulst (eds.), Management Sciences, Models and Techniques, Vol. 2. Oxford: Pergamon Press.
  1965 "The causal texture of organizational environments." Human Relations (18) :21–31.
Fiedler, F.E.
  1964 "A contingency model of leadership effectiveness," in Berkowitz (ed.), Advances in Experimental Social Psychology, Vol. 1. New York and London: Academic Press.
  1967 A Theory of Leadership Effectiveness. New York: McGraw-Hill.

740   Frank A. Heller

Fleishman, E.A., E.E. Harris and H.E.E. Burtt
  1955   "Leadership and supervision in industry." Ohio State University, Bureau of Educational Research. Monograph No. 33.
French, J.R.P. and B. Raven
  1959   "The bases of social power," in D. Cartwright (ed.), Studies in Social Power. Ann Arbor, Michigan: Institute for Social Research.
Friend, J.K. and W.N. Jessop
  1969   Local Government and Strategic Choice. London: Tavistock Publications.
Galbraith, K.
  1967   The New Industrial State. Boston: Houghton Mifflin.
Gerth, H.H. and C.W. Mills (eds.)
  1947   From Max Weber: Essays in Sociology. London: Routledge and Kegan Paul.
Gibb, C.A.
  1958   "An interactional view of the emergence of leadership." Australian Journal of Psychology (10):101–110.
Haire, M., E. Ghiselli and L. Porter
  1966   Managerial Thinking. New York: McGraw-Hill.
Heller, F.A.
  1964   Integrated Manpower Development: A Successful Case Example. Buenos Aires: Argentine Productivity Centre.
  1969a "The managerial role in the effective use of resources." Journal of Management Studies (6):1–14.
  1969b "Group feedback analysis: a method of field research." Psychological Bulletin (72):108–117.
  1970   "Group feedback analysis as a change agent." Human Relations (23): 319–333.
  1971a Managerial Decision Making: A Study of Leadership Styles and Power-Sharing Among Senior Managers. London: Tavistock Publications.
  1971b "Social and technical aspects of manpower utilization." Management Education and Development (1):111–123.
  1973   "Leadership, decision-making and contingency theory." Industrial Relations (12):183–199.
  1975   "Group feedback analysis as a method of action research," in A.W. Clark (ed.), Experiences in Action Research. London. To be published.
Heller, F.A. and L.W. Porter
  1966   "Perceptions of managerial needs and skills in two national samples." Occupational Psychology 40(1, 2):1–13.
Heller, F.A. and B. Wilpert
  1974   "Limits to participative management: task, structure and skill as contingencies—a German-British comparison." Mimeographed. Tavistock Institute of Human Relations (SFP4146).
Heller, F.A. and G. Yukl
  1969   "Participation and managerial decision-making as a function of situational variables." Organizational Behavior and Human Performance (4):227–241.
Hemphill, J.K.
  1950   "Relations between the size of the group and the behavior of 'superior' leaders." Journal of Social Psychology (32):11–22.

Herbst, P.G.
  1962   Autonomous Group Functioning. London: Tavistock Institute of Human Relations.
Herzberg, F., B. Mausner, R.O. Peterson and D.F. Capwell
  1957   Job Attitudes: Review of Research and Opinion. Pittsburgh: Psychological Services of Pittsburgh.
Herzberg, F., B. Mausner and B. Snyderman
  1959   The Motivation to Work. New York: Wiley.
Hickson, D.J., C.R. Hinings, C.A. Lee, R.E. Schneck and J.M. Pennings
  1971   "A strategic contingency theory of intraorganizational power." Administrative Science Quarterly (16):216–229.
Hill, W.
  1973   "Leadership style: rigid or flexible." Organizational Behavior and Human Performance (9):35–47.
Hill, W. and D. Hughes
  1974   "Variations in leader behavior as a function of task type." Organizational Behavior and Human Performance (11):83–96.
Hinings, C.R., D.J. Hickson, J.M. Pennings and R.E. Schneck
  1974   "Structural conditions of intraorganizational power." Administrative Science Quarterly (19):22–44.
Inkson, J.H.K., D.S. Pugh and D.J. Hickson
  1970   "Organization context and structure: an abbreviated replication." Administrative Science Quarterly (15):318–329.
Jaques, E.
  1956   Measurement of Responsibility. London: Tavistock Publications.
Kepner, C.H. and B.B. Tregoe
  1965   The Rational Manager: A Systematic Approach to Problem Solving and Decision-Making. New York: McGraw-Hill.
Kingdon, D.R.
  1973   Matrix Organization. London: Tavistock Publications.
Koreman, A.K.
  1966   "Consideration, initiating structure and organizational criteria—a review." Personnel Psychology (19):349–361.
Lammers, C.
  1973   "Two conceptions of democratization in organizations," in E. Pusić (ed.), Participation and Self-Management. Vol. 4. Zagreb, Yugoslavia: Institute for Social Research, University of Zagreb.
Lawrence, P.R. and Lorsch, J.W.
  1967a   "Differentiation and integration in complex organizations." Administrative Science Quarterly (12):1–47.
  1967b   Organization and Environment: Managing Differentiation and Integration. Boston: Harvard Business School.
Leavitt, H., L. Pinfield and E. Webb (eds.)
  1974   Organizations of the Future: Interactions with the External Environment. New York: Praeger.
Likert, R.
  1961   New Patterns of Management. New York: McGraw-Hill.
  1967   The Human Organization. New York: McGraw-Hill.
Lowin, A.
  1968   "Participatory decision-making: a model, literature critique and pre-

742 FRANK A. HELLER

scription for research." Organization Behavior and Human Performance (3):68–106.
McGregor, D.
1960 The Human Side of Enterprise. New York: McGraw-Hill.
1967 The Professional Manager. New York: McGraw-Hill.
March, J.G.
1955 "An introduction to the theory and measurement of influence." American Political Science Review (49):431–451.
March, J.G. and H.A. Simon
1958 Organizations. New York: Wiley.
Marples, D.L.
1967 Studies of managers—a fresh start?" Journal of Management Studies
(4):282–299.
Marrow, A.J., D.G. Bowers and S.E. Seashore
1967 Management by Participation: Creating a Climate for Personal and
Organizational Development. New York: Harper & Row.
Maslow, A.H.
1943 "A theory of human motivation." Psychological Review (50):370–396.
Miles, R.E.
1964 "Conflicting elements in managerial ideologies." Industrial Relations
4(1):77–91.
1965 "Human relations or human resources?" Harvard Business Review
(July–August):148–163.
Miles, R.E., K. Roberts and L.V. Blankenship
1968 "Organizational leadership, satisfaction and productivity: a comparative analysis." Academy of Management Journal (11):402–414.
Miller, D.C. and W.H. Form
1964 Industrial Society: The Sociology of Work Organizations. Second Edition. New York: Harper & Row.
Mulder, M.
1971 "Power equalization through participation." Administrative Science
Quarterly (16):31–38.
Mulder, M. and H. Wilke
1970 "Participation and power equalization." Organizational Behavior and
Human Performance (5):430–448.
Parsons, T.
1963 "On the concept of political power." Proceedings of the American
Philosophy Society (107):232–262.
Participation and Self-Management
1972 Six Volumes. Report of the First International Sociological Conference
–73 on Participation and Self-Management. Institute for Social Research,
Zagreb, Yugoslavia.
Paul, W.J. and K.B. Robertson
1970 Job Enrichment and Employee Motivation. London: Gower Press.
Perrow, C.
1970 "Departmental power and perspective in industrial firms," in M.N.
Zald (ed.), Power in Organizations. Nashville: Vanderbilt University
Press.
Pettigrew, A.
1973 The Politics of Organizational Decision-Making. London: Tavistock
Publications.

Phesey, D., R. Payne and D. Pugh
   1971   "Influence of structure at organizational and group levels." Administrative Science Quarterly (16) :61–73.
Porter, L.W.
   1964   Organizational Patterns of Managerial Job Attitudes. American Foundation for Managerial Research.
Porter, L.W. and M.M. Henry
   1964   "Job attitudes in management: perceptions of the importance of certain personality traits as a function of job level." Journal of Applied Psychology (48) :31–36.
Pugh, D.S.
   1969   "Organizational behavior: an approach from psychology." Human Relations (22) :345–354.
Pugh, D.S., D.J. Hickson, C.R. Hinings, K.M. Macdonald, C. Turner and T. Lupton
   1963   "A conceptual scheme for organizational analysis." Administrative Science Quarterly (8) :289–315.
Pugh, D. and D. Phesey
   1968   "Some developments in the study of organizations." Management International Review (8) :97–107.
Pyle, W.C.
   1970   "Monitoring human resources—on line." Michigan Business Review (July) :19–32.
Reddin, W.
   1970   Managerial Effectiveness. New York: McGraw-Hill.
Reiman, B.
   1973   "On the dimensions of bureaucratic structure: an empirical reappraisal." Administrative Science Quarterly (18) :462–476.
Ritchie, J.B. and R.E. Miles
   1970   "An analysis of quantity and quality of participation as mediating variables in the participation decision-making process." Ann Arbor: University of Michigan. Mimeographed.
Roberts, K.H.
   1970   "On looking at an elephant: an evaluation of cross-cultural research related to organizations." Psychological Bulletin (74) :327–350.
Roberts, K.H., G.A. Walter and R.E. Miles
   1971   "A factor analytic study of job satisfaction items designed to measure Maslow need categories." Personnel Psychology (24) :205–220.
Rus, V.
   1974   "The external and internal influences affecting industrial enterprises." Yugoslav papers presented to the 8th World Congress of the International Sociological Association at Toronto, August. Printed: University of Ljubljana.
Sadler, P. and B. Barry
   1970   Organizational Development. London: Longmans Green.
Salancik, G. and J. Pfeffer
   1974   "The bases and uses of power in organizational decision-making: the case of a university." Administrative Science Quarterly (19) :453–473.
Schneider, J. and E. Locke
   1971   "A critique of Herzberg's incident classification system and a suggested

744   FRANK A. HELLER

revision." Organizational Behavior and Human Performance (6) :441–457.

Scott, M.M.
1964 "Who are your motivated workers?" Harvard Business Review (42) : 73–88.

Seeman, M.
1953 "Role conflict and ambivalence in leadership." American Journal of Sociology (18) :373–380.

Simon, H.A.
1957 "A behavioral model of rational choice," in H.A. Simon (ed.), Models of Man. New York: Wiley.

Sirota, D. and M. Greenwood
1971 "Understand your overseas work force." Harvard Business Review (January–February) :53–60.

Starbuck, W.
1972 "Organizations and their environments," Mimeographed. International Institute of Management, Berlin. Also in M.D. Dunnette (ed.), Handbook of Industrial and Organizational Psychology. Chicago: Rand McNally College Publishing Co., 1976.

Stewart, R.
1970 Managers and Their Jobs. London: Pan Books.

Stogdill, R.M.
1948 "Personal factors associated with leadership: a survey of the literature." Journal of Psychology (25) :35–71.

Stogdill, R.M., C. Shartle and Associates
1956 "Patterns of administrative performance." Ohio Studies Personnel Research Monograph No. 81.

Strauss, G.
1963 "Some notes on power-equalization," in H. Leavitt (ed.), The Social Science of Organizations. Englewood Cliffs, New Jersey: Prentice-Hall.
1968 "Human relations 1968 style." Industrial Relations (7) :262–276.

Tannenbaum, A.
1957 "The distribution of control in formal organizations." Social Forces (136) :44–50.
1962 "Control in organizations, individual adjustment and organizational performance." Administrative Science Quarterly (7) :236–257.
1968 Control in Organizations. New York: McGraw-Hill.

Tannenbaum, A., B. Kavčič, M. Rosner, M. Vianello and G. Wieser
1974 Hierarchy in Organizations. San Francisco: Jossey-Bass.

Taylor, D.W.
1965 "Decision-making and problem solving," in J.G. March (ed.), Handbook of Organizations. Chicago: Rand McNally.

Taylor, R. and M.D. Dunnette
1974 "Relative contribution of decision-maker attributes to decision process." Organizational Behavior and Human Performance (12) :286–298.

Thompson, J.
1967 Organizations in Action. New York: McGraw-Hill.

Tiffin, J. and E. McCormick
1942 Industrial Psychology. Englewood Cliffs, New Jersey: Prentice-Hall.

Trist, E.L. and K.W.Bamforth
  1951 "Some social and psychological consequences of the longwall method of coal-getting." Human Relations (4) :3–38.
Trist, E.L., G.W. Higgin, H. Murray and A.B. Pollock
  1963 Organizational Choice. London: Tavistock Publications.
Udy, S.
  1965 "The comparative analysis of organizations," in J.G. March (ed.), Handbook of Organizations. Chicago: Rand McNally.
Viteles, M.
  1969 "Critical evaluation of Herzberg's two factor theory." International Review of Applied Psychology (18) :5–10.
Vroom, V.H.
  1964 Work and Motivation. New York: Wiley.
  1970 "Industrial social psychology," in G. Lindzey and E. Aronson (eds.), Handbook of Social Psychology. Vol. 5. Reading, Mass.: Addison-Wesley.
Vroom, V.H. and P. Yetton
  1973 Leadership and Decision-Making. Pittsburgh: University of Pittsburgh Press.
Walker, K.
  1974 "Workers' participation in management—problems, practice and prospects." International Institute of Labour Studies (12) :3–35.
Webb, E.J., D.T. Campbell, R.D. Schwartz and L. Sechrest
  1966 Unobtrusive Measures: Nonreactive Research in the Social Sciences. Chicago: Rand McNally.
Weber, M.
  1947 The Theory of Social and Economic Organization. Glencoe, Ill.: Free Press.
Whyte, W.F.
  1969 Organizational Behavior. Homewood, Ill.: Dorsey Press.
Wilkins, L.
  1967 "Information and decisions regarding offenders." Paper presented at the National Symposium on Law Enforcement Science and Technology, Chicago, March.
Wilpert, B. and F.A. Heller
  1973 "Power sharing at senior management levels." Omega (1) :451–464.
  1974 "Decision-making in German and British companies." Paper to the 18th International Congress of Applied Psychology, Montreal, August.
Wispe, L.G. and K.E. Lloyd
  1955 "Some situational and psychological determinants of the desire for structured interpersonal relations." Journal of Abnormal and Social Psychology (51) :57–60.
Wofford, J.C.
  1971 "Managerial behavior, situational factors and productivity and morale." Administrative Science Quarterly (16) :10–17.
Woodward, J.
  1965 Industrial Organization: Theory and Practice. London: Oxford University Press.

[15]

Managerial Decision Making: An international comparison*

F. A. HELLER
Tavistock Institute of Human Relations, London
B. WILPERT,
Padagogische Hochschule Berlin
and International Institute of Management, Science Center
Berlin, and Research Collaborators**

This paper describes research on influence and power sharing among senior levels of management in successful modern organizations. Results from eight different countries fail to sustain any clear "culturological" explanation. National differences, however, are important and account for 10–15 per cent of the variance, while differences between sectors (dominant technology) account for 5–10 per cent of the variance in decision-making patterns.

Skill emerges as a major factor in all countries in explaining variations of centralized or participative decision-making between dyads of boss-subordinates. We call this a situational or contingency factor. Several ways of measuring skill in relation to job needs are used. Both subjective and objective measures show a very consistent reliable pattern. In general, it can be said that when skills are low or seen to be low, centralized decision making is preferred to participation.

Contingency or situational approaches to organizational behavior are replacing monistic or universalistic positions (Staehle, 1973) but are in some danger of becoming a "bandwagon". It was to be expected, therefore, that they

* The study was financed from several sources. The Social Science Research Council (UK) and the International Institute of Management (Berlin) made the major contributions.

** The following researchers collaborated in this study as the main contributors in addition to the authors of this paper: P. Docherty, The Economic Research Institute at the Stockholm School of Economics, Sweden; P. Fokking, Erasmus University Rotterdam, The Netherlands; J. -M. Fourcade, Centre d'Enseignement Supérieur des Affaires, France; W. t'Hoft, Erasmus University Rotterdam, The Netherlands; B. Roig-Amat, Instituto de Estudios Superiores de la Empresa, Universidad de Navarra, Spain; T. D. Weinshall, Tel-Aviv University, Israel. Each center was responsible for funding and supervising its own field work. Statistical and computing consulting services were provided by R. Mays, Civil Service College, London and M. James, Research Resources Ltd., London.

50   *F. A. Heller & B. Wilpert*

would soon come under severe criticism. Moberg and Koch (1975) warn
against recent precocious and megalomaniac attempts to aggregate different
situational approaches and to present them as integrated theoretical positions.
Such holistic demands, they argue convincingly, would destroy the very basis of
contingency thinking, falling into the universalistic trap instead of contributing
"to a mid-range theory of organizations between 'universal truths' and
everything depends".

A second criticism advanced against contingency approaches is the claim
that they represent a mechanistic, deterministic view of the world where
variables such as technology, organizational structure, environmental turbulence, and task characteristics unequivocally define behavioral outputs. The
freedom of relevant actors to choose certain strategies in the pursuance of
specific goals is seen as either non-existent or at best so limited that people
emerge as puppets in a network of contingency relations (Crozier and Friedberg,
1976). Such a view of contingency statements overlooks the fact that most
contingency statements are statements of probability rather than all-encom-
passing iron laws. Besides, it appears to be very virtue of situational propositions that they enable a researcher or actor to include individual needs,
strategies and characteristics in an analysis as constituent elements of the
situation. Contingency views attempt to probe the specific ranges of applicability of theoretical propositions including the preference structures of actors.
They become a means of scanning the environment for significant regularities.

A third attack is launched against contingency approaches on the basis that
they are basically conservative. It is alleged that they describe the *status quo*
non-prescriptively and assume that it is "the optimal fit" of, let us say, structure
and environment. This means that contingency theories accept underlying value
premises uncritically (Miller, undated).

Since there are many different contingency models, it is not appropriate to
attempt a detailed defense or to make out a case for the intrinsic value of
contingency views. One can point out, however, that the ultimate test of any
theory is its capacity to predict events, and this is the critical ingredient for
facilitating directed, purposeful change. In relation to the present research
project, we would claim that the findings, on the role of skill as a mediating
variable for instance, help to predict where participation is likely to occur and
how to increase its value. In our opinion, the significance of contingency or
situational approaches lies in its heuristic modesty (Bass *et al.*, 1975). It could
even be argued that, in the last analysis, any good theory must specify the
conditions under which it operates and consequently takes on a contingency
framework (Moberg and Koch, 1975).

Our research was designed as a way of studying the effects of several sets of
variables indirectly or interactively influencing a specific social behavior: the
interaction patterns of two interlocking management levels in organizational
decision-making. We thereby reverse the traditional approach to leadership and
decision-making which tended to inquire into the consequences of certain
decision-making styles in terms of their economic and social consequences for
the organization and its members. Rather, we intend to identify key contingency
relationships and their relative impact on behavior that practitioners and
theoreticians consider critical for the survival and growth of organizations.

MANAGERIAL DECISION MAKING   51

FRAMEWORK OF THE STUDY

The research spans several systematic levels of analysis (Heller, 1973). It ranges from a macro-level (ω-variables) with countries constituting distinctive units of comparison, moving to meso-level where the effects of industrial sectors or predominant technologies (δ-variables) are studied, and finally includes a micro-level with organizational micro-structure (γ-variables), task (β-variables) and person-related variables (α-variables) serving as focal points for analysis (see figure 1).

METHODS

The whole study comprised over 1,500 senior managers in 129 large companies from eight countries: France, Germany, The Netherlands, Israel, Spain, Sweden, U.K., U.S.A. The sample is made up from economically successful and "progressive"[1] companies from thirteen industrial sectors. The companies were generally chosen from among the largest of their respective industrial sector in each country. They range from continuous-flow production (e.g., refinery, paper production), large batch production (e.g., tele-communication equipment production, packaging industry) to small-batch production (e.g., airplane production) to service industries (e.g., public transport systems, banking) and retailing. (For a detailed description of the sectors cf. Heller, 1971; Wilpert, 1977). Approximately one-half of the managers belong to the highest level immediately below the chief executive, or

Figure 1

MODEL OF ASSUMED CONTINGENCY RELATIONSHIPS*
* (from Wilpert 1977)

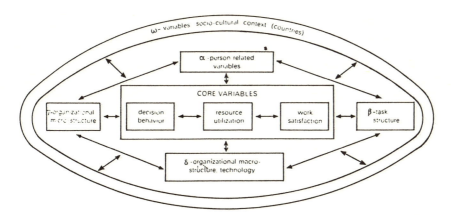

[1] "Progressive" was defined as a combination of techno-economic success and openmindedness of management towards modern managerial practices.

the board of management[2]. A deliberate attempt was made to cover 100 per cent of all managers of this first level (L1). The other half (L2) consists of the most senior immediate subordinate of Level 1, i.e., their formal deputies or closest co-workers. The average of the matched managers in our sample for Level 1 is 46.6 years (L2:42.9), with an average tenure in the company of 16.6 years (L2:14.9 years). On average, they held their present job for 5.7 years (L2:5.1) and had command over 521 (L2:193) employees in their respective departments.

An important and unusual feature of this research is the way the senior-subordinate dyad is used to obtain independent corroboration of behavioral as well as attitudinal measures. The senior level's description of the amount of influence shared between it and the next level down can be checked against the subordinate's description of the same behavior. Similarly, we can compare and contrast the skill judgements of both levels when they relate to the same set of data, namely, the job requirements at L 1 and L 2. The dyadic measurement unit can also be used to obtain independent *cross-level judgments* that avoid "social desirability" distortion. For instance, the senior manager's judgment of job requirements for both levels can be correlated with the senior man's decision styles as described by his subordinate (see Table 7). The senior manager's judgment of his subordinate's potential for promotion can be compared with the subordinate's description of the senior man's power-sharing behavior (see Table 8).

This paper presents only a part of the study. For certain statistical comparisons our international sample is reduced to make it more valid for comparative purposes. When each senior-level manager is matched to his most experienced immediate subordinate, we call this a dyadic sample. Furthermore, when comparisons are made between our sample of countries, we reduce the industrial sectors from thirteen to eight in order to ensure close matching. Our smallest sample consists of seventy comparable companies and 1250 managers in 625 matched dyads of senior and subordinate managers. Sometimes comparison with U.S. data had to be omitted because certain instruments were developed only after the U.S. study had been completed.

The method of data collection was Group Feedback Analysis (Heller, 1969), a combination of structured questionnaire technique and immediate feedback of part of the questionnaire data to the group of respondents from one managerial level in a given company. An extensive discussion of the level's results followed the feedback. The data were fed back anonymously with individual answers, means and distributions so that each participant was aware of his/her answers and could compare them with those of his/her colleagues. The same was later repeated with the participating managers of the other levels. The very lively discussions and interpretations (usually lasting one hour, but sometimes up to four hours) were tape recorded for later content analysis.

The complete research was based on fourteen questionnaires. These are described in Heller, 1976 and Wilpert, 1977. Here we confine ourselves to

---

[2] In the case of Germany, where sometimes boards of management constitute the chief executive level, the highest level in our study could be perceived as formally reporting to such a board.

findings which relate to six questionnaires, Forms 2, 3, 5, 6, 7, 11.[3]

FORM 2. Job Performance Requirements contains 12 items (5-point Likert-type scales) comparing the job performance requirements of one level with those of the other level and asked which job required more or less of, e.g., technical competence. Both levels answer the same question.

FORM 3. Skill Acquisition Time includes the same 12 items as Form 2, and requested answers from each dyad partner on how much time the L 2 manager would need to acquire the competence needed to do the L 1 job successfully. The subordinate (L 2) estimates how long he needs to acquire the skills needed by the senior manager. The senior (L 1) also estimates the time his subordinate needs to acquire the senior's skills.

FORM 5. Specific Decision Questionnaire[4] contains 12 decision items of general relevance to a manager. The items were grouped according to three decision types: SUB-decisions relating to a senior manager's immediate subordinate; DEPT-departmental decisions; EMP-decisions relating to employees working for L 2. L 1 was asked to report the relative frequency in percentage of his using one of the following decision methods which are assumed to constitute an influence-power sharing continuum (IPC):

   I. own decision without detailed explanation to subordinates;
   II. own decision with detailed *ex post* explanation to subordinate (in writing or through meetings);
   III. own decision with prior consultation of subordinate;
   IV. joint decision with subordinate;
   V. delegation of decision to subordinate.

L 2 was asked to describe the superior's decision behavior on the same scale.

FORM 6. General Decision Questionnaire asks L 1 and L 2 to describe their own general decision behavior "in all important questions they are responsible for" on the same accumulative percentage scale as in Form 5.

FORM 7. Lateral Decision Questionnaire asks for a similar self-judgement on decision making in cooperation with colleagues on the same level. The senior manager describes his collaboration with colleagues and the subordinate level manager similarly describes his lateral decision behaviour.

The ordinal scales of Forms 5, 6, and 7 were transformed to a continuous variable with a maximum of 5.0 ('all decisions taken without explanation or

---

[3] Analyses of Forms 2 and 3 are conducted with composites based on factor analyses. For internal consistency measures, see Appendix. Form 5 has theoretical composites. Individual items were used from Forms 6, 7 and 11.
[4] This form was an adaptation of a questionnaire devised by Blankenship and Miles, 1968.

consultation with subordinates) and a minimum of 1.0 (delegation of all decisions). The transformation is done through a weighting of the respondents' percentages given for each decision style such that the percentage of style I is multiplied by 5; II by 4 . . . and V by 1. The sum of the products then is divided by 100. A high value, therefore, signifies centralized decision making, that is to say, a lack of power and influence for the subordinates. The distribution of this 'Decision Centralization Score' (DCS) is reasonably smooth with no marked bunching of integer values.

FORM 11.Formal Skill Qualifications is a 12-item questionnaire on training and educational background.

The questionnaires were translated from the English original into the various vernaculars. The translation was checked through independent re-translations and minor accommodations after pretests in each country. Where appropriate, questionnaires were factor analyzed to form composite indices (if the comparison of α-values of composites and overall averages of a form suggested this). In addition, means for all questions were used for further statistical analyses.

The final data base consists of two different sets[5] depending on the purpose of a given analysis: (1) The full population of more than 1500 managers from 129 companies of 13 industrial sectors in several countries; and (2) The subset of data based on 625 complete dyads of managers of eight common industrial sectors[6] in which we were able to collect data in seven participating countries.

In this paper bivariate analysis is used to investigate the different impact of macro-, meso- and micro-levels of decision styles. These results are reported in the next section. Further work is now being done using multivariate analysis including regression to quantify the relative weight necessary to estimate style scores from these levels of variables.[7]

FINDINGS

Macro-level: Country Context

A comparison of the average decision-making patterns of managers from the various countries reveals quite consistent results across the various measures we used. One-way analysis of variance using Decision Centralization Scores (DCS) shows that decision behavior of managers is significantly influenced by their national contexts (Tables 1 and 2). About 10–15 per cent of the variance in decision-making patterns can be explained by overall country effects.

This may be considered as a partial corroboration of the alleged 'cul-

---

[5] Wherever possible we use also data from a previous U.S. study (Heller, 1971) for comparisons.

[6] For list of sectors, see Tables 4 and 5.

[7] Heller, Mays, and Wilpert, "The Use of Contingency Models in a Multi-national Study of Managerial Behavior." Mimeographed. Tavistock Institute of Human Relations, 1977.

MANAGERIAL DECISION MAKING   55

true-bound" thesis (Child, Kieser, 1975) holding that organizations differ as a consequence of cultural (national) conditions and antecedents. We prefer to use the term national rather than cultural, since in the majority of studies, including our own, culture has not been defined separately from national boundaries (Roberts, 1970).

Given that we find significant differences in the overall regime (managerial power and influence sharing) of comparable organizations in different

Table 1

COUNTRY AND MANAGERIAL DECISION MAKING: L 1
One-way ANOVA, DCS Values. Intl. Dyad File[8]

	Department Decisions (DEPT)	Employee Decisions (EMP)	Subordinate-related Decisions (SUB)	All Specific Decisions (SPEC)	General Decision Making (F6)	Lateral Decision Making (F7)
U.S.A.	3.31	2.56	3.46	3.09	2.70	2.31
	(62)	(58)	(60)	(48)	(20)	(20)
U.K.	3.33	2.61	3.40	3.05	2.95	3.20
	(64)	(71)	(59)	(51)	(79)	(79)
Netherlands	2.69	2.45	3.20	2.74	2.84	2.24
	(40)	(40)	(42)	(28)	(52)	(52)
Germany	2.99	2.77	3.43	3.03	2.85	2.92
	(53)	(48)	(55)	(39)	(66)	(65)
France	2.58	2.26	3.15	2.59	2.63	2.40
	(34)	(38)	(38)	(28)	(45)	(42)
Sweden	2.39	2.27	3.03	2.55	2.53	3.00
	(57)	(54)	(51)	(47)	(60)	(59)
Israel	2.91	2.49	3.36	2.85	3.08	2.79
	(33)	(30)	(31)	(25)	(41)	(41)
Spain	2.68	2.42	3.45	2.75	3.00	2.88
	(36)	(30)	(32)	(25)	(47)	(47)
Means	2.91	2.49	3.32	2.25	2.83	2.92
(Total N)	(379)	(369)	(368)	(291)	(410)	(405)
F—Ratio	11.105	2.487	4.882	7.346	4.766	3.463
Approximate percentage variance explained by country effect	17	6	8	15	7	5

[8] Number of respondents varies whenever one member of a dyad did not respond to one of the items and due to eight sector reduction. N is given in brackets.

TABLE 2

COUNTRY AND MANAGERIAL DECISION MAKING: L 2
One-way ANOVA, DCS Values. Intl. Dyad File[9]

	Department Decisions (DEPT)	Employee Decisions (EMP)	Subordinate-related Decisions (SUB)	All Specific Decisions (SPEC)	General Decision Making (F6)	Lateral Decision Making (F7)
U.S.A.	3.56 (61)	2.19 (54)	3.23 (50)	3.09 (36)	2.96 (20)	2.41 (20)
U.K.	3.19 (58)	2.44 (64)	3.20 (53)	2.89 (39)	2.98 (76)	3.42 (79)
Netherlands	3.43 (34)	2.30 (36)	2.82 (35)	2.77 (24)	2.78 (52)	3.10 (52)
Germany	2.56 (49)	2.33 (47)	2.86 (33)	2.47 (24)	2.88 (66)	2.96 (65)
France	2.50 (36)	2.21 (39)	3.06 (35)	2.56 (27)	2.68 (45)	2.57 (41)
Sweden	2.18 (57)	2.26 (52)	3.03 (47)	2.50 (41)	2.56 (60)	3.18 (58)
Israel	3.52 (29)	2.38 (27)	3.04 (27)	3.03 (17)	3.19 (41)	3.03 (41)
Spain	1.95 (34)	2.29 (31)	2.90 (24)	2.31 (16)	2.85 (47)	2.63 (47)
ϕ	2.87 (358)	2.30 (350)	3.04 (304)	2.72 (224)	2.85 (407)	3.00 (403)
F–Ratio	23,979	0,803 n.s.	3.131	8.634	4.580	4.943
Approximate percentage variance explained by country effect	32	7	6	22	7	8

countries, the next question to be asked is whether characteristic patterns of differences emerge.

Taking the average DCS scores of the total sample of managers as the dividing line between countries with "participative regimes" and countries with "centralized regimes" we see that the U.K., Israeli and German L 1 managers describe themselves rather consistently as using the most centralized decision methods (Table 3). This self-judgment is corroborated by the judgments of their immediate subordinates describing their superiors' behavior in the case of the U.K. and Israeli managers. British managers are particularly consistent, one could almost say insistent, on describing the decision behavior at the two top

[9] Number of respondents varies whenever one member of a dyad did not respond to one of the items and due to eight sector reduction. N is given in brackets.

Table 3

**DEGREE OF DECISION CENTRALIZATION ACCORDING TO COUNTRY
L 1 describes own; L 2 describes decision-making of L 1 (Form 5)**

Low Centralization	L 1 MEAN[10]	High Centralization
Netherlands France Sweden* Spain	DEPT	United Kingdom* Germany U.S.A.*
France Sweden Spain	EMP	United Kingdom Germany U.S.A.
Netherlands France Sweden*	SUB	United Kingdom* Germany U.S.A.* Spain
Netherlands France Sweden* Spain	SPEC	United Kingdom* Germany U.S.A.*
France Sweden* U.S.A.	F6	United Kingdom* Israel* Spain*
Netherlands France U.S.A. Israel	F7	United Kingdom Sweden

	L 2	
France* Sweden* Spain* Germany*	DEPT	United Kingdom* Netherlands* Israel* U.S.A.*
France U.S.A.	EMP	United Kingdom Israel
Netherlands Spain Germany	SUB	United Kingdom U.S.A.
France Sweden Spain* Germany	SPEC	United Kingdom* Netherlands Israel* U.S.A.*

[10] Countries with DCS-scores within .05 of MEAN were left out (about one standard error).

Table 3 *(Contd.)*

Low Centralization	L1 Mean[10]	High Centralization
Netherlands	F6	United Kingdom*
France		Israel*
Sweden*		
U.S.A.		
France*	F7	United Kingdom*
Spain*		Netherlands
U.S.A.*		Sweden

* According to Scheffee-Test: Asterisked countries are significantly different from asterisked countries of the opposite group.

levels of their companies as highly centralized! On the basis of the overall DCS values on specific decisions of U.S. managers, we would usually have to locate them among those using the highest degrees of centralized decision making. On the other end of the influence power-sharing continuum appear the Swedish and French managers as employing comparatively decentralized decision-making methods.

Another interesting phenomenon is the difference between the description of decision-making of senior and subordinate levels. There is a tendency for subordinates to describe the dyadic decision pattern as less centralized than the description of the same decision pattern described by the senior manager. In Table 3, this comes out particularly clearly for the German sample of L 2 managers who describe their superior's behavior as relatively decentralized. These results reverse the more usual findings that subordinates describe their superiors' behavior as relatively more centralized than the description given by superiors (for instance, Vroom and Yetton, 1973; Ritchie and Miles, 1970).

A few observations may be appropriate at this stage relating our findings to those of other authors. The cultural cluster thesis of Haire, Ghiselli and Porter (1966), that managerial attitudes seem to fall into recognizable cultural clusters of countries is not supported by our findings. The type of country grouping that emerges from our data suggests that distinctive categories in terms of Nordic, Anglo-Saxon, and Latin-European countries do not exist in decision behavior. German, and sometimes Spanish managers, would have to be grouped with Anglo-Saxon managers; and French, together with Swedish managers, would be grouped together with the Dutch. The marked differences attributed to German and Anglo-Saxon managerial systems in terms of decision centralization and influence power-sharing (cf. Ruedi and Lawrence, 1970; Grosset, 1970; Granick, 1962, 1972; Child and Kieser, 1975) are not verified by our findings. German and British L 1 managers describe their decision behavior basically in similar, namely centralized, terms. If we can use our data for a transatlantic comparison of managerial behavior, we would have to reject the once-famous managerial gap thesis (Servan-Schreiber, 1967) which claims that higher productivity of U.S. firms in comparison to European ones can be explained by the greater degree of delegation and participation among hierarchial levels of U.S. firms. If anything, we would have to group American managers with the most centralized European managers.

MANAGERIAL DECISION MAKING   59

Table 4

INDUSTRIAL LABOR (DOMINANT TECHNOLOGY AND MANAGERIAL DECISION MAKING) L1
One-Way ANOVA, DCS-Values, Intl. Dyad File

Sector	DEPT	EMP	SUB	SPEC	F6	F7
1. Electronics	2.82 (73)	2.33 (70)	3.42 (74)	2.88 (67)	2.76 (63)	2.96 (63)
2. Retailing	3.39 (42)	2.64 (40)	3.38 (38)	3.07 (29)	2.94 (39)	2.82 (38)
3. Public Trans.	2.81 (51)	2.59 (48)	3.30 (50)	2.84 (35)	3.04 (63)	3.14 (60)
4. Packaging	3.19 (37)	2.59 (35)	3.27 (37)	2.97 (32)	2.82 (36)	2.52 (36)
5. Banking	3.03 (56)	2.65 (55)	3.31 (58)	2.91 (35)	2.92 (80)	3.22 (80)
6. Tele. Comm.	2.62 (46)	2.30 (45)	2.23 (42)	2.70 (37)	2.77 (49)	2.65 (48)
7. Paper	2.72 (35)	2.34 (39)	3.36 (35)	2.71 (26)	2.69 (38)	2.73 (38)
8. Refinery	2.73 (39)	2.54 (34)	3.21 (34)	2.76 (30)	2.59 (42)	2.96 (42)
Means (Total N)	2.91 (379)	2.49 (369)	3.32 (368)	2.86 (291)	2.83 (410)	2.93 (405)
F-Ratio	4.541	2.735	.92 n.s.	1.894 n.s.	2.903	2.287
Approximate percentage variance explained by sector effect	8	5	1	4	4	3

Meso-level: industrial sector/dominant technology

One of the critical contingency elements for organizational functioning is often assumed to be the dominant technology of an organization (Woodward, 1965; Thompson, 1967; Perrow, 1967, 1970). We have no specific measurements of technology, but the distinct sectors (see Table 4) use, on average, different technologies. Comparing the decision-making of managers in the eight sectors for which we have comparable data, we come to the conclusion that industrial sector or dominant technology does indeed have an impact on managerial behavior (Tables 4–5). Some 5–10 per cent of the variance in decision behavior can be explained on the basis of managers belonging to companies in a particular sector or with a particular technology. Service

Table 5

INDUSTRIAL SECTOR DOMINANT TECHNOLOGY AND MANAGERIAL DECISION MAKING: L 2
One-Way ANOVA, DCS-Values, Intl. Dyad File

Sector	DEPT	EMP	SUB	SPEC	F6	F7
1. Electronics	2.67	2.11	2.89	2.59	2.62	2.91
	(69)	(70)	(61)	(53)	(63)	(63)
2. Retailing	3.27	2.56	3.14	2.89	2.99	2.72
	(38)	(34)	(36)	(21)	(39)	(38)
3. Public Trans.	2.95	2.48	3.17	2.92	2.94	2.72
	(55)	(50)	(40)	(33)	(63)	(60)
4. Packaging	3.17	2.36	3.26	2.88	2.84	3.32
	(31)	(33)	(33)	(20)	(36)	(36)
5. Banking	2.84	2.53	3.07	2.72	2.99	3.36
	(51)	(52)	(40)	(24)	(79)	(78)
6. Tele. Comm.	2.76	2.20	3.05	2.73	2.77	2.85
	(41)	(41)	(35)	(27)	(49)	(48)
7. Paper	2.99	2.16	2.97	2.75	2.83	2.93
	(38)	(38)	(31)	(24)	(38)	(38)
8. Refinery	2.48	2.02	2.85	2.42	2.71	3.12
	(35)	(32)	(28)	(22)	(40)	(62)
Means	2.87	2.30	3.04	2.72	2.85	3.00
(Total N)	(358)	(350)	(304)	(224)	(407)	(403)
F-Ratio	2.572	4.476	2.517	2.649	2.496	3.021
Approximate percentage Variance explained by sector effect	4	8	5	7	4	5

companies, on the whole, tend to have managers who decide in a comparatively more participative fashion, with banking managers taking the lead. The same is true for electronics companies with highly-developed, intensive technologies (Thompson, 1967), while managers dealing with continuous flow technologies appear on the side of higher centralization.

Micro-level: dyadic skill requirements and resources

One of the guiding hypotheses of our research was that objective and perceived skill requirement and skill availability have a major impact on the decision-making process. A non-parametric test of this assumption was employed by splitting the managers into three approximately equal groups on the basis of each variable, for instance "high", "medium" and "low" education, and cross-tabulating with other variables. Table 6 shows the results tabulating

Table 6

THE RELATIONSHIP BETWEEN VARIOUS MEASURES OF SKILL (EDUCATION, etc) AND MANAGERIAL DECISION MAKING[11]

FORM 11	Level 1 N=763 — FORM 5						Level 2 N=783 — FORM 5:					
Skills, Education, etc.	DEPT	EMP	SUB	SPEC	FORM 6	FORM 7	DEPT	EMP	SUB	SPEC	FORM 6	FORM 7
Number of professional institutions person belongs to	K0017	C025			C0190 K0000	K0015	K0207	K0001	K0070	K0155	C0000 K0000	
Journals taken	K0001	K0002	K0213	K0141	K0000		K0282	K0000	K0230	K0000	K0000	K0107
Journals read	C0003 K0000	C0000 K0001	C0000 K0005	C0246 K0003			K0082				K0082	
Educational level	C0000 K0000	C0000 K0000	C0218 K0000	C0194 K0000	C0001 K0000	K0145	C0051 K0001	K0013	C0227 K0001	K0133	C0000 K0000	K0019
Number of outside courses attended		K0169		K0092			K0036	K0040			K0043	K0002
Number of inside courses attended	C0010 K0000	K0019	K0008	C0001 K0002			C0011 K0000	C0163 K0000	K0024	C0155 K0000	C0004 K0000	K0002

[11] This table gives figures only when results are significant above the 5 per cent level. The letter C stands for chi square test; K for Kendall's non-parametric correlation coefficient tau. An entry of K = 0017 means that the correlation is significant at the level of 17 in 10,000. If only noughts are shown, the significance level is better than 1 in 10,000. Similarly for chi square. All relationships shown are negative, i.e. the higher the level of education and skill, the more participative is decision-making (low degree of centralization)

skills and educational background measures against the various assessments of decision styles (Forms 5, 6, and 7: Chi square (C) and Kendall's tau (K)). Results are shown only if they are significant above the 5 per cent level. It can be seen that there is a high degree of consistency in these relationships for both senior levels of management. When skills and educational qualification are high, decision-making is decentralized or participative. This is equally true for both levels and is strongest for the variable measuring formal educational qualifications.

Similar strong evidence comes from the data on the relationship between perceived skill requirements (Form 2), skill availabilities, and decision-making (Table 7). The more demanding a L 1 manager perceives his job to be, compared to his subordinate's job, the more will he be inclined to decide in a centralized rather than in a participative fashion. The result, in Table 7, shows parametric correlations, the non-parametric results being equally consistent and significant.

Table 7 shows results relating to one of the two levels separately. We also have results comparing data from L 1 with data from L 2 (cross-level analysis). In many respects, cross-level data is more reliable since it avoids social desirability and order effect. For instance, we can correlate the senior manager's judgments about job skill differences with his subordinate's description of the decision methods used. Such a table would be the same as Table 7, except that the decision styles on the right-hand side are described by Level 2. The statistical results are very similar, but show slightly smaller correlations coefficients (but all significant above the 1 per cent level).

A substantially different analysis of the relationship between skill and decision making comes from Form 3. Managers are asked to estimate the time it

Table 7

L 1 PERCEPTIONS OF SKILL REQUIREMENTS FOR HIS JOB COMPARED TO THOSE OF HIS SUBORDINATE AN L1 DECISION BEHAVIOR
Correlation Co-efficients (Pearson).
International Dyad File (N=625).

Job performance requirements as judged by L1 (Form 2)	Decision styles described by L 1				
	DEPT	EMP	SUB	SPEC	F6
Entrepreneurial competence[12]	−.23	−.22	−.20	−.25	−.29
Technical competence	−.17	−.21	−.19	−.22	−.22
Interpersonal competence	−.27	−.21	−.15	−.26	−.28
Average	−.27	−.28	−.24	−.32	−.35

Note: Scale values of skill requirements scales run from 1 = very much more needed to 5 = very much less needed. Significance: all correlations are significant beyond the 1 per cent level.

[12] For items in the various factors, see Appendix.

MANAGERIAL DECISION MAKING   63

TABLE 8

L 1 PERCEPTION OF L 2'S PROMOTIONAL FEASIBILITY (SKILL ACQUISITION TIME NEEDED) AND L 1 DECISION BEHAVIOR.
Cross-Level Correlation-Coefficients
(Pearson). International Dyad File (N = 625).

	L 2 perception of L 1 decision making			
L 1 perception of skill acquisition time for L 2 (Form 3)	*DEPT*	*EMP*	*SUB*	*SPEC*
Entrepreneurial skills	—	.08+		.11--
Technical competence	10+	.12++	.15++	.20+-
Interpersonal competence	n.s.	n.s.	n.s.	n.s.
Average	—	.10+	.10+	.16++

Note on significance: + = sign 5 per cent
                         ++ = sign 1 per cent

would take their subordinate to acquire the skills necessary to carry out the senior man's job (promotion feasibility). We hypothesized that when this time estimate was high, centralized decision methods would be used. This assumption is supported by cross-level analysis. (Table 8).

The findings on skill requirements (Form 2) and on skill learning times (Form 3) are complementary. Highly centralized decision making is related to a low estimation of skills needed in a subordinate's job; similarly, it is related to a low estimation of a subordinate's capacities to acquire the skills needed in the L 1 job. Hence, it can be concluded that objectively-measured skills, as well as subjective skill estimates in the dyadic relationship, must be considered to be among the most crucial factors in the understanding of influence and power sharing in modern organizations. These results support the human resources model and the findings of Ritchie and Miles (1970) that a superior's confidence and trust in his subordinates is an important aspect of the participation process.

DISCUSSION AND CONCLUSION

The literature on comparative management and industrial relations is divided between cultural convergence and divergence protagonists (Hofstede and Kassem, 1976; Dore, 1973). It seems likely, however, that, apart from the difficulty of justifying the use of the term "culture", clusters of countries probably vary with the subject matter under investigation and for reasons we do not yet understand fully. Two views are frequently put forward. One suggests that certain countries have traditionally shown similarities of managerial or organizational behavior, for instance, "Latin" countries, or "Nordic" countries. The other view holds that similarities and differences between countries are related to their economic success or stage of development. The first explanation leans towards a natural selection model which "posits that environmental factors select those organizational characteristics that best fit the environment." The second explanation reflects a resource dependence model which claims "that organizations seek to manage or strategically adapt to their environments" (Aldrich and Pfeffer, 1976:79). We do not believe that the evidence in favor of either model is completely convincing. In fact, it may very well be that both models are partially in evidence in every country (Weinshall, 1972).

A previous research team attempted to re-draw the map of the world by revising geographic distances between countries on the basis of their similarity in managerial decision-making attitudes (Haire, Ghiselli and Porter, 1966:ix). The attempt was daring and ingenious, but almost certainly premature (Barrett and Bass, 1976). International comparative work will in future have to pay more attention to different systems levels of organizational functioning (Negandhi and Prasad, 1971). Attention has to be paid to external as well as internal organizational variables at the same time. External indices such as labor market structure, patterns of socialization through family, educational system and on-the-job socialization, turbulence, etc., will have to be considered. One might then discover that similar behavior is not so much a function of "Cultural" likeness (being "Nordic," for instance) as of similar phenotypes based on substantial genotypical differences. An interesting move in this direction was taken by Ajiferuke and Boddewyn (1970) who successfully used eight external indicators (including level of education and life expectancy) in a multiple regressional analysis of the Haire *et. al.* (1966) micro-level data.

The research presented in this paper used two external indicators: country and industrial sector. We see that significant country differences were present, but we cannot yet explain the reason for this. Labelling these differences "cultural" certainly does not help. The significant differences due to the economic-sector variable, however, could bear some resemblence to the "functional niche in the interorganizational division of labor" (Aldrich and Pfeffer, 1976:99), which appears to be a fairly universal explanatory phenomenon that cuts across national boundaries.

We need a framework that links up various explanatory levels from the individual to the wider society. Recent models take a useful step in this direction (Miles *et al.*, 1978; Weinshall, 1976). They postulate a series of relationships between a company's problem-solving activity, its structure, the strategies it adopts in dealing with its environment, and the managerial philosophies which direct choices of behavior. The models do not cover variables such as the economic sectors country or culture, but concentrate on the links among market behavior, organization structure, and managerial processes. One of these models further attempts to relate these variables to managerial choices between human relations and human resources models (Miles, 1965).

Our data gives considerable support to human resources model thinking. Managers seem to adjust their decision behavior to their perception of skills among subordinates. Where skill resources are great, participative decision making is significantly more prevalent than in circumstances when skill resources are low or seen to be low. This finding is now well established in previously published results from American, British and German samples (Heller, 1971; Heller and Wilpert, 1977; Wilpert, 1977).

The relationship between skill and participation is of practical importance for two reasons. In the first place, it prevents or minimizes the practice of using participation to give people "a feeling" of it, rather than the reality which implies a measure of influence sharing (Strauss, 1963). What Etzioni (1969) has called "inauthentic participation" is based on the naive assumption that pretending to give people influence, by consultation for instance, will keep them happy. When the objective is to use people's skills rather than to keep them happy, genuine participation has to be used.

The second practical consequence of our finding relates to training. If participative decision-making is (in part) a function of skill resources, then increasing skills is a way of increasing participation. In contrast, it is probably true that training packages designed to increase participative behavior as such are likely to increase inauthentic participation with all the negative practical and ethical consequences this implies (Clarke and McCabe, 1970; Cummings and Schmidt, 1972).

On the theoretical level, the link between the use of skills and participative decision-making is congruent with the view that skill utilization is a motivating factor. Argyris and Schon (1974) have pointed to this possibility when they argue for the idea that "man is also motivated by a sense of competence and a need to be effective." They see "one source of human energy is psychological success with challenging opportunities; thus, effectiveness may be connected with psychological health" (Argyris and Schon, 1974:x). The connection between skill and utilization, participative decision-making, effectiveness and psychological health is certainly worth exploring.

REFERENCES

Ajiferuke, M., and J. Boddewyn. "Socioeconomic Indicators in Comparative
1970   Management." *Administrative Science Quarterly*. 15:453–458.
Aldrich, H. E., and J. Pfeffer. "Environments of Organizations." *Annual Review of
1976   Sociology*. 2:79–105.
Argyris, Ch., and D. A. Schon. *Theory is Practice: Increasing Professional Effectiveness*.
1974   San Francisco: Jossey-Bass, Inc.
Barrett, G. V., and B. M. Bass. "Cross-Cultural Issues in Industrial and Organizational
1976   Psychology." In Marvin Dunnette (ed.), *Handbook of Industrial and
          Organizational Psychology*: 1639–1686. Chicago, Ill.: Rand McNally.
Bass, B., and E. Valenzi. "Contingent Aspects of Effective Management Styles." In
1974   J. Hunt and L. Larson (eds.), *Contingency Approaches to Leadership*:
          130–152. Carbondale and Edwardsville, Southern Ill.: University Press.
Bass, B., E. Valenzi, D. Farrow, and R. Solomon. "Management Styles Associated with
1975   Organizational Task, Personal, and Interpersonal Contingencies." *Journal of
          Applied Psychology*. 60:720729.
Bavelas, J. B. "Systems Analysis of Dyadic Interaction: The Role of Interpersonal
1975   Judgement." *Behavioral Science*. 20:213–222.
Blankenship, L. V., and R. E. Miles. "Organizational Structure and Managerial Decision
1968   Behavior." *Administrative Science Quarterly*. 13:106–120.

Brossard, M., and M. Maurice. "Betriebliche Organisationsstrukturen im interkulturellen
1974   Vergleich." *Soziale Welt.* 25:432–454.
Child, J., and A. Kieser. "Organization and Managerial Roles in British and West-
1975   German Companies—an Examination of the Culture-Free Thesis." Institut für
          Unternehmensführung, Free University Berlin, Working Paper.
Clarke, A. W., and S. McCabe. "Leadership Beliefs of Australian Managers." *Journal of*
1970   *Applied Psychology.* 54:1–6.
Crozier, M., and E. Friedberg. *L'acteur et le Système.* Paris: Le Seuil.
1977
Cummings, L., and St. M. Schmidt. "Managerial Attidues of Greeks: The Roles of
1972   Culture   and   Industrialization." *Administrative   Science   Quarterly.*
          17:265–272.
Dore, R. *British Factory—Japanese Factory.* London: George Allen & Unwin.
1973
Etzioni, A. "Man and Society: the Inauthentic Condition." *Human Relations.*
1969   22:325–332
Granick, D. *The European Executive.* London: Weidenfeld and Nicholson
1962
Grosset, S. *Management: American and European Styles.* Belmont, Cal.: Wadsworth
1970   Publ.
Haire, M., E. Ghiselli, and L. W. Porter. *Managerial Thinking: An International Study.*
1966   New York, London, Sidney: John Wiley.
Heller, F. A. "Group Feed-back Analysis: A method of field research." *Psychological*
1969   *Bulletin.* 72:108–117.
————. *Managerial Decision Making: A Study of Leadership Styles and Power*
1971   *Sharing among Senior Managers.* London: Tavistock Publications.
————. "The Decision Process: Analysis of Power Sharing at Senior Organizational
1976   Levels." In R. Dubin (ed.), *Handbook of Work, Organization and Society:*
          687–745. Chicago: Rand McNally.
————. "Leadership, Decision-Making and Contingency Theory." *Industrial*
1973   *Relations.* 12:183–199.
————. "Infrastructures of Organizational Power: A Process Model", *International*
1974   *Institute of Management,* Preprint I/74–59. Berlin.
Hofstede, G., and S. Kassem. *European Contributions to Organization Theory.* Assen,
1976   Netherlands: Van Gorcum.
Jago, A. G., and V. H. Vroom. "Perceptions of Leadership Style: Superior and
1975   Subordinate Descriptions of Decision-making Behavior." In J. G. Hunt and
          L. Larson (eds.), *Leadership Frontiers:* 103–120. Kent, Ohio: Kent State
          University Press.
Jago, A. G., and V. H. Vroom. "Hierarchical Level and Leadership Style." *Organizational*
1977   *Behavior and Human Performance.* 18:131–145.
Marrett, C. B., J. Hage, and M. Aiken. "Communication and Satisfaction in
1975   Organizations." *Human Relations.* 28:611–626.
Miles, R. E. "Human Relations or Human Resources?" *Harvard Business Review.*
1965   43:148–163.
Miles, R. E. and C. C. Snow. *Organization, Strategy, Structure and Process.* New York:
1978   McGraw-Hill.
Millar, J. A. "Contingency Theory, Values and Change." *Mimeographed,* undated.
Moberg, D. J., and J. L. Koch. "A Critical Appraisal of Integrated Treatments of
1975   Contingency Findings." *Academy of Management Journal.* 18:109–124.
Negandhi, A. and B. Prasad. *Comparative Management.* New York: Appleton Century
1971   Croft.

MANAGERIAL DECISION MAKING 67

Perrow, C. "A Framework for the Comparative Analysis of Organization." *American*
1967   *Sociological Review*. 32:194–208.
————. *Organizational Analysis: A Sociological View*. Belmont, Cal., London:
1970   Wadsworth Publ.
Pfeffer, J., and G. R. Salancik. "Determinants of Supervisory Behavior: A Role Set
1975   Analysis." *Human Relations*. 28:139–154.
Pye, L. W. "Mao Tse-Tung's Leadership Style." *Political Science Quarterly*.
1976   91:219–235.
Ritchie, J. B. and R. E. Miles. "An Analysis of Quantity and Quality of Participation as
1972   Mediating Variables in the Participative Decision-Making Process."
         Personnel Psychology. 23:347–359.
Roberts, K. "On Looking at an Elephant: An Evaluation of Cross-Cultural Research
1970   Related to Organizations." *Psychological Bulletin*. 74:327–350.
Ruedi, A., and P. R. Lawrence. "Organizations in Two Cultures." In J. W. Lorsch and
1970   P. R. Lawrence (eds.), *Studies in Organizational Design*: 54–83. Homewood,
         Ill.: Irwin.
Servan-Schreiber, J.-J. *Le Défi Américain*. Paris: Editions Denoel.
1967
Staehle, W. H. *Organisation und Führung sozio-technischer Systeme. Grundlagen einer*
1973   *Situationstheorie*. Stuttgart: Enke Verlag.
Strauss, G. "Some notes on power equalization." In H. J. Leavitt (ed.), *The Social*
1963   *Science of Organizations*: 39–84. Englewood Cliffs, N.J.: Prentice Hall.
Tagiuri, R. and L. Petrullo. *Person Perception and Interpersonal Behavior*. Stanford, Cal.:
1958   Stanford University.
Thompson, J. D. *Organizations in Action: Social Science Basis of Administrative Theory*.
1967   New York: McGraw-Hill.
Vroom, V. H. and Ph. W. Yetton. *Leadership and Decision-Making*. Pittsburgh, Pa.:
1973   University of Pittsburgh Press.
Weinshall, T. D., The Industrialization of a Rapidly Developing Country—Israel, in:
1976   Robert Dubin (ed.), *Handbook of Work, Organization and Society*. Chicago,
         Ill: Rand McNally.
Weinshall, T. D. (ed.). *Culture and Management*. London: Penguin Books.
1977
Wilpert, B. and F. A. Heller. "Power Sharing at Senior Management Levels." *Omega*.
1973   1:451–464.
Wilpert, B. *Führung in deutschen Unternehmen*. Berlin, New York: W. de Gruyter.
1977
Woodward, J. *Industrial Organization: Theory and Practice*. London: Oxford University
1965   Press.

Name Index

Physical activity for patients

A ~~This book is to be~~ prescription

Edited by

Archie Young
Professor of Geriatric Medicine, University of Edinburgh

Mark Harries
Consultant Physician, Northwick Park Hospital

ROYAL COLLEGE OF PHYSICIANS

2001

Acknowledgements

This publication is based upon a conference held at the Royal College of Physicians on 8 June 2000. We would like to thank all those who played a part in organising the conference.

The Royal College of Physicians is pleased to acknowledge generous support towards the cost of production of this book from **The Virgin Healthcare Foundation**.

Cover photograph: Ulrike Preuss

Royal College of Physicians of London
11 St Andrews Place, London NW1 4LE

Registered Charity No. 210508

ISBN 1 86016 1286

Typeset by Dan-Set Graphics, Telford, Shropshire
Printed in Great Britain by The Lavenham Press Ltd, Sudbury, Suffolk